Religious Dogmas and Customs of the Ancient Egyptians, Pythagoreans and Druids

Religious Dogmas and Customs of the Ancient Egyptians, Pythagoreans and Druids

The Origin, History and Purport of Freemasonry

by
John Fellows

Athens ‡ Manchester

Religious Dogmas and Customs of the Ancient Egyptians,
Pythagoreans and Druids. The Origin, History and Purport of
Freemasonry.

Published by: Old Book Publishing Ltd

Book Cover Design: Old Book Publishing Ltd

Copyright © 2011 Old Book Publishing Ltd
All rights reserved.

Title of original: An Exposition of the Mysteries, or Religious Dogmas
and Customs of the Ancient Egyptians, Pythagoreans, and Druids.
Also: An Inquiry into the origin, history, and purport of freemasonry.

Originally published in 1835

Copyright © 1835 John Fellows

ISBN−10: 1-78107-006-7
ISBN−13: 978-1-78107-006-2

EDITOR'S NOTE

Old Book Publishing Ltd takes care in preserving the wording and images of the original books. For this reason we have invested in technology that enables us to enhance the quality of such reproduction. This investment helps overcome problems encountered when reproducing old books, such as stains, coloured paper, discolouration of ink, yellowed pages, see-through and onion skin type paper.

This reproduction book, produced from digital images of the original, may contain occasional defects such as missing pages or blemishes due to the original source content or were introduced by the scanning process.

These are scanned pages and the quality of print represents accurately the print quality of the original book, though we may have been able to enhance it.

As this book has been scanned and/or reformatted from the original we cannot guarantee that it is error-free or contains the full content of the original.

However, we believe that this work is culturally important, and despite its imperfections, have elected to bring it back into print as part of our commitment to the preservation of printed works.

AN

EXPOSITION OF THE MYSTERIES,

OR

RELIGIOUS DOGMAS AND CUSTOMS

OF THE ANCIENT

EGYPTIANS, PYTHAGOREANS, AND DRUIDS.

ALSO: AN INQUIRY INTO THE ORIGIN, HISTORY, AND PURPORT OF

FREEMASONRY.

BY JOHN FELLOWS, A. M.

L'Unity de Dieu etait le grand Dogme de tous les Mysteres.

NEW-YORK:

PRINTED FOR THE AUTHOR, AND SOLD BY GOULD, BANKS AND CO.

1835

ENTERED according to Act of Congress, in the year 1835, by JOHN FELLOWS, in the Clerk's Office of the District Court of the United States for the Southern District of New-York.

EXPLANATION OF THE FRONTISPIECE.

The two Pillars represent two imaginary columns, supposed to be placed at the equinoxes, to support the heavens. The one on the left is called Boaz, and indicates Osiris, or the Sun: the one on the right is called Jachin, and designates Isis, the symbol, both of the earth and its productions, and of the Moon.

The Arch, supported by the two pillars, is a representation of the semicircle made by the apparent course of the sun in the upper hemisphere, from Aries to Libra inclusive; from whence originates the name of the *royal arch* degree of masonry.

The Seven Stars, are the Pleiades, "a small platoon of stars, says Pluche, very remarkable, most known, and easiest to be distinguished, of all the constellations. They were particularly useful to regulate the informations given to the disciples of the priests, by means of an atlas." "They were, says Bailey, very famous among men, because they intimate the season of the year."

The Blazing Star is Anubis, the Dog-star; whose rising forewarned the Egyptians of the approach of the overflowing of the Nile. Hence the great veneration in which it was held by them, and which has descended to the Freemasons.

The G indicates Geometry, the knowledge of which was of vast importance to the Egyptians in measuring their lands,—the boundaries of individual property being removed by the inundation of the Nile. This science, consequently, was considered by them *divine;* and acquired a sort of mystical union with the Deity. The G, however, was not intended as the initial of the word God, that term being unknown to the Egyptians.

The Square and Compass, as instruments in the science of geometry, became an emblem of *justice;* because through their means, every one had his "old land-marks" restored to him.

The Cornucopia, or Horn of Abundance, was a symbol used by the Egyptians to denote the sun's being in the sign *Capricorn*, when the harvest was gathered, and consequently an abundance of provisions laid up in store.

The Armorial Bearings are those of *royal arch* masonry; for an explanation of which, see Cherubim, page 243.

The Checkered Flooring, called *mosaic* or *musaic work*, represents the variegated face of the earth in the places where the ancients used formerly to hold their religious assemblies. This imitation was made when temple-worship was introduced, to reconcile the people to the change. For the origin of the term *mosaic*, or *musaic work*, see page 288.

The Cenotaph, or Mock-Coffin, used in the anniversaries, is typical of the death of the sun in the inferior hemisphere, under the name of Osiris; who is personated by the Hiram of masonry.

The Mysterious Trunk, on the left of the coffin, is a copy of those used by the ancients for a deposition of memorials of past events; and the *box*, on the right, is the form of those used by Freemasons for a similar purpose.

Among the emblems of masonry, in Cross's Chart, is the figure of a *Key*, which is also generally displayed in masonic Monitors. The key was the attribute of Anubis, the Dog-star, in aftertimes denominated Mercury, and indicated the closing of one year, and opening of another; because the Egyptians formerly commenced the year at the rising of this star. Its employment was afterwards extended to the opening and shutting the place of departed spirits. The Popes of Rome, consequently, now claim it as their appropriate badge of office. The meaning of this symbol not having been preserved in the lodge, is there assigned to its Treasurer.

ADVERTISEMENT.

As some works, frequently alluded to in this volume, may not be familiar to readers in general, it is requisite to describe them more particularly than was convenient to do when making references to them. In fact, often the names of the authors only are mentioned; of such, therefore, I will here give the titles more fully, with the dates of the editions.

The work of Bailey, from which many quotations are made, is entitled "An Universal English Dictionary of Words, and of Arts and Sciences, illustrated with 260 cuts." London, 1759. This is a continuation of his etymological dictionary, but entirely distinct from that work.

"An Exposure of Freemasonry;" published in London, 1825, in a periodical, entitled "The Republican," edited by Richard Carlile.

"Light on Masonry." By Elder David Bernard: Utica, 1829. This work contains an exposition of 48 degrees of Freemasonry.

"A Ritual of Freemasonry, illustrated with numerous engravings." By Avery Allyn: Boston, 1831. This volume treats of 33 degrees of the order.

Volney's Ruins, here made use of, is the New-York edition of 1828.

ERRATA.—Many errors, which may appear in some copies, were corrected after a few sheets were struck off. Those which mar the sense, and mistakes in the spelling of classical words, as well as others in the learned languages, which the general reader could not correct, will alone be taken notice of.

For Et foror and conjux, Page 22, Line 13, read, Et soror et conjux.—p. 28, l. 10, repofitum and Ofiridis; repositum, [Osiridis.—p. 11, l. 38, Nemefis; Nemesis.—p. 30, l. 32, Jevov; Jehov.—p. 35, l. 26, that their founder of colony; that founder of their colony.—p. 40, l. 9, Dionyisus; Dionysius.—p. 41, l. 10, Sabio; Saboi.—p. 49, l. 27, Hannadi; Hannabi.—p. 52, l. 12, Dœdalus; Dædalus.—p. 56, l. 7, Pegassus; Pegasus.—p. 56, l. 13, Stabro; Strabo.—p. 86, l. 14, covering; convening.—p. 86, l. 15, That; Thus.

N. B. *Ibid.*, page 152, line 10, refers to Moore's Epicurean, to which the preceding extract from Dupuis should have been credited.

The running title of Ch. III, should have commenced at page 142, instead of 156.

In page 318, the Defence of Freemasonry is referred to as having been before noticed, whereas that article was printed subsequently.

The extract commencing at page 333, and ending at 335, should be credited to Fontenelle's History of Oracles.

CONTENTS.

CHAPTER I.

Dogmas and Customs of the Ancient Egyptians   1-97

CHAPTER II.

Origin, Nature, and Object, of the Ancient Mysteries; abridged from Bishop Warburton's Divine Legation of Moses; with notes and remarks, pointing out their identity with Freemasonry, etc.   100-141

CHAPTER III.

An Examination of Virgil's Sixth Book of the Eneid: in which it is shown, that the allegorical descent of Eneas into Hell, is no other than an enigmatical representation of his initiation into the Mysteries   142-177

CHAPTER IV.

The Metamorphosis of Apuleius: and the Amour of Cupid and Psyche. Also: a Sketch of the Life and Doctrines of Pythagoras, the founder of the sect that bore his name: and the Doctrines and Customs of the Druids, the priests of the ancient Britons   178-224

CHAPTER V.

Opinions and Observations of learned writers on Freemasonry, who are in full communion with the order   225-257

CHAPTER VI.

An Inquiry into the Origin and History of Freemasonry   258-274

CHAPTER VII.

Analysis of Freemasonry; in which the symbols, and original intention of the Institution, are explained   275-356

CHAPTER VIII.

Miscellaneous Articles.—Ceremonies observed in laying the corner stone of Freemasons' Hall, London, 1775; and at its Dedication in 1776.—Antimasonic Writers.—Barruel and Robison.—The Illuminati.—Horrors of the American Revolution.—Defence of Masonry.—Conclusion.   357-403

INDEX TO CHAPTER I.

A.	Page.	J.	Page.
Animals become symbolical	31	Jehov, Ammon, Neptune, Pluto	34
Anubis, Thos, Æsculapius	37		
Atlas, Hyades, Pleiades	45	**M.**	
Apollo, Muses, Graces	54	Memorials of past events	25
Argus,	58	Menes	35
Apis, Mnevis	70	Moloch, Baal, Adonis, Achad	39
Auguries	81	Mercury, Hermes, Camillus	46
		Metamorphoses, Phantoms	63
C.			
Cabiri	53	**N.**	
Circé	59	Nyobe	57
Conjuration	85		
		O.	
D.		Osiris, the sun, 13. Resurrection of	15
Dionysius, Bacchus	40		
Dædalus	82	**P.**	
Dog-days, why so called	90	Phenix, origin of the fable of	48
		Proteus	61
E.		**S.**	
Egyptian Mysteries	74	Symbolical writing	5
		Symbolical ceremonies	25
F.		Syrens	62
Funeral symbols and ceremonies	31	Saturn	67
		Semiramis	69
G.		Sesostris	70
Genealogy of the Gods	64	Sibyls	83
		Science of Ancient Egyptians	91
H.			
Harpocrates	24	**T.**	
		Typhon or Phyton	72
I.			
Isis, symbol of the earth	18	**U.**	
		Usages common to all nations	4

DEGREES IN FREEMASONRY, OF WHICH NOTICE IS TAKEN IN THIS VOLUME.

	Page.
Degree of Entered Apprentice,	281
" Fellow-craft	292
" Master Mason	294
" Select Master	307
" Most Excellent Master	311
" Royal Arch	324
" High Priesthood	339
" Knight of the Eagle	343
" Knight of Kadosh	344
" Order of Noachites	352
" Rosycrucian	400

INTRODUCTION.

The original object of the secret rites of freemasonry has been a subject of inquiry for upwards of six hundred years, and the enigma seems not to have been satisfactorily solved. The initiated, as well as those without the pale of the order, are equally ignorant of their derivation and import. *What mote it be?* is a question as difficult of solution now as when first propounded by king Henry VI. of England.

The intention of this work is to endeavor to unravel the intricate web in which the mystery is involved, by tracing the order back to its source, and, by showing its intimate connection and similitude to institutions more ancient, put it beyond a doubt, that it sprang from, and is a continuation of the rites and ceremonies observed in those establishments.

Had a work, taken notice of by the Abbe Barruel, fallen into the hands of the editor, he would probably have been saved much trouble in the prosecution of this research.—" We recommend, says he, to our reader to peruse the treatise of a most learned and zealous mason, dedicated *Demen die es Verstehen*, or *To those who can understand*. He leaves no stone unturned throughout antiquity to prove the identity of the ancient mysteries of Eleusis, of the Jews, of the Druids, and of the Egyptians, with those of freemasonry."

In pursuance of this course, it becomes necessary to take a transient view of the dogmas and customs of Egypt in the remotest periods of its history; for it appears evident, that this country was the salient point from which the religious observances of the ancient world commenced.

What are emphatically called the *mysteries*, is but another name for religion; and an exposition of what they consisted, is of course embraced in the subject as forming a parallel with the rites of masonry. Independent of the main design of the work, these topics in themselves possess great interest as matters of curiosity; which is enhanced by observing the close affinity which they bear to the practices of the masonic order at the present day.

" Among all the ancient nations which have been distinguished in history, there is none more worthy of our notice than the kingdom of Egypt. If not the birth-place, it was the early protector of the sciences; and cherished every species of knowledge, which was known or cultivated in remote times. It was the principal source from which the Grecians derived their information; and, after all its windings and enlargements, we may still trace the stream of our knowledge to the banks of the Nile." (New Edinb. Ency.)

Whatever may be thought of the doctrines of the mysteries, they enforced the principles of morality by the most terrific scenical representations of the torments of the wicked on the one hand, and of the most pleasing spectacles of the happiness of the righteous on the other, in a future life. These scenes are faintly copied in royal arch masonry, and the same morals, in like manner, inculcated.

The writer is not a devotee to the mystic rites of the craft; he is not prepared to vindicate the outrages committed by individuals of the order, instigated by a fanatical zeal for the protection of frivolous ceremonies; nor will he apologize for the use that m y have been made of the fraternity to promote the views of political aspirants. If any improper influence in this respect, has been employed, as is asserted, he does not hesitate to pronounce it anti-masonic—against the rules of the order; for both religion, on which itself was originally founded, as well as politics, are totally excluded from the lodge.

The most material and best founded objection that has been brought against masonry, is the oaths which it imposes upon the brethren. They are shocking to the taste of the present age: their continuance was an enormous blunder in the revivers of the order in 1717. They were then no longer necessary. Masonry contains nothing which at that time rendered its members amenable to the laws of England.

The false construction put upon these oaths, has implicated the order in the foulest deeds; and perhaps caused the masonic obligations to be considered paramount to legal oaths administered in courts of law, and thus perverted the course of justice. The only means, therefore, of avoiding this evil, and of wiping away the stain at present attached to the society, is a total abandonment of the oaths.*

However desirable this may be to many of the brethren, it is

---

* "At the very threshhold of our mysteries, an oath of secrecy, extremely minute in all its details, and tremendous in its sanctions, has from time immemorial been exacted of every candidate. It is not to be supposed that such an oath had no foundation at first. It would argue a profligacy incredible, to invent one so sacred and inviolable merely for the sake of swearing it. Nor does such a solemnity comport with the design or practices of any association of architects whatever. For what is there, or what could there ever have been, in the art of building, or in the whole circle of science merely, that could require or even warrant so appalling an obligation? Neither does it agree with the present state of the institution; for masonry harbors no treasons nor blasphemies. Its designs at the present day are not only innocent, but laudable. It requires us to fear God and promote the happiness of man. The inventors of this oath, then, must have most unpardonably trifled with the awful solemnity of such an engagement, if, at the time of its institution, there did not exist a cause, proportionate, at least in some degree, to the precautions used against its violation. (Vid.—The way to words by things, or an attempt at the retrieval of the ancient Celtic, in a volume of tracts in the library of Harvard College.) What this cause was, we can determine only by probable conjecture. But we may presume that it must have originated in some great personal danger, if not death, apprehended to members of the institution from the populace, if their secrets were laid open to the world. Every mason, by reflecting on these hints, will satisfy his own mind, that at the first constitution of our fraternity, its great object was *not* solely the advancement of the arts, still less of architecture alone."—(Greenleaf's Brief Inquiry into the Origin and Principles of Freemasonry.

resisted by others on the absurd and superstitious notion, that no alterations can take place in "the *ancient land-marks*" of the institution; which, like the laws of the Medes and Persians, must remain eternally the same: when, notwithstanding, within about fifty years, the old inclosures have been broken down, and the boundaries of the order extended so as to include an immense territory beyond the ancient limits.

After this unqualified reprobation of the oaths, I confidently assert, that nothing is taught or practised in the lodges contrary to the strictest morals. The exposition of the ritual by those even who are inimical to the order, proves the fact. And, as has been often urged, if there were no other testimony, the characters of many of those who are known to be members, is a sufficient guarantee that nothing improper would be tolerated.

If it be said, that a partial feeling is created among the brethren, that operates injuriously to the public good, it may be answered, that the same objection may be urged against all associations of individuals, whatever may be their views and intentions.

This partiality, by the way, has been the cause of relieving many in distress, and even saving the lives of valuable citizens. A case of this kind happened in the American revolutionary war, which is often alluded to by masonic writers. Col. McKenstry was taken prisoner by the Indians, who were preparing to put him to a cruel death. In this emergency, he gave the masonic sign of distress, which induced a brother mason, a British officer, to interfere and save his life.

While this transaction reflects honor upon the officer as a *mason*, it at the same time leaves an indelible stain upon his character as a *man*, which equally attaches to his *king* and *government*. What! employ savages as auxiliaries in war, and then stand by and look coolly on, while they amuse themselves in *tomahawking* and *scalping* their prisoners, unless the latter can give the talismanic signal, and pronounce the *Shibboleth* of masonry?—But as kings are considered by their subjects not to be moral agents, but looked upon as minors or idiots *who can do no wrong*, the prime minister at the time, lord North, and his principal adviser, lord Sackville, must bear the bulk of the odium.

This rule of masons to grant aid to each other under certain circumstances, was probably derived from the laws of Egypt: by which, "He who had neglected or refused to save a man's life when attacked, if it were in his power to assist him, was punished as rigorously as the assassin: but if the unfortunate person could not be succoured, the *offender* was at least to be impeached, and penalties were decreed for any neglect of this kind. Thus the subjects were a guard and protection to one another; and the whole body of the community united against the designs of the bad."—(Rollin's Anc. Hist.)

Some apology for the awful oaths administered in masonic lodges, is perhaps due on the score of precedent; which has in all times greatly influenced the customs and government of the world, and sometimes sanctified principles the most absurd and pernicious.

The *mysteries* were protected by the most severe oaths in Greece and Rome, and, no doubt, were equally so in Egypt, the place of their birth. And, moreover, in the two former countries, if not in the latter, revealing the secrets of these mysteries was punished with death by the laws.

For this there was a substantial reason: the greater mysteries taught the doctrine of one Supreme God, and that polytheism was an error; admitting, at the same time, that the sun, moon, and stars, were minor divinities under the superintendence of the one Supreme. The belief, however, in Hero-gods was so engrafted on the minds of the ignorant multitude, that it was feared the open promulgation of a doctrine in opposition to that faith, would lead to disturbances in the state that might produce great evil. This mystery consequently was confided only to a chosen few of the most intelligent, under the sanction of an oath and the penalties of the law.

When freemasonry was first established in England, soon after the edict of Canute, in the beginning of the eleventh century, (as is presumed,) prohibiting *in toto* the Druidical worship, the strongest oaths were required to bind the initiated to secrecy : for had the real intent of its founders been known, it would doubtless have cost them their lives.

That Canute was superstitious, and of course vindictive, is evident from his having made a pilgrimage to Rome, through excessive religious zeal, in 1030 ; and, therefore would, no doubt, have punished the Druids for an infraction of his edict with merciless cruelty.

By the incorporation of the Danes with the nation, (says Lingard, in his History of England,) the rites of paganism had again made their appearance in the island. Canute forbade the worship of the heathen gods, of the sun or moon, of fire or water, of stones or fountains, and of forests or trees.

This ferocious and sanguinary warrior, in 1030, made a pilgrimage to Rome. On the road he visited the most celebrated churches, leaving every where proofs of his *devotion* and liberality. In his return he proceeded immediately to Denmark, but despatched the abbot of Tavistock to England with a letter, describing the object and issue of his journey. In this letter he says, " It is long since I bound myself by my vow to make this pilgrimage ; but I had been hitherto prevented by affairs of state, and other impediments. Now, however, I return humble thanks to Almighty God, that he has allowed me to visit the tombs of the blessed apostles,

Peter and Paul, and every holy place within and without the city of Rome, and to honor and venerate them in person. And this I have done, because I had *learned from my teachers*, that the apostle St. Peter received from the Lord the great power of *binding* and *loosing*, with the *keys* of the *kingdom of heaven*. On this account I thought it highly useful to solicit *his patronage* with God."

He concludes his letter as follows: "Lastly, I entreat all my bishops, and all the sheriffs, by the fidelity which they owe *to me* and to God, that the church dues, according to the ancient laws, may be paid before my return, namely : the *plow-alms*, the *tithes* of *cattle* of the present year, the *Peter-pence*, the *tithes* of *fruit* in the middle of August, and the *kirk-shot* at the feast of St. Martin, to the parish church. Should this be omitted, at my return, I will punish the offender by exacting the whole fine appointed by law. Fare ye well."

Furthermore, it may be remarked, that the customs of the times in which I am endeavoring to show that masonry was established, sanctioned the most horrible oaths.

"The multiplicity of oaths in the judicial proceeding of the middle ages,* (says Dr. Henry, in his History of Great Britain, v. iii, p. 425,) had the same effect that it will always have, of diminishing men's veneration for them, and giving occasion for frequent perjury. The legislators of those times employed several devices to prevent this, by awakening the consciences, and keeping alive the religious fears of mankind. With this view, their oaths were couched in *the most awful forms of words that could be invented;* and these forms were frequently changed, that they might not lose their effect by becoming too familiar."

Many who have written with great asperity against masonry, under false impressions of its general tendency, have doubtless

---

* The middle or dark ages are described as comprehending the thousand years from the taking of Rome by the Goths, in the middle of the fifth century, to the taking of Constantinople, by the Turks, in the middle of the fifteenth century.—Edit.

been actuated by the purest motives, whilst others, such as the Abbe Barruel and Professor Robison, have been instigated by the most malignant political prejudices. I shall take some notice of these two writers in the sequel.

AN

EXPOSITION

OF THE

MYSTERIES, &C.

CHAPTER I.

DOGMAS AND CUSTOMS OF THE ANCIENT EGYPTIANS.

It will be attempted, in this work, to show that the mysteries and ceremonies of the celebrated order of Freemasons are derived from the religious dogmas and customs of ancient nations, particularly those of Egypt, where the foundation of the whole machinery of religious mysteries, as far as is known, was first laid.

In order, therefore, to attain a comprehensive view of this subject, it becomes necessary to be well informed of the rites, customs, and ceremonies, of the ancient inhabitants of that famous country. And as the Abbe Pluche, in his *History of the Heavens*, has treated more minutely of these topics, and explained them more satisfactorily, than any other author that has fallen under my observation, I shall commence this volume with extracts from his work.

Critical histories of the fabulous gods of Paganism, under the semblance of truth, have been transmitted from age to age, and been generally received as narratives of real facts. Pluche has unveiled many of these poetical fictions, and pointed out the source from which they were derived.

My limits will not permit me to give the whole of his expositions; but, on account of the great merit of the work, with which, it is presumed, but few American readers are acquainted, I have not confined the selections merely to such parts as have a particular bearing upon the subject in hand.

As the author is little known in America, I will give an abstract of a sketch of his life and writings, contained in *La Biographie Universelle*, Paris, 1830.

Anthony Pluche, a celebrated writer, was born at Reims, in 1688; and obtained the appointment of Professor of Languages, in the University of that city. Two years afterwards, he passed to the chair of Rhetoric, and was raised to holy orders. The bishop of Laon, (Clermont,) becoming acquainted with his talents, gave him the presidency of the College of his diocese. By his assiduity and science, the institution was much improved; when particular circumstances occurred that troubled his tranquility, and obliged him to relinquish his employ. The Intendant of Rouen confided to him the education of his son, at the request of the celebrated Rollin. The Abbe Pluche having fulfilled this trust with success, left Rouen for Paris, where he gave, at first, lessons on Geography and History. Through the notice of distinguished authors, his name soon became celebrated, and he sustained that celebrity by his works.

He gave successively, to the public,—first, the Spectacle de la Nature, (Nature Displayed,) in 9 volumes, 12mo. This work, equally instructive as agreeable, is written with much clearness and elegance. Second, The Histoire du Ciel, (History of the Heavens,) in 2 vols., 12mo. In this work is to be found two parts, almost independent of each other. The first contains learned researches upon the origin of the poetical heavens. This is nearly a complete mythology, founded upon new and ingenious ideas. The second is the history of the opinions of philosophers on the formation of the world. The author here shows the uncertainty of systems the most accredited. Besides a diction noble and well turned, one here finds an erudition that does not fatigue. As to the ground of the system exposed in the first part, Voltaire calls it, probably with reason, the *Fable of Heaven*. Third, La Mécanique des Langues, Paris, 1735, in 12mo. He here proposes a means more short for learning languages. Fourth, Concorde de la Geographie des differens ages; Paris, 1764, in 12mo.

Plan of the Work.

I FIND myself under the necessity of oversetting, or unravelling, fables, in order to establish truth. The men most celebrated, who have treated of the formation of the heavens and of the earth, or of their mutual relations, were pagans, philosophers of different nations, and sacred writers. Those systems which have been given by the Egyptians, Phenicians, the Greeks, and Romans, are obscured by fabulous recitals, and by metamorphoses full of absurdity. Although they were the most ingenious and polished of all people, they formed ideas so strange on the government of the heavens, and on the powers which sustain the human species, that there is no need to combat them with argument; they carry their own refutation with them. But, from the depth of this frightful darkness, it is possible to elicit light. Through these fictions, I find a fact, the explication of which shows us what has given birth to fables; it is the development of them. The first fixed point, is the signification of the names and figures which have served, from the highest antiquity, to characterize the sun, the moon, and the stars, according to their different situations. The usages of the ancients, and the inspection of nature, will aid us in discovering the sense, the knowledge of which will lead us immediately to perceive the enormous abuse that has been made of the institutions of the first men, and place in sufficient light the origin of the idolatry of our fathers.

Another effect of this research, is to teach us, that the same mistake which has peopled the heavens with chimerical divinities, has given birth to a multitude of false pretensions on the influences of the heavenly bodies, and the errors which still tyrannise over most minds. If our history of the heavens produces no other benefit than the discovery of the mistakes which have precipitated the human race into errors that disgrace it,—the consequences of which still disturb the repose of society,—this will undoubtedly be an advantage sufficiently satisfactory.

My remarks may be useful to youth, by unveiling to them those fabulous personages which they hear so often mentioned. I have still greater hopes, perhaps with too much presumption, that this small essay might be of some use to teachers themselves. I should think myself happy to have assisted their work, by some views which they might afterwards improve and proportion to the wants of their disciples. Teachers, however well qualified, generally want leisure to undertake researches of any considerable length; and the more judicious they are, the more disagreeable is it to them, to be for a long series of years handling fables almost always absurd or scandalous, without being recompensed for the tiresomeness of these ridiculous stories, by the satisfaction of being able at least to find out the origin of them. . I here derive all the branches of idolatry from one and the same root. I endeavor to show, that the same mistake has given birth to the gods, goddesses, metamorphoses, auguries, and oracles. The fables thus reduced to their true value, will amuse without danger; and the masters possibly will like and adopt a principle, whose great simplicity puts it within the reach of children themselves.

The chief benefit I should be glad to reap from my labor, would be the facilitating the study of nature, and even that of religion, in restraining the said study within the bounds of possibility and necessity, both which are still of no small extent.

The engravings accompanying the work are all drawn from the monuments of antiquity. They are marked as follows:—all those found in *Antiquity Explained*, by Montfaucon, with an M; those collected by Cartari, with a C; those which are on the vase of agate of St. Denys, with a V; and those which are taken from the table of Isis, published by Pignorius, with a T.

Usages Common to All Nations.

We are sometimes amazed at the conformity found in many respects between the practices of the Hebrews, and those of the nations given over to the grossest idolatry. Most of the learned, in order to account for such a similitude of usages, say that false religions only copied and mimicked the true; and from the conformity of some particulars of mythology with sacred history, they think themselves authorized to affirm, that the heathens had the communication of the holy scriptures, or must have frequented the company and imitated the Hebrews.

Other learned men, and among the rest, Sir John Marsham, in his *Rule of Times*, being sensible how much unknown to, and as it were, separated from other nations, the Hebrews were,—how much disliked by those that knew them,—and of course, how little fit they were to serve them as models, and finding, moreover, from a multitude of evident proofs, that the sacrifices, the ceremonial, and the very objects themselves, of idolatry, were prior to Moses and the holy scriptures, they have maintained, that the laws and the ceremonies of the Hebrews were an imitation of the customs of Egypt and the neighboring nations, but adapted to the worship of one God.*

---

* Great use is made of the Bible, in the ceremonies of masonry; which may be accounted for by the conformity in the customs of the Hebrews with those of more ancient nations, from which the masonic order is derived.—*Edit.*

Symbolical Writing.

The Egyptians, even the most ancient of them, were acquainted with the signs of the Zodiac. Their monuments, which are known to be of the earliest antiquity, are covered with figures, among which those of the crab and the wild goat, of the balance and the scorpion, of the ram and the bull, of the kid, the lion, the virgin, and the rest, are frequently found.

The twelve symbolical names, which signify the twelve portions, both of the year and the heavens, were a prodigious help towards regulating the beginnings of sowing, mowing, harvest, and the other works of mankind.

It was found very convenient, to expose in public a small figure, or a single letter, to notify the exact time when certain general works were to be begun in common, and when certain feasts were to be celebrated. The use of these figures appeared so convenient, that they by degrees extended it to more things than the order of the calendar. Several symbols, fit to inform the people of certain truths, by some analogy or relation between the figure and the thing they had a mind to have understood, were devised.

This method of saying or showing one thing, to intimate others, is what induced among the eastern nations the taste of allegories. They preserved, for a long time, the method of teaching every thing under symbols, calculated, by a mysterious outside, to excite curiosity, which was afterwards recompensed by the satisfaction of having discovered the truths which they concealed. Pythagoras, who had travelled among the eastern nations, thence brought that custom to Italy.

Ham, and those of his descendants who came to inhabit the banks of the Nile, and the whole Lower Egypt, first tried to cultivate the earth according to the order of the year, and in the manner used in other countries; but no sooner were they ready to cut down their harvest, in the driest season of the year, and without the least appearance of rain,[*] but the river swelled, to their great amazement: it flowed on a sudden over its banks, and took from them those provisions which they thought themselves already sure of. The waters continued to rise to the height of twelve, fourteen, or even *sixteen* cubits,[†] covered all the plains,

---

[*] Never does it rain in the Delta, (Lower Egypt,) in the summer, and but rarely and in small quantities during the whole course of the year.—*Volney's Travels.—Edit.*

[†] In the time of Herodotus, sixteen cubits were necessary, or at least fifteen, to overflow the Delta. The same number was sufficient in the time of the Romans. Before the time of Petronius, says Strabo, plenty was not known in the Delta, unless the Nile rose to *fourteen* cubits.—Ibid. (*Edit.*)

the plains, carried away their cattle, and even the inhabitants themselves. The inundation lasted ten or eleven weeks, and oftentimes more.

It is true, the overflowing left on the land a mud which improved it; but, the difficulty of obtaining a harvest, since the summer the only time proper for it, brought the storm and the inundation, caused Ham to quit both the lower and the middle Egypt, and retire to the higher. He there founded the city of Thebes, originally called Ammon-no, Ammon's abode. But many, finding it inconvenient to remove from lower Egypt, which after the retiring of the waters, was throughout the remaining part of the year like a beautiful garden, and a delightful place to dwell in, endeavored to fortify themselves against the return of the waters.

They observed from one year to another, that the overflowing was always preceded by an Etesian (annual) wind, which blowing from north to south, about the time of the passage of the sun under the stars of the crab, drove the vapors towards the south, and gathered them in the middle of the country, (Ethiopia, now Nubia and Abysinia) whence the Nile came; which there caused plentiful rains, that swelled the waters of the river, and brought on the inundation of lower Egypt.

But they wanted the means of knowing exactly the time when it should be necessary for them to be prepared for the inundation. The flowing of the river beyond its banks happened some days sooner or later, when the sun was under the stars of the lion. Near the stars of Cancer, though pretty far from the band of the zodiac towards the south, and a few weeks after their rising, they see in the morning one of the most brilliant, if not the largest star of the whole heaven, ascending the horizon. It appeared a little before the rising of the sun, which had rendered it almost invisible for a month or two before. The Egyptians then pitched upon the rising of this magnificent star as the infallible sign of the sun's passing under the stars of Leo, and of the beginning of the inundation. That star became the *public mark*, on which every one was to keep a watchful eye, not to miss the instant of retiring to the higher grounds. As it was seen but a very little time above the horizon, towards the dawning of the aurora, which becoming every instant clearer, soon made it disappear, it seemed to show itself to the Egyptians, merely to *warn* them of the overflowing, which soon followed.

They then gave this star two names having a very natural relation to the helps they borrowed therefrom. It *warned* them of the *danger;* whereupon they called it Thaaut or Tayaut, the dog; they called it also the *barker*, the *monitor*, in Egyptian, *Anubis;* in Phenician, *Han-*

nobeach; which, by-the-by, shows the analogy there was between these two languages, notwithstanding the diversity of many words, though chiefly in the pronunciation, which made them appear quite different. The connection of this star and the rising of the river, caused the people to call it commonly the Nile-star, or barely the Nile. In Egyptian and in Hebrew, Sihor; in Greek, Scirios; in Latin, Sirius. The Egyptians gave it besides, but in latter times, the name of Sothis or Thotes, which is the same with his other name, Thot, the *dog*, with a different pronunciation.

The inhabitants, retiring into their towns on the warning of the northern wind and the dog-star, remained idle for two months or more, till the waters were perfectly drained. Therefore, the *prudence* of the Egyptians, before the overflowing, chiefly consisted in observing the termination of the vernal winds, the return of the northerly which began with the summer, and at last the *rising* of the *dog-star*, which circumstance was to them the *most remarkable point of the heavens*.

During their inaction, after the rising of the river beyond its banks, their attention was directed to the observance of the return of the southerly winds, more moderate than those of the spring, and which facilitated the flowing of the river towards the Mediterranean, by the conformity of their blowing with its direction, which is from south to north;* and also to measuring the depth of the river, in order to regulate their husbandry according to the quantity of mud, which was always proportioned to the degree of the increase.

I will here remark, that the *Anubis* or *Dog-Star*, so useful to the ancient Egyptians, is the *Blazing-Star* of masonry; and, although the craft are ignorant of its origin as a masonic symbol, they are actually taught the moral drawn from its original emblematical use.

"*The blazing-star represents* that *prudence* which ought to appear conspicuous in the conduct of every mason; but is more especially commemorative of the star which appeared in the east, to guide the wise men of Bethlehem, to proclaim the birth and the presence of the Son of God." (Allyn, p. 47.)

What connection can possibly exist between a *star* and *prudence*, except allegorically in reference to the caution that was indicated to the Egyptians by the first appearance of *this star*, which warned them of approaching danger?

Mr. Converse, in his explanations of the intention of this emblem in his Symbolical Chart, observes, "*Approaching evil* is frequently averted by a *friendly admonition.*" Pluche, in a part of his work not quoted above, says, "The names given to this public sign were Anubis *the barker, the giver of advices,* or Tahaut the *dog*." The meaning then that has been handed down to masons of their blazing-star, completely identifies it with Anubis the dog-star.

---

* See Plutarch de Isid. and Osiris.; also M. De Mallet's description of Egypt.

The advice given to the ancient Egyptians by this star was undoubtedly very important to them, but it cannot be of the least advantage to the masons of Europe or America.

As to the allusion to *the star that guided the wise men to Bethlehem*, every intelligent and candid mason will acknowledge its absurdity; because he must know, that the principles and dogmas of freemasonry, contained in the ancient mysteries from which it is derived, existed long before the birth of Jesus Christ.

Webb, in his "Monitor," says, "The Mosaic pavement is emblematic of human life, chequered with good and evil; the beautiful border which surrounds it, those blessings and comforts which surround us; and which we hope to obtain by a faithful reliance on divine providence, which is *hieroglyphically* represented by the *blazing-star* in the center."

This symbol is peculiarly, if not exclusively, applicable to the Egyptians who inhabited the Delta, who by placing a reliance on the warning providentially given by this star, and in consequence retiring to the high ground with the produce of their agriculture, might enjoy the comforts that surrounded them.

The same necessity which rendered the Egyptians astronomers, made them also painters and writers. The inspection of the heavens had taught them at last how to regulate their tillage, so strangely crossed by that disposition which was peculiar to Egypt. The custom of giving symbolical names to the objects that served them as rules, most naturally led them to delineate in a rude manner the figures of these symbols, in order to inform the nation of the works in common to be done, and of the annual events with regard to which it was dangerous to misreckon. This service was performed by a number of persons appointed for that purpose and maintained at the public expense, whose duty it was to study the revolutions and aspects of the heavenly bodies, and to communicate the necessary information to the people.

Such is the original of the *sacerdotal order* so ancient in Egypt; the chief functions of which always were the study of the heavens and the inspection of the motions of the air. Such is the origin of the famous tower where that company was lodged, and where the characters of the several works and the symbols of the public regulations were carefully delineated. Which symbols appeared in time very mysterious, when the meaning of them was forgotten. That tower, the structure of which has caused so much criticism, was at that time, without any affectation of mystery, called the *Labyrinth*, that is, the tower, the palace.

Now, if we would in a reasonable manner unriddle some of the most usual of the Egyptian symbols, we ought to consult the wants of the Egyptian colony. It is there we are naturally to look for the meaning of the figures which were exposed to the eyes of the whole nation assembled.

The hawk and the hoop were the names and the symbolical figures given the two winds, the return whereof the Egyptians were most concerned to observe. The hawk signified the Etesian northerly wind, which, in the beginning of the summer, drives the vapors towards the south, and which covering Ethiopia with thick clouds, there resolves them into rains, and makes the Nile swell all along its course. The hoop, on the contrary, signified the southerly wind which promoted the draining of the waters, and the return of which proclaimed the measuring of the lands and the time of sowing. I must here produce some analogy and some peculiar resemblance, between a hawk and a northerly, a hoop and a southerly wind.

Naturalists observe, that the hawk delights in the north; but that at the return of mild weather, and when she casts her feathers, she makes southward with her wings spread, and looks towards the place whence a warm air comes, which may assist the falling of her own feathers, and restore her the beauties of youth. In times of the remotest antiquity, and even before Moses, the Arabians, who were the neighbors and allies of the Egyptians, had an idea of the hawk in all respects like that which naturalists give us. In the conversation which God had with Job, and in which he shows, that it is not man, but the Creator, who, by a special providence, has varied all the parts of nature, and to good purpose has regulated the inclinations of animals: *Does the hawk*, says he to him, *by thy wisdom shake her old feathers, to get rid of them, and stretch her wings towards the south?* (*Job*, 39. 29.) This bird then, on account of the direction of its flight at the return of the heats, was the most natural emblem of the annual wind, which blows from north to south about the summer solstice, and which on account of the effects of this direction was of so great importance to the Egyptians.

The hoop on the contrary makes her way from south to north. She lives upon the small worms, an infinite number of which are hatched in the mud of the Nile. (*Diod. Sic. Biblioth. lib.* 1.) She takes her flight from Ethiopia into Higher Egypt, and from thence towards Memphis, where the Nile divides. She always follows the course of the Nile as it retires within its banks, qite down to the sea. From this method of hers, she was perfectly fit to characterize the direction of the south wind.*

---

* A passage in Shakspeare's Hamlet seems evidently to allude to the hawk and hoop, or hoopoe, of Egypt. Hamlet says, "my uncle-father, and aunt-mother are deceived." G. "In what my lord?" Ham. "I am but mad *north-north west:* when the wind is *southerly,* I know a *hawk* from a *handsaw.*" Thomas Capell, editor of the Oxford edition of Shakspeare, changes handsaw to *hernshaw,* which renders the passage intel-

The warning given by the dog-star being their most important concern, the Egyptians from its rising, anciently dated the beginning of their year, and the whole series of their feasts. Wherefore, instead of representing it under the form of a star, which might not distinguish it from another, they delineated it under the figure relative to its function and name. They called it the star-dog, the door-keeper, the star which opens or shuts, closing one year as it were, and opening another. When they had a mind to express the renewal of the year, they represented it under the form of a door-keeper, easy to be distinguished by the attribute of a *key*; or else they gave it two heads back to back; the one of an old man, which marked the expiring year, and the other of a young one which denoted the new.

When the people were to be warned of the time of their retreat at the approach of the inundation, instead of the two heads, they then put on the shoulders of a human body, the head of a dog. The attributes or subordinate symbols, added thereto, were the explication of the warning it gave. It was in order to give the Egyptians to understand, they were to take with them a store of provisions, and repair with all speed to the high ground, or their raised terraces, and there to remain quiet by the water side, that Anubis had on his arm a kettle or porrige-pot, *wings* on his *feet*, in his right hand, or under his arm a large *feather*, and behind him a tortoise or duck, both amphibious animals, which live on the earth and by the water side.

The Egyptians expressed the several increases of their swelling river, by a column marked with one, two or three lines in form of a cross, and surmounted with a circle, the symbol of God, to characterize providence, which governs this important operation. More commonly, instead of a column, they made use of a pole terminated like a T, or crossed with one or more transverse pieces. To abridge these remarks, they were often contented with one small cross;—which put upon a vessel or elsewhere might signify the increase of the water.

---

ligible. Hernshaw or hern is but another name for heron, of which there are various species; the tufted or crowned heron is also denominated hoopoe. This kind is very rare in Europe, but in Africa, they associate in great numbers. They feed upon worms, and, in Egypt, follow, as above stated, the retreat of the Nile. See Rees's Cycl.

Hamlet, though feigning madness, yet claims sufficient sanity to distinguish a hawk from a hernshaw, when the wind is *southerly;* that is, in the time of the migration of the latter to the north, and when the former is not to be seen.

If it be said that Shakspeare was not probably acquainted with the customs of these migrating birds of Egypt, I answer, that several of the works of Plutarch, who gives a particular account of that country, were translated into English, by Thomas North, in about the middle of the sixteenth century, and no doubt were known to Shakspeare, whose Hamlet was first published in 1596.—*Edit.*

It is certain that the *Mikias*, or column marked as above stated, to signify the progress of the water, became in Egypt the *ordinary sign* of the *deliverance from evil*. They hung it on the *neck of sick persons*, and put it in the hand of all *beneficial deities*. Mr. Gordon, Secretary of the Society for the encouragement of learning, has given us in the seventh plate of his collection, the amulets and preservatives which he has observed in the Egyptian monuments; many of which are perfectly like the measure of the Nile.

They painted the devastation made by the overflowing water under the figure of a dragon, of a crocodile, a hippopotamus, or a water monster, which they called ob,* that is, swelling, an overflowing; and which they afterwards called Python, the enemy.†

Another method of communicating to the people information respecting the inundation, seems to have been by publicly exposing three vessels or measures, being pitchers of unequal capacities, well known to the people without any proclamation or messengers, which served to show them the increase and diminution of the Nile. Two things persuade me that this is the meaning of these vessels or bulging measures, so commonly found in the Egyptian monuments. One is the name given them; the other is the attributes annexed. The name *canob* or *canopus* given to these vessels, is grounded on the use made of them. *Canob* signifies *the fathom of the dragon*, the measure of the overflowing. From—*Cane*, a perch, a fathom, a rod or cane to measure; and from—*ob*, the dragon.

The canopi are very commonly terminated by one or two crosses. The top of the vase is also oftentimes surmounted with several bird's heads, to signify and characterize the several winds which they know, and which either assisted or retarded the increase or the lowering of the waters, sometimes they put upon the canopus the head of a dog, to signify the state of the river or the time of the rising of the dog star. At another time they put thereon the head of a maid, to mark out the state of the Nile under the sign of the virgin, and at the approach of the draining or retiring of the water.

---

*——— ob. Levit. 20, v. 27.

† Mount Cassius, to the foot of which the inundation of the Nile extended, a little above the ancient City of Pelusium or the modern Damietta, derives its name from a word which signifies the *bound* or term of this inundation; and the sandy coast near it was called Cassiobe for the same reason. And it was because the lake Sirbon, or *Sirbonis*, which is near it, was still full of the remains of the inundation when Egypt was quite dry, that it was said *Python* had gone to die in this lake. It was moreover so full of bitumen and of oily or combustible maters, that it was imagined that Jupiter had their pierced him with a thunderbolt, which filled all the great morass with sulpher.

It appears that the ancient Egyptians, after they had ascertained the great benefit of the inundation when they were properly prepared for it, changed the name of their Evil Genius, the Water Monster from *ob** to *Python ;* which had reference to the deadly effects of the miasmata arising from the stagnant waters left upon the low lands after the retiring of the inundation. "Ovid makes the serpent *Python* spring from the steams of the mud which the deluge had left upon the earth ; and in this, he is plainly making an allusion to *Typhon,* whose name is the same by a simple transposition. In making *Python* spring from the slime of the deluge, does not the Poet point out thereby the noxious steams which rise in *Egypt* after the waters of the Nile have subsided. In fine, when he says that *Apollo* slew him with his arrows, does he not conceal under this emblem, the victory of *Orus* over *Typhon,* or at least the triumph of the sun beams over the vapors of the Nile ?" (Mayo's Myth. vol. ii. p. 47.) Python, says Bailey, is derived from *pytho,* Gr. to putrify. The serpent Python's being slain by Apollo, is thus interpreted : by Python is understood the ruins of waters ; but Appollo (that is the sun) dispersing the vapors by his arrows (that is his beams) slew this serpent.

Typhus, a species of continued fever, has the same origin. "It may be occasioned (says Hooper, in his Medical Dict.) by the effluvia arising from either animal or vegitable substances in a decayed or putrid state : and hence it is, that in low and marshy countries it is apt to be prevalent, when intense and sultry heat quickly succeeds any great inundation."

The convenience of that language, which rendered itself intelligible to the eyes, and in some sense made animals and even stones themselves to speak, by degrees became more common. It was extended to every thing. The symbolical writing soon served as the rule of morals, as well as the regulation of husbandry. It was made use of to perpetrate among the people, the knowledge of the most important truths, and to inculcate their principal duties.†

The character of the Egyptian writing designed to signify God, was not a simple flame or blaze, as was the general usage of the East but a circle, or rather a sun. They added to the circle or solar globe several marks, or attributes which served to characterize so many different perfections. For instance, in order to indicate that the Supreme Being is the author and preserver of life, they annexed to the circle sometimes two points of flame, but more commonly one or two serpents. This animal was always, among the Egyptians, as in other countries, the symbol of life and health. Not because the serpent makes itself look young again, by every year casting its old skin,

---

* The descendants of Africa, in the West Indies, still retain the name of *ob*, or *obi*, by whose aid they pretend to magical powers.—*Edit.*

† The custom of conveying moral instruction by symbolical figures has descended to the masons, that is, a show of it is kept up by them, but without being seriously regarded. The practice is now a mere *dead letter* ; showing, however, the force of habit in continuing a custom no longer needed. Too much light is now abroad in the world, to require the *square* and *compasses,* to direct men in their duties. The continuance of these old practices notwithstanding, is of use in pointing out the origin of the institution that observes them.—*Edit.*

but because among most of the eastern nations, as the Phenicians, Hebrews, Arabians, and others, with the language of whom that of Egypt had an affinity, the word *heve* or *heva* equally signifies the life, and a serpent. The name of *him who is*, the great name of God *Jov* or *Jehova* thence draws its etymology. *Heve* or the name of the common mother of mankind comes likewise from the same word.

It is from this word that the Latins made their *ævum*, the life and the *ave*, which is a wish of good health.

St. Clement of Alexandria, observes, that the word heva, which is known to signify the life, likewise signifies a serpent. And it is barely on a double meaning of the word hevi or heva, that the metamorphosis of Cadmas and Hermione into serpents is grounded, (Ovid, Metam.) They were of the country of the Hevians.

Macrobius has informed us that the serpent was an emblem of health, *salutis draco*, speaking of Esculapius. When Moses lifted up a brazen serpent in the wilderness, the afflicted Hebrews understood, that it was a sign of preservation.[*]

To express the wonderful fecundity of providence, they added to the symbolical circle the figures of the most fruitful plants, and most commonly two or three large leaves of the banana-tree.

The solar year.—Osiris.

The year relates to three principal objects. To the course of the sun ; the order of the feasts of each season, and to the works in common to be done. Let us begin with the symbols of the sun.

That luminary, as it was the grandest object in nature, had also its peculiar character or mark in the symbolical writing. It was called Osiris. This word, according to the most judicious and most learned among the ancients,[†] signified the inspector, the coachman, or the leader, *the king*, the guide, the moderator of the stars, *the soul of the world, the governor of nature.* From the energy of the terms of which it was composed, it signified in general the governor of the earth, which amounts to the same sense. And it is because they gave that name and function to the sun, that it was expressed in their writing

---

[*] In one of the modern degrees of masonry, entitled *The Brazen Serpent*, the *Jewel* is a serpent entwined upon a cross pole, in form of a T, about which are the Hebrew characters——which signify *one who shall live*. The *covered* word is John Ralp, the founder of this degree. The *sacred* word is Moses. This degree has reference to the deliverance of the Israelites, from captivity. (Benard,)—*Edit.*

[†] Plutarch de Isid, and Isirid, and Macrob, Dux and princeps, moderator luminum, reliquorum, mens mundi, and emperatio.

sometimes by the figure of a man bearing a scepter, sometimes by that of a coachman carrying a whip, or plainly by an *eye*.*

They were often contented with setting down the marks of his dignity, such as a scepter surmounted with an *eye*, or a scepter with a serpent twined round it, the symbol of life which the sun maintains, or barely the whip and the scepter united; sometimes the royal *cap* of Osiris on a throne, with or without a scepter.

The Egyptians every where saw, and especially in the place of their religious assemblies, a circle or the figure of the sun. Near the sun, over the head of the symbolical figures, were seen sometimes one or two serpents, the symbol of life, sometimes certain foliages, the symbols of the bounties of nature; sometimes scarabeus's wings the emblem of the variations of the air. All these things being connected with the object of their adorations, they entertained a sort of veneration for the serpent, which they besides saw honorably placed in the small chest that was the memorial of the state of the first men, and the other ceremonies whose meaning began to be lost.

Having already contracted a habit of confounding the Most High with the sun, they by little and little mistook the symbol itself of the sun, the Osiris, the mederator of the year, for a man. Osiris, from the letter or symbolical personage he was before, becoming in the minds of the people a real person, a man who had formerly lived among them, they made his history to relate to the attributes which attended the figure. So soon as Egypt was possessed with the ridiculous notion, that the statues of Osiris, Isis, and Horus, which served to regulate society, by their respective significations, were monuments of their founders; that Osiris had lived in Egppt, and had been intered there, they framed stories agreeable to this belief. For want of a tomb containing in reality the body of Hammond or Osiris, they were contented with a cenotaph, an empty tomb. A vast concourse of people gathered near these pretended tombs, and with pomp celebrated an annual feast there. Plutarch often mentions the feasts of Osiris's tomb, and informs us, that when the Egyptians were reproached with placing in heaven gods whose tombs they showed, their reply was, that the bodies of these gods had been embalmed and interred in Egypt; but that their souls *resided among the stars.*

---

* " Eye and sun are expressed by the same word in most of the ancient languages of Asia." (Ruins p. 159.)
This is one of the emblems of masonry, called *the all seeing eye*, and said to represent the true God; whereas it is nothing more than a symbol of the sun made use of by the ancient Egyptians, and from them descended to the masons.—*Edit.*

These tombs, tho merely representative, were become a necessary part of the ceremonial. The Cretians, being of Egyptian extraction, had their own feast of Osiris or Jehov, the feast of their god, and of course the empty tomb was inseparable from that solemnity.*

Death and Resurrection of Osiris.

The author here gives a complex figure, copied from the collection of Mountfaucon and which, he says, is painted on a mummy at the Austin-fryar's of La Place des Victoires, representing the death and resurrection of Osiris, and the beginning, progress, and end of the inundation of the Nile.

The sign of the lion is transformed into a couch, upon which Osiris is laid out as dead; under which are four canopi of various capacities, indicating the state of the Nile at different periods. The first, is terminated by the head of the dog-star, which gives warning of the approach of the overflow of the river; the second by the head of a hawk, the symbol of the Etesian wind, which tends to swell the waters; the third by the head of a Heron, the sign of the south wind, which contributes to propel the water into the Medeterranean sea; and the fourth by that of the Virgin, which indicates that when the sun had passed that sign, the inundation would have nearly subsided.

To the above is superadded a large Anubis, who with an emphatic jesture, turning towards Isis who has an empty throne on her head, intimates that the sun, by the aid of the lion, had cleared the difficult pass of the tropic of Cancer, and was now in the sign of the latter, and, altho in a state of exhaustion, would soon be in a condition to proceed on his way to the South; at the same time, gives to the husbandman the important warning of retireing to avoid the inundation. The empty throne is indicative of its being vacated by the supposed death of Osiris.

The raising of grand master Hiram, in the third degree of Masonry, by the "*grip or paw of the Lion,*" (the terms used in that operation) who, as the story goes, had been murdered by three fellows of the craft, is evidently copied from this fable of the death and resurrection of Osiris. The position of the master Mason, when in the act of raising Hiram, is a fac simile of that of Anubis over the body of Osiris.

Mr. Pluche seems not to have had an adequate conception of the fabled death of Osiris, and consequently to have mistaken the purport of the figure now under consideration I therefore offer the foregoing explication as the result of my investigation of the subject.

Mr. Pluche candidly acknowledges that he had doubts of his understanding the intention of the picture which he endeavors to expound; for he says, immediately after giving his explanation, "But it would be a rashness in me to presume to write any longer in Egyptian, when I am not as yet over sure of my skill in reading it. Let us first of all confirm ourselves therein, and again try the application of our principles to some other monuments." He adds, in a note, "We shall in another place explain why this figure is used about a dead body, when we show how the sense of these symbols came to be preverted."

This he afterwards attempts to do as follows;—

"Thus being gradually come to ascribing divinity, and offering their worship to the ruler, representing the functions of the sun, they to complete the absurdity, took him

---

* The coffin of Hiram has a place among the emblematical figures of masonry.—*Edit.*

for the first of their kings. Thence this odd mixture of three inconsistent notions, I mean of God, of the Sun, and of a dead man, which the Egyptians *perpetually confounded together.*"

The cause of their thus confounding them is easily accounted for, when the supposed death of Osiris, the sun, and God of the Egyptians, is taken into consideration.

It must be understood that the sun was supposed to be in insurmountable difficulties at both the solstices, which caused as great lamentations as his victories and reappearance afterwards, did rejoicings. What led to these apprehensions when he was in the summer solstice, is well explained, in Rees's Cyclopædia, as follows:—

"Orus or Horus,* a famous Deity of Egypt, which, as well as Osiris, was an emblem of the sun. Macrobius, who informs us why the Greeks gave Horus the name of Apollo, says, in the mysteries (Saturn, lib. 1,) they discover us a *secret* which ought to be *inviolable, that the sun arrived at the upper hemisphere, is called Apollo.* Hence we may infer, that this emblematical Deity was no other than the star of day, passing through the signs of summer. As Apollo among the Greeks was called the Horus of the Egyptians, as to his skill both in Medicine and divination, he was regarded as the same person, and called by the ancients Horus-Apollo.† The Allegory of Horus has been thus explained. The wind *Rhamsin* makes great ravages in Egypt in the spring, by raising whirlwinds, of burning sands, which suffocate travellers, *darken the air, and cover the face of the Sun, so as to leave the earth in perfect obscurity.* This circumstance *represents the death of Osiris, and the reign of Typhon.* When the sun approaches the sign of the lion, he changes the state of the atmosphere, disperses these tempests, and restores the northerly winds, which drives before them the malignant vapors, and preserve in Egypt coolness and salubrity under a burning sky. *This is the triumph of Horus over Typhon,* and his glorious reign. As some natural philosophers have acknowledged the influence of the moon over the state of the atmosphere, they united her with this god to drive away the usurper from the throne. The priests considering Osiris as the father of time, might bestow the name of his son on Horus, who reigned three months in the year.

Jablonski, who has interpreted the epithet of *Arueri,* which the Egyptians gave to Horus, pretends that it signifies *efficatious virtue.* These expressions perfectly characterize the phenomina which happened during the reign of this god. It is in summer, in fact, that the Sun manifests all his powers in Egypt. It is then that he swells the waters of the River with rains, exhaled by him in the air, and driven against the summit of the Abysinian Mountains; it is then that the husbandman reckons on the treasures of agriculture. It was natural for them to honor him with the name of Arueri, or efficatious virtue, to mark these auspicious effects."—(Savery's Letters in Egypt, etc.)

The reasons which the inhabitants of northern climates have for lamenting the absence of the sun when in the southern hemisphere, is thus beautifully portrayed by Dupuis:

"We have, in our explication of the labors of Hercules, considered the sun principally as the potent star, the depository of all the energies of nature, who creates and measures time by his march through the heavens, and who, taking his departure from the summer solstice

---

* Authors write this name differently: in the Greek, from which it seems to be copied, the first letter, omega, is aspirated.—*Edit.*
† "Orus was more particularly Osiris in his second state, and therefore represented by the Egyptians as a child."—(Holwell,s Myth. Dict.)—*Edit.*

or the most elevated point of his route, runs over the course of the twelve signs in which the celestial bodies move, and with them the different periods or revolutions of the stars, under the name of Osiris or of Bacchus, we shall see this beneficent star, who, by his heat, in spring, calls forth all the powers of generation; who governs the growth of plants and of trees; who ripens the fruits, and who dispenses to all seeds that active sap which is the soul of vegetation, and is the true character of the Egyptian Osiris and the Greek Bacchus. It is above all in spring-time that this humid generator developes itself, and circulates in all the rising productions; and it is this sun, by its heat that impels its movements and gives its fertility.

"We may distinguish two points in the heavens which limit the duration of the creative action of the sun, and these two points are those where the night and the day are of equal length. All the grand work of vegetation, in a great part of northern climates, appears to be comprised between these two limits, and its progressive march is found to be in proportion to that of light and heat. Scarcely has the sun, in his annual route attained one of these points, than an active and prolific force appears to emanate from his rays, and to communicate movement and life to all sublunary bodies, which he brings to the light by a new organization. It is then that the *resurrection* of the great god takes place, and with his that of all nature. Having arrived at the opposite point, that power seems to abandon him, and nature becomes sensible of his weakness. It is Atys, whose mutilation Cybele deplored; it is Adonis, wounded in the virile parts, of which Venus regretted the loss; it is Osiris, precipitated into the tomb by Typhon, and whose organs of generation the disconsolate Isis never found.

"What picture more effectual to render man sorrowful than that of the earth when, by the absence of the sun, she finds herself deprived of her attire, of her verdure, of her foliage, and when she offers to our regard only the wreck of plants dried up or turned to putrefaction, of naked trunks, of arid lands without culture, or covered with snow; of rivers overflowed in the fields, or chained in their bed by the ice, or of violent winds that overturn every thing. What has become of that happy temperature which the earth enjoyed in the spring and during the summer? that harmony of the elements, which was in accord with that of the heavens? that richness, that beauty of our fields loaded with grain and fruits, or enameled with flowers whose odour perfumed the air, and whose variegated colors presented a spectacle so ravishing. All has disappeared, and the happiness of man has departed with the god, who, by his presence, embellished our climes; his retreat has plunged the earth into mourning from which nothing but his return can free her.

"He was then the creator of all these benefits, since we are deprived of them by his departure; he was the soul of vegetation, since it languished and ceased as soon as he quitted us. What will be the term of his flight and of his descent into other regions? Is he going to replunge nature into the eternal shade of chaos, from whence his presence had drawn it?'

"Such were the inquietudes of these ancient people, who, seeing the sun retiring from their climate, feared that it might one day happen that he would abandon them altogether: from thence arose the feasts of Hope, celebrated at the winter solstice, when they saw this star check his movement, and change his route to return towards them. But if the hope of his approach was so sensibly felt, what joy would not be experienced when the sun, already remounted towards the middle of heaven, had chased before him the *darkness* which had encroached upon the *light*, and usurped a part of its empire.* Then the equilibrium of the day and the night is reëstablished, and with it the order of nature. A new order of things as beautiful as the first recommences, and the earth, rendered fruitful by the heat of the sun, who had renewed the vigor of youth, embellishes herself under the rays of her lord." (Abrégé de l'Origine de tous les cultes, p. 142.)

The civil year.—Isis.

We might here reasonably enough call the order of the feasts the ecclesiastical year, since they were religious assemblies. But this order of the days appointed for working or for religious purposes being the rule of society, we shall call it *the civil year.*

The figure of the man, who rules over every thing on earth, had been thought the most proper emblem to represent the sun, which enlivens all nature: and when they wanted a characteristic of the production of the earth, they pitched upon the other sex. The changes of nature, the succession of seasons, and the several productions of the

---

* I will here remark, that all the talk put into the mouth of Masonic candidates about *wanting light and more light*, relates to a physical and not to a mental benefit: it has reference to the light of the sun. In fact, on taking the bandage from the eyes of a candidate, the blaze of many tapers is exhibited before him in satisfaction of his desires, with this declaration of the master, "And God said let there be light, and there was light." These ceremonies are emblematical of the sun's return to the northern hemisphere.—*Edit.*

earth, which no doubt were the subject of the common thanksgivings, might easily be expressed by the several dresses given this woman.*

When the sacrifice was intended to be made in the day, Isis was dressed in *white*, but if in the night she was dressed in *black*. They put a sickle in her hand to denote the time of harvest. When the purpose of a feast was to remind the people of the security afforded by their dwellings, Isis was crowned with small towers. † To intimate the winter neomenia, the head of Isis was covered with little fillets and with skins sewed together ; sometimes with feathers ranged one over the other, or with *small shells neatly set by each other.* ‡ There were sometimes on the head of Isis a craw-fish or crab, sometimes the horns of a wild goat, according as they had a mind to signify

---

* "On comparing the different explanations given by Plutarch, and other ancient writers, it will appear that Osiris is the type of the active, generating and beneficent force of nature and the elements ; Isis, on the contrary, is the passive force, the power of conceiving and bringing forth into life in the sublunary world. Osiris was particularly adored in the sun, whose rays vivify and impart new warmth to the earth, and who on his annual return in the spring, appears to create anew, all organic bodies. Isis was the earth, or sublunary nature, in general ; or, in a more confined sense, the soil of Egypt inundated by the Nile, the principle of all fecundity, the goddess of generation and production. United to one another, Osiris and Isis typify the universal being, the soul of nature, the Pantheus of the Orphic verses. * * * *

"The Egyptians solemnized, at the new moon of Phamenoth (March,) the *entrance of Osiris into the moon*, which planet he was believed to fecundate, that it might in turn fecundate the Earth. (Plut. de Is et os.) Finally, on the 30th, of Epiphi, (24th, of July,) the festival of the *birth* of *Horus* took place, (of Horus the representative of Osiris, the conqueror of Typhon,) in the second great period."—Anthon's Lemp. Class. Dict. Art. Isis.)

The first conquest of Osiris over Typhon was at the winter solstice, and then the birth of a renewed sun was celebrated ; the second conquest, as above stated, was attributed to Horus, which, or rather Horus Apollo, as before observed, was the name given to the sun when in the northern hemisphere, or at least after his passing the summer solstice.

One of the grand festival days of masons is on the 24th., of June. The cause of this variation from the ancient custom arises from the precession of the equinoxes, which has caused the northern solstice to occur on that day, when the sun is in the sign Cancer ; whereas it was in Leo (July 24th,) that this solstice took place in ancient times during 2160 years. This is the reason why the Egyptians consecrated this animal to the sun, while in its full strength, and as the forerunner of the summer solstice, of the rise of the Nile and its succeeding overflow, which caused the fertility of Egypt. (See "Truth drawn from Fables" by Dr. Constantio.)

† It is a little remarkable, that one of the significations given to tower, is high *head-dress*.—*Edit.*

‡ This is Mosaic work, and was no doubt intended to represent in anticipation the variegated face of the earth in the approaching season, after the sun had changed his course to return to the northern hemisphere.—*Edit.*

either the entering of the sun into the sign cancer, or the feast that was solemnized at his entering into that of Capricorn. In Egypt, where the inhabitants can with certainty judge of the product of the year by the state of the river, they proclaimed a plentiful crop by surrounding Isis with a multitude of breasts; on the contrary, when the presage of fertility were not favorable, they exposed an Isis with a single breast; thereby to warn the people, to make amends for the smallness of the harvest by the culture of vegetables, or by some other industry.

All these changes had each its peculiar meaning, and Isis changed her dress as often as the earth.

Next to the symbolical *king*, or the emblem of the sun, the Egyptians had no figure that appeared more frequently in their assemblies than *Isis*, the symbol of the earth, or rather the sign of the feast that were successively characterized by the productions of the earth in each season.

In looking for the origin of this woman, they ran into the same mistake which had caused them to take the governor of the earth, the symbol of the sun, for Ammon their common father. Isis was looked upon as his wife : she partook of the titles of her husband ; and being in their opinion raised to a real person and a considerable power, they invoke her with confidence : they gave her the honorable titles of the Lady, the Queen, the Governess, the common Mother, the Queen of heaven and earth.*

What contributed most to seduce the Egyptians, was the frequent joining of a crescent or a full moon to the head-dress of Isis. Thence they took occasion to give it out that Osiris's wife, the common mother of the Egyptians, had the moon for her dwelling place.

" It was formerly a general custom to make sacrifices and public prayers upon *eminent places*, and more especially in groves, to shelter the people from the heat of the sun. When the Isis which proclaimed the feasts, and whose figures were one of the finest parts of the ceremonial, was once become the object of it, and had been looked upon as the dispenser of the goods of the earth, of which she still bore the marks ; her several representations, which only foreboded abund-

---

* The Roman Catholics seem to have borrowed from the Egyptians the style of their address to the Virgin Mary, which is as follows ;—
 " Holy Mary—Holy Mother of God—Mother most amiable—Mystical rose—Tower of David—Tower of ivory—Gate of Heaven—Morning Star—Queen of Angels—Queen of Virgins,—Queen of all Saints," etc.—*Edit.*

ance and joy, becoming most agreeable to the people, always eager and credulous on that head, the false sense attributed to these figures made them pass for the surest means of obtaining plentiful harvests. These images were worshipped with solemnity, and placed in the finest words. Crouds of people flocked to the religious feasts of the lovely queen who loaded them with blessings. No doubt they had every thing from her. The coolness and beauty of the place where she was worshipped, had no less an influence on the assistants than the attire of the goodness, and instead of calling her the queen of heaven, they often styled her *the queen of the groves.*"

She also became the queen of herds, Asteroth, the great fish, or queen of fishes, Adirdagal, or by way of excellence the queen Amalcta Appherudoth.

The Greeks softened the sound of these words, and gave them the inflection and turn of their own language. The queen of herds became Astarte; that of fishes became Atergatis, and the mother of corn became the Aphrodite of the Cyprians and the Greeks. The name Appherudoth, the mother of harvests, changed into that of Aphrodite, was no more than an empty sound void of all meaning. But it seeming to the Greeks to be derived from a word in their tongue, which signified the froth of the sea they thereupon built the wonderful story of the goddess engendered of the froth of the sea, and suddenly springing out of the bosom of the watery main, to the great amazement both of the gods and men.

They represented the Amalcta Aphrodite, the queen of harvest, holding with her left hand a long goat's horn, out of which they make ears of corn, vegetables, and fruits to spring. She had a sickle or some other attiribute in her right hand; and thus they united without any reason the mark of the opening of the harvest, together with the horn of the wild goat, which signified anciently the end of all harvests, and the beginning of winter. This is then the plain original of the horn of abundance, and of the Amalthean goat. That horn being always full, (a privilege it evidently had) could not but proceed from a goat which had done some important service to mankind. They contrived that this goat had been nurse to Jupiter. But the god and the nurse are both alike. The one existed as little as the other. This single instance is fully sufficient to prove that most of the tales of the poets are little stories grounded on quibbles of the same kind, and invented only to have something to say upon figures always presented at certain feasts, but no longer understood. They made all these figures so many tutelar deities.

The common people have at all times and in all countries, been fond of quibbles, equivocations, and puns. If the change of figure has often made several gods of one and the same symbol diversified, a simple variety of names, nay the difference of pronunciation, has more than once produced a like multiplicity. The Isis mistaken for the queen of heaven, or for the moon, was called Echet, Hecate, or Achate, *the only, the excellent.* (Inter ignes luna minores.) Among some people of Syria, the same symbol, by a slight inflection of name, was called Achot, *the sister.* The same whom they had already made the wife of Jehov, or of the sun, or of Jupiter, (for these are still but one) became also his sister.

—Ego quæ di vum incedo regina, Jovisque
Et foror and conjux———

She afterwards became the daughter of the same Jupiter; and then the mother of all the gods. All this medley of states and genealogies evidently proceeds from the diversity of the attributes and names given to one and the same symbol.

It is not more difficult to guess, how the same Diana is sometimes a terrestrial deity, sometimes the moon, and sometimes the queen of hell. By her first institution she had a relation to the earth, and marked out her productions. The false interpretation that was given to the crescent and the full moon which she bore over her head to proclaim the feasts, caused her to be taken for the moon ; and at last the time during which she remains invisible, that is, between the last phasis and the return of the new, put it beyond all doubt that she was gone to take a turn in the abode of Ades, or the invisible, that is, to the empire of the dead.

But what contributed most to the strange notions people framed to themselves of this triceps Hecate, which was at the same time the earth, the moon, and the wife of Pluto, is this. So soon as the first phasis of the new moon was perceived in the evening, ministers for that purpose went and proclaimed it in all the cross-ways and public places, and the feast of the neomenia was celebrated either that very evening or the next day, according to the institution of places. When the sacrifice was to be made at night, they put an owl near the figure that proclaimed it. The Isis then was called *Lilith*, that is the owl; and this visibly is the origin of that nocturnal lilith of whom so many tales have been told. A cock was put in the room hereof, when the sacrifice was to be made in the morning. Nothing could possibly be more simple or more convenient than this practice. But when the deified Isis had once been looked upon as a woman, or a queen dwelling in the moon, and there governing the heaven in conjunction with Osiris or Adonis, the proclamation of the return of the new moon, which was a thing extremely plain before, assumed a mysterious and stately air. Hecate was become invisible for many days; her return was expected with ceremony. The goddess at last left the empire of the dead, to come again into the heavens. Imagination had a vast field to expatiate here, and Hecate never failing to visit successively those two districts, it could not be doubted but she ruled both in heaven and in the invisible abodes. On the other hand, they could not but be sensible of the palpable relation she had to the earth and its productions, whereof she always bore the several marks either on her head or in her hands. She then became the threefold Diana (*triceps Hecate*) which is at one and same time, the earth; the moon or the lady of heaven; and the queen of hell.

Tergeminamque Hecaten, tria virginis ora Dianæ

The ancient proclamation of the new phasis, which was made with a loud voice, to proclaim the beginning of the neomonia, insensibly degenerated into loud shrieks, which they gave out of mere superstition and custom at the entrance of cross streets. They saluted the goddess of the dead, at her coming out of the horrid mansions. The music and the notions agreed with and suited each other. But the ancient proclamation of the neomenia, was the origin of those devout and meritorious roarings,

Nocturnis Hecate triviis ululata per urbes.

All the heathen antiquity, after it had confounded the symbol of the new moons and of the feasts relating to the several seasons of the year, with the star that regulates society by its phases, ascribed to the moon an universal power over all the productions of the earth, and generally over all the operations of men. They likewise fancied, that she was perfectly well acquainted with future things, and that she never appeared without foreboding by certain marks what was to befal husbandmen, families, and whole kingdoms. People have not as yet fully shaken off the persuasion they anciently had of the influences and presages of the moon.

A like respect was paid to the Neomenia, or New Moon by the Hebrews. Dr. Adam Clarke, in his history of the ancient Israelites, gives the following statements in substance of this matter.

"As the Moon regulates the months, so does the Sun the year. The division which we make of the year into twelve months, has no relation to the motion of the moon. But it was not so with the Hebrews: their months are lunar, and their name sufficiently shows it. They call them *Jarchin*, which comes from *Jarac*, which signifies the moon.

The moment in which the conjunction between the sun and moon is made, can only be known by astromical calculation, because she does not then appear; and as the Hebrews were little skilled in this science, they began their months at the first *phasis*, or first appearance of the moon, which required no learning to discover. This was an affair in which the great *Sanhedrim* were concerned, and the different phases of the Moon were painted upon the hall in which they assembled. It belonged to them to choose men of the *strictest probity*, whom they sent to the tops of the neighboring mountains, and who, no sooner perceived the new Moon, but they came with all speed, even on the *Sabbath day itself*, to acquaint the Sanhedrim with it. It was the business of that council to ascertain whether the moon had appeared, and to declare it: which was done by pronouncing these words, *the feast of the New Moon, the feast of the New Moon ;* and all the people were informed of it by the sound of trumpets. To which ceremony David alludes, when he says, *blow up the Trumpet in the New Moon, in the time appointed, on our solemn feast-day.*—Psalms. 81. v. 3."

The masonic pillar Jachin, which represents Isis, the figure of whom, was exhibited at each neomenia, is undoubtedly derived from Jurchin, the name given by the Hebrews to their months.

Bailey relates some curious customs which formerly prevailed in regard to the moon.

"The common people, he says, in some counties of England, are accustomed at the prime of the Moon, to say; *It is a fine Moon, God bless her*; which some imagine to proceed from a blind zeal, retained from the ancient Irish, who worshipped the Moon, or from a custom in Scotland, particularly in the Highland, where the women make a courtesy to the New Moon; and some English women do still retain a touch of this gentilism, who sitting upon a gate or stile the first night of a moon, say,

"All hail to the Moon, all hail to thee;
I prithee, good Moon, declare to me,
This night who my husband shall be."

In New England, where most of the ancient usages of the mother country have been perpetuated, it is considered an ill omen to observe the first appearance of the Moon over the left shoulder; but when seen over the right, particularly if the beholder has money in his pocket, it is deemed a presage of good luck. It is not unfrequent upon such occasions to prefer a petition for what is most desired, and great confidence is entertained in its being granted.

Thus it appears that the Moon has been the innocent cause of much superstition from the earliest time to the present day, and that the term "*moon struck*," possesses a legitimate origin.

Harpocrates.

The Egyptians did not fail to put in places consecrated to the public exercises of religion, the symbol of the prosperities of their tillage. They placed a figure, sinking under the burden of the goods he had reaped, in the assembly of all the feasts that were solemnized after the harvests of corn, wine, fruits, and vegetables. He carried on his head the natural marks of a plentiful harvest, viz. *three pitchers* of either wine or beer, surmounted with three loaves, and accompanied with leaves, vegetables and several fruits. The bread, wine, etc., wherewith they deck his head, lay immediately on the two great horns of a wild goat. They could not possibly mark out in a more simple and less mysterious manner, the perfect plenty which the husbandman enjoys in the beginning of winter, when the sun passes under the sign Capricorn.

He is most commonly seen with a single pitcher instead of three, and with one goat's horn instead of two;* or with the circle accompanied with large banana leaves, or with some other symbol. The Greek sculptors, who did not much like these enormous head dresses disposed the whole with more comeliness and decorum. They placed the goat's horn in one of the hands of the figure, and made some fruits come out of it.

Symbolical ceremonies. Memorials of past events.

The symbolical writing so commonly and usefully imployed to teach in a compendious and popular manner the most important truths for the preserving of good manners, and promoting the good of mankind, served also from the beginning to preserve the memory of histories, and publicly to expose the object or the motives of the feasts to which some great event had given occasion.

The ancients always opened their festivals and public prayers with woes and lamentations for what they had lost ; though they were used to conclude the same by a general repast, where singing, the sound of instruments, and joy succeeded their mourning. Whence it comes, that the cries usual in the most ancient feasts, even those which in process of time became expressions of joy, and set forms of acclamations, being traced up to the primitive origin, signify nothing but tears and expressions of grief addressed to Almighty God. Such were the cries, io Bacche, hevoe Bacché, io triumphé, io pæan. This word io, jeov, jevoe, hevoe, is the name of God, and signifies the *author of life, he that is.* Bacché comes from *bechè* tears. *Baccoth* signifies *lamentations.* The women who lament the death of Adonis in Ezekiel are called Bacchants, *meboccoth,* women mourners. Triumphé comes from, *teroweh,* which the western nations pronounced triumphe ; there being no letter whose pronunciation was more difficult and more varied than the oin. That word triumphe signified groans and sobs. It afterwards signified the public prayer, and finally

---
* Cross's masonic chart represents two cornucopiæ or goat's horns, and one pitcher ; three, however, of the latter, as before observed, are used in the ceremonies.—*Edit.*

the singing of the assemblies, as may be seen Ps. 89.* All these words joined to the name of God, were short expressions by which the people excited each other to have recourse to God in their distress, and to direct their prayers and cries to him. The whole of these, was like the Latin and French expressions, *Deo gratias, Dieu mercy, adieu.*

The object and motives of this mournful practice are more easy to be discovered among the Egyptians than among the other nations; not only because the Egyptians having been less mingled with other people, have made fewer alterations in their ancient customs; but also because their practices being strictly connected with public and certain symbols engraved in stone, or carried in ceremony at the feasts, they were better fixed or less disfigured in Egypt than in other parts of the world. There they lamented with Isis the death of the governor which had been taken from them, and killed by a dragon rising from under the ground, and by a water monster. They then rejoiced for the resurrection of Osiris; but he was no longer the same and had lost his strength.

The Fgyptians, and most of the eastern nations, had an allegory or picture, which became famous, and which is every where met with. It represented the water monster slain, and Osiris restored to life; but there sprang out of the earth hideous figures, who endeavored to dethrone him. They were monstrous giants, one of which had many arms; another pulled up the largest oaks; and a third had in his hands the fourth part of a mountain, which he flung against heaven. They were all distinguished by some singular attempt, and by frightful names, the most known of which were Briareus, Othus, Ephialtes, Enceladus, Mimas, Porphyrion, and Rouach or Rœchus. Osiris got the better of them; and Horus, after he had been very much abused by Rœchus, happily got rid of his pursuits, by appearing before him with the *jaws* and *claws* of a *lion.*

I might be thought here to offer a mere fable; But to show that this picture is historical, and that all the personages which compose it are so many symbols, or significant characters, representing the hardships of the first men, and in particular the unhappy state of husbandry in Egypt, it will be sufficient here to translate the peculiar

---

* Blessed are the people that know the joyful sound, they shall walk, O Lord, in the light of thy countenance. For thou art the glory of their strength; and in thy favor our horn shall be exalted. For the Lord is our defence; and the holy one of Israel is our king. How long, Lord? wilt thou hide thyself forever?"

names given to each of these giants. Briareus signifies *the loss of serenity*; Othus, *the diversity of seasons*: Ephialtes, *great gatherings of clouds*, Enceladus, *the havocks of great overflowing waters spread*: Porphyrion, *the earthquakes* or *the fracture of the land*, Mimas, *the great rains*; and Rœchus, *the wind.**

As to the figure of Horus who assumes the *head* and *claws of a lion*, to rid himself of the *wind* that ruined all his hopes; it is a symbol peculiar to the husbandry of the Egyptians.

Thus the necessity of personifying the objects they wanted to paint very soon introduced the use of allegorical pictures, and of fabulous recitals. They at that time could not write otherwise than by delineating the figures of the objects intended. But they thought themselves masters of ordering the whole, in the manner they judged the fittest to make an agreeable impression, and to be well understood. The difficulty of conveying the ideas of intellectual things into the mind by the eye, first made them have recourse to symbolical figures: the use of these figures afterwards authorized the taste of fictions. But what was obscure in them was cleared by the simplicity and propriety of the names given each peice. I could produce new instances of this in the fables of Andromeda and Bellerophon, which are pure allegories, the interpretation of which must be deduced from the signification and meaning of the names of all these personages. But this would take us off too much from that part of the ancient writing and of the public ceremonies that related to the representation of past disasters, and to the regulations of mankind.

Altho, Mr. Pluche has actually shown the cause of the lamentations and after rejoicings to have been occasioned by the loss and subsequent restoration of Osiris the sun, still he attributes the allegory to the misfortunes that had happened to mankind in consequence of a general flood. His remarks upon this head are omitted.

The ancients not only expressed certain truths by figures delineated on stone; they also joined to these figures dramatic ceremonies, wherein the objects and the names of the actors were significant, and served to recall the memory of things past.

The feast of the ancient state of mankind, assumed a more shining form in Egypt and Syria, by means of the symbolical figures, which had been multiplied there much more, than any where else. This feast having become common to all nations, on this account deserves a more

* The author gives in notes, the originals of the above names, which are omitted.

ample illustration, than what has already been said about it. We cannot explain the symbols of it, without casting a useful light upon an infinite number of monuments remaining in our hands, and which have hitherto been looked upon as unintelligible.

They carried at this feast a basket or small chest, that contained the monuments of the progresses of husbandry. The chest was neither mysterious nor significant in itself. It only served to receive the memorative symbols of things past.

First, they found therein the mark of the weakening of Osiris, and of the loss of fecundity. (*In cista* or *capsula repofitum erat Dionysii* (*Ofiridis*) *pudendum. S. Clem. Alex. cohortat, adgentes. p.* 6. *edit. Oxon.* From the Phenician word, —— *ouervah* or *orvia, pudendum*, they made *Orgia*, a name given the ancient rural feasts. They were called in Greece *Phallica*, which has the same meaning. The indiscretion of that symbol gave birth to all sorts of extravagances and licentiousness.

Then came sesameseeds, heads of poppies, pomegranates, bay-berries, branches of fig-tree, dry stalks, cakes of several kinds of corn, salt, carded wool, cakes of honey and of cheese, and finally a *child* a *serpent* and a winnowing van. See this enumeration in St. Clem. Alexand. and in *Potter's Antiquity of Greece, vol.* 1. *Grecian festivals.* The whole was accompanied with a flute, or some other musical instrument.

The drum or flute, which was inseparable from the celebration of the feasts, was the symbol of gratitude, which on certain days invited men to meet together, to praise God in concert. The small chest, the van, in which they afterwards found so many mysteries, (*Mystica vannus.* Virg. Georgic. See *l'Antiq. expliq. and the agate, in the treasury of St. Denys.*) and the whole representation here enumerated, passed from the Egyptians to the Phenicians, and by their means spread far and wide. Nothing is more commonly found in the monuments of the heathen feasts, than a small chest, a van, a *serpent*, a *human head*, and a flute or a drum.

When the feast representing the ancient state of mankind and the progresses of industry was celebrated, both the figure of the earth and that of work obtained several names in different countries. But we find the same purpose and the same relations in all these names. The Isis representing the earth, was called Ceres, Themis, Nemefis, Semele Mnemosyne, and Adrastia.

We shall bestow an entire article upon the explanation of the symbol of Ceres. The Isis surnamed Nemesis simply signified the earth preserved from the waters. Semele signified the *representation* of the ancient condition of men ; and Mnemosyne is no more than a bare translation of the same word into Greek. Torches were always carried next to Ceres, or the symbol of the mourning earth, and this caused Isis thus accompanied to be called Themis, Themisto, and Adrastia, which three names signify all *the excellency of fire*.

A multitude of ancient monuments testify to us the use of the little portable chest, of the van, the child and the serpent. They added to these figures the sorry grains on which they in the beginning had been obliged to feed, and the marks of the crosses they had been necessitated to overcome.* (See the antiquities of Greece collected by Dr. Potter, Vol. i. And Clem. Alexander. *Cohort. ad Gent.*)

The persons who in the public ceremony carried the chest wherein all these memorials were contained, likewise assumed to themselves significant names, and made a part of the representation. They became actors, and every thing concurred with the symbolical pieces, to convey certain truths into the minds of the spectators.

The representative child was called simply the child, *liber*, the beloved son ; sometimes the child author of life and subsistence, *liber pater* ; sometimes the child of the representation, *ben, Semeleh* ; sometimes Horus, Erichthonius, Harpocrates, Bacchus, Apollo, Icarus. He bore many other names, whereof we shall give an explication, in the particular enumeration of the feasts of the several nations.†

It is known from the testimony of Diodorus Siculus, and from the conformity of the Athenian laws with the Egyptians, that the first inhabitants of Attica were an Egyptian colony. We have even several

---

*Every royal arch chapter of masons is supplied with a similar chest ; to which great consequence is affectedly attached. It contains, besides other testimonials of times past, something resembling, and which is declared to be, manna, the food upon which the Israelites are said to have subsisted during their wanderings in the wilderness.

Among the emblems of masonry are likewise the skeleton or skull of the human head, as well as the figure of a serpent. But the original intention of these symbols are probably now unknown to the fraternity.

" The Jews also had, at the *east end* of every school or synagogue, a chest called Aaron, or *ark*, in which was locked up the pentateuch in manuscript, written on vellum in *square characters*, which by express command, was to be delivered to such only as were found to be *wise* among them."—(Colcott Disq. on Masonry, p. 72.)

It is probable that this chest also contained memorials of the wretched state of the Israelites while in the wilderness. The letters, above mentioned, were probably the same as the royal arch ineffable characters, which consist of right angles in various atitudes, with the addition of a dot.—*Edit.*

†The author makes this child the symbol of work ; and as the sun bore the name of Apollo, or Horus Apollo, when in the northern hemisphere which is the time for carrying on the labors of husbandry in this region, there may be a propriety in the application.—*Edit.*

proofs, that it originally came from the city of Sais, so famous for its olive-trees. Among the ceremonies which these foreigners brought from Egypt into Greece, they remark the little chest, which according to the custom of their original country, contained the symbolical figures of agriculture. Three young Athenian women carried in their feasts a basket, wherein lay a child and a serpent.

*Infantemque vident exporrectumque draconem.**

The three maids that carried this child had names relating to husbandry, the symbols of which they bore in their hands. They were called *Herse, Pandrosos,* and *Aglauros*. The signification of these names unveils the whole obscurity of the enigma. It is enough for us thereby to understand, that it is to the alternative of the *rain*, the *dew*, and the *fair weather*, that husbandry is indebted for the life it affords us. Let the imagination of poets wander upon the rest, and, according to their custom, look into a symbol to them become unintelligible, for the matter of an insipid metamorphosis.

In order to render these representations more complete, they did not in Egypt, forget any more than in other places, the necessity, the first men had been under, of defending their houses and the fruits of the earth, from wild beasts. They preserved the memory of this particular circumstance by a kind of hunting which they renewed every three years, throughout the East. The same feast was not celebrated every year, because wild beasts did not multiply from one year to another so as to alarm the neighborhood. This hunting being only a representation and not much in earnest, it made the sanctity of feasts degenerate into tumultuous ramblings, which were succeded by the greatest disorders.

It is true, they began by a sacrifice, and the invocation of the true God ; as may be easily proved from their warlike cries, that signified, *The Lord is the mighty; the Lord is my strength ; Jo Saboi,*† *Deus mihi exercitus. The Lord is an host to me ; the Lord is my guide ; Jevov nissi ; Jo nissi, Dio nissi ; Deus vexillum mihi, Deus mihi, dux esto. Exod.* xvii: 15. And Moses built an altar, and called the name of it *Jehovah-nissi.* It is not time yet to convert the Dionissi, which was only a prayer, into a man's name, and of it to make the Dionysius of the

---

* *Ovid. Metam. of Erichthonius.*

† *Saboi*, with, perhaps, some variations in the pronunciation, is a common expression with country people, to set dogs upon cattle.—*Edit.*

Greeks. All words which we find again in the mouth of the Hebrews, because their tongue and religion were originally the same with that of the other nations. The latter have altered their notions, while the *form of prayers still remained the same.*

Animals become Symbolical.

From the knowledge we now have of the genius and taste of the eastern nations, and chiefly of the Egyptians, for symbolical figures and significant ceremonies, we are authorized to think, that the singular practices observed among them were so many emblems of certain astronomical, moral and other truths. We no longer run any risk in saying, that the ram which they reverenced in Thebais and Libya, the bulls they respected at Memphis and Heliopolis, the kids honored at Mendes, the lion, the fishes and other animals which they worshiped in several provinces, were very plain symbols in their first origin. They were no more than the ancient signs of the Zodiac, and the different marks of the situations of the sun. They distinguished the neomenia of one month or of another, by annexing the figure of the celestial animal into which the sun then entered, to the Isis which proclaimed that feast; and instead of a bare picture, they introduced into the feast the animal itself, the living animal relating thereto. The dog being the symbol of the dog-star, which formerly opened the year; they put a living dog at the head of the whole ceremonial of the first neomenia. It is Diodorus, who recounts this fact, as having been an eye-witness of it. They therefore took the habit of calling these neomeniæ the feast of the ram, the feast of the bull, of the dog, and of the lion.

Funeral symbols and Ceremonies.

There was near the Egyptian towns a certain ground appointed for the common burying-place. Diodorus Siculus, (*Biblieth. l.* 1.) informs us how these tombs were regulated, and in an exact description of the burying-place at Memphis, the largest and most frequented of all, relates all that was practised there. According to his recital, the common burying place, was on the other side of the lake called Acherusia, from —— *acharie, after,* and from —— *ish, man,* comes, —— *achariis ultima hominis* the last condition of man, or rather what follows the death of man. They also say —— *acheron, postremum, conditio ultama.* The dead person was brought to the shore of that lake, and to the foot of a tribunal consisting of several judges, who inquired into his life and conversation. When he had not faithfully observed the laws, the body was left unburied, and very likely was thrown into a sort of lay-stall or ditch called Tartarus. This word may come from the *Chaldaic*, —— *tarah, præmonitio*, doubling the word. Diodorus informs us, that there was near a town, at a small distance from Memphis a leaking vessel, into which they incessantly poured Nile water; which could signify nothing but endless tortures and remorses. And this single circumstance gives room to think, that the place where the unburied bodies were thrown, was set round with frightful representations.

When no accuser appeared, or he who deposed against the deceased was convicted of falsehood, then they ceased to lament the dead person, and his encomium was made. (*Diod.*) They, for instance, commended his excellent education, his respect for religion, his equity, moderation, chastity and other virtues. His birth, which was supposed to be the same with all men, was never allowed as any merit in him. All the assistants applauded these praises, and congratulated the deceased, on account of his being ready to injoy an eternal repose with the virtuous.

There was on the shore of the lake a severe and incorruptible water-man, who by order of the judges, and never upon any other terms, received the deceased into his boat. The very kings of Egypt were treated with the same rigor, and were not admitted into the bark, without the leave of the judges, who sometimes deprived even them of burial. The water-man carried the body on the other side of the lake, into a plain embellished with meadows, brooks, groves, and all the rural ornaments. This place was called Elizout, or the Elizian fields, that is, *full satisfaction, an habitation of repose* or *of joy.* There was at the entrance of that abode the figure of a dog with three pair of jaws, which they called Cerberus. The whole ceremony ended by thrice sprinkling sand over the opening of the vault wherein they had put the corpse,* and by bidding him thrice† adieu.

All these words and practices almost every where copied, were so many instructions addressed to the people. They gave them to understand by all these ceremonies, as by so many speeches or very significant symbols, that death was followed by an account which we were to give of our life before an inflexible tribunal: but that what was indeed dreadful to the wicked, was only a passage into a happier

---

*The custom of throwing thrice sand upon the corpse is now become universal. *Injecto ter pulvere.* Horat. carm. l. 1. od. 28.
†*Magna manes ter voce vocavit.* Æneid. 6.

state for the good. Wherefore death was called the deliverance. (*Pelitah*, or rather, *pelouta*, alleviation, deliverance. Wherefore Horace looks upon that passage as the end of evils.

Levare functum pauperem laboribus. Carm. l. 2. od. 18.) It is likewise called in French *le trepas*, that is, the passage to another life. The boat of transportation was called tranquility, (*beri, tranquilitas, serenitas*. Whence comes,——*baris*, Charon's bark. *Diod. Sic.*) because it carried over, none but the just; and on the contrary the waterman, who inflexibly refused those whom the judges had not acquitted, was called *Wrath*, (*Charon*. Exod. 15; 7.) or the vengeance.

As to the earth thrown upon the corpse, and the tender adieus of the relations, they were no more than natural duty and a simple expression of their regrets. But they were not contented with paying them by the way this honor: They also put at the entrance of the cemetery and over the door of the deceased's tomb the symbol of the value and tender affection they had for their departed relation. The dog, being of all animals the most addicted to man, is the natural emblem of friendship and attachment. They gave the figure of the dog three heads or throats, to express the three cries they had made over their friend's grave, according to the custom which granted that honor to none but good men. Therefore this figure, thus placed near the tomb and over the head of the new-buried person, signified his having been honored with the lamentations of his family, and with the cries which friends never failed to come and utter over the grave of him whom they had valued and cherished for his good qualities. The meaning of this symbol is no longer a riddle, after its name has been translated. They called it *Cerberus*, that is in plain terms, the cries of the grave.*

It is neither easy nor reasonable to pretend to explain all the symbols and ceremonies of antiquity, before we are convinced that most of the singular figures used on the most solemn occasions, were in their first original no more than significant symbols and instructive ceremonies. It is enough for us that this is true of many of them; which I flatter myself I have shewed in this first essay of explanation of the ancient writing, since the explication I give of it is simple, plain, and strictly connected both with the common notions and the wants of the first men.

The Egyptians, who had contracted a habit of adoring the sun as God, as the author of all good, and looked on Osiris as their founder, ran headlong into a third abyss. They, from a confused remem-

---

*From ——— *ceri* or *cri*, which has the same sense in French, and from —— *ber*, the vault, the grave —— *cerber*.

brance, and an universal custom, knew that this figure of Osiris related to the sun, and it was indeed nothing else in its first institution. They besides saw the circle the character of God placed frequently enough on Osiris's forehead. They then perpetually joined the idea of Hammon with that of the sun, and both these with that of God. They no longer honored God nor the sun, without singing at the same time the favors of Osiris or Hammon. The one was still inseperably connected with the other; which made them give out, that Hammon or Osiris had been transported into the sun, there to make his residence, and that he thence continually protected Egypt, taking a delight in pouring a greater plenty upon the country inhabited by his offspring, than on any other land in the universe. Thus being gradually come to ascribing divinity, and offering their worship to the ruler representing the functions of the sun; they, to complete the absurdity, took him for the first of their kings. Thence this odd mixture of three inconsistent notions, I mean of God, of the sun, and of a dead man, which the Egyptians perpetually confounded together.

Jehov, Ammon, Neptune, Pluto.

That religion which grossly indulged the self-love and vanity of the Egyptians, easily found favor, and took root in the minds of the people. The rest of the symbols took the same turn. They inquired who was the Poseidon or Neptune, that is, the marine Osiris, the symbol of the annual return of the fleets; and they made of him a god who delighted in the sea, as Osiris did in the heaven. The funeral Osiris who declared the anniversary of funerals, had also his own history: and as all the ceremonies belonging to burials, instead of being taken in their true sense, that is, as public instructions upon the state of the just, after death, had by degrees been looked upon as pictures of the real treatment given to the dead under ground and in delightful gardens: they, of Pluto or of the symbol of the deliverance of the just, made a god, who presided over the abodes of the dead.

The pretended god Neptune, (*Herodot, in Euterp.*) who became the favorite deity of the maritime nations, was almost unknown to and hardly worshiped among the Egyptians, who hated the sea, and who living in plenty of every thing, hardly ever went out of their own country. On the contrary, as they were very exact in the outward practice of their religious ceremonies, the funeral anniversaries which were frequently repeated, rendered Pluto much more renowned among them.

We often see round the head of the Egyptian Pluto a radiant

crown, and round his body a serpent sometimes accompanied with the signs of the zodiac; which evidently signifies the duration of one sun, that is, of one year. And it is plain here, that the author of the Saturnals, who pretended that Pluto and many other gods were originally nothing but the sun, had great reason to think so, since Jupiter, Ammon, Neptune, and Pluto, are in reality no more than the symbol of one solar year diversified according to particular circumstances. They did not quite lose sight of the unity of their origin in making persons of them: for they made them three brothers, who, as they said, had divided the empire of the world between them.

Ham or Hammon being commonly called *God* Jehov, Jehov-Ammon, the city of Thebes where he had dwelt longest, and which they anciently called Ammon's abode, (*Ammonno*) was afterwards called *the city of God.* (*Diospolis.*)

This word Jehov, in its primitive use, signified the *father of life, the supreme being.* The Greeks translated it by that of *Zeus* or *Dios*;* and the Romans by that of *Deus*: all names having the same sense, if they be not the same sound diversified according to the pronunciation of different people. They sometimes joined to it the name of father, which was but an interpretation of it, and called him Diospiter or Jovpiter. The Ammon which by a stupid kind of love was confounded with God, and with Osiris or the star moderator of seasons, became the famous Jov-Ammon or the Jupiter-Ammon, and had always the first honors paid to him, after the other symbols had in like manner been converted into so many celestial personages and powerful deities. The reason of this pre-eminence is founded on their having annexed the idea of that their founder of colony to the most brilliant of all their symbols, I mean, their Osiris.

The establishment of the laws. Menes

The rural works not being resumed in Egypt, till after the Nile had quitted the plain, they, for this reason, gave the public sign of husbandry the name of Moses or Museus (saved from the waters;) and on the same account, the moons during which Horus Apollo, or husbandry, continued his exercises, went also by the same name.

About the end of autumn, the inhabitants being freed from the works of the field, manufactured in their night—work the line thread and

---

*They sometimes changed this word into that of *zen*, which comes from *zan* and *zao to live.* Which makes the same sense.

cloth, which were one of their chief riches. The sign which was the publication of it, took thence the name of Linus, which signifies *watching, the setting up in the night.* (——Lyn, to watch.) The star that lights the night has on this account retained the same name, and so has the matter itself that was manufactured during those watchings.

This sign has evidently given birth to the tales of Linus, Museus, Orpheus, Picus, Ganymede, and many other pretended heroes or legislators, of which it is needless to pretend to determine and fix the chronology and the above.

The custom they had, to publish the several regulations concerning polity, by the several postures of the son of Osiris, caused him to be commonly called Menes, that is, *the rule of the people.* The Egyptians from this new title took it into their heads, that Menes had been their legislator, the author of their polity, the orderer of their year, the founders of their laws. For this reason, they put this imaginary founder at the head of all the lists of the kings of their several provinces.

The name of Moses or Museus was very properly given to the public sign of the revival of husbandry. This word, which signified *the drying up,* made part of the calendar : it was the summary and the substance of a statute of polity. It was every year in the mouth of the people, after the re-entering of the river within its banks. It was not then a man's name. But if Menes and Museus are but one and the same thing ; if they are only the names of the same sign ; what then becomes of the first king of Egypt, the foundation of their history ? He, from that moment, loses all his reality.

Two of the most learned men among the ancients, Eusebius in his evangelical preparation, and St. Clement in his exhortation to the Gentiles, by preserving and handing down to us the ancient set-form whereby they incited those that were initiated into the mysteries to imbibe religious sentiments and love work, have helped us to find out exactly what the famous Menes was. The instructions given therein for good conduct, are addressed to work itself. It is called *the son of the star of the day,* because husbandry can do nothing without the sun. Again, it is called Museus ; because in Egypt, whence this set-form came, husbandry did not resume its operations but till after the retiring of the waters. In short, it is surnamed Menes * in the same set-form, that is rule of the people. Therefore, this pretended founder of the Egyptian monarchy has not more reality in him than his father

---

* Harken thou, O Menes Museus, son of the star of the day.

Osiris, the ancient character of the sun, nor more than Museus another character of the revival of the tilling of the lands and of the operation of sowing.

Anubis, Thot, Æsculapius.

The falsity of the ancient history of Egypt is completely demonstrated by the abuse they further made of the fourth key of their symbolical writing. It was the figure of a man with a dog's head, wearing oftentimes a pole with one or two serpents twisted about it. The meaning and intention of the public sign exposed in the assembly at the rising of the dog star, was to advise the people to run away and give attention to the depth of the inundation, in order to rule their ploughing accordingly, and to secure their lives and subsistence. The names given to this public sign were Anubis *the barker, the giver of advices* or Tahaut *the dog*, or Æsculapius *the man-dog*. * It was still the same meaning or the same public sign; but they were three names for one and the same thing. A sufficient ground for them to derive from thence three personages of their history, the chronology whereof will be still lengthened by this means. They make their demi-god Anubis to reign before Menes, without telling us where. They make Thot or Thaautes son of Menes, their second king of Egypt. They make him a counsellor to Menes. They ascribe to him the introduction of the letters, the invention of music and dancing, with a great many other fine discoveries; the foundation of which is because the dog-star opened the year, brought along with it a new series of feasts, and appeared at the head of all the letters or symbolical figures which expressed the annual order. Though Æsculapius was as yet no more than the sign of the canicular star, the Egyptians made him a third king, who had applied himself to the procuring the preservation of his subjects by the study of physic; a notion that had its origin from the preservation of life which was expressed by the serpents twisted about the measure of the Nile. Such is the origin of the serpent of Epidaurus, and the very plain reason for which the serpent has always been inseparable from the god of physic, to which art both the man and the animal had originally no manner of relation. Several historians quoted by sir John Marsham in his rule of times (*Chronicus Canon.*) attributed the inven-

---

* From —— *aish man*, and from —— *caleph dog*, comes —— *æsaleph the man dog*. The Greeks called him *astrokuon, the* star-dog.

tion of the letters to Æsculapius as well as to Tahaut. Which was doing them justice, the one not being different from the other. Marsham is most earnestly angry with those who have thus confounded things and altered history, by attributing to Æsculapius the invention which is the glory of Thot. This he patches up to the best of his power. But it was very superfluous, here to have recourse to means of reconciliation; since Æsculapius or *the man-dog*, and the Tahaut, or the dog-star, as well as Anubis, were no more than the names of one figure that was exposed in the assembly of the people, to warn them of the appearance of that star, the rising of which would soon be succeeded by the inundation.*

The Gods of Egypt communicated to Asia and Europe by the Phenicians.

Egypt always was and still is the most fruitful country in the world. The harvest, which is almost certain there, and by much exceeds the wants of the inhabitants, occasioned great quantities of corn to be amassed there, which in barren years were the resource of the Arabians, the Canaanites, the Syrians, and the Greeks. Travelers whom need or curiosity had drawn thither, and the Phenicians especially, who inhabited but a small maritime coast near mount Libanus, and had no granary so certain as Egypt, were all equally struck with the polity that reigned in every part of that beautiful country, with the gentle temper of the inhabitants, the mysterious outside of the ceremonies and feasts which were with much pomp celebrated there, and finally with the plenty which they looked upon as miraculous in a country where it never rained. The notion they had of that river whose source remained concealed, and whose overflowings seemed to them contrary to the common course of nature, made them say, that God himself poured these beneficial waters on Egypt. (*Fluvius à Deo missus.* Odyss. 4.) The Egyptians represented this marvel by the figure of God, that is, by a sun out of whose mouth a river sprung;† and the foreigners as

---

* Æsculapius was sometimes represented either standing, or setting on a throne, holding in one hand a staff, and grasping with the other the head of a serpent: at his feet a *dog* lay extended. On some ancient monuments we see him with one hand applied to his beard, and having in the other a knotted staff encircled by a serpent.— *Anthon's, Clas. Dict.—Edit.*

† For this reason it was, that they gave God or the sun among other titles that of ———— *pheob Phœbus* or *Phoibos* which signifies the *mouth of Ob*, that is the *source of the overflowing*, from the two words, ———— *pheb, os,* the mouth, and ———— *ob* the swelling, the overflowing; it is the ancient name they gave to the Nile overflowing its banks.

well as the Egyptians every where gave it out, that so singular a prosperity was the reward of the piety of the inhabitants. Nay, the Phenicians perhaps and the Canaanites at first received from the Egyptians and used the symbolical characters among themselves. The introduction of the common writing must have caused them to lose the sense without suppressing the figures; so that these symbols being always a part of the ceremonies, and publicly exposed at feasts, every body annexed to them the notion or history he thought carried the greater likelihood with it. Thus Egypt was the cup wherein the poison of idolatry lay, and the Phenicians are the people, who, by traveling all over the world, have presented this fatal cup to the greater part of the western nations. For the same reason it is, that the names of the gods and the words made use of in the heathen feasts, have so sensible an analogy with the Phenician language.

Travellers and merchants, during their sojourn in Egypt, were undoubtedly struck with the outward shew of the feasts and the abundance that seemed to be the result of them. They did not carry home this multitude of symbols and practices which they understood nothing of but they seldom failed to look with veneration upon the three or four chief symbols which the Egyptians honored as beneficial powers, and as the authors of all the good they enjoyed.

The governor, the woman, the child, and the messenger, or the giver of advices, always appearing in their feasts, though with some variety; foreigners used themselves chiefly to these three or four objects, the most distinguished of the whole worship: and the Phenicians, whom constant necessity always brought again to the port of Pharos, were the first who made use of the same ceremonial, and celebrated the same feasts in their own country. The circle of the sun, accompanied with serpents and foliages, or with large wings to represent the intelligence which is the mover of all things, the master of the air, the dispenser of seasons and harvests, though always placed at top of the noblest symbols, however less attracted the eyes than did the brilliant figure of the governor of the earth, or the several dresses given the mother and the beloved child. Nothing contributed more to humanize, as I may say, the idea of God, or rather to make men refer their worship and adorations to beings like ourselves.

Moloch, Baal, Adonis, and Achad.

The god, or rather the figure of the sun, which the Egyptians called *Osiris*, or the governor of the earth, assumed other names in other places. The eastern nations who had adopted him, and who looked on their temporal advantages as the effect of this devotion, called him *Moloch* or *Melchom*, that is the king; some, *Baal* or *Adonai*, or *Adonis*, or *Hero*,* all which names signify *the lord*. Others called him *Achad*,† which the old inhabitants of Latium have rendered by that of *Sol, unicus* ; and others finally named him Baalshamain or Beelsamen ‡ *the lord of the heavens*. But it was always the sun which these figures of a king and these names immediately signified.

Dionyisus, Bacchus.

In the times when things were expressed by symbols, and the several parts of these symbols were varied to be the better understood, far from being designed to conceal any mystery; the figure of Horus changed its name and attributes according to the exigency of the circumstances in which it was employed. The first use it was applied to in certain feasts was *the representation of past events*. The second was the instruction and *the regulations* fit for the people.

The representation of the ancient state of mankind consisted, not only in the commemorative signs that were carried either upon a winnowing van or in the small chest before mentioned : they joined thereto ceremonies or set forms of prayers regarding the same intention. They, in these feasts, invoked the name of God with great lamentations. They called him the mighty, the life, the father of life. They implored his assistance against wild beasts, and made show of giving them chace, running hither and thither, as if they were going to attack them. They even did it in good earnest completely armed.

It was the custom to say with a sigh : *Let us cry unto the Lord*, io terombe, *or* disterombe. Let us cry before the Lord, or *God see our tears*, io Bacche, io Baccoth. *Thou art the life, the author of being. Thou art God and the mighty:* Jehova, hevan, hevoe, and eloah. They chiefly said in the east : *God is the fire and the principle of life. Thou art the fire ; life proceeds from thee* : hu esh : atta esh.* All these words and many others, which were the expressions of grief and

---

* See the name of *hero* in that sense in the interpretation of the obelisk of Ramesses in Ammian Marcellin, or in Marsham's rule of times. From that *hero*, the Latins made their *herus* and *hera*, the lord, the lady. The Philistines called him the lord of men, *marnas*, from the word *maran*, which signifies the master, and from *as* which signifies man. And this comes to the sense of the foregoing names.

† ———— *achad, unicus*, and by a softened pronunciation, *adad*, one, the only. The ancient kings of Syria, who styled themselves his children, assumed the name of *Ben-adad* son of God. *See Macrob. Saturnal.*

‡ ———————— *Dominus cœlorum.*

§ Hu esh — *ipse est ignis*, Deuteron, 4 : 24. *Atta esh, tu vita es*. See Strabo, 1, 10.

adoration, became so many titles, which the people, without understanding, gave to this child or imaginary deity. He was then called Bacchos, Hevan, Evoe, Dithyrambus, Jao, Eleleus, Ves, Attes. They knew not, what all this signified : but they were sure that the god of the feast delighted in all these titles. They never failed to give them him, and thus these expressions became cries of joy, or extravagant roarings.

When people went about pursuing the wild beasts that thwarted the endeavors of husbandmen, they cried aloud : *Lord thou art an host to me*, io Sabio. *Lord ! be my guide*, io Nissi, or with a different accent Dionissi.* Of these warlike cries, which were repeated without being understood, they made the names of Sabasius and Dionysius

Of all these names, that were most used in Italy was Baccoth. The delicate ear of the Greeks, who could not indure harsh sounds, gave the preference to the name of Dionysius. These several titles (and the series of them was long) gave birth to as many histories Thus they called this god Dionysius, because he was son of Jehov or Jupiter, and born at Nysa an Arabian city. He was named Evius, because, as he was fighting with one of the giants, Jupiter encouraged him in the Greek language, and——————But if we now are sure of truth, why should we busy ourselves in enumerating such sorry tales ? We are no way concerned to hear all the nonsense, which the want of understanding these names † has caused to be built upon each of them.

Let us now pass on to the retinue of Bacchus. We shall there find a proof, that Bacchus was no more than a mask or figure, and not any man that ever existed.

When the arts were once invented, the remembrance of the roughness of the first ages, and the comparison of the hardships which mankind had at first experienced with the conveniences and inventions of latter times, rendered the rural feasts or the feasts of the representation of the ancient state of men, more brisk and lively than all the rest.

One of the most essential points of this feast was then to appear

---

* The supplications in Masonry are similar to the above. In the degree of royal arch, the following ejaculations are utered :—"Lord I cry unto thee : make haste unto me : give ear unto my voice. Mine eyes are unto thee O God the Lord ; in thee is my trust ; leave not my soul destitute. I cried unto thee, O Lord ; I said, thou art my refuge, and my portion in the land of thé living. Attend unto my cry ; for I am brought very low : deliver me from my persecutors ; for they are stronger than I. Hear my prayer, O Lord ; give ear to my supplications ;fin thy faithfulness answer me and in thy righteousness."—(Webb.)—*Edit*.

† These fables may be seen in the hymns attributed to Orpheus and Homer ; in the poems of Hesiod and Ovid ; in the hymns of Callimachus ; in the mythologies of *Noel le Comte*, and others.

there covered with skins of goats * bucks, tygers, and of other tame and wild animals. They smeared their faces with blood, to bear the marks of the danger they had run and the victory they had obtained.

Instead of a child of metal mysteriously carried about in a chest, they by degrees contracted a custom of choosing a good fat jolly boy, to play the part of the imaginary god. They in process of time gave him a chariot; and to render the whole more admirable, the pretended tygers offered to draw him, whilst the bucks, and goats were jumping and capering round him. The assistants *disguised* and *masked* in this manner had names agreeable to what they were doing. They were called Satyrs, a word which signifies *men disguised* † or Fauni, that is *masks*. These etymologies which are very plain, and strictly connected with what precedes, are still confirmed by the usage which the assistants at these rural feasts observed of consecrating to Bacchus, and of suspending on the tree under which they made their last station, the mask of bark or other matter, wherewith they had covered their face, that they might have a share in the ceremony. The feasts of Bacchus have been abolished by the preaching of the gospel; but we see the remains of them among us in our winter rejoicings. It is the same concern, and, with no great difference, the same idolatry ‡

Those who followed or attended the chariot of Bacchus, were called Bacchants, that is, mourners, because the feast began with woes and complaints, and with frequent invocations on the assistance of God.

The woman, who carried the small chest or the sacred baskets, or at least a thyrsus,§ which was sometimes a javelin, in memory of the first chaces; sometimes a torch of resiny wood, were called Menades Thyades, and Bassarides. They were named Menades, which signi-

---

* This is what the Latins expressed by *Thyasos inducere* : to form choruses of people dressed like goats and rams. —— *thiasim 'hirci et arietes,* Genes. 30; 35.

† ——*fatur,* hidden, disguised,—— *panim* or *phanim, facies, prosopa, personæ, oscilla, masks.* Those panim or hideous masks could not fail frightening your children. For this reason it *is,* that fears occasioned by appearances of evil void of reality, have been called *terreurs paniques, panick terrors.* Such is evidently the origin of the name given to the god of Mendes, *viz.* Pan, in whose horns and hair the philosophers thought they had found a very noble emblem of general nature. Those who are fond of these admirable conceptions, may look out for them in the allegoric explications of Plutarch, Iamblichus, Psellus, the emperor Julian, and Plato.

‡ I have rend in an English paper, that anciently it was not unusual for a wag, on the first of January, to burst into a neighbor's house disguised in an ox's hide, including that of the head with the horns attached.—*Edit.*

§ Thyrsus, a rod or lance twisted round with ivy, which was put into the hand of the soldiers of Bacchus, or of those who celebrated his festivals. Ovid describes them as wound about with vine branches.

The Jews do at this day carry a sort of Thyrsii or something like them, in the feasts of *Tabernacles* and especially in the *Hosanna Rabba.* They are branches of willow, myrtle and palm-tree, bound up together with citrons or oranges, which they wave or push in a *religious manner* towards the four quarters of the world.—(Bailey.)—*Edit.*

fies, the *women who carry the public signs*, because the feasts or the regulations, and all the sacred figures inseparable from them, were in the ancient language called *Manes*, that is, regulations. This the Greeks rendered *Thismoi*. The extravagant attitudes of these mad women, who strove to outvie each other by the lamentations and representing gestures authorized by custom, were thence called *Maniæ*. These women again were called the Thyades, that is *vagrant* or *wandering*, when they dispersed themselves in the mountains like so many huntresses. They were called Bassarides or grape-geatherers, because these feasts were celebrated after vintage, and when new wine began to be drinkable.*

After the vagaries and the whole train, at last appeared an old man upon an ass, who advanced with a sedate countenance, offering wine to the tired youth, and inviting every body to take some rest.†

If any body should complain that this explication of the origin of the Bacchanals does not establish a relation sufficiently sensible between wine and the feasts of Bacchus, who from all antiquity, has been looked upon as the inventor and propagator of the vine, whereas we reduce it to the proclamation of a few instructions, which the people stood in need of; I shall reply, that the feasts of Bacchus and Ceres are every where styled among the Greeks and Romans, the feasts of the *regulations;* because they confusedly remembered, that the purport and intention of the figures of Isis and Horus was to regulate the conduct of the people. And I shall at the same time desire such, to take notice of what Horus carries over his head at the solemnity of the Pamylia, or at the beginning of the winter. Among other objects capable of pleasing, there appear *three large pitchers of wine*. This was the finest part of the ceremonial: and the feasts where this liquor was drunk in plenty could not but be the most brisk and most enlivened of all.

I have considerably abridged the preceding article. That the Bacchus honored in the processions here described was not, as the author states, a man that ever lived, is very evident; but that the figure representing him was merely *a symbol of husbandry* as he endeavors to show, is not so clear. The festivals were religious thanksgivings, in

---

* After the virgins, followed a company of men carrying poles at the end of which were fastened *phalloi*. The heads of these men were crowned with ivy and violets, and their faces covered with other herbs. They marched *singing songs* upon the occasion of the festival.—Anthon's Lemp, class Dict.—*Edit.*

† Ibat pando Silenus asello.

"It was the custom, at the celebration of the Eleusinian mysteries, as we are told by the Scoliast on the place, to have what was wanted in those rites, carried upon Asses. Hence the proverb, *Asinus portat mysteria*."—Warb, Div. Leg.—*Edit.*

which grateful acknowledgments were rendered for the favors received from the hand of divine providence, and the image intended to represent the god who was supposed to bestow these blessings, was ceremoniously carried in procession. The Bacchanals were similar to the feasts noticed in the memorials of past events, with trifling variations arising from a difference of taste, and misconceptions in the conveyance of customs from one country to another.

The Roman Catholic processions of the *Host* are of the same nature as the above, and no doubt the custom, like most of the practices of the church of Rome, has been derived from the ancient pagan ceremonies. The catholic processions, it seems, are conducted with more mystic, solemn pomp than those of the ancients, but the ruffian assaults of the guards or assistants in this affair, of persons walking in the streets, who are not even within the pale of their order, for neglecting to fall upon their knees, on the passage of the host, is more outrageous than the extravagancies of their prototype.

The masonic processions are identically the same thing as the Bacchanals, but got up with more taste and refinement, owing to the influence of civilization. In these are carried, besides other articles, which will hereafter be enumerated, a box or chest, called the lodge, about which much secrecy is pretended, and which is kept covered from the eyes of the profane or uninitiated. The utmost decorum is observed, and no person is annoyed for not paying homage to the sacred contents of of the mysterious chest.

The author himself in the next article to the foregoing, has told us who Bacchus really was, and which fully explains the understanding that should be applied to these Bacchanalian processions ; as follows :—

———

The scepter and empire of heaven and earth fell to the share of Osiris. The chariot, the whip, and the reins were assigned to Apollo ; whence it is that we so commonly find in one god the characters of another. The Horus Apollo, who was only related to the rural year or the order of works, was the more easily mistaken for the sun which rules nature, that they put the whip and the attributes of the sun into the hands of the Horus, in order to shorten and abbreviate the marks of the solar year, and of the works suitable to each season. Thus Horus became the same with the Moloch of the Ammonites, the Ádonis of Byblos, the Bel of the other Phenician cities, and the radiant Belenus honoured in Gaul. This driver of the chariot, which gives light to the world, is the son of Jupiter ; but the son of Jehov the son *par excellence, liber*, is no other than Horus, Bacchus or Dionysius. Osiris, Horus, Apollo, Bacchus, and the sun, are then confounded. This the author of the Saturnals has sufficiently demonstrated. Virgil himself makes no distinction between Bacchus and Appollo or the sun, when he gives Bacchus and Ceres or Isis the government of the year and the light.

    ———Vos, ó clarissima mundi
    Lumina, labentem cœlo quæ ducitis annum,
    Liber et alma Ceres.—   Georgic. I.

Atlas. The Hyades and Pleiades.

Atlas, according to the fable, was an ingenius master af astronomy a doctor who knew nature in general, and gave information about it. Homer gives us Atlas as a very learned god, who knew all the obliquities of the coasts, and all the depths of the sea. Virgil ascribes to the informations of the great Atlas the knowledge men had acquired of the moon, the eclipses of the sun, and the whole order of nature. The name signifies a support, (——— *atlah*, support, prop,) which gave occasion for the invention of the metamorphosis of the doctor Atlas into a *column* or high mountain, that props up the arch of the heavens.

The Phenicians in the voyages they repeated every third year to Tarshish, that is, to Cadis, and to Bœtica, (now Andalusia) through the Red-Sea, and in carrying on the commerce of all the coasts of Africa, often saw the highest mountain of Mauritania, whose top is generally covered with snow, and seems joined with the heavens. The name of Atlas or column given to that mountain, caused the fable of Atlas to be applied to it. They said he was king of Mauritania a great astrologer and geographer, who at last was by the gods changed into a high mountain, reaching from the earth to the heavens.

The Hyades or Huades, who took their name from the figure V, which they form in the forehead of the celestial bull, and the Pleiades, which are that small platoon of stars so remarkable, near the foregoing, are the most known and the easiest to be distinguished of all the constellations of the zodiac. They particularly were of use to regulate the informations given to the disciples of the priests by means of an Atlas, that is, of a Horus bearing a celestial sphere. Atlas humanized, became the father of the Hyades and Pleiades; and Orion which rises immediately after them, easily passed in the imagination of the fabulists for a libertine, who incessantly pursues them.

Among the other fables which the Phenician travellers were sufficiently at leisure to devise in their courses, or to recount when they came home, the two finest doubtless are those of the garden of the Hesperides, and of Atlas freed by Hercules of the burden of the celestial globe. What can be the origin of the first? Three nymphs placed round a tree that bears golded apples, of which they have the disposition and management; a dragon that watches to interdict the use of and access to this admirable fruit, to any other; a wild goat that browzes on the grass at the foot of the tree; or instead of the goat, a horn of abundance placed either at the foot of the tree or in the hand of one of the three nymphs. This is the picture of the garden of the Hesperides.

The picture is nothing more than the ancient symbol of the rich commerce of which the Phenicians made the preparations in winter. It was the commerce of Hesperia or of the western countries, particularly of Spain, whence they drew exquisite wines, rich metals, and that superfine wool which the Syrians dyed in purple, (See *Diod, and Strab,* or *Spect, de la nat, vol.* 4. *part* 2, *dialog.* 2.) They brought back the finest corn from the coast of Africa ; and when they went round the continent through the Red Sea, they exchanged all sorts of ironware, knives, and edge-tools, for ebony and other precious woods, for *gold dust* and provisions of all kinds. This branch of their commerce was the most esteemed of all. It was the chief object that did then take up the thoughts of the Phenicians ; nor did they fail to expose the *public sign* of it in the assemblies. One may easily guess at the meaning of that tree which afforded such precious things. The great dragon that surrounded the tree, turned the mind of the beholders to the subsistence and benefits whereof it was the sign. The capricorn, or barely one horn of this animal placed at the foot of the tree, was the character of the season. The three moons during which the companies were formed, had their name of Hesperides, or Hesperia, as well as all the West, from the word which signifies *the good share, the best lot.* (——*esper,* 2 Sam. 6 : 19)

The *public sign,* used upon this occasion, was doubtless three golden balls, having reference to the three moons, personified by three nymphs, in which the companies were formed, the figure and color corresponding with those of the full moon. An allusion may also be made to the *gold dust* and other precious articles, *the best lot,* which the Phenicians received in exchange for their merchandise.

The Lombards, the money-lenders of former times, are said to have adopted this sign for their offices ; and pawn-brokers still use it, to designate their profession. I am sensible that some writers conjecture the golden apples of the Hesperides to be nothing more than oranges ; but it is hardly probable that an article of so little value, in a mercantile point of view, should have given rise to the fable.

Hercules is a name of the sun, and his releaving Atlas of his burden, alludes to his dissolving the snow with which Atlas or the mountain of Moritania was loaded.

Mercury, Hermes, Camillus.

We have now a pretty large number of very famous men and women, which we, methinks, have an acquired right to strike out of history. We must no longer inquire into their country, antiquity, or genealogy, since we have proved that they all of them are nothing more than the Osiris, the Isis, and the Horus of Egypt ; that is, the three principal keys of the ancient writing, or the simbols of the solar, the civil, and the rural year.

We know a fourth key, *viz.* the Thot or Taaut, that is the dog. Thence again springs a multitude of kings and gods, of whom we shall in few words find out and explain the names, ranks, and imployments.

The Egyptians in after-times, no doubt, made him one of their kings, who had been transported into this fine star. They give him as the son of Menes, and the grandson of Osiris, and ascribe the invention of the symbolical characters to him. They say, that he was the counsellor of Menes, whom he assisted in the regulation of their feasts. But this fine story had no other foundation than the report that went among the Egyptians of old, that Thot introduced the Manes, and renewed the proclamations. And indeed he opened the year, since that always began at the rising of the dog-star ; whence the first of their months had the name of Thot. It was out of mere superstition, that the Egyptians forbore calculating exactly the sacred or civil year, when they began to know that besides the 365 days, there remained a quarter of a day to be added to complete the revolution of a year. Four quarters of a day overlooked, made a whole day in four years' time ; and neglecting to intercalate that day at the four years' end, and to reckon 366, instead of 365, their civil year on this account began one day too soon, and by retrogradation differed a whole day from the calculation of the natural year. The beginning of the sacred year went successively therefore through every one of the days of the natural year in the space of 365 times four years, which make 1460 years. They fancied they blessed and made all the seasons to prosper, by making them thus enjoy one after another the feast of Isis, which was celebrated along with that of the dog-star ; though it was frequently very remote from that constellation : and it was in consequence of the ancient custom of celebrating the feast of Isis, or the renewal of the year at the exact rising of the dog star, that they afterwards, in whatever season that feast might fall, to be sure, introduced, not only the figure of a dog, but even real and live dogs, which always preceded the chariot of Isis (*Diod, l.* 1.) ; a circumstance which I beg my reader to take a particular notice of. Thus in aftertimes they took a special pleasure in introducing a marvellous and mysterious air into every thing. The calculation just mentioned, and many others which they had received from the priests their predecessors, were things of the utmost plainness. They, in process of time, mistook them for the durations of the several kings whom they quartered in the dog-star and other celestial bodies. One had lived 1460 years; another had reigned so many thousands of years together. The astronomical observations grounded on several suppositions and combinations of the stars, were one of the chief imployments of the priests. These calculations found in the registers of the most laborious among the learned, being always joined with names of men, such as Anubis, Thot, Menes, Osiris, and others whom they lodged in the stars, passed for the term of the terrestrial life of these gods. Such is indeed the true origin of that antiquity of the Egyptian history, which they trace back so very high. Their ancient kings are nothing more than the names of the stars; and the pretended duration of their lives, is only a supputation of the time necessary to bring again a planet to that point of the heavens from which it had begun its course. Thus they made as wrong a use of their astronomical computations as they had done of their writing.

Let us not, in mentioning the retrogradation of the feast of Isis and the return of that feast at the rising of the dog-star at 1460 years' end, omit one observation, *viz.* that they looked upon the 1461st year as privileged, as a year of *plenty and delights*. It was because this so important an event, according to them, concurred with the desired Etesian wind, that they expressed the whole by a bird of singular beauty, that raised admiration more than any of the rest, and returned to Egypt after an absence of 1460 years, (*Tacit, Annal,* 6.) They farther said, that this bird came thither to die upon the altar of the sun, and that out of its ashes there rose a little worm, that gave birth to a bird perfectly like the preceding. They called it Phœnix, which signifies the advantage they pretended was annexed to the concurrence of the opening of the year with the real rising of the dog-star; I mean *the most delightful plenty* (——*phonek, deliciis abundans.* Prov. 26; 21.) We then have here again another emblematic figure converted into a wonder which it would have been a crime to doubt of.*

The dog-star has already afforded us two deities, one residing in the fine star near Cancer, under the name of Thot or of Anubis, and very well employed in swelling and sinking the river Nile, the other wholly intent upon physic, and entirely taken up with the care of people's

---

* Bailey observes, that "a Phœnix, hieroglyphically, was pictured to signify a reformation;" which corroborates our author's hypothesis, for there was a complete reformation of the calendar, according to the Egyptian calculation, at the end of the above mentioned period.—Edit.

health under the name of Æsculapius. Next to Anubis and Æsculapius, let us now see the Camillus of the Heturians, the Janus of the Latins, the Hermes of the Greeks, and the Mercury of the Phenicians, all of them rising out of the same figure. The observation of the dogstar was not only justly denoted by the figure of a serpent, the symbol of the life it had procured the Egyptians, but having besides procured them abundance or rather a superabundance of corn, which enabled them to help foreigners and to enrich themselves by the selling of their commodities, the figure of Anubis was often accompanied by a full purse the sight whereof filled the people with joy ; and this procured it the new title of Mercury, which signifies *the dealer*, or *the intriguing*, *the cunning*, or only *commerce*.

A new proof that Mercury was no more than a symbol of the dogstar or of the warning of the retreat, and not a man that ever taught or invented any thing, is, that they put into his hand the mark of the swelling of the Nile, and at his feet the wings, intimating the necessity of escaping the inundation by a speedy flight.

The mark of the rising of the water was a pole crossed ; a very plain symbol indeed ; and the serpent twisted round it had, in the hand of this figure, no other meaning than elsewhere. It always signified the life, the subsistance. When double, it denoted subsistance in very great plenty, and such as was sufficient both for the Egyptians and foreigners. This pole was terminated with two little wings ; the symbol of the wind that regulated the increase of the waters. All which significations were forgoten, and *the monitor* becoming a god as well as the other figures, they changed his name of Anubis, the barker, into that of Hannadi, the orator. (*Hannobeah*, Isai. lvi. 10.) His gesture and the stick he had in his hand helped on this metamorphosis. It was taken for the mark of a leader, an embassador. Hence the title of *guide*, of *inspector of the roads*, of messenger of good news, and so many the like that were given Mercury, and of which we find a collection in Geraldi's history of the gods. Hence came the roads under his protection, and of placing his statue at the entrance of the highways. But what can be the origin of the name of Caduceus given to Mercury's rod ?

In the East, any person preferred to honors bore a sceptre* or staff

---

* The proof of this is frequently met with in Scripture. When the tribes murmured at seeing the priesthood settled in the family of Aaron, the chiefs of the tribes received orders to bring their scepters into the tabernacle. The scepter of Levi borne by Aaron was found in bloom the next day ; and the Scripture observes, that the other chiefs took back their scepters or staves of command.

of honor, and sometimes a plate of gold on the forehead called *cadosh* or *caduceus*, * signifying a sacred person, (———*cadosh sanctus, separatus*.) to inform the people that he who bore this rod or mark was a public man, who might go hither and thither freely, and whose person was inviolable. Such is the origin of the name given to *Mercury's wand*. Thus they made the guide of travelers, the interpreter, (——— *interpres, nuncius sacer*,) and deputy of the gods, of a figure whose office they confusedly knew was to warn people of being gone. Being wholly ignorant of the relation between this long measure and the Nile, it was every where converted into an embassador's staff, that there might be some connexion between the envoy and the wand he carried.

Instead of the measure of the Nile, they very often put into his hand a key, and gave him two faces, one of a young man, the other of a man in years; incompassing the whole with a serpent having his tail in his mouth. The serpent symbol of life or of time, here signifies the year that makes a perpetual circle, and the revolution of the stars coming again to the point of the heavens from which they began their course the year before. Our door-keeper who here shuts up the concluding year, and opens the new, is no other than the dog-star, whose rising or disengaging from the rays of the sun pointed out the new solar year. I say solar, or natural, because it happened for reasons before stated, that the beginning of the sacred year went through every one of the seasons. But they still observed the custom of making the god Anubis who was the *door-keeper of the feasts*, to precede the pomp of Isis, which was the first feast of the year; whence it appears, that the whole was rather astronomical than historical. This undoubtedly is the Janus of the Latins, who had the same attributes with the name of door-keeper. His ordinary companion good king Picus, with his hawk's head, has

---

* A similar plate decorated the chief priest of the Israelites. 'The high-priest wore a plate of gold upon his forehead, on which were engraven these two words *Kodesch layhovah*, that is *Holy to the Lord*. It was tied with a purple or blue ribbon to his tiara, which was made of linen, like those of the other priests, and was only distinguished from them by this plate and ribbon. There was in every synnagogue a sort of *minister*, who read the prayers, directed the reading of the law, and preached, he was called *chazan*, that is, *inspector* or bishop. See Dr. A. Clark's Hist. Israel p. 286-7.

There is a degree in masonry called " a chapter of the grand *Inspectors* of lodges, or grand elected knights of *Kadosh*?" who seem to have borrowed their title and functions, as *Inspectors*, from those of the Egyptian Mercury. The badge borne by Mercury appears to be alluded to by the manner of answering the question, " *Are you Kadosh*?" upon which the person questioned places his hand upon his forehead, and says, " yes, I am." The sacred words are *Nekam Adonai*; which probably have the same signification as the words engraved on the plate worn by the Jewish high priest; Adonai or Adonis meaning lord.—This degree will hereafter be particularly noticed.

The miter worn by the high priest of masonry, in the royal arch degree, is surrounded with the words *holiness to the lord.*—*Edit.*

so much the air of an Egyptian, that we cannot doubt but that Egypt not Latium, was the country of both.

Anubis considered as a symbol, was in reality the rule of the feasts, and the introducer of all the symbolical figures that were successively shown to the people during the whole year. When a god, he was made inventor and regulator of these feasts. Now these solemnities were called the *manes*, that is, *the regulations, the signs, the ensigns*, because the figures there presented to the assistants were originally designed to regulate the works of the people. This they made the noblest function of Anubis; and it was with regard to this frivolous opinion, that the pomp of Isis was always preceded by a dog. But the neomeniæ of each season, and the particular feasts that went before or that followed each harvest having peculiar names that distinguished them, the general word of *manes*, ensigns or images, was still the name of the funeral assemblies, which were frequently repeated, and the names of manes, images simaulcres, and dead persons were confounded. Thus Mercury, who *opened and shut* the manes,(———, manium dux, ductor animarum,) became the leader of the dead. He conducted the souls with a high hand. The king or the shepherd must indiscriminately follow the troop. He opened the melancholly abodes to them, shut these again without remorse, and took away the key, not permitting any one to escape. (*Tum virgam capit. Hac animas ille evocat orco.*) This again is what the Phenicians and the Arcadians meant, when they called him Cyllenius, a word which signifies the shutting or *one that concludes* the year, and who *finishes for ever* the duration of life.

The people were persuaded, that he invented music, the lyre, wrestling, and all the exercises that form the body because all these things being inseperably annexed to the ancient feasts, he was thought the regulator of them as well as of the feasts, he of course introduced every thing belonging to them.

As to the genealogy of Mercury, it confirms all we have said. He is the son of fair Maia, and grandson of Atlas. Maia is the Pleias or the cluster of stars known even by the vulgar, and placed on the back of the bull. The eastern nations called these stars Mæah, which signifies the *hundred, the multitude.* The Greeks sometimes retained their first name, and called them Maia; sometimes translated this word by those of Pleiades and Pleione, which likewise signify *the multitude.* These so very remarkable stars being most fit to regulate the study of the heavens, and being the first that struck the eye before the rising of the dog-star, of which they thus became the forerunners;

they, together with the Hyades, were the first in the knowledge of which the Egyptian priests took care to instruct their young pupils, in the sphere of Atlas. This symbol being once become a god, all his instructions were embellished with histories as well as he. The stars, that served as a rule to know the others by, became the beloved daughters of doctor Atlas. Maia disengaged herself at that time from the rays of the sun in Gemini, that is, in the month of May, to which she seems to have given her name. The finest star that clears itself a month or somewhat more after from the rays of the sun, is the dog-star or the Anubis, of which they were pleased to make Maia the mother, because the star of Anubis was the first that succeeded her.

Dædalus.

It was the custom in Egypt to say, when the dog-star or Anubis was represented with large hawk's wings, that the water would be of a sufficient height, and there would be a certainty of a plentiful harvest. On this occasion Anubis was called Dœdalus, which signifies a *sufficient height*, or a sufficient depth.

All the ancients agree that Dœdalus was an ingenius architect. They ascribe to him the invention of the *compasses* and the *square*. They farther add, that to him mankind is indebted for statuary; they even characterize the nature of the progress which this noble art made under him, by circumstances which render the thing very credible. *Before Dædalus*, and to his very time, according to Diodorus Siculus. " Statues had their eyes shut, and their hands close to their sides. But Dœdalus taught men how to give them eyes, to separate their legs, and to clear their hands from their body. Which procured him the general admiration.''

But by misfortune, both the history and the statues with their feet united, become the proof of the origin I here assign to Dœdalus. The compasses and square, of which he is made the inventor, are no other than the compasses and square that were put into the hands of Anubis or Horus, to warn the husbandmen to be in readiness to measure their lands, to take angles in order to distinguish them from the lands of others. Thus he was made the inventor of the symbolical instruments they saw in his hands. The statues whose hands and feet are frequently swathed, and which are found in the cabinets of our virtuous, are no other than the statutes of Osiris, Isis, and Horus, such as they were presented to the people at the time of the inundation. There was nothing then to be done, and the inaction was universal. The intire cessation of the rural works could not be better intimated, than by a Horus swathed or deprived of the use of his feet by the inundation, and using only his arms to point out the measure of the water, a vane to shew the wind, another instrument to take angles, and a horn to proclaim the general surveying.

The Cabiri of Samothracia.

The three principal figures of the Egyptian ceremonial were carried to Berytus in Phenicia, and thence into several Islands of the Ægean sea. Their worship became very famous, especially in Lemnos, and in the island of Samothracia, which lies very near it. They were called there the Cabiri, (———— *cabirim, potentes*,) meaning the powerful gods: and their name of Cabiri, which is Phenician, was as much used in Egypt as in Phenicia itself: which is a standing proof of the mixture of the Phenician terms with the Egyptian language, if the ground of both be not exactly the same.

The figures of these gods being originally designed to make up a certain sense, by a collection of several pieces that very seldom meet together, could not but have a very odd, if not a very ridiculous air in the eyes of such as did not understand their meaning. The foliages, horns, wings, and spheres, so commonly found on the heads of Osiris, Isis and Horus, could not but amaze or raise the laughter of such as were not accustomed to them. Herodotus observes, that the Cabiri, as well as the same figure of Vulcan, were the diversion of Cambyses, when he entered their temple and that of the forging deity.

They often add to these a fourth god, whom they sometimes call Mercury, sometimes Camilus or Casmilus, which among the Heturians and in Latium signified a minister or a messenger. In all which it is plain, that we again meet with the four principal keys of the ancient Egyptian writing, changed on account of their human figure into so many *tutelar and powerful* gods.

The names of the Cabiri, with their significations, are thus given in Anthon's Class. Dict. :—"Axieros is said to have signified in Egyptian, *the all powerful one ;*—Axiokersos is made to denote *the great fecundator ;*—Axeokersa is consequently the *great fecundatrix ;* and Casmilus *he who stands before the deity, or he who beholds the face of the deity*."

The first answers to the Supreme Intelligence; the second to Osiris the sun; the third to Isis; and the fourth to Anubis.

Apollo, the Muses, and the Graces.

Notwithstanding the variety which the caprice of private men and the difference of tastes have introduced into the Egyptian ceremonial, and among the signs that served to proclaim whatever was of concern to the public, we find every where the same grounds, because the wants of all men were the same, and their practices were founded on these wants. After the sense of those emblems had been so far perverted as to change the significant figures into so many deities solely taken up with the care of supplying all the wants of the Egyptians, or of informing them of all their concerns; each province paid special worship to one or the other of the figures. For instance, in some places they honored Apollo holding in his hand a lyre. This so very plain a symbol of the feasts, having been taken for a deity presiding over harmony,* the other figures which attended him to denote the several circumstances of each season, were taken in a sense agreeable to the notion they had framed to themselves of Apollo. The nine Isises which proclaimed the neomeniæ, or the first days of every one of the nine months, during which Egypt is freed from the inundation, bore in their hands symbols peculiar or suitable to each of these months; as for instance, a pair of compasses, a flute, a trumpet, a mask, or some other attribute, to denote the feast that preceded the surveying of the lands that had been overflowed, or some other solemnity. All these figures in reality informed men of what they were to do. They had a general confused remembrance that these were their functions. But being once become goddesses, people imagined that they had the superintendance of music, geometry, astronomy, and of all sciences. They were united in a chorus to the musician Apollo; and instead of seeing in the instruments they bore the peculiar characters of the feasts and works of each month, men took them for the specific marks of all fine and delicate arts, and even helped on this fancy, by adding a part of the emblems. They were called in Egypt the Nine Muses: which

---

* The author, it seems, was not sensible of the propriety of this title; but none could be more appropriate for the inhabitants of the northern climates to bestow upon Apollo, the sun of the upper hemisphere. Dupuis, as before noticed, has well described the complaints that would naturally occur, in consequence of the absence of the sun in the winter season: "What has become of the happy temperature which the earth enjoyed in the summer? that *harmony* of the *elements* which accorded with that of the heavens? that richness, that beauty of our fields," etc.

Apollo restored this happy state of things, and might, therefore, very properly be styled a *deity presiding over harmony*. "The god of the sun became also the god of music by a natural allusion to the movements of the planets and the mysterious harmony of the spheres." (Anthon's Class. Dict.)—*Edit.*

signifies the nine months *rescued from the waters*, or *delivered from the inundation:* an etymology whose exactness is demonstrated in the name of Moses, or Mose, which signifies *saved from the waters, disingaged, freed from the waters.* Such was the common name they always retained. But the Greeks, among whom this chorus of deities was introduced, gave each of them a proper name. Those names if they are taken out of their language, conformably to the ridiculous notions they entertained of these figures, are no manner of information to us, and are not worth our translating. Near the nine Isises that denoted the nine months in which people might go up and down, and act at liberty, appeared also the three Isises, that represented the three months during which the water remained on the plains, and hindered the free correspondence of one city with another. They were drawn sometimes in swathings, and incapable of making any use either of their feet or arms; sometimes half women and half lizards, or half fishes; because men must then remain on the land by the water-side. In fine, (and this last form was more to the liking of the Greeks,) they were represented as three idle sisters, without any attribute, holding one another by the hand; because they denoted the inaction of the three months of inundation, that succeeded each other without interruption. And as these three months broke off the ordinary correspondence of one city with another, at a time when they had not as yet raised the, magnificent causeways that have since been made; the three Isises proclaiming the neomeniæ, of these months of total separation, were called *Cheritout*,* that is, the *divorce*, the time of *the separation.* This word had a relation of sound with the word *eharites*, which in Greek signifies sometimes *the thanksgivings*, sometimes *the favours*, or *a courteous behaviour*. Which gave occasion to the Greek poets to imagine, that these three goddesses presided over gratitude and outward charms.

Notwithstanding all the care every city had taken in the month of June to supply itself with necessary provisions, they could not on many occasions do without the assistance of each other, and they had recourse to the conveniency of barks and sails. The bark with its sail was represented in Egypt and Phenicia under a figure of a winged steed. On this account it was that the people of Cadis, who were originally of Phenician extraction, anciently gave a ship, whether large or small,

---

* From —— *charat. abscindere*, comes —— *cheritout repudium, scissio*, the interruption of commerce. See the word *Cheritout*. Isai. 50: 1. & Deut. 24: 1.

the name of a horse;* and speaking of their barks, they called them their horses. What can be then the meaning of Pegassus, or the winged horse set by the side of the three Graces and the nine Muses? If these goddesses preside over gratitude and the sciences, our winged horse becomes unintelligible. But if our Charites are the three months of separation, or the interruption of the free correspondence of one city with another, in this case indeed Pegassus comes to our assistance; and if the nine Muses are the nine figures that publish what is to be done during the nine months in which Egypt is freed from the waters, then indeed the winged horse, that is, the boat, becomes a symbol of the end of navigation, and of the return of the rural works. They therefore gave this figure the name of Pegassus, which signifies *the end of navigation*,† according to the style of the Phenician people testified by Stabro, *the conveniency of navigation*.

An Egyptian or Phenician colony, that had all these figures in the ceremonial of its religion, brought them along with it to Phocis in the neighborhood of Mount Parnassus and of Delphos. They had for certain no meaning there, being no way related to any thing belonging to that country. But they had been long honored, together with their president Apollo, as so many bountiful deities: which was sufficient to perpetuate the use of these figures, and of the pretty stories which had been devised to account for all.

It will not be improper, in order to strengthen what has been said, to observe, that in the ancient figures the three Graces are often seen under the conduct of Mercury, because the rising of the dog-star in Egypt is succeeded by the three months of inundation; and the nine Muses under the conduct of Apollo, because Horus, or working, makes its use and benefit of the nine following months.

But why did this Apollo pronounce oracles, and foretel future events? This was its first destination and appointment. Horus served only to inform people by his attributes, of what was to be done or expected according to the winds and years. People never forgot, that these figures were the signs and regulaitons that guided the works of man: but when they were once made gods; instead of lookng upon them as convenient indications and tokens, whereby persons of great experience regulated

---

* *Gaditarorum mercatores ingentibus uti navibus, pauperes parvis, quas equos appellent.* Strab. geograph. l. 2, p. 99. edit. *Reg.*
† From — *pag, cessat, otiatur;* and from —— *sus, cursor, navis,* comes —— *pegasus. navigationis intermissio.* The head of a steed put on the shoulders of Isis, (*Pausan, in Arcad.*) with a fish in one hand and doves in the other, was evidently the proclamation of a feast that opened the navigation, when the sun left the sign Pices, and brought on the Zephyrs, the gentleness of which was denoted by the dove.

the works of the people, and beforehand pointed out to them what was to be done from one month to another, they fancied that these figures were acquainted with future events, and gave informations about them.*

The author, it appears to me, is here in error. Apollo was a god, the sun, before the invention of the symbols that indicated his movements in the heavens, and the state of the seasons, which regulated the labors of man. Nor do I perceive the propriety of naming these symbols Horus, or Apollo, any other appelation would answer equally well. When Appollo had become personified by means of the popular religion that governed the opinions of men at the time, he then, "Instead of being the god from whom eminate fecundity and increase, is a simple shepherd, conducting the herds of another. Instead of dying and arising again to life, he is ever young. Instead of scorching the earth and its inhabitants with his devouring rays, he darts his fearful arrows from his quiver of gold. Instead of announcing the future in the mysterious language of the planets, he prophesies in his own name. Nor does he any longer direct the harmony of the spheres by the notes of his mystic lyre, he has now an instrument, invented by Mercury and perfected by himself. The dances too of the stars cease to be conducted by him; for he now moves at the head of the nine muses, the strings of his divine cithara, the divinities who preside each over one of the liberal arts." (Constant, de la Religion.—Anthon's Class. Dict.)

Nyobe.

Niobe, the poets say, proud of her own fruitfulness insulted Latona, but Appollo punished her by slaying her *fourteen children* with his arrows. She never could be comforted; and the gods out of compassion changed her into a rock. Latona or the lizard, or the figure which is half woman and half lizard, signifies the retreat of the Egyptians to the higher grounds.†

Nyobe signifies the sojourn of the enemy, or of the river overflowing the plain. From —— *nuah*, habitares to sojourn; and from —*ob*, exundation, tumor, comes ——— *Nyob*, mora exundationis.

The insult Nyobe gives Latona is the necessity she lays the Egyptians under of flying like amphibious animals, to terraces surrounded with water. The *fourteen children* of Nyobe, are the *fourteen cubits* that mark the several increases of the Nile, (Strab. l. 17.) These

---

* Possibly this has procured Horus-Apollo the title of *Pœan* or *Pœana, revelator, the interpreter of hidden things, the oracle*. It is the same name Pharoah gave Joseph in his tongue. He called him (*Genes.* 41 : 45 ;) *tsaphat pœanach, the interpreter of sacred things*. These Egyptian words have a vast relation with the two of the Phenician language which signify the same thing, — to observe, to perceive, and — *tsaphan* to hide.

† The figures of Anubis and Isis are sometimes attended by a tortoise, a duck, or an amphibious lizard. The nature of these animals is to keep within reach both of the land and water, which are frequently necessary to them, and to get to higher ground as the water rises. This was the symbol borne by the Egyptian Isis at the approach of the overflow, and she was then called Leto, or Latona, which is the name of the amphibious lizard. This Isis, having the head and shoulders of a woman, with the paws, body and tail of a *leto* or lizard, is found in the monuments of antiquity.

fourteen cubits are still seen represented by fourteen children, disposed one above another upon the feet and arms of the figure of the Nile, now standing in the Tuileries.

Niobe, in short, is changed into a stone. Here lies the equivocation. The sojourn of the enemy becomes the preservation of Egypt, *shelav*. But the same word, disguised by a slight alteration into that of *shelaw*, signifies a stone, (—— *shelav*, salus, —— *shelaw*, silex.) Understanding no longer what was meant, by the mother of the fourteen children, changed into preservation, or become the preservator of Egypt, they metamorphosed her into a rock, and her eyes into two fountains, that continue to shed tears for the death of her dear family.

The following remarks of Mr. Mackey are ingenious and plausible. If his derivation of Tantalus be correct, it completely developes the origin of this celebrated personage.

"Nyobe was the symbol of the Nile; whose *fourteen children* show that the water of the Nile rose *fourteen cubits* above the land, which being dried up by the rays of the sun, it was said that Appollo, that is, the sun, slew the fourteen children with his arrows. Ovid reckons up the pedigree of Nyobe with much precision, and tells us her father's name was *Tantalus*.

"The lower part of Egypt, that is, the Delta, was formerly a gulf of the sea, which was filled up in the run of some thousand ages by the sediment brought down by the Nile from Ethiopia. Nyobe then is the daughter of a high country; but Ethiopia on account of its being a high country, is called in their language, *Tandalus*, from *Tan* a country, and *dalah* high. Thus Tantalus, a high country, was the father of Nyobe, a low country—the sediment of the one having produced the other.

"It is further said, that Tantalus was punished in hell with eternal thirst, while he stood *chin deep in water*. But do we not know that Tandalus, that is, Ethiopia is an *arid* country, notwithstanding all the fertilizing water of the Nile runs through it."

Although it rains in Ethiopia for several months almost continually, a portion of the year is said to be very dry and sickly.

Argus.

The explication of the foregoing fable * assists us in the understanding another, which, puerile as it is, has often exercised the greatest poets and the best painters: I mean the fable of Argus.

Juno, provoked at the conduct of her husband, took from him fair Isis, and having turned her into a heifer, committed her to the vigilance of Argus, who had a hundred eyes, some of which were awake, while the rest slept. But Mercury by his songs lulled all the eyes of the guardian asleep, and carried off Isis. What can this tale relate to? If I am not mistaken, the origin of it is this:

---

* That of the Argonauts, which is shown pretty conclusively by Dupuis, contrary to our author's explication, to be purely astronomical.—Edit.

Weaving was famous at Athens, in the island Amorgos, and in Colchis, as well as in Egypt.

Isis, the symbol of feasts, when she proclaimed the neomeniæ, and other solemnities of the winter and the spring, was attended by a Horus fit to characterize the kind of work which was to last for six months together. This figure was covered all over with eyes, to mark out the peculiar kind of work which is done by night; and it was because this Horus intimated the necessity of watching to forward the making of cloth, that he was called *Argus*, which means *the weavers work*.* The Isis, after having quitted the horns, of the wild goat, whereby she denoted the winter, assumed during the whole spring those of a heifer, because it is properly the passing of the sun under the sign of the bull, that constitutes in the temperate zone the true beauty of that delightful season. The vernal Isis, the handsome heifer, thus remained several months together under the eyes of Argus, or by the side of the open-eyed Horus, till the latter was removed, and the heifer carried away by Mercury; that is, till the nightly works, spinning and the making of cloth, were over, by the rising of the dog-star or Anubis. The people jesting upon these figures, forged the fable of Isis changed into a heifer, of her guardian Argus, and of the notable exploit of Mercury, who on this account was surnamed Argiphontes, the murderer of Argus. We find in Pierius, that the Egyptians gave also the name of Argus to the peacock that was by the side of Juno or Isis; and in the mythologists, that Juno, after the death of Argus, took the eyes he had about him, and therewith embellished the tail of the bird that was consecrated to her. This peacock placed near Isis, is only an attribute fit to denote the beginning of the nightly works, by an agreeable imitation either of the starry heaven, or rather of a multitude of eyes kept incessantly open. The name of Argus, viz. of *weaving*, it then went by, is a proof of this, and shews the intention of the ensign.

Circé.

The same Isis carried into Italy with her several attributes, gave birth to a fable of quite another turn. There she became the sorceress Circe, who with her wand turned men into lions, serpents, birds, swine and any other figure she was pleased to give them. From what can men imagine stories like this? The mythologists thought she was an

---

* ——— *argoth* or *argos*, *opus textrinum*, the weavers work. Thence are derived the words ——— *ergon*, *opus*, and *ourgla*, generally used to express all kinds of work, that of spinning and making of cloth being the most common.

emblem of voluptuousness, that brings men down to the condition of beasts. It was difficult to say any thing more reasonable, when they neglected to inquire into the true origin of these fictions. Circe is no other than the Egyptian Isis, who sometimes with a measure of the Nile, sometimes with a weaver's beam, a distaff, or a lance, always appeared with some distinction in the public proclamations. She was always accompanied with the figures of Horus and others, that varied from month to month, and often from day to day. She was the principal part of the enigma, to which all the other enigmatic emblems were subordinate. She was every where to be met with, and had always by her side and under her wand, sometimes a man with a dog's head, sometimes a lion, then a serpent or a tortoise, sometimes a whole child, at another time a child's head upon the body of a serpent, and successively the animals of the zodiac, and others, that denoted the return of the different rural works. In a word, she converted all that were near her into several animals. The Isis and her whole attendance was then really a riddle to be found out, an emblem to be explained. But what signifies Circe? Even *the wrapper, the enigma, (circ, involucrum.)*

Let us proceed farther. Isis very probably was not called Circe on any other account but that of the *circ*, or solar circle she commonly wore over her head. That circle was the emblem of the Supreme Being, of whom Isis proclaimed the several feasts. But why was this sun called *circ, the enigma?* It is because God could not be painted and a disc was the enigma of God. It was the enigma *par excellence the circ.* The place in Italy, to which this Isis with her circle over the head was brought and honored of old, is still called *Monte Circello.* To proclaim certain feasts or sacrifices, that were celebrated perhaps in the evening at the rising of the new moon, or in the morning at the rising of some star, or of the planet Venus, when it is admirably splendid, a little before the dawning of Aurora, they put over the head of Isis instead of the disc of the sun, that of a star, or of the known planet, a crescent, or a full moon. These figures, and the prayers that were sung in the old language at the return of each feast, made them imagine that Circe, by her inchantments, or by some mysterious words, had the power of making the stars and the moon come down upon the earth. It is equally evident, that the several foliages she bore in her hand, or over her head near the figure of the moon or of some other plannet, made, the people say, that the properties of these plants were admirable ; and that it was from a knowledge of their virtues that Circe was able to make both heaven and earth submit to her power. The figure seemed to intimate this, and they believed it.   This afterwards became the privilege of common witches; and the people is still persuaded, that the sorceresses at their pleasure dispose of heat, cold, hail, and all nature. This figure of Circe, which ignorance from an enigma or popular ensign had converted into a witch that turns men into several animals, and has the power of displacing the stars, relates very sensibly to the enigmatic attributes of Isis, which were a sun, the moon, some stars, certain extraordinary plants, and animals very often of a monstrous kind.   The rest of the fable, by its conformity with this interpretation, completes the demonstration of its exactness.   Circe, or Isis, was so far really the proclamation of the year, that she put on such clothes and dresses as were agreeable to the four seasons.   To announce the begining of spring, that overspread and enamels the earth with flowers and verdure, she wore carpets of different colors.   To denote the beginning of summer, which nourishes us, she bore in her hand a basket and a loaf; to proclaim the autumn, she bore a cup; and at the begining of winter she bore a chafing-dish, or a stove with its foot.   These four figures gave birth to the fable mentioned by Homer, (*Odyss. v.* 350.) that Circe had four maids, one of which spread the carpets of several colors to recive the guests, the second prepared the table, and put large baskets upon it, the third presented the cups, and the fourth kept up the fire on the hearth.

Proteus.

Proteus was the sign denoting the exchange of the Egyptian products for flocks, metals, wine, and other commodities which Phenician ships brought into the island of Pharos, the only Egyptian port formerly of safe and easy access.   These vessels there took in their provisions of corn, flax, and all the productions of Egypt.   The annual return of those ships to the confines of Egypt, was proclaimed by an Osiris called Neptune.   The Egyptians, who hated the sea, did not worship Neptune ; but they retained his name, which signifies *the arrival of the fleet*, and gave it to the borders of Egypt or the sea coast.   This we have from Plutarch.   Proteus going to Pharos to supply the *marine steeds* (the vulgar name for ships or vessels) with every thing, can be no other than the sale the Egyptians went to make of their commodities, on the arrival of the Phenecian barks.   This is confirmed by the name Proteus, which signifies nothing but *the abundance of fruit and the productions of the earth.* *   From the name

* From ——— peri, *fructus*, comes ——— *poret*, copia fructuum. Genes. 49. 22.

Poret or Proteus evidently proceed the French words *port* and *porter* because the fruits of the earth were the first object of transportation from one coast to another. The feigning that Proteus, on his arival at the port of Pharos, assumed many figures, arose from the variety of the commodities there offered for sale by the Egyptians.

The Syrens.

All Greece and Italy were by degrees filled with colonies and customs originally derived from Egypt or Phenicia; but the ritual, of which Egypt itself had forgotten the meaning so far as to take Osiris and Isis for deities, was infinitely more disfigured among other nations; and when a single part of the Egyptian religion was any where introduced, it grew darker and darker, for want of being connected with the other practices that served to compose the whole. The three Isises that proclaimed the feasts during the three months of inundation, being presented to the inhabitants, who seemed to become amphibious by their long dwelling by the water-side, were sometimes half-women, and half-lizard, or half-women and half-fish. One of them had in her hand an instrument of music rounded at top, and called Sistrum, which was the symbol of the hymns, dances, and of the universal joy that appeared throughout Egypt, when the Nile was of requisite height. They sung and danced at that time, as is still practised in Cairo, and all over Egypt, on the like occasion. They called the woman that carried the sistrum, *the singer of hymns*, because her function was to publish the good news, and the hymns of the great feast. This is then the origin of the Syrens on the coast of Naples, whose name signifies to *sing hymns*. (From ——— *shir hymnus*; and from ——— *ranan, canere.*) The figure given to all the three is exactly that of our Isis. The number of the Syrens answers to that of the three months of inundation; and the sistrum borne by one of them has, through ignorance, been converted into a looking-glass. As to what is said, that they devoured the strangers, that presumed to come too near in order to hear them; this fable is grounded on what was given out, that the three Isises of the summer were fatal to foreigners, whom the gross and marshy air of Egypt used to carry off, when they exposed themselves too much to it. M. de Maillet, and all travellers, agree that the air of the houses is then suffocating, that no one can bear it and that every body has tents on board the boats, to injoy a little coolness. It is therefore evident, that it was of very great moment to foreigners to avoid the three Syrens. Let us not leave this matter without observing, that this number of four nymphs for the four seasons, that of three for the moons of each season apart, that of nine for the nine months during which they work in Egypt, their attire, their functions, and names, are things very plain, connected with each other, and equally agreable both with nature and the monuments. Messieurs Bochart Huet, le Clerc, and other learned men, have thought upon these several subjects in a very ingenious, and even sometimes very judicious manner. But what they have said of them is destitute of connection. Facts do not favor their opinion; and when they have made a few mythologies accessible by the help of a first key, they cannot lead us any further without having recourse to a new key, or without wresting the sense of every thing. If we use but one single key, and the bare idea of a sign is sufficient to introduce a sense, and some relations between figures so utterly incoherent, is it not because we are indeed arrived at their true original, and have found out the common and general intention from which they sprung?

The Metamorphoses, and the Phantoms.

After these instances of fables evidently proceeding partly from Egyptian figures and partly from the popular expressions, equivocations, or proverbs occasioned by the sight of these figures; we have acquired a privilege of asserting in general that from the same source, metamorphoses, phantoms, and oracles sprung.

All and every one of the Egyptian figures had been established only to proclaim the feasts and works to come. When they were become so many gods, all these deities had the privilege of foretelling future events; whence it happened, according to Herodotus, (*In Euterp. num.* 52.) that Jupiter, Minerva, Apollo, Diana, Mars, and above all Latona, pronounced oracles to the Egyptians. The oracle of Latona became the most notable, because really Latona being originally no other than the Isis, half-woman half-lizard, or the virgin Erigone united to a lizard's body, to mark out the exact height of the increases of the Nile, she was the most consulted of any figure. All eyes were fixed upon this measure. They addressed to Latona every day and every hour. When she was at last made a goddess, the people who consulted her imagined, that she knew every thing. But we shall treat of this matter apart, as there is nothing in point of which it is so difficult to make men cast off their ancient prejudice, as the predictions of futurity.

The same source from which the oracles sprung, has given birth to phantoms. The gods which men had forged to themselves, being for the most part hideous and monstrous figures, and the apprehension of the evil they were reputed capable of doing, having a greater share in the religion of nations than confidence and the love of justice; men represented to themselves their own deities, and the powers which they dreaded, only under the ideas of figures bristling with serpents, armed with claws or horns, very often with yawning wide-open jaws, and with such an aspect as could not but corrupt the imagination and reason of children. These empty phantoms fostered in them a childish terror, that lasted as long as their lives.

It is no longer any task to guess at the general origin of metamorphoses. Egypt is evidently the source of them. A man with a dog, wolf or lion's head; a woman, who, instead of feet, has a lizard or a fish's tail; a child with the body of a serpent, and other the like figures invented to supply the wants we have mentioned, being no longer understood, they imagined as many fables and miraculous changes as there were of these compound figures. This relish for surprising stories became universal in Phenicia, then in Greece, and all the world over. The least equivocation, historical facts abriged, short and proverbial expressions, all in short gave birth to some miraculous transformations.

This would be the proper place to explain the whole series of the metamorphoses, and to recall them severally to their peculiar originals. I even conceive how several of them might be accounted for in a very plain manner. But it is enough for us to know how this odd taste came to take root in Greece and other places. The particular examination of these innumerable extravagances would become tiresome to my readers; and far from being willing to clog them with a new train of Phenician etymologies, I am really very much afraid of having already transgressed bounds, though I was indispensably obliged to follow this method. It is with ancient languages as with geometry; they must be made use of when there is necessity; but it is ridiculous to treat of needless matters, merely for the sake of making a show of erudition and geometrical learning.

The Genealogy of the Gods.

Though the Egyptians, by introducing great mysteries where there were none, have disfigured history and religion, yet we cannot deny, them the glory of good regulations for polity and public order. Whatever was necessary, and must be done in common, was not left to the free-will of private persons, but fixed to a certain time of the year, and proclaimed by public signs.

In the beginning of the spring, or at the return of the first heats, which in Egypt come on in February, they cleansed their goods, houses and stables. Every thing in a decayed state, being of no use to the Egyptian lands which the Nile sufficiently improved, was consumed by fire.

This general purification was proclaimed by an Isis and a Horus, who had names agreeable to to the work of the season. The Horus, was called Our * or Ourim, *the fire, the fire-brands ;* and the Isis was called Obs, † or Ops, mould *or hoariness.* These purifications which were transmitted from coast to coast, are still in use all over Europe towards the return of the fair weather in February or March ; and the custom of lighting fires in the evening on certain days in the spring for that purpose appointed, is still the amusement of youth in a multitude of cities and villages, where they faithfully observe the old rubric without knowing the reason of it. Even in Egypt, where the solemn feasts, falling back one day every fourth year, appeared in seasons to which they had no longer any relation, they forgot the motive of the institution of the feast of the fire-brands, but they were always faithful in the observation of it.

In the evening the inhabitants of Sais began their great feast with an illumination. So soon as the neighboring towns saw it, they lighted the like fires. Each did the same one after another, and all Egypt took a part in the feast by a general illumnination. (*Herodot. in Euterp. n.* 50.)

The moon of February, besides the visitation of houses, proclaimed two other operations. The one consisted in scouring the canals and chanels of the Nile; and the other, which immediately preceded the harvests, was the decision of law-suits.

The priests, during the year, appeared but seldom in public, except at the times of religious affairs. But they went out in the spring, that is, in February, and met to judge the differences of private persons, that these might afterwards freely go about their respective works.

The scouring of the ditches and canals was proclaimed in the assembly of the neomenia, by an Isis that was called Tite, or Tetis,

---

* ——— *our*, whence the Latins derived their word *ouer* or *ver*, the spring. They had also their *Februa*, that is, their general purifications in the month of February, which had its name from thence.

† From ——— *abash, putrescere, mucidum fieri,* comes ——— *obs, mucor, petrudo.* ——— *obsu pherudot*, the rotten corn. *Joel* i. 17.

and by an Horus whose name was Titan, that is, *the mud*, the raking up of the earth. (——— *tit, cænum, lutum.**

The assembly of the priests to judge the people was proclaimed by a Horus with a great beard, and a scythe in his hand. He was indifferently called Sudec, Keren, Chiun, and Cheunna, or Saterin; and by an Isis with many breasts, and encompassed with the heads of animals. This Isis was on this occasion called Rhea. The Horus with his great beard denoted the assembly of the ancient men. The *scythe* in his hand denoted *hay-making* and the *harvest*, which immediately followed the assize. They called this figure Sudec or *stadic, justus,*) which means the just; Crone, (——— *keren, splendor,*) that is, *the glory, the dignity the majesty* ; or *the crown*, that is the circle of the judges; Chiun or Cheunna, which means *the assembly of the priests* ; in short, Soterim, ———*soter, judex, soterim* or *sotrim, judices* and *principes*. Joshua i. 10: sometimes *executores, satellites,* or Setrum, which signifies the *judges*, or *the execution of the judgments.*†

After the decision of the law suits of private persons, and while the people were busy about cutting down and threshing the corn, the judges continued to hold their sessions, to provide by general regulating for all the exigencies of the state ; and it was on account of their being assembled the rest of the year till the rising of the dog-star in June or July, that the characteristick of the judgments, *viz.* the old man armed with a scythe, remained in his place, till they saw a new Osiris, a new sun, that is, till the new year. We shall see the strange fables to which this particular circumstance gave birth.

They by degrees lost the meaning of these plain figures and names, that were in use at the feasts in which the whole was become an invariable ceremonial. The current or the running writing caused the sense of them to be neglected ; on the other hand, nothing contributed more to make it forgotten than the custom of not reckoning exactly the sacred year, and of always putting the beginning of it back a whole day every fourth year ; so that the feasts and figures relating to the operations of the spring, being placed in autumn or winter, and so of the rest, they no longer understood any thing of what this multitude of

---

* 'Father Pezron derives the name Titan from the Celtic, *Tit* the earth, and *Den*, a man.'—*Bailey. Edit.*

† 'Justice (among the Israelites,) was administered by two sorts of officers *Shophetim* and *Soterim*, established in every city, by the command which God gave to Moses Deut. xvi. 18.) These posts were given to Levites, and there were six thousand of hem in David's time (1 Chron. xxiii. 4.) Dr. Adam Clarke's, Hist. Isrcal, p. 164,—*Edit*

figures meant. All being taken for so many men and women whose apothesis was celebrated, the people assigned to them a genealogy agreeable to the order of their feasts. Osiris and Isis, who began the year, were the two great deities that held the first rank and from whom they made the secondary gods and goddesses already spoken of, to descend. But from whom shall Orisis and Isis, that is, Jupiter and his wife, proceed? They, as well as their brothers Neptune and Pluto, are the children of that venerable old man, who, of all the signs exposed, was what appeared the longest towards the end of the year, and whose place Jupiter afterwards took. According to the primitive order, a new Osiris and a new Isis, or the posted signs of the new year, appeared again in June or July. According to the order of later times, all these figures, it is true, succeeded each other in the same manner, but in seasons and months to which they had no longer any just relation. Thus Sudec, or Cronos, or Saturn, became father of Jupiter and Isis. Saturn, Rhea, Tetis and Titan were their forefathers. The Titans were looked upon as the children of *Ur*, or *Urane*, and of *Ops*. Several genealogists go no further. Others, as Diodorus, make Urane and Ops the children of Acmon. The Egyptians, in their genealogy, go back even to Vulcan. Now Acmon, the brazier, and Vulcan are but one and the same thing.

Thus all these great personages that have peopled heaven, whom every country flattered themselves with having had for their inhabitants, to whom poets have attributed tragical adventures, and all the accidents of humanity; these great conquerors, the histories of whom our learned men are incessantly sifting, even so far as to penetrate into the political concerns that prompted them to act, prove at last to be, as well as Cancer, Capricorn, the balance, or the sphinx, mere ensigns or public marks and figures posted up to direct the people, and regulate the feasts and public works all the year round.

Saturn.

Again I find a proof of the same truth in the observations which the fable of Saturn naturally offers to my mind.

Instead of painting him with a scythe, to signify that the sessions of the judges are to be held in the time of harvest and hay-making, we sometimes find him represented with eyes before and behind, (*Sanchoniathon in Euseb, præp, Evangel.*) some of which are awake, and the others asleep; and with four wings, two of which are spread and two closed; which marked out the penetration and continuance of the work of the judges, who relieved each other by succession night and day, to dispatch the affairs of the people and those of the state, without making any one to linger under prejudicial and destructive delays. A new proof of Saturn's being a judge, or the symbol of justice, whose penetration nothing can escape, is that the poets, and above all, Homer, most commonly calls him the penetrating, the sagacious, the subtil, the quick-sighted Saturn. Again it was, because Saturn in its original, signified *the execution of the judgments*, or the punishment of criminals, that they usually said, Saturn carried away somebody, and demanded his victim every year. Thence came the opinion they had, that Saturn would be worshipped by the effusion of human blood, and the barbarous custom which every where spread, making its way from Phenicia into Africa, and thence throughout Europe.

It was because Saturn or Chrone had a necessary relation to the *equity* of the judgments, that were passed without any respect of persons, that Saturn was said to have reigned with perfect gentleness and integrity. They said farther, that a perpetual spring reigned in his time, because the sessions of the judges were anciently inseparable from the finest month of the year: such is constantly the month of February in Egypt.

The custom of reckoning 365 days for the year, without intercalating one day at four years end, by degrees displaced all the feasts, and made people forget that the figures there exposed related to the circumstances of the season.

In imitation of this usage, justice was anciently administered in Europe in the finest of our months, *viz*. in May. We still find in a multitude of places remains of this custom, in the practice observed by the farmers of the duties and receipts of lords, of setting up branches with their leaves on, or a green arbour before the chief or manor-house, where the assizes were held formerly, and where executions of criminals were made. But all this preparation is grounded on the circumstance of the season in which justice was administered in remotest antiquity; it was in the finest of our months. The above mentioned green arbor is still called the May, and the terms of magistrate and majesty seem to be borrowed from the name of the month in which these venerable assemblies were held in Europe.*

* This month has received its name from the Pleias anciently called Maia, which then disengaged itself from the rays of the sun, distant thirty degrees and passing under Gemini.

We again find a sensible token of the relation Saturn had to the judicial functions of the sacredotal order, in the disposal of the public treasure and the archives in the temple of Saturn. (*Festus, et Lil. Greg. Girald. syntagm.* 4.) This was an imitation of the method of the Egyptians, who anciently put the public treasure and the records of the genealogies of families in the tower or labyrinth under the custody of the priests.

In fine, there is no better proof that people were perfectly ignorant of the sense of the figures mistaken for deified personages, than the notion which the Greeks framed to themselves of Saturn when he was brought into their country.

The name of Chrone under which he was known to them, very plainly signified the majesty of the judicial assemblies, the crown or circle of the judges. But not knowing what this figure and its intention were, and finding a relation of sound between the name of Chrone and that of Chronos which among them signified *time* they interpreted, the whole symbol in that sense. The age of the figure squared with this incomparably well. But what were they to do with the scythe he carries in his hand? Why, he shall use it to cut down every thing. Above all, the stones which they made him to devour in Syria, seemed to distinguish him perfectly well. Time consumes every thing, and preys upon the very stones.

The following judicious remarks, from the Myth. Dict. of W. Howell, B. D. support the hypotheses of Pluche, in regard to the manner in which names have been appropriated to individual persons that never had existence.

Semiramis.

The wonderful actions of Ninus and Semiramis may be read in divers historians, Herodotus, Strabo, Diodorus Siculus, Ctesias, etc. The accounts are inconsistent and incredible; and indeed what credit can be given to the History of a person, Semiramis, the time of whose life cannot be ascertained within 1535 years? for so great is the difference of the extremes of the following numbers.

According to Syncellus she lived before Christ 2177, years, Patavius makes the term 2060, Helvicus, 2248, Eusebius 1984, Mr. Jackson, 1964, Abp-Usher, 1215, Philo Biblius from Sanchoniathon 1200, Herodotus about 713.

The history of Ninus and Semiramis is in great measure founded upon terms, which have been misconstructed; and fictions have been invented in consequence of these mistakes. Under the character of Semiramis we are certainly to understand a people called Semarim, a title assumed by the ancient Babylonians. They were called Semarim from their ensign, which was a dove, expressed Semiramis. It was used as an object of worship, and esteemed the same as Rhea, the mother of the gods. It was a common mode of expression to call a tribe or a family by the name of its founder: and a nation by the head of the line. People are often spoken of collectively in the singular under such a patronymic. Hence we read in Scripture, that Israel abode in tents ; that Judah was put to the worst in battle, etc. When it was said, that the Ninevite performed any great action, it has been ascribed to a person called Ninus, the supposed founder of Nineveh. But we may be assured, that under the character of Ninus and Ninyas, we are to understand the Ninevites ; as by Semiramis is meant a people called Samarim : and the great actions of these two nations are in the histories of these personages recorded. But writers have rendered the account inconsistent, by limiting, what was an historical series of many ages, to the life of a single person.

The Ninevites and Samarim did perform all that is attributed to Semiramis, and Ninus. They did conquer the Medes and largely extended their dominions. But these events were many ages after the foundation of the two kingdoms.

It is said of this ideal personage, that she was exposed among rocks ; but delivered and preserved by Simma, a Shepherd ; and was afterwards married to one Menon ; she is likewise said to have constructed the first ship. Now Simma is a personage made out of Sema, or Sama, *the divine token.* Menon is the deus Lunus, under which type the Ark was reverenced in many regions : and as it was the first ship constructed, with which the history of the Dove was closely connected they have given to Semiramis the merit of building it.

Sesostris.

The history of this personage has been admitted as credible by the most learned writers and chronologists ; though they cannot determine the era of his reign within a thousand years. Notice has been taken under several articles of the supposed conquerors of the earth ; and among them of the reputed deities of Egypt, under the names of Osiris, Perseus, etc. These are supposed, if they ever existed, to have lived in the first ages of the world, when Egypt was in its infant state; and Sesostris is made one of the number. He is by some placed before Orus ; and by some after. He is also represented under the different names of Sethos, Sethosis, Sesoothis, Seconthosis, and Sesostris.

Osiris is said to have conquered the whole earth ; then Zeus, then Perseus, then Hercules, all nearly of the same degree of antiquity ; if we may believe the best mythologists. Myrina comes in for a share of conquest in the time of Orus. After her Thoules subdues the whole from the eastern ocean to the great Atlantic ; and as if nothing had been performed before, Sesostris succeeds, and conquers it over again. By comparing the histories of ancient personages together, we may perceive that they bear a manifest similitude to one another ; tho' they are attributed to different persons. Sesostris was Osiris ; the same as Dionysius, Menes, and Noah.

Origin of Apis and Mnevis.

Nothing could be more convenient or more ingenious than the astronomical language, which immediately characterized each season and the works peculiar to it, by making the governor of the earth enter into the twelve signs of the zodiac, whose names had a just relation to what successively passes upon the earth in the course of a year. Nothing so gross, on the contrary, or so pitiful as the historical sense which the people afterwards anexed to this language; and such is evidently the origin of the ridiculous doctrine of the transmigration of souls, which Pythagoras brought to Italy as a rare discovery.

Generally all the animals of which the stars bear the name, were looked upon with veneration by the Egyptians, as having been the first retreats of their gods, and as being very possibly appointed for that of their dead parents. People never looked without a religious awe upon those in which they knew Osiris and Isis had resided, such as the ram, the bull, the heifer, the goat, and the lion. Their ancient custom of carrying ceremonially at the feasts of certain seasons, the animal whose name the house into which the sun entered, went by, disposed the people of certain provinces to honor particularly the animal carried at the feasts that concurred with the conclusion of their harvest.

Chance having produced a calf at Memphis which had some spots nearly in the figure of a circle or crescent, symbols so much reverenced among them, this singularity was taken by them for the characteristic of Osiris and Isis stamped upon the animal which their gods had an affection for: and that this was an apparition of the governor, a visit which the protector of Egypt deigned to make them. This miraculous calf, after having served preferably to any other at the ordinary ceremonial, was lodged in the finest place in Memphis. All his motions were judged prophetical, and the people flocked to him with their offerings. He received the great name of *Apis*, which means the mighty, the powerful god.

They took great care after his death to replace him with another that had nearly the same spots. When the marks desired were not neat and exact, they were improved with a pencil.

They even seasonably and after a certain time prevented the indecency of his death, by leading him in ceremony to a place where they drowned and then interred him very devoutly. This melancholy ceremony was intermixed with torrents of tears, and was emphatically called *Sarapis*, or the retreat of Apis, (—— *sur, recedere;* ———*sar abir, recessit Apis.* Vid. Judic. xvi: 20.), a name which was afterwards given to Pluto the infernal Osiris. After the burial of Apis, his successor was sought for. Thus was this strange devotion perpetuated. A powerful motive contributed greatly to it, *viz.* it was lucrative.

The inhabitants of Heliopolis, who made a separate dynasty, or a kingdom different from that at Memphis, thought themselves too much in the favor of the sun whose name their capital bore, not to partake of his visits or those of his son. They therefore soon had the sacred ox as well as those of Memphis. They called him Menavis or Mnevis which is the same thing as *Menes the mighty*, or the same with Menophis; and in choosing this magnificent name for him, they supposed other qualities and other functions in him no less capable of drawing crowds of people thither.

Phyton or Typhon.

Osiris being become the common father of the Egyptians, was by degrees looked upon as the principle from which all the good that happened to Egypt sprung; in like manner, Phyton, when he was become the name of the symbol that signified the havock of waters, was looked upon as an ill-minded spirit, as a principle fond of thwarting, perpetually intent upon crossing and prejudicing them. They made him the principle of all disorder, and charged him with all the physical evils they could not avoid, and all the moral evils which they did not care to lay to their own charge. Hence came the doctrine of the two opposite principles, equally powerful, incessantly striving against each other; (*Plutarch, de Isid. and Osir.*,) and alternately vanquished and victorious. This doctrine, which from the Egyptians was handed down to the Persians under the names of Oromazes and Arimazes, is altogether different from ours, according to which God, conformably to the adorable views of his providence, employs the ministry of the spirits who have persevered in a state of uprightness, and leaves a certain measure of power to those who are fallen from it.

The aversion of the Egyptians for this Phyton their imaginary enemy, and according to them incessantly intent upon vexing them, went so far, that they no longer dared to pronounce his name. However, we find it entire in the language of the Hebrews who had dwelt in Egypt, and had contracted the habit of calling by that name the most mischievous of serpents, that is, the asp. (—— *peten.*) The entire name of Phyton or Python, is found again in the most ancient and most celebrated fables of paganism. There we see this terrible monster engaged with the god who enlightens the world, and spreading desolation every where.

Nothing has been more celebrated in antiquity than the victory of the sun; nothing more abhorred than Phyton, when, from a painted monster, he was become a being intent upon doing mischief. The Egyptians fearing to defile themselves by the bare pronouncing of that detestable name, retained the letters of it, and converted them into that of Typhon.*

We have seen how the cross, as well entire as abridged, was the mark of the increase of the Nile, because it was the measure of it. When confined in the hand of Osiris, in the claws of the hawk, or the hand of Horus, it very plainly signified the overflowing of the Nile regulated by the sun, strengthened by the wind, and subject to fixed rules. This cross which in their vulgar writing, as likewise in the ancient Hebraic characters, in the Greek and the Latin alphabet, was the letter Tau.

That the cross or the T suspended by a ring, was taken by the Egyptians for the deliverance from evil, we may assure ourselves by consulting their practices, which are the surest interpretation of the opinion that governed them.

They hung it round the neck of their children, and of their sick people. They applied it to the strings or fillets with which they wrapped up their mummies, where we still find it. What can in their ideas signify a T placed near those of to whom they wished health and life, if not the deliverance from the disease and death, which they hoped to obtain by these superstitious practices.

Hence we see how strangely they misapplied those figures, which in their first institution related to the Nile, to husbandry, and to things totally foreign to the applications of succeeding times. This very probably is an introductive key, wherewith one might strive to explain part of the meaning which the Egyptians of the later times have given to their sacred writing.

This custom of the Egyptians appeared so beneficial and so important, that it was adopted by other nations. The children and the sick most commonly wore a ticket, wherein was a T which they looked upon as a powerful preservative. In process of time other characters were substituted in the room of the letter T, which was at first engraved on this ticket, but of which the other nations understood neither the meaning nor the intention. They often put a serpent in it, an Harpocrates, or the object of the devotions in vogue; nay sometimes ridiculous figures, or even some that were of the utmost indecency. But the name of Amulet, (*Amolimentum malorum.*), that was given to this

---

*Some people even at this day, have a reluctance to pronounce the common English name of this *prince of darkness.* They call him the *de'il*, the *old nick*, *old harry*, &c. Edit.

ticket, and which signifies *the removal of the evil*, most naturally represents the intention of the Egyptians, from whom this practice came.

The above mentioned practice, we have seen, arose from the instrument used for measuring the height of the inundation of the Nile, being an abridgement of it, and which was considered the salvation of Egypt. A like veneration is bestowed upon this figure, that is, the cross, by Roman Catholics : which, like other customs of the ancients, has probably been adopted by them without understanding its origin, and which they attribute to a different source. A spell, which they no doubt consider more potent, however, is now generally used instead of the cross. This is called gospels, and consists of short passages extracted from the gospels by a priest, which is enclosed in a piece of silk, and tied round the necks of children, going to bed.

The same superstition prevails among the Mahometans.

Dr. Hume, in Walpole's memoirs, speaking of modern Egypt, says, "The general remedy in cases of fever and other kinds of illness, is a saphie from a priest, which consists of some sentence from the Koran written on a small piece of paper and tied round the patience's neck. This, if the sick man recovers, he carefully preserves by keeping it constantly between his scull-caps, of which he generally wears two or three. Saphies are very commonly used by the Mahammedans, being considered to possess much efficacy for the body as well as the soul, and occupy the same place in the estimation of the superstitions as did the frontlets of the Jews and the phylacteries of the early Christians." Quoted in Russell's View of Egypt, p. 324, New-York edition.

In regard to the sacred writing of the Egyptians, it is not improbable that its characters were originnally formed from the figure of the Nilometer, consisting of right, angles and thence considered sacred.

The Egyptian Mysteries.

We must not expect, we are told, that the priests of Isis, or Plutarch, or any other travellers who heard them talk, can be able to give us any information about the true sense and meaning of their symbols. It was a *mysterious theology* ; which they took great care not to divulge. Those who were initiated therein, engaged themselves by an *oath* never to communicate to the people any part of what had been revealed to them. Does not Herodotus often tell us, that he is permitted upon no account whatever, to reveal the names and the honors that were destined and annexed to certain deities, or what these deities were ? The secret in this point being inviolable, are we to wonder that they have not explained themselves on the grounds which concern us ; and can we judge of what they have not revealed ?

Let us then see, (and this shall be the conclusion of our essay upon the Egyptian religion) what these mysteries so much spoken of were ; and, if possible let us penetrate into these secrets, in spite of the *veils and barries* intended to render them inaccessible.

Among the ancient Egyptian figures, there were some which could not well be mistaken for celestial gods, and of which it was difficult to lose the meaning, having at first been of infinite use to the people. Such were, for instance, the serpent, the canopus, and the hawk. We see therefore, from the interpretation given of them by the grammarian Horapollo, that in the fourth century the Egpytian priesst still expressed the life or eternity of their gods by a serpent encompassing thme : (*Serpentem aureum Diis suis circumponunt.*) that they represented the overflowing of the Nile by *three piichers*, and denoted the wind by a hawk spreading her wings. *Accipiter alis in aere protensis ventum significat.* Ibid. But the people having once forgotten the sense of the *sacred writing*, and taken human figures for celestial powers, never gave over inventing histories ; and the priests who preserved this writing, adapted it to their histories, which renders it worthy, of contempt, and altogether different from the ancient as to the meaning.

The priests at first retained a part of the primitive explications. Thence comes the mixture of great and little in the Egyptian theology and in the Eleusinian which was the same. In there more than any where remained the ancient footsteps of the truths, which constituted the principal ground-work of the religion of the patriarchs.

But it would have been dangerous for the Egyptian priests to attempt undeceiving the people and divert them from the pleasing thought that Osiris and Isis were two real personages, and were besides of their country and the protectors of Egypt. This chimera and all the others in appearance were authorized by the agreement of the monuments with the common phrase. The actions of Osiris and Isis were incessantly mentioned. The people believed what they saw and what they heard. The perpetual recital of as many historical facts, as there were figures and ceremonies exhibited, completed their errors, and rendered them invincible.

If *our councils* and the most venerable of our bishops have had so much ado to abolish among the people the belief of certain legends unworthy the *majesty* of our religion, and which were connected with no monument capable of countenancing them ; how can we conceive that the Egyptian priests were able to take from a people immersed in ignorance and cupidity, the extravagant stories which universal custom offered to their minds on sight of the personages and animals wherewith the places of their assemblies were filled ? It is much more natural to think, that the priests themselves, like the rest, yielded to the persuation of being under the patronage of their ancestors transported into the stars, and now the moderators of the sun, the moon, and of all nature. The people, in their fanatic enthusiasm, would have torn in pieces any that should have dared to deny the history of Osiris and Isis. Truth was then altered and obscured by the very priests. They first accustomed themselves to these notions, because it was dangerous not to comply with them and afterwards became themselves the most zealous defenders of them. The whole came on by degrees. They first complied with the common language, because they thought they could not stem the torrent ; but they studied in private what they could collect of the interpretation of the ancient writing. Thus they at once admitted both the popular stories and the explications that demolished them : they only took care to require profound *secrecy* from those whom they would *instruct* in a more solid manner.

Thus instruction assumed a mysterious and important air, without altering any thing in what the people believed. It only mentioned a a more perfect state, and a kind of knowledge of which none became capable till after many trials and efforts which suited not the common fort of men. Thus they avoided exciting the fury of the people.— This was already a crying injustice in those priests to detain truth captive, and to appropriate it exclusively to themselves.

* So criminal a disposition could not but occasion a still greater impairing of truth. And really every thing degenerated more and more every day. The *probation* of the disciples, and the oath of an inviolable secrecy, being very remarkable practices, were perpetuated with great exactness. The ceremonial part easily supports itself in all religions, and is often embellished rather than diminished, because it is of no importance to the passions, which it never disturbs, and sometimes really indulges. It was not with truth and instruction as with the ceremonial. They were disfigured from age to age, sometimes through the ignorance of the priests, sometimes by their averice, but principally by their fondness for systematic reveries, with which the most subtil among them tried to explain the symbolical writing ; and of which they were much fonder than of a few plain and over simple truths, which their predecessors were contented to teach them.

Therefore danger and fear first gave birth to the secrecy of the Egyptian instructions, and have converted the practices, of the ancient ceremonial of the public religion, into so many mysteries, to the knowledge of which none could be admitted but such as had given proofs of a profound respect for the objects of religion, of a perfection which common men could not attain, and of an unconquerable taciturnity. But then those who were initiated thought themselves of a *class superior to the rest of men*, and their condition appeared worthy the envying. The priest being sure of the discretion of their disciples, might very well acknowledge to them the grossness of the meaning which the people annexed to these symbols. But their shameful connivance suffered error to get so much ground, that the piety of the initiated themselves sunk into a *mere ceremonial*; and the small remains of truths, which subsisted amongst so many fabulous stories, remained there stifled as it were, and without any useful effect. The priests themselves out-did the popular superstitions; and out of custom, and from *interested views* preserved the preparatory ceremonies, and the religion of silence, that gave the people a high notion of the ministers, and of their learning.

I have given the literal translation of most of the terms made use of in these mysteries. Neither the Greeks nor the Romans understood the meaning of them, because they are Phenician. The very name mystery being also a Phenician word, which signifies a *veil*, an *invelopement*,* we are, on this very account, authorized to look out in the Chananean language for the meaning of the other terms made use of in the mysteries. But if the terms used in the Eleusinian feasts shall perfectly concur with the sense I have ascribed to the pieces that were most in use in the symbolical writing and ceremonies, the result will evidently be, that the figures originally appointed to instruct the people have been converted into so many imaginary gods, and that we have obtained the true original of allthese inhabitants of the poetical heaven.

The Ceres of Sicily and Eleusis is no other than the Egyptian Isis, brought intothose places by Phenician merchants, who made themselves rich by transporting the corn of Lower Egypt into the places whither the scarcity of provisions drew them, and generally on the different coasts of the Mediterranean, where they had offices, and establishments. The ceremonial of the rural feasts had in their hands taken a turn somewhat different. The mother of harvests there lamented her daughter, instead of bewailing her husband, as the Egyptian ritual would have it This excepted, the ground and intention were the same.†

---

*———— mistar, et ———— mistor, *velamen, absconsio, latibulum*. *Psl*. 10 : *Isa*. 4 : 6.
†Cicero, on the "Nature of the Gods, makes the following remarks upon this subject; " The sovereignty and power over the earth is the portion of a god, to whom we, as well as the Greeks, have given a name that denotes riches; in Latin Dis, in greek Plu-

The feasts instituted in honor of Ceres were called Thesmophoria, whose principal parts may be reduced to three, viz. the *preparations* the *processions*, and the *autopsia*, or the sight of truth.

The preparations, the long enumeration of which may be read in Meursius, (*Græcia Feriata*,) had for their object the frugality, *chastity* and *innocence* that were necessary to the worshippers. The processions consisted in the carriage of the *sacred baskets*, wherein they inclosed a child and a golden serpent, a van, grains, cakes, and all the other symbols of which we have made the enumeration in another place.

If in the feasts of Ceres or Isis, men carried to an extravagant excess the form of the gestures and situations, the scrupulous recitals of the *set-forms* of *prayers*, the length of the vigils, outward purity, abstinence, the forbearance of all pleasures, and the shunning all manner of distraction; it is because the whole of religion was reduced to these *outward practices*. Those who observed them knew neither the motive nor the purport or destination of them. It was no longer any but an artificial devotion, or the skeleton of the ancient religion. But any upright unprejudiced mind will easily discern in them the intentions of the first founders, who knew the full value of rule, the beauty of order, and the benefit of recollection,

A long description of all the purifications and other ceremonies that filled up the first of the nine days of devotion consecrated to Ceres, would have tired out my readers, and is no part of my plan, which chiefly aims at obtaining the origin of these establishments. It will be the same with the long procession formerly made from Athens to Eleusis, and with the several marches peculiar to each of the nine days. The Greeks had built the particulars of this minute ceremonial upon the little adventures that composed the wonderful story of the migration of Ceres into their country.

But this my reader is acquainted with. What was carried in the

---

ton, because all things arise from the earth and return to it. He forced away Proserpine, in Greek called Persephone, by which the poets mean the seed of corn ; from whence their fiction of Ceres, the mother of Proserpine, seeking for her daughter, who was *hid from her*. She is called Ceres, which is the same as Geres, a gerendis frugibus, from bearing fruit, the first letter of the word being altered after the manner of the Greeks ; for by them she is called *Demeter*, the same as Gemeter," that is mother earth."

Pluche derives Persephone thus, from — *peri*, fruit, corn, and — *saphan*, to hide, comes ——— *persephoneh*, the corn lost.

It may be remarked, that the flambeau or torch which Ceres, according to the fable is said to have carried night and day in search of her daughter Proserpine, is a symbol of the lost sun, without whose aid no fruit or corn could be found or produced.—Edit

feasts of Ceres at Eleusis, is the same that was carried in the feasts of Isis. Let us, therefore, pass on to the explication of the autopsia, or the manifestation of truth, which was in a manner the last act of this representation, and was the whole purport of the mysteries. After a horrid darkness, lightnings, thunder claps, and an imitation of what is most shocking in nature, the serenity which at last succeeded, discovered four personages magnificently dressed, and whose habits were all mysterious.

The most brilliant of all, and who was especially called the Hierophant, or the expounder of sacred things, was dressed so as to represent the being that governs the universe. The second was the *flambeau bearer*, and had relation to the sun. The third, who was called the *adorer*, and who kept near an altar, represented the moon. The fourth was called the *messenger of the gods*, or Mercury, which corresponds to the Egyptian Anubis, with his dog's head and measure of the Nile, accompanied by two serpents, and is nothing but the *wholesome advice* which the dog-star timely gives to men, to make off, at the increase of the waters, and thereby secure their subsistence.

Nothing could be better contrived than these magnificent ceremonies whereby the Egyptians incessantly recalled to the minds of the assistants the belief of the first men concerning the judgment of God, and the hopes which are to quiet the minds of the just at the approach of death.

What an indestructible tradition attended with constant practices had been able to preserve of the ancient doctrine, proved at last so very opposite to the popular notions, that the priests thought themselves under the necessity of using much circumspection, and of having recourse not only to the trial of their desciples, but also to the oath of secrecy. The reason of the priests themselves went astray in this labyrinth of obscure signs and mysterious practices. Then came on systems. One looked out among all this apparatus of ceremonies and fables for a complete set of physics.

Another tried to find out a complete body of moral and instructive maxims, under the color of the most scandalous fables. Others imagined they had found the most profound metaphysics therein.— Nor does the simplicity of the Egyptian, appear by much so shocking as the sublime nonsense of a Platonic, who sees Monades and Triades every where; who, in a figure of Isis exposed in the middle of an assembly of husbandmen, finds the archetpye world, the intellectual world, and the sensible world ; or who seeks in the feet of a goat the picture of universal nature; or who finds out in the horn of an ox the efficacy of the impressions of his imaginary genii.

Thus the learned, from a habit of diving into matters, and of looking out for extraordinary explications, have perplexed a subject of itself very simple.

A few regular assemblies excepted, in which by public authority were preserved some footsteps of truth together with some ancient customs, the whole went on from bad to worse, from the liberty of embelishments and interpretations. The gods were multiplied in the popular discourses as much as the symbols, and even in proportion to the different names given one and the same symbol. Oftentimes the minutest equivocations, proceeding from a variety in the pronunciation, the diversity of dresses of the same figure, nay a bare change of place, a trifle added or retrenched, gave birth to a new god.

We may see in Plutarch's treatise, but above all in Eusebius's Evangelical Preparation, the strange variety of adventures and employments which the Africans, the Phenicians, and the Phrygians attributed to the same gods. The celestial court was not the same in Egypt as in Greece. In Egypt it was Osiris that gave light to the world. In Greece Osiris or Jupiter was freed from that care. The sceptre and thunderbolt were left to him; but the chariot of the day was given to Horus or Apollo, who in his quality of symbol of the rural works bore by way of abbreviation the marks of the situation of the sun, or the characteristic of the season.

Jupiter could neither do every thing, nor be every where. Lieutenants were then given him, each with separate districts. Every thing assumed a settled form. The histories of the gods were composed; and by attributing to them what each nation in particular was pleased to publish on their account; by adding thereto the histories of the ministers of the temples, and those of the kings who had favored their worship; but chiefly by excusing the disorders of women on account of the pretended disguises of these gods possessed with their charms; they formed that monstrous lump, of mythology, in which it is no wonder that we find no sense, no coherency, no order of place or time, nor any kind of regard either to reason or good manners. Though the major part of these fabulous recitals be utterly extravagant; yet as they have made part of the strange theology of our forefathers, men have at all times endeavored to find out the true origin of them. I have ventured my own conjectures on the same subject; because they appeared to me to amount nearly to a certainty, and the whole might be unravelled with no less decency than benefit. It is no longer so with regard to the minute particulars of these extravagances. The collection of them would be the matter of very large volumes; and there is indeed no subject upon which it will be more lawful to set bounds to one's knowledge.

The foregoing article has been very much curtailed as it is intended to give a full account of the ancient mysteries from bishop Warburton's Divine Legation of Moses; in which the subject is treated of more at large, and in some respect evidently with a better understanding of it than the Abbè Pluche possessed.

The horrors exhibited at the commencement of the ceremony were intended to represent the condition of the wicked in another life, and the closing scene portrayed the abode of the blessed; the miseries of Tartarus and the happiness of Elysium were contrasted; and being pronounced by holy priests, in whom the vulgar in barbarous ages placed implicit confidence, to be a true picture of what actually takes place in a future state of existence, must have produced a most powerful effect.

This scene is imitated in the royal arch degree of masonry, originally with the same view as the archetype; and as in the original mysteries, it forms the last act or degree of ancient masonry. The candidates, are kept in the dark by being hoodwinked; thunder and lightning are represented by the firing of pistols, rolling cannon balls, etc. In the conclusion, the aspirants are brought to light, and presented to what is called the *grand council*, consisting of three personages denominated high priest, king, and the holy scribe; on whose decorations some hundred dollars are expended, in order duly to prepare them to sustain the exalted characters allotted to them. These three are the principal persons of the drama. The fourth, and next in dignity, is styled the *captain of the host*; " who is stationed at the right hand of the grand council, and whose duty is, to receive their orders, and see them duly executed."

The high priest corresponds with the hierophant of the mysteries, the king with the flambeau bearer, the sun, who was deemed the *king* and governor of the world; the *holy* scribe with Isis, the adorer, hence the attribute holy applied to him; and the captain of the host, with Anubis Hermes or Mercury, the messenger of the gods. The identity of these institutions cannot be mistaken.

The Auguries.

My readers, ever so little conversant in ancient history, may remember to have often seen the Romans, the Sabines, the Hetrurians, the Greeks, and many other nations, very careful in never attempting any important undertaking, without previously consulting the birds, and drawing favorable or ill consequences, sometimes from the number and kind of the birds that traversed the air, sometimes from the quarter whence they began their flight, and the different course they took. We may likewise remember, that in order not to be obliged to wait long for a bird which chance may not immediately offer, the priests of the false deities had introduced the custom of the sacred chickens, brought into the middle of the assembly of the people in a cage, for the magistrates gravely to observe their ways and motion. They had reduced into an art, and refered to constant and settled rules, all the consequences to be drawn with regard to futurity, from the several methods in which these whimsical animals let fall or swallowed the food offered to them. Have not the priests of paganism, either out of interested views, or from an infatuation for these chimerical rules, a thousand times spoiled or put a stop to the most important and best concerted undertakings, out of regard to a fowl that had refused her meat? Augustus and many other persons of understanding, have without any fatal consequences despised the chickens and divination. But when the generals in the times of the republic had miscarried in any enterprise, the priest and people cast the whole blame of it on the heedlessness with which the sacred chickens had been consulted, and more commonly still, on the general's having preferred his own forecast to that of these fowls. Nor can one indeed without some indignation, see these dangerous sillinesses continue in the highest esteem and credit among people full of magnanimity, and the greatest genius seemingly making serious apologies for them.

Tully has handed to us a good saying of Cato, who declared that one of the most surprising things to him was, how one soothsayer could look another in the face without laughing. I do not doubt but this judicious orator, when he was discharging his functions as a priest of the auguries, was always ready to change his countenance whenever he happened to see any of his colleagues walking with a grave stately air, and lifting up the augural staff. He was perfectly sensible of the vanity of these practices. After having observed in the second book of divinition, that the Romans had never been concerned in a matter of greater consequence than that of the quarrel between Cæsar and Pompey, he freely confesses, that the augurs, aruspices, and oracles, had never been more frequently consulted; but that the answers, whose number was endless, had not been followed by the events they foretold, or else had been succeeded by such as were quite contrary. However, Tully, notwithstanding this confession, which wholly demolishes the art of prediction, yet out of politic views defends the practice of it. He preferred leaving the people in their error, to the risk of provoking them, by endeavouring to free them from a pernicious and criminal superstition.*

---

* It may be presumed that the *risk* which Cicero was unwilling to hazard in this

Anciently, or at the time of the institution of the symbols, men, before sowing, or planting, used to say; *let us first consult the birds.* Nor was there any thing better understood. People were satisfied when they had observed this custom with care. These birds signified the winds, the observation and course of which determined the propriety of rural works. But men, in process of time, very earnestly invoked the birds themselves.

The cock commonly placed by the side of Horus and Anubis or Mercury, very plainly signified what was to be done in the morning, as the owl marked out the assemblies that were to be held in the evening. Cocks were then made so many new monitors foretelling futurity; and the owl acquired in this matter a talent which many people earnestly contend she is still possessed of. When this bird, which is an enemy to light, happens to shriek as she passes by the window of a sick person, where she perceives it, you never can beat it out of their head, that this shrieking, is a foreboding of his end.

Origin and Falsehood of the Sibyls.

It is from a sensible abuse in astronomy or of the custom of consulting certain stars, that the oracles of the Sibyls were introduced. Harvest has always been the great object of the desires and attention of all nations. In order therefore to regulate the manuring of their lands, their plowing, sowing, and the other operations of concern to the bulk of society, men had their eyes fixed on the virgin that bears the ear of corn, and which is the mark of the time of harvest. They observed how far the sun was remote from it, and on this account they generally used to consult and have recourse to the virgin ; a language as reasonable as the practice expressed by it. They at first gave this constellation the name Shibyl Ergone* *the reddening ear of corn,* because it is exactly the circumstance for which men wait to begin their harvest, and because their crop ripens when the sun draws near this collection of stars.

They afterwards called it sometimes Sibyl, sometimes Erigone.

---

ease, was the loss of popularity, and the emolument arising from the priestly office. Self-interest, in all ages of the world, has been the moving principle of action with the cunning and designing, to impose upon the credulity of ignorance. Observing the feeding or flight of birds, or inspecting the entrails of a bullock, thereby to predict future events, is not more ridiculous, nor less creditable to the understanding of the human species, than some practices that might be mentioned, which are in vogue at the present day.—*Edit.*

* From ——— *Shibul,* or ——— *Shibolet, spicæ*; and from ——— Dan. 5 : 7. Erigone *purpura.* The purple ear of corn, *Spica rubescens.*

This name Erigone rendered in Greek by that of Erytra, which corresponds to it, and signifies *red*, gave birth to the Erytrean Sibyl. There was certainly an advantage in consulting her, and her answers were very just to regulate husbandry so long as she was taken for what she was, that is, for a cluster of stars under which the sun placed himself at the time which brought on harvest, and reddened the ear of corn. And because the Egyptian harvest did not fall under that sign, but under the Ram or the Bull, it is, that Egypt flocked to the oracles of Ammon or of Apis, and had so particular an affection for Isis with the horns of a heifer, the ancient proclamation of their harvest; whereas all the east consulted the Erytrean Sibyl, in order to be assured of a plentiful crop. This language became the matter of fables. Our maid changed from a sign to a prophetess, had no doubt the most perfect knowledge of futurity, since people came from all parts to ask her questions. The excessive wickedness of mankind at last obliged her to quit their abodes, to go, and in the heavens take possession of the place due to her. Many countries assumed to themselves the honor of having given birth to this sibyl: nor would it be a hard matter to find seven instead of one. All the current predictions, among which some strokes of the prophecies addressed to the Hebrews, are found, in time passed for the answers of these sibyls.*

The American reader should be aware that the term corn is used in England, as a generic term for all seeds that grow in ears. The French word, here translated corn, is blé, which signifies grain, wheat; blé de Torquie or d' Inde, means maize, Indian corn. Wheat as it ripens puts on a reddish hue: which is not the case with Indian corn, although red ears are sometimes found among it. Grain, in English, seems the most proper term, for the genus of the different species.

In masonic lodges, the master is stationed in the east, representing Osiris the sun; and the senior warden in the west, representing Isis or Virgo, the sign of harvest; his duty is to pay the craft their wages, which alludes metaphorically to the reward the husbandman receives in the produce of his labor, when the sun arrives at this sign. This is indicated by a painting representing a sheaf of wheat, which is hung back of this officer's chair. The pass word of the fellow-craft, at this station, to entitle him to pay, is *shibboleth, the reddening ear of wheat.* Can any thing more conclusively point out the astronomical cast of free-masonry.

It must have been at a very remote period when the Egyptian harvest occurred, as above stated, during the passage of the sun, either under the sign of the ram or the bull. Volney, in his travels in Egypt and Syria, observes:

"As the sun approaches the tropic of Capricorn, the winds becomes variable and tempestuous; they most usually blow from the north, the north-west, and west, in

* See upon this subject the excellent remarks of P. Catrou on the fifth eclogue of Virgil.

which points they continue during the months of December, January, and February, which is the winter season in Egypt, as well as with us. The vapour of the Medeterranean, condensed by the coldness of the atmosphere, descends in mists and rains."

Conjuration.

I am still to inquire into the origin of an art far more important than all the foregoing. This is necromancy, the art of calling up the spirits of the dead, and of making them speak.* The reader will not be displeased here to find the key of the occult languages, and to be acquainted how magicians went about asking questions of hell, and conversing with the devils.

A respect for the human body which was believed to be destined for a better state to come, and one day to rise from the dust, induced the first nations to inter the dead in a decent manner, and always to join to this melancholy ceremony, wishes and prayers, which were expressions or a profession of their expectation.

Funeral assemblies were the most frequent, because men died every day, and these meetings were repeated on every anniversary. They were not only the most common, but also the most regular.

Every thing was simple in the ancient feasts. Men met upon some high and remarkable place. They made there a small pit, wherein to consume the entrails of the victims by fire. They made the blood to flow into the same pit. Part of the flesh was *presented* to the *ministers of the sacrifice*. They boiled the rest of the offering immolated, and eat it, sitting near the fire. By degrees they swerved from this simplicity.

What had been approved on some important occasion, afterwards passed into custom, and became a law. The number, the characters, and the histories of the objects which men took for gods, afterwards gave birth to a thousand varieties, which appeared very important rites and necessary precautions. Whoever should have neglected one single point of the ceremonial prescribed, had nothing less than the plague or famine to apprehend. Whenever the gods in that case were contented with only sending a transitory tempest or some furious beast among them, the fault was reckoned very cheaply atoned for. Each feast having its proper service and decorations had a peculiar name. It was not

---

* The science of communing with departed spirits, supposed to have been lost for many centuries, is believed, by the Swedenborgians, to have been communicated to the founder of their sect, Emmanuel Swedenborg. He asserts, that in the year 1743, the Lord manifested himself to him by a personal appearance, and at the same time opened his spiritual eyes, so that he was enabled constantly to see and converse with spirits and angels.—*Edit.*

thus with the funeral assemblies: nothing was changed in them. They were void of joy and decoration. Men went on with practising what had ever been done. The families in intering their dead, were accustomed to a common rubric which was perpetual. It is then in the service of the funerals especially, that we may again find the principal of the usages of primitive antiquity. At these solemnities they continued to make a ditch, to pour out *wine, oil, honey, milk,* or some other liquors in use, to shed the blood of the victims,* to roast their flesh, to eat it in common sitting round the pit or hearth, and discoursing of the virtues of him they came to lament. These assemblies continued to bear the name given to all solemn convenings.

While the other feasts, on account of the diversity of the ceremonies, were called Saturnalia, Dionisiaca, Palilia, etc. the funeral assemblies were simply called *the Manes,*† that is, the covering or regulation. That the *Manes* and the *dead* became two synonymous words, or were indifferently used, one for another. And as the things which gave names to the feasts, were generally become the objects of an extravagant worship; the *Manes* or the *dead* became likewise the object reverenced in the funeral ceremonies. The strange facility with which the minute parts of the universe were deified, is a hint to us how the custom was introduced of directing prayers, vows, and religious worship to the dead whom they had loved, whose praises were celebrated, and who were thought to enjoy the most refined knowledge, after they had, together with their body, cast off the frailties of humanity.

The ancient sacrifices were not only eucharistical. In the times when the Most High was as yet worshipped, they were looked upon as an alliance contracted with him, and whereby they engaged themselves to be faithful to him. I shall here mention neither the reasons nor any instances of it. The former are palpable, and the scripture abounds with the latter.

All nations, when they sacrificed either to the gods they had framed to themselves, or to the dead whose memory was dear to them, thought they entered into an alliance, conversed, and familiarly eat with them. But this familiarity engrossed their thoughts most particularly in the funeral assemblies, in which they were as yet full of the memory of the

---

* *Inferimus tepido spumantia cymbia lacte,*
Sanguinis et sacri pateras. Æneid. 5.
See the same ceremonies in the anniversary of Anchises. Æn. 5.
† From ——— *manim, distributiones, vices, reditus, solemnitas.* This name was given to the symbolical figures. In particular it remained the name of the image of the dead person which characterized a funeral assembly.

persons whom they had tenderly loved, and who, as they thought, took always a great part in the concerns of their family and country.

We have heretofore observed, how cupidity and ignorance having rendered all men indifferent as to justice, had led them astray as to the object of their worship, and had afterwards converted every part of it into so many means of being relieved of in their illness, instructed in futurity, and provided all proper means to succeed in all their undertakings. Every object in nature spoke to them. The birds in the heaven, the serpents and other animals on the earth, a simple rod in the hand of their minister, and all the instruments of religion, were so many oracles and prophetical signs. They read the stars, and the gods spoke or revealed their intentions to them from one end of nature to the other. This *covetousness* and *gross religion*, which applied to the gods merely to ask them questions *in matters of interest*, was no less inquisitive and thought it had a right to be still better served in the funeral sacrifices than in all the rest. Men in these ceremonies thought they had to deal with affectionate gods, which, on account of the concern they still had in the prosperity of their family, could not but inform them in time, of whatever might be of service or detrimental to them. The whole apparatus of the funerals was then again interpreted in the same manner, as that of the other feasts, and the whole was converted into so many methods of divination.

The ceremonies of the *Manes*, though they were but the bare practices of the assemblies of the primitive times, being in every respect different from those observed in the other feasts, appeared so many different methods of conversing with the dead, and of obtaining the desired information from them. Who then could doubt but it was in order familiarly to converse with their ancient friends, that men sat down round a pit, into which they had thrown the oil, the flour, and the blood of the victim they had killed to their honor? How could it be doubted, but that this pit so different from the altars set up and pointing towards heaven, was a suitable ceremony, and peculiarly belonging to the dead? The dead evidently took pleasure in these repasts, and especially in what was poured into the pit for them. Doubtless they came to consume the honey and the liquors which disappeared from thence; and if their friends were contented with offering them liquors only, no doubt it was because their condition as dead persons would not admit of gross foods. Men were then so extravagantly credulous as to believe that the phantoms came to drink and voluptuously to relish these liquors, while their relations feasted on the rest of the sacrifice around the pit. After the repast in common between the dead and the living, came the interrogation, or particular calling up of the soul, for which the sacrifice was appointed, and who was to explain her mind. Every body is sensible that an inconvenience attended the ceremony, it being to be apprehended that the dead might crowd about the ditch, to get a share in this effusion which they were so very greedy of, and leave nothing for the dear soul, for whom the feast was designed. This was provided against. The relations made two ditches. In one they threw in wine, honey, water and flour, to amuse the generality of the dead : in the other they poured out the blood of the victim then to be eaten in common by the family. They sat upon the brink of the latter, and with their swords near them, they kept off by the sight of these instruments, the crowd of dead who had no concern in their affairs. They on the contrary invited and called up by his name the deceased, whom they had a mind to cheer and consult. They desired him to draw near. The dead seeing that there was there no security for them, flocked and swarmed round the ditch, the access to which was free, and politely abandoned the other to the privileged soul, who had a right to the offering, and who knew the bottom of the affairs about which she was to be consulted.

The questions made by the living were distinct and easy to be understood. The answers, on the contrary, though very certain, were neither so quick, nor so easy to be unraveled. But the *priests* who had been *taught* in their labyrinth how *to understand the voice of the gods* the answers of the planets, the language of the birds, the serpents and the mutest instruments, easily understood the dead, and became their interpreters. They reduced it into an art, whose most necessary point and what best suited the condition of the dead, was silence and darkness. They retired into the deeper caves : they fasted and lay upon the skins of the sacrificed beasts. When they waked or after a watch, which, was fitter to turn their brains than to reveal hidden things to them, they gave for answers the thought or dream which had most affected them. Or they opened certain *books* appointed for that use :* and the *first words* which offered at the opening of them, were precisely those

---

* A similar custom is still practised by some superstitious people; who, when in doubt what they ought to determine in particular circumstances, open the bible, and the first passage that strikes their eyes, is expected to intimate the proper course.—*Edit.*

of the prophecy expected: or in short, the priest and sometimes the person himself who came to consult, took care, at going out of the cave, to listen with attention to the very *first words* he could possibly hear, from what part soever they proceeded, and they were to him in lieu of an answer. These words for certain had no manner of relation or connexion with the business in hand; but they were turned so many ways, and the sense of them so violently wrested, that they must needs have given way some small matter. Commonly enough they had in appearance some relation to it. They sometimes, instead of the foregoing methods, had recourse to what they called *sortes, viz*: a number of tickets on which there were some words written at random, or some verses already current or newly coined. These tickets being thrown into an urn, they were stirred very well together, and the first ticket that was drawn, was gravely given to the distressed family, as the means to make them easy. Methods of divination were multiplied without end. The whole of religion was almost converted into so many methods of knowing futurity. See the dissertation of Vandale upon the heathen oracles. See the history of the oracles. This matter has been sufficiently treated upon by the learned: it would be needless to resume it.

It is evident that the practices above mentioned were extremely fit every where to spread this extravagant persuasion, which is still preserved among the people, that we may converse with the dead, and that they often come to give us advices.

If I can again supply my readers with the proofs of this custom, or rather of this perverse abuse of the funeral ceremonies; I shall, methinks, have sufficiently shown, that the opinions of men upon the gods, the dead, and the answers that may be obtained from either of them, are nothing but a literal and gross interpretation made of very plain signs, and of still plainer ceremonies, whose purport was to express certain truths, and to fulfil certain duties.

Because all nations flocked to *high places*, there to shed the blood of the victims into a trench, and to converse with a dead person, by keeping off others by the sight of a sword, it is, that, scripture so often, and in so express a manner, forbids the Israelites to assemble upon *high places*, or, (which was frequently the same thing) to hold their assembly near the blood, or to eat sitting round any pit sprinkled with the blood of the victims. The seventy interpreters knowing perfectly, that this was what drew the people to the high places, having very well translated this passage of Leviticus, xix. 26. and other the like by these words, —— ye shall not go and eat upon the *mountains.* Here to eat is the same thing as to sacrifice.*

In concluding my extracts and remarks on the interesting works of the Abbé Pluche, I will take some notice of what he says of the *dog-days*; which are continually recorded in Almanacs, when probably neither the authors nor readers, know any thing of their origin, or the propriety or use of their being retained in such registers.

According to our author, the rising of the dog-star, was generally accompanied with what the Egyptians called the Etesian northern wind, that continued to blow for about *forty days* in succession. When this wind failed to occur at this period, or was too light to be of use in causing the swelling of the Nile to a sufficient height, a general sadness of the people ensued. The probability, therefore, is, that while the inhabitants remained idle on the high ground, watching the progress of the inundation, these forty days were passed very much, in fasting and other acts of devotion to gain the favor of their gods in this respect. Indeed the author relates a story that prevailed among the Cretians, that corroborates this opinion; which is, that through the displeasure of the gods, this wind was not permitted to blow for a considerable time; "but after repeated *sacrifices,* the gods at length granted the return of the Etesian wind, and its constant blowing, during the *forty days* that followed the rising of the *dog star,* called the dog-days; which again brought abundance upon the earth." The people, he says, in another place, "were warned to observe the dog-days."

Volney remarks that, "about the end of July, during all the month of August, and half of September, the winds in Egypt remain constantly in the north, and are moderate; brisker in the day, however, and weaker at night."

The dog-days, in callenders calculated for the United States, are generally noted as commencing on the 30th of July, and ending on the tenth of September, making forty two days.

It is highly probable that the Roman Catholic Lent has grown out of this ancient custom in regard to the dog-days; accommodated however, in respect to the time of its observance, to the circumstances of countries differently situated to that of Egypt. Such an essential change in the usual habit of living, is, no doubt, very detrimental to health, and probably causes the premature death of thousands annually. The requirement of abstinence from meat on Fridays and Saturdays, is founded upon the same principle.

A breach of this rule of the politico-religious church of Rome, is placed in the list of damning sins, in a ritual issued, even under the reign of the Emperor Napoleon, with his signature attached, ordering its observance by all Catholics throughout his dominions.

Thus the fastings and mortifications originally got up to appease the fickle and vindictive gods of paganism, have, without the least propriety or reason, been incorporated into the systems of some sects of professed Christians.

By this establishment the catholic is required to abstain from eating meat for forty days, except by special indulgence granted by a priest. Those therefore, to whom it is inconvenient to pay for indulgences, are under the necessity of restricting themselves to fish and vegetable diet during the above term.

---

* Masonic writers say, "their brethren used to meet on the highest hills." This declaration applies to the predecessors of freemasons, but not to the craft; whose assemblies were always held in a lodge-room, guarded by a member at the door, with a drawn sword.

The *first word spoken,* on raising the dead body of Hiram, was to be substituted for the lost master mason,s *word,* provided it was not found upon him. This idea is evidently copied from the superstitious practices mentioned above, at the funeral anniversaries.— *Edit.*

I will here observe, that personages which Mr. Pluche declares to be mythological, never having had existence, will be considered by other writers, quoted in this work, as real historical persons. Some of his hypotheses in other respects, may also be contrary to the doctrines of authors here cited. I shall generally pass such discrepances without comment, leaving the reader to form his own opinion.

To Abbé Pluche's account of Egypt, I will add a few extracts from a recent and very valuable work, entitled, "A View of Ancient and Modern Egypt, by the Rev. Michael Russell, L L. D.

Literature and Science of the Ancient Egyptians.

In Egypt the use of the hieroglyph was not entirely superseded by the invention of an alphabet. For many purposes connected with religion, and even with the more solemn occupations of civil life, the emblematical style of composition continued to enjoy a preference; on a principle similar to that which disposes the Jew to perform his worship in Hebrew, and the Roman Catholic in Latin. There appears also to have been a mixed language used by the priests, partaking at once of hieroglyphics and of alphabetical characters; which, in allusion to the class of men by whom it was employed, was denominated hieratic. Hence, in process of time, the Egyptians found themselves in possession of three different modes of communication—the hieroglyphic, properly so called, the hieratic, and the demotic or common. This distinction is clearly recognized in the following well-known passage extracted from the works of Clemens Alexandrinus.

Those who are educated among the Egyptians, says he, learn first of all the method of writing called the epistolographic; secondly, the hieratic, which the sacred scribes employ; and, lastly, the most mysterious description, the hieroglyphic, of which there are two kinds,—the one denoting objects, in a direct manner, by means of the initial sounds of words; the other is symbolical. Of the symbolical signs one class represents objects by exhibiting a likeness or picture; another, by a metaphorical or less complete resemblance; and a third, by means of certain allegorical enigmas. Thus,—to give an example of the three methods in the symbolical division,—when they wish to represent an object by the first, they fix upon a distant resemblance: such as a circle, when they want to indicate the sun, and a crescent when their purpose is to denote the moon. The second, or metaphorical, allows a considerable freedom in selecting the emblem, and may be such as only suggests the object by analogous qualities. For instance, when they record the praises of kings in their theological fables, they exhibit them in connexion with figurative allusions which shadow forth their good actions and benign dispositions. In this case the representation is not direct but metaphorical. Of the third method of symbolical writing the following will serve as an example: they assimilate the oblique course of the planets to the body of a serpent, but that of the sun to the figure of a scarabæus.

In reference to the knowledge actually acquired of the literature of ancient Egypt by means of the late discoveries in hieroglyphics, we are not entitled to speak in boastful or very confident language. The wasting hand of time, which has rendered its effects visible even on the Pyramids, has entirely destroyed the more perishable materials to which the sages of Thebes and the magicians of Memphis may have committed the science of their several generations. We know, too, that the bigotry of ignorance and of superstition accomplished, in many cases, what the flood of years had permitted to escape; for which reason we must not estimate the extent of acquirement among the wise men of Egypt by the scanty remains of their labors which have been casually rescued from accident and violence. From Diodorus Siculus we receive the information that in the tomb of Osymandias were deposited twenty thousand volumes,—a number which is reduced by Manetho to three thousand five hundred and twenty-five,—all of which, on account of their antiquity or the importance of their subjects, were ascribed to Thoth or Hermes, who, it is well known, united in his character the intelligence of a divinity with the patriotism of a faithful minister.

Of these works, which unquestionably belong to a very remote antiquity, we have a short account supplied by a Christian bishop, Clemens of Alexandria, who appears to have devoted much attention to the learning of the ancient Egyptians. "In that country," he tells us, "every individual cultivates a different branch of philosophy,—an arrangement which applies chiefly to their holy ceremonies. In such processions the singer occupies the first place, carrying in his hand an instrument of music. He is said to be obliged to learn two of the books of Hermes; one of which contains hymns addressed to the gods, and the other the rules by which a prince ought to govern. Next comes the Horoscopus, holding a clock and the branch of a palm-tree, which are the symbols of astrology. He must be completely master of the four books of Hermes which treat of that science. One of these explains the order of the fixed stars; the second, the motion and phases of the sun and moon: the other two determine the times of their periodical rising. Then follows the Hierogrammatist or *sacred scribe*, with two feathers on his head, and, a *book* and ruler in his hand, to which are added the instruments of writing, some ink and a reed. He must know what are called hieroglyphics, and those branches of science which belong to cosmography, geography, and astronomy, especially the laws of the sun, moon, and five planets; he must be acquainted with the territorial distribution of Egypt, the course of the Nile, the furniture of the temples and of all consecrated places. After these is an officer denominated Stolistes, who bears a square-rule as the emblem of justice, and the cup of libations. His charge includes every thing which belongs to the education of youth, as well as to sacrifices, first-fruits, *hymns, prayers*, religious pomps, festivals, and commemorations; the rules for which are contained in ten books. This functionary is succeeded by one called the prophet, who displays in his bosom a jar or vessel, meant for carrying water,—a symbol thought to represent the deity, but which, more probably, had a reference to the sacred character of the Nile. He is attended by persons bearing bread cut into slices. The duty of the prophet, [as president of the mysteries, according to Volney's citation of this passage,] made it necessary for him to be perfectly acquainted with the ten books called sacerdotal, and which treat of the laws *of the gods*, and of the whole discipline of the priesthood. He also presides over the distribution of the sacred revenue; that is, the income arising from the performance of pious rites, and dedicated to the support of religious institutions. Hence, there are forty-two books of Hermes, the knowledge of which is absolutely necessary; of these, thirty-six, containing the whole philosophy of the Egyptians, are carefully studied by the persons whom we have mentioned; and the remaining six are learned by the Pastophori, or inferior priests, as they belong to anatomy, to nosology, to instruments of surgery, to pharmacy, to the diseases of the eye, and to the maladies of women." (Clemen. Alexandrin. Strom. lib. vi. p. 633.)

This distribution of the sciences does not enable us to determine either the principles on which they were founded or the extent to which they were pursued. We possess a better criterion in the perfection to which the people of Egypt, at a very early period, had carried some of those arts which have a close dependence upon scientific deductions. The prodigies of Thebes could not have been accomplished by a nation ignorant of mathematics and chymistry; nor could the pyramids, the obelisks, and the monolithic temples, which still meet the eye of the traveler in almost every spot between Elephantiné and the mouths of the Nile, have been raised without the aid of such mechanical powers as have their origin in the calculations of philosophy.—(See p. 133, Harper's Ed.)

Here we have the archetype of masonic processions, on festival days and other important occasions. I shall hereafter give a detailed account of those which took place in London, on laying the corner stone and on the dedication of Freemasons' Hall. We see here also the original of the square rule, as a masonic symbol. It was, in Egypt, an emblem of justice, because it was the means by which was ascertained the boundaries of lands that had been obscured or carried away by the inundation. We here moreover recognise the holy or *sacred* scribe of a royal arch chapter, with a *book* and ruler in his hand. The original book, containing the laws of Egypt relating to sacrifices and other matters appertaining to religion, not having been preserved, masonry substitutes for it the Bible, which is opened at the beginning of the gospel of St. John, and with the square and compasses laid thereon, is ceremonially carried in the processions.

The *jar* or vessel spoken of, was undoubtedly one of the Cannopi which indicated the different heights of the Nile, and for this reason acquired a sanctity among the people. The three pitchers carried in masonic processions no doubt originally alluded to the Egyptian cannopi.

As to the learning, so much boasted of by the craft, and which seems to be claimed by them as an inheritance from their predecessors, it is to be feared, that it remains buried in the the *tomb of Osymandias*. The hymns or odes and songs, as well as prayers are retained in great abundance, and compose an essential part of the masonic ceremonies.

Attributing the authorship of twenty thousand, or even three thousand five hundred and twenty-five volumes, to Thoth or Hermes, is an evidence of his being a fictitious character, and corroborates the opinion of Pluche on the subject. Jamblichus, however, puts this matter beyound controversy; he says : "Hermes, the god who presides over language, was formerly very properly considered as common to all priests ; and the power who presides over the true science concerning the gods is one and the same in the whole of things.

Hence our ancestors dedicated the inventions of their wisdom to this deity, *inscribing all their own writings* with the name of Hermes. (Taylor's trans. p. 17·)

Volney, who, in his Ruins, quotes part of the foregoing extract from Clemens observes, that Mercury [who is the same as Hermes] is the Janus of the Romans, the Guianese of the Indians, and it is remarkable that Yanus and Guianese are synonymous. In short, it appears that these books are the source of all that has been transmitted to us by the Greeks and Latins in every science, even in alchymy, necromancy, etc. What is most to be regretted in their loss is that part which related to the principles of medicine and diet, in which the Egyptians appear to have made considerable progress and useful observations."

Remains of the Ancient Arts, in various parts of Egypt.

Dendera, which is commonly identified with the ancient Tentyra, presents some very striking examples of that sumptuous architecture which the people of Egypt lavished upon their places of worship. The gateway in particular which leads to the temple of Isis has excited universal admiration. Each front, as well as the interior, is covered with sculptured hieroglyphics, which are executed with a richness, a precision, elegance of form, and variety of ornament, surpassing in many respects the similar edifices which are found at Thebes and

Philoe. The height is forty-two feet, the width thirty-three, and the depth seventeen. "Advancing along the brick ruins," says Dr. Richardson, "we came to an elegant gateway or propylon, which is also of sandstone, neatly hewn, and completely covered with sculpture and hieroglyphics remarkably well cut. Immediately over the centre of the door-way is the beautiful Egyptian ornament usually called *the globe*, with serpent and wings, emblematical of the glorious sun poised in the airy firmament of heaven, supported and directed in his course by the eternal wisdom of the Deity. The sublime phraseology of Scripture, 'the Sun of Righteousness shall rise with healing on his wings,' could not be more emphatically or more accurately represented to the human eye than by this elegant device. The temple itself still retains all its original magnificence. The centuries which have elapsed since the era of its foundation have scarcely affected it in any important part, and have impressed upon it no greater appearance of age than serves to render it more venerable and imposing.* To Mr. Hamilton, who had seen innumerable monuments of the same kind throughout the Thebaid, it seemed as if he were now witnessing the highest degree of architectural excellence that had ever been attained on the borders of the Nile. Here were concentrated the united labors of ages, and the last effort of human art and industry, in that uniform line of construction which had been adopted in the earliest times.

The portico consists of twenty-four columns, in three rows; each above twenty-two feet in circumference, thirty two feet high, and covered with hieroglyphics. On the front, Isis is in general the principal figure to whom offerings are made. On the architrave are represented two processions of men and women bringing to their goddess, and to Osiris, who is sitting behind her, globes encompassed with cows' horns, mitred snakes, lotus flowers, vases, little boats, *graduated staffs*, and other instruments of their emblematical worship. The interior

---

* The knowledge of astronomy leads to the interpretation of hieroglyphical characters, since astronomical signs are often found on the ancient Egyptian monuments, which were probably employed by the priests to record dates. On the ceiling of the portico of the temple among the ruins of Tentyra, there is a long row of figures of men and animals, following each other in the same direction; among these are the twelve signs of the zodiac, placed according to the motion of the sun: it is probable that the first figure in the procession represents the beginning of the year. Now the first is the Lion as if coming out of the temple; and it is well known that the agricultural year of the Egyptians commenced at the solstice of summer, the epoch of the inundation of the Nile: then if the preceding hypothesis be true, the solstice at the time the temple was built must have happened in the constellation of the lion; but, as the solstice now happens 21° 6' north of the constellation of the Twins, it is easy to compute that the zodiac of Tentyra must have been made 4000 years ago.—Diss. on Mech. of the Heav. by Mrs. Somerville.—Edit.

of the pronaos is adorned with sculptures, most of them preserving part of the paint with which they have been covered. Those on the ceiling are peculiarly rich and varied, all illustrative of the union between the astronomical and religious creeds of the ancient Egyptians; yet, though each separate figure is well preserved and perfectly intelligible, we must be more intimately acquainted with the real principles of the sciences, as they were then taught, before we can undertake to explain the signs in which they were embodied.

The sekos, or interior of the temple, consists of several apartments, all the walls and ceilings of which are in the same way covered with religious and astronomical representations.

The rooms have been lighted by small perpendicular holes cut in the ceiling, and, where it was possible to introduce them, by oblique ones in the sides. But some idea might be formed of the *perpetual gloom* in which the apartments on the ground-floor of the sekos must have been buried, from the fact, that where no sidelight could be introduced, all they received was communicated from the apartment above; so that notwithstanding the cloudless sky and the brilliant colors on the walls, the place must have been always well calculated for the mysterious practices of the religion to which it was consecrated. On one corner of the roof there was a chapel or temple twenty feet square, consisting of twelve columns, exactly similar in figure and proportions to those of the pronaos. The use to which it may have been applied must probably remain one of the secrets connected with the *mystical* and sometimes cruel service in which the priests of Isis were employed.

Towards the eastern end of the roof are two separate sets of apartments, one on the north and the other on the south side of it.

The ceiling of the next room is divided into two compartments by a figure of Isis in very high relief. In one of them is the circular zodiac; in the other a variety of boats with four or five human figures in each; one of whom is in the act of spearing a large egg, while others are stamping with their feet upon the victims of their fury, among which are several human beings. Near this scene a large lion, supported by four dog-headed figures, each carrying a knife, may be regarded as an additional type of the sanguinary purposes for which the apartment was used. The walls of the third room are covered with the several representations of a person,—first at the point of death lying on a couch; then stretched out lifeless upon a bier; and finally, being embalmed.

The western wall of the great temple is particularly interesting for the extreme elegance of the sculpture.

Here are frequent representations of men who seem prepared for slaughter or just going to be put to death. On these occasions one or more appear, with their hands or legs tied to the trunk of a tree, in the *most painful* and distorted attitudes.

In a small chapel behind the temple, the cow and the hawk seem to have been particularly worshipped, as priests are frequently seen kneeling before them presenting sacrifices and offerings. In the centre of the ceiling is the same front face of Isis in high relief, illuminated, as it were, by a body of rays issuing from the mouth of the same long figure, which, in the other temples, appears to encircle the heavenly bodies. About two hundred yards eastward from this chapel is a propylon of small dimensions, resembling in form that which conducts to the great temple, and, like it, built in a line with the wall which surrounds the sacred enclosure. Among the sculptures on it which appear of the same style but less finished than those on the large temple, little more is worthy of notice than the frequent exhibition of human slaughter by men or by lions. Still farther towards the east, there is another propylon, equally well preserved with the rest, about forty feet in height, and twenty feet square at the base. Among the sacred figures on this building is an Isis pointing with a reed to a graduated staff held by another figure of the same deity, from which are suspended scales containing water animals, the whole group perhaps being an emblem of her influence over the Nile in regulating its periodical inundations.—*Ibid. p.* 166.

The signs of the zodiac portrayed in the center of the roof of freemasons' hall, London, it appears, are in accordance with the astronomical decorations of the ancient temples of Egypt. Celestial and terrestrial globes also compose a part of the masonic emblems.

The author seems not to be aware that the Isis, pointing with a reed to a graduated staff, was directing the attention of the Egyptians to the Nilometer or measure of the inundation, so important to their well being. This measure in after times, as before noticed, became an ensign of office, Mercury's wand, and as such has been adopted by masonry.

The cruelty supposed to be connected with the Egyptian mode of worship, as indicated by the appearance of persons under torture, the reader will find in the sequel, were nothing more than sham representations of the punishments said to be inflicted upon the wicked in another life. The contrast displayed in the death of a virtuous character, carefully embalmed, clearly points out the intention of these representations. The appartments where these awful figures were portrayed, were, no doubt, the first into which candidates for initiation into the mysteries were introduced.

CHAPTER II.

ORIGIN, NATURE, AND OBJECT, OF THE ANCIENT MYSTERIES;
ABRIDGED FROM BISHOP WARBURTON'S DIVINE LEGATION OF
MOSES; WITH NOTES AND REMARKS, POINTING OUT THEIR
IDENTITY WITH FREEMASONRY, ETC.

It is proper to premise, that the author uniformly refers to the works of the writers which he quotes, and generally gives the passages in the original language in which they were written. His quotations from the Eneid, the Metamorphosis of Epuleius, and some other works, given in the Latin language, are here rendered into English. A few Greek passages in his work are also given in translation, and all Greek terms are put in Roman characters for the benefit of the general reader.

An abstract of the author's remarks, introductory to his treatise on the Mysteries, is first given, as follows:

So inseparable, in antiquity, were the ideas of *law-giving* and *religion*, that Plutarch, speaking of the preference of atheism to superstition, supposes no other establishment of divine worship than what was the work of the legislator. "How much happier would it have been, says he, for the Carthagenians, had their first law-giver been like Critias or Diogoras, who believed neither gods nor demons, rather than such an one as enjoined their *public sacrifices to Saturn.*"

But here it will be necessary to remind the reader of this previous truth, that there never was in any age of the world, from the most early accounts of time, to this present hour, any civil-policied nation or people who had a religion, of which the chief foundation and support was not the doctrine of a future state of rewards and punishments; *the Jewish people only excepted.* This I presume, our adversaries will not deny. Mr. Bayle, the indulgent foster father of infidelity, confesses it in the fullest manner, and with the utmost ingenuity; "all the religions of the world, whether true or false, turn upon this grand pivot, that there is an *invisible judge* who punishes and rewards *after this life*, the actions of men, both of thought and deed. From thence it is supposed the principal use of religion is derived," and thinks it was the utility of that doctrine which set the magistrate upon inventing a religion for the state. "It is the principle motive that incited those who invented it." (Dict. Crit. and Hist. Art. Spinoza Rem. E.)

The Egyptians were the first people who perfected civil policy, and established religion: they were the first too, who deified their kings, law-givers and public benefactors. This was a practice invented by them, who in process of time, taught the rest of the world their mystery.

The attributes and qualities assigned to their gods, always corresponded with the nature and genius of the government. If this was gentle, benign, compassionate and forgiving; goodness and mercy were most essential to the deity; but if severe, inexorable, captious or unequal, the very gods were tyrants; and *expiations, atonements, lustrations*, and *bloody sacrifices* composed the system of religious worship.

> Gods partial, changeful, passionate, unjust,
> Whose attributes were rage, revenge and lust,
> Such as the souls of cowards might conceive,
> And formed like tyrants, tyrants would believe.

The first step the legislator took, was to pretend a mission and revelation from some god, by whose command and direction he had framed the policy he would establish. In a word, there is hardly an old lawgiver, on record but what thus pretended to revelation, and the divine assistance.

The universal custom of the ancient world was, to make gods and prophets of their first kings, and law-givers. Hence it is, that Plato makes legislation to have come from God, and not from man.

Aristotle, in his maxims for setting up, and supporting a tyranny, lays this down for one "to seem extremely attached to the worship of the gods, for that men have no apprehension of injustice from such as they take to be religious, and to have a high sense of providence.* Nor will the people be apt to run into plots and conspiracies against those, whom they believe the gods will in turn, fight for, and support." And here it is worth noting, that, anciently, tyrants, as well as law-givers gave all encouragement to religion; and endeavored to establish their irregular wills, not by convincing men that there was no just nor unjust in actions; but by persuading them that the privilege of *divine right* exempted the tyrant from all moral obligation.

Porphyry quotes an express law of Draco's concerning the mode of divine worship. "Let the gods and our own country heroes be publicly worshipped, according to the established rites; when privately, according to every man's abilities, with terms of the greatest regard and reverence; with the first fruits of their labors, and with annual libations." Andocides quotes another of Solon, which provides for the due and regular celebration of the *Eleusinian Mysteries.* Athenæus does the same. And how considerable a part these were of divine worship, and of what importance to the very essence of religion, we shall see hereafter.

---

* This principle is beginning to be understood, and acted upon, by some of our leading patriots in the American republic.—Edit.

The second step the legislators took to propagate and establish religion, was to make the general doctrine of a providence, with which, they prefaced and introduced their laws, the great sanction of their institutes.

Thus Zaleucus begins his preface: "Every inhabitant whether of town or country, should first of all be firmly persuaded of the being and existence of the gods: which belief he will be readily induced to entertain, when he contemplates the heavens, regards the world, and observes the disposition, order, and harmony of the universe; which can neither be the work of blind chance, nor of man. These gods are to be worshiped as the cause of all the real good we enjoy. Every one therefore should so purify, and possess his mind, as to have it clear of all kinds of evil; being persuaded that god is not honored by a wicked person, nor acceptably served, like miserable man, with sumptuous ceremonies, or taken with *costly sacrifices*, but with *virtue only, and a constant disposition to good and just actions.*"

And much in the same fashion does Charondas introduce his laws.

In imitation of this practice, Plato likewise, and Cicero both preface their laws with the sanctions of religion. And though these two great men were not, strictly speaking, law-givers in form; yet we are not to suppose that what they wrote in this science, was like the dreams of the sophists, for the amusement of the idle and curious. They were both well practised in affairs, and deeply conversant in human nature; and they formed their speculative institutes on the plan, and in the spirit and views of ancient legislation; the foundation of Plato's being the *Attic Laws*, and the foundation of Cicero's the *Twelve Tables*.

Plato makes it the necessary introduction to his laws, to establish the being and providence of the gods by a law against *sacrilege*. And he explains what he means by sacrilege, in the following words; "Either the denial of the being of the gods: or, if that be owned, the denial of their providence over men; or, thirdly, the teaching, that they are flexible, and easy to be cojoled by prayer* and sacrifice." And afterwards: "It is not of small consequence, that what we here reason about the gods, should by all means be made probable; as, that they *are;* and that they are good; and that their *concern for justice takes place of all other human considerations*. For this, in our opinion, seems to be the noblest and best preface that can be made to a body of

---

* Plutarch, in his treatise of Isis and Osiris, remarks, that "In Crete there was a statue of Jupiter, without ears. The Cretians judging it fit that he who is the ruler and lord of all things, should hear no one."—See Taylor's Translation Jamb. p. 248. Edit.

laws. In compliancy with this declaration, Cicero's preface to his laws is conceived in the following terms: "Let our citizens then be, first of all firmly persuaded of the government and dominion of the gods; that they are the lords and masters of the world; that all things are disposed by their power, direction, and providence; and that the whole race of mankind is in the highest manner indebted to them; that they are intimately acquainted with every one's state and condition; that they know what he does, what he thinks; with what disposition of mind, and with what degree of piety he performs the acts and offices of religion; and that, accordingly, they make a distinction between the *good* and *evil*."

And then follow the laws themselves; the first of which is conceived in these words: "Let those who approach the gods, be pure and undefiled; let their offerings be seasoned with piety, and all *ostentation of pomp omitted*: the god himself will be his own avenger on transgressors. Let the gods, and those who were ever reckoned in the number of celestials, be worshipped: and those likewise, whom their merits have raised to heaven: such as Hercules, Bacchus, Æsculapius, Castor, Pollux, and Romulus. And let chapels be erected in honor to those qualities, by whose aid mortals arrive thither, such as *reason, virtue, piety* and *good faith*."—De Legg. lib. ii. c. 8.

Institution of the Mysteries.

The next step the legislator took, was to support and affirm the general doctrine of a providence, which he had delivered in his laws, by a very circumstantial and popular method of inculcating the belief of a future state of rewards and punishments.

This was the institution of the *mysteries, the most sacred part of pagan religion*: and artfully framed to strike deeply and forcibly into the minds and imaginations of the people.

I propose, therefore, to give a full and distinct account of this whole matter: and the rather, because it is a thing little known or attended to: the ancients who wrote expressly on the mysteries, such as Melanthius, Menander, Hicesius, Sotades, and others, not being come down to us. So that the modern writers on this subject are altogether in the dark concerning their origin and end; not excepting Meursius himself; to whom, however, I am much indebted, for abridging my labor in the search of those passages of antiquity, which make mention of the Eleusinian Mysteries, and for bringing the greater part of them together under one view.—(Eleusinia: five de Cereris Eleusinæ sacro.)

To avoid ambiguity, it will be proper to explain the term. Each of the pagan gods had, besides the *public* and *open*, a *secret worship* paid unto him; to which none were admitted but those who had been selected by preparatory ceremonies, called *initiation*. This secret worship was termed the *Mysteries*.

But though every god had, besides his open worship, the secret likewise; yet this latter did not every where attend the former; but only there, where he was the patron god, or in principal esteem. Thus when in consequence of that intercommunity of paganism, which will be explained hereafter, one nation adopted the gods of another, they did not always take in at the same time, the secret worship or mysteries of that god; so, in Rome, the public and open worship of Bacchus was in use long before his mysteries were admitted. But on the other hand, again, the worship of the stange god was sometimes introduced only for the sake of his mysteries: as, in the same city, that of Isis and Osiris. Thus stood the case in general, the particular exceptions to it, will be seen in the sequel of this dissertation.

The first and original mysteries, of which we have any sure account, were those of Isis and Osiris in Egypt; from whence they were derived to the Greeks, under the presidency of various gods, as the institutor thought most for his purpose; Zoroaster brought them into Persia, Cadmus and Inachus into Greece at large, Orpheus into Thrace; Melampus into Argis, Trophonius into Bœotia, Minos into Crete; Cinyras into Cyprus, and Erechtheus into Athens. And as in Egypt they were to Isis and Osiris; so in Asia they were to Mithras, in Samothrace to the mother of the gods, in Bœotia to Bacchus, in Cyprus to Venus, in Crete to Jupiter, in Athens to Ceres and Proserpine, in Amphissa to Castor and Pollux, in Lemnos to Vulcan, and so to others, in other places, the number of which was incredible.

But their end, as well as nature, was the same in all; to teach the doctrine of a *future state*. In this, Origen and Celsus agree, the two most learned writers of their several parties. The first, minding his adversary of the difference between the future life promised by Christianity, and that taught in paganism, bids him compare the Christian with what all the sects of philosophy, and all the mysteries, among Greeks and Barbarians, taught concerning it: and Celsus, in his turn, endeavoring to show that Christianity had no advantage over Paganism in the efficacy of stronger sanctions, expresses himself to this purpose; " But now, after all, just as you believe eternal punishments, so do the ministers of the sacred rites, and those who initiate into, and preside in the mysteries."

And that nothing very heterodox was taught in the mysteries concerning a future state, I collect from the answer Origen makes to Celsus, who had preferred what was taught in the mysteries of Bacchus on that point, to what the Christian religion revealed concerning it. lib. iv. p. 167.

They continued long in religious reverence: some were more famous and more extensive than others; to which many accidents occurred. The most noted were the Orphic, the Bacchic, the Eleusinian, the Samothracian, the Cabiric, and the Mithriac.

Euripides makes Bacchus say, in his tragedy of that name, that the *Orgies* were celebrated by all foreign nations, and that he came to introduce them among the Greeks. And it is not improbable, but several barbarous nations might have learned them from the Egyptians long before they came into Greece. The *Druids of Britain who had, as well as the Brachmans of India, divers of their religious rites from thence, celebrated the Orgies of Bacchus, as we learn from Dyonisius the African.* And Strabo, having quoted Artemidorus for a fabulous story, subjoins, "But what he says of Ceres and Proserpine is more credible, namely, that there is an island near Britain, where they *perform the same rites to those two goddesses as are used in Samothrace.*" (Strabonis Geor. lib. iv.) But of all the mysteries, those which bore that name, by way of eminence, the *Eleusinian*, celebrated at Athens in honor of Ceres, were by far the most renowned; and in process of time, eclipsed, and, as it were, swallowed up the rest. Their neighbors round about very early practised these mysteries to the neglect of their own; in a little time all Greece and Asia Minor were initiated into them; and at length they spread over the whole Roman empire, and even beyond the limits of it. "I insist not, (says Tully) on those sacred and august rites of Eleuris, where, from the remotest regions, men come to be initiated." And we are told in Zosimus, that "these most holy rites were then so extensive, as to take in the whole race of mankind." Aristides calls Eleusis the common temple of the earth. And Pausanias says, the rites performed there as much excelled all other rites, instituted for the promotion of piety, as the gods excelled the heroes.

How this happened, is to be accounted for from the nature of the State which gave birth to these mysteries. Athens was a city the most devoted to religion of any upon the face of the earth. On this account their poet Sophocles calls it the sacred building of the gods in allusion to its foundation. Nor was it a less compliment St. Paul intended to pay the Athenians, when he said, " Ye men of Athens, I perceive that in all things ye are too superstitious." (Acts, xvii. 22.) And Josephus tells us, that they were universally esteemed the most religious people of Greece. Hence, in these matters, Athens became the pattern and standard to the rest of the world.

In discoursing, therefore of the mysteries in general, we shall be forced to take our ideas of them chiefly from what we find practised in the Eleusinian. Nor need we fear to be mistaken; the end of all being the same, and all having their common *original* from Egypt.

To begin with the general purpose and design of their institution. This will be understood, by showing what they communicated promiscuously to all.

To support the doctrine of a providence which, they taught, governed the world, they enforced the belief of a future state of rewards and punishments, by all kinds of methods. But as this did not quite clear up the intricate ways of providence, they added the doctrine of a metempsychosis, or the belief of a prior state, as we learn from Cicero, and Porphyry, the latter of whom informs us, that it was taught in the mysteries of the Persian Mithras. This was an ingenious solution, invented by the Egyptian lawgivers, to remove all doubts, concerning the moral attributes of God, and so, consequently to establish the belief of his providence, from a future state. For the lawgiver well knew how precarious that belief was, while the moral attributes of God remained doubtful and uncertain.

In cultivating the doctrine of a future life, it was taught, that the *initiated*, would be happier in that state than all other mortals: that while the souls of the profane, at their leaving the body, stuck fast in mire and filth, and remained in darkness, the souls of the initiated winged their flight directly to the happy islands, and the habitations of the gods. This promise was as necessary for the support of the Mysteries, as the Mysteries were for the support of the doctrine. But now, lest it should be mistaken, that initiation alone, or any other means than a virtuous life, entitled men to this future happiness, the Mysteries openly proclaimed it as their chief business, to restore the soul to its original purity. " It was the end and design of initiation, says Plato, " to restore the soul to that state, from whence it fell, as from its native seat of perfection." They contrived that every thing should tend to show the necessity of virtue, as appears from Epictetus. "Thus the mysteries became useful, thus we seize the true spirit of them, when we begin to apprehend that every thing therein was instituted by the ancients, for instruction and amendment of life." Porphyry gives us some of those moral precepts, which were enforced in the mysteries, as to honor their parents, to offer up fruits to the gods, and to forbear cruelty towards animals. In pursuance of this scheme, it was required in the aspirant to the Mysteries, that he should be of a clear and unblemished character, and free even from the suspicion of any notorious crime. (Libanius Decl. xix.) To come to the truth, he was severely interrogated by the priest or hierophant, impressing him with the same sense of his obligation to conceal nothing, as is now done at the Roman confessional.

As appears from the repartee which Plutarch records, in his *Laconic Apothegms of Lysander*, when he went to be initiated into the Samothracian mysteries, "he was required, by the hierophant, to confess every wicked act that he had committed during his whole life."

Why initiation into these mysteries is called, inquiring of the oracles will be seen afterwards.

Hence it was, that when Nero, after the murder of his mother, took a journey into Greece, and had a mind to be present at the celebration of the Eleusinian mysteries, the consciousness of his parricide deterred him from attempting it. (Sueton. Vita Neron. cap. 34.) On the same account, the good Emperor M. Antoninus, when he would purge himself to the world of the death of Avidius Cassius, chose to be initiated into the Eleusinian mysteries, it being notorious, that none were admitted into them, who labored under the just suspicion of any heinous immorality. This was originally a fundamental condition of initiation, observed in common by all the mysteries.

During the celebration of the mysteries, they were enjoined the greatest purity, and highest elevation of mind. "When you sacrifice or pray, says Epictetus in Arrian, go with a prepared purity of mind, and with dispositions so previously disposed, as are required of you when you approach the ancient rites and mysteries." And Proclus tells us that the mysteries and the initiations drew the souls of men from a material, sensual, and merely human life, and joined them in communion with the gods. Nor was a less degree of purity required of the initiated for their future conduct. They were obliged by solemn engagements to commence a new life of strictest piety and virtue ;

into which they were entered by a severe course of penance, proper to purge he mind of its natural defilements. Gregory Nazianzen tells us, " that no one could be initiated into the mysteries of Mithras, till he had undergone all sorts of mortifying trials, and had approved himself holy and impassible." The consideration of all this made Tertullian say, that, in the mysteries, "truth herself took on every shape, to oppose and combat truth." Omnia adversus veritatem, de ipsa veritate constructa esse. Apol. cap. 47.) And Austin, "that the devil hurried away deluded souls to their destruction, when he promised to purify them by those ceremonies, called initiations."

The initiated, under this discipline, and with these promises, were esteemed the only happy men. Aristophanes, who speaks the sense of the people, makes them exult and triumph after this manner : " On us only does the sun dispense his blessings, we only receive pleasure from his beams; we, who are initiated, and perform towards strangers and citizens all acts of piety and justice." And Sophocles, to the same purpose, " Life, only is to be had there; all other places are full of misery and evil." " Happy, says Euripides is the man who hath been initiated into the greater mysteries, and leads a life of piety and religion." And the longer any one had been initiated, the more honorable they deemed him. It was even scandalous not to be initiated, and however virtuous the person otherwise appeared, he became suspicious to the people, as was the case of Socrates, and, in after-times of Demonax. No wonder then if the superior advantages of the initiated, both here and hereafter, should make the mysteries universally aspired to. And indeed, they soon grew as comprehensive in the numbers they embraced, as in the regions and countries to which they extended. Men, women, and children, ran to be initiated. Thus Apuleius describes the state of the mysteries even in his time : " There was an influx of a crowd of those who had been initiated in the *sacred rites* of the goddess, consisting of men and women of every degree and of every age, resplendent with the *pure whiteness of linnen garments.*"

The pagans, we see, seemed to think *initiation* as necessary, as the Christians did *baptism.* And the custom of initiating children appears from a passage of Terence, to have been general.

Nay, they had even the same superstition in the administration of it which some Christians had of baptism, to defer it to the approach of death; so the honest farmer Trygæus, in the Pax of Aristophanes;

" I must be initiated before I die."

The occasion of this solicitude, is told us by the scholiast on the

Ranæ of the same poet. "The Athenians believed, that he who was initiated, and instructed in the mysteries, would obtain divine honors after death; and therefore all ran to be initiated. Their fondness for it became so great, that at such times as the public treasury was low, the magistrate would have recourse to the mysteries, as a fund to supply the exigences of the state. "Aristogiton, says the commentator on Hermogenes, in a great scarcity of public money, procured a law, that in Athens, every one should pay a certain sum for his initiation."

Every thing in these rights was mysteriously conducted and under the most *solemn obligations to secrecy.** Which, how it could agree to our representation of the mysteries, as an institution for the use of the people, we shall now endeavor to show.

They were hidden and kept secret for two reasons:

First—Nothing excites our curiosity like that which retires from our observation, and seems to forbid our search. Of this opinion you will find the learned Synesius, where he says, " the people will despise what is easy and unintelligible, and therefore they must always be provided with something wonderful and mysterious in religion, to hit their taste and stimulate their curiosity." And again, "the ignorance of the mysteries preserves their veneration; for which reason they are entrusted to the cover of night."

On these principles the mysteries were framed. They were kept secret, to excite curiosity: they were celebrated in the night to impress veneration and religious horror.† And they were performed with variety of shows and representations, (of which more hereafter) to fix and perpetuate those impressions. Hitherto, then, the Mysteries are to be considered as invented not to deter, but to invite the curiosity of the people. But,

Secondly—They were kept secret from a necessity of teaching the initiated some things, improper to be communicated to all. The learned Varro in a fragment of his book of *religions*, preserved by St. Augustin, tells us that "there were many truths, which it was inconvenient for the state to be generally known; and many things, which, though false, *it was expedient the people should believe;* and that therefore the Greeks shut up their mysteries in the silence of their sacred inclosures."

Now to reconcile this seeming contradiction, of supposing the mys-

---

* This obligation of the initiated to secrecy was the reason that the Egyptian hieroglyphic for them, was a grasshopper, which was supposed to have no mouth. See Horapollo Hyeroglyph. lib. ii. cap. 55.
† Euripides, in the Bacchantes, act. ii. makes Bacchus say, that the orgeries were celebrated in the night, because darkness has something solemn and august in it, and proper to fill the mind with sacred horror.

teries to be instituted to invite the people into them, and at the same time to keep them from the people's knowledge, we are to observe, that in *the Eleusinian* rites there were two *mysteries*, the *greater* and the *less*. The end of the *less* must be referred to what we said of the institutor's intention to invite the people into them; and of the *greater*, to his intention of keeping some truths from the people's knowledge. Nor is this said without sufficient warrant: antiquity is very express for this distinction. We are told that the lesser mysteries were only a kind of preparatory purification for the greater, and might be easily communicated to all. That four years was the usual time of probation for those greater mysteries; in which, as Clemens Alexandrinus expressly informs us, *the secrets were deposited*.

However, as it is very certain, that both the greater and lesser mysteries were instituted for the benefit of the state, it follows that the doctrines taught in both, were equally for the service of society; only with this difference, some without inconvenience, might be taught promiscuously, others could not.

On the whole, the secret in the lesser mysteries, was some hidden *rites and shows* to be kept from the open view of the people, only to invite their curiosity; and the secret in the greater, some *hidden doctrines* to be kept from the people's knowledge, for the very contrary purpose. For the shows common both to the greater and lesser mysteries, were only designed to engage the attention, and raise their devotion.

But it may be worth while to inquire more particularly into the *hidden doctrines* of the greater mysteries, for so religiously was the secret kept, that the thing seems still to lie involved in darkness. We shall therefore proceed cautiously; and try, from the obscure hints dropped up and down in antiquity.

"Pandere res alta terra et caligine mersas."

Lay open things hidden in the deep earth and in obscurity.

To begin with a passage of Clemens Alexandrinus: "After these, (namely, lustrations,) are the lesser mysteries, in which is laid the foundation of the hidden doctrines, and preparations for what is to come afterwards."

But there was one insuperable obstacle to a life of purity and holiness, the vicious examples of their gods. Ego homuncio hoc non facerem? (Could not I, a sorry fellow, be permitted to do this thing)*

---

* Terence, Eun. act. iii. sc. v.—Euripides puts this argument into the mouth of several of his speakers, up and down his tragedies. Helen, in the fourth act of *the Trojan Dames*, says, "How could I resist a goddess, whom Jupiter himself obeys?" Ion, in his play of that name, in the latter end of the first act, speaks to the same purpose;

was the absolving formula, whenever any one was resolved to give a loose to his passions. And the licentious rites, in the open worship of their gods, gave still greater encouragement to these conclusions. Plato, in his book of laws, forbids drinking to excess; unless, says he, during the feast of Bacchus, and in honor of that god. And Aristotle, in his politics, having blamed all lewd and obscene images and pictures, *excepts those of the gods*, which religion had sanctified.

Now the mysteries professed to exact nothing difficult of the initiated, which they would not assist him to perform. It was necessary, then, to remedy this evil; which they did by striking at the root of it. So that, such of the initiated as were judged capable, were made acquainted with *the whole delusion*. The mystagogue taught them, that Jupiter, Mercury, Bacchus, Venus, Mars, and the whole rabble of licentious deities, were only dead mortals, subject in life to the same passions and infirmities with themselves, but having been, on other accounts, benefactors to mankind, grateful posterity had deified them, and, with their virtues, had indiscreetly cannonized their vices.* The fabulous gods being thus routed, the supreme cause of all things naturally took their place. Him they were taught to consider as the creator of the universe, who pervaded all things by his virtue, and governed all by his providence. But here it must be observed, that the *discovery of this supreme cause* was made consistent with the notion of local tutelary deities, beings superior to men, and inferior to God, and by him set over the several parts of his creation. This was an opinion universally holden by antiquity, and never brought into question by any theist. What the aporreta overthrew, was the vulgar polytheism, the worship of dead men. From this time, the initiated had the title of Epoptes, by which was meant *one that sees things as they are and without disguise;* whereas, before he was called Mystes, which has a contrary signification.

But besides the prevention of vice, the detection of the national gods

---

and in the fifth act of Hercules Furens, Theseus comforts his friend by the examples of the crimes of the gods. See likewise his Hyppolitus, act. ii. sc. ii. The learned and ingenious Mr. Seward, in his tract of *the conformity between popery and paganism*, has taken notice of a difficult passage in this tragedy, which he has very ably explained, on the system here delivered of the detection of Polytheism in the sacred mysteries.

* When St. Austin, (Civ. de', lib. ii. cap. 7, 8) had quoted the Ego homunico hoc non facerem, to show what mischief these stories did to the morals of the people; he makes the defenders of paganism reply, that it was true, but then these things were only taught in the fables of the poets, which an attention to the mysteries would rectify; this the father cannot deny; but observes however, that in the then corrupt state of the mysteries the remedy was become part of the disease; "Nolo dicere illa mystica quam ista theatrica esse turpiora."

had another important use, which was to excite men to heroic virtue, by showing them what honors the benefactors of nations had acquired, by the free exercise of it. And this, as will be shown hereafter, was the chief reason why princes, statesmen, and leaders of colonies and armies all aspired to be partakers of the *greater mysteries.*

Thus we see, how what was taught and required in the lesser mysteries, became the foundation of instruction in the greater; the obligation to a good life there, made it necessary to remove the errors of vulgar polytheism here; and the doctrine of a providence taught previously in those, facilitated the reception of the sole cause of all things, when finally revealed in these. Such were the truths which Varro, as quoted above, tells us it was expedient for the people to know.* He supposed, indeed, the error of vulgar polytheism to be so inveterate, that it was not to be expelled without throwing society into convulsions. But Plato spoke out, he owned it to be "difficult to find the father and creator of the universe; and, when found, impossible to discover him to all the world."—(In Timæo.)

Besides, there was another reason why the institutors of the mysteries, who were lawgivers, should be for keeping this truth a secret. They had had, themselves, the chief hand in the rise of vulgar polytheism. They contrived it for the sake of the state; and to keep the people in awe, under a greater veneration for their laws. This polytheism the poets had depraved, by inventing or recording vicious stories of the gods and heroes, which the lawgivers were willing to have stifled. And they were only such stories, that, in their opinion, as may be seen in Plato, made Polytheism hurtful to the state.

That this accounts for the secret in the greater mysteries, is no precarious hypothesis, raised merely on conjecture, I shall now endeavor to show.

First, from the clear evidence of antiquity, which expressly informs us of these two particulars. That the errors of polytheism were detected, and the doctrine of the unity taught and explained in the mysteries. But here it is to be observed, that when the ancients speak of mysteries indefinitely, they generally mean the greater.

---

* These two were the truths which the pontifex Scævola, said were to be kept hid from the people. "It is recorded in books that Scævola, a very learned pontiff, argued that three kinds of gods had been handed down to us, one by the poets, another by the philosophers, the third by the rulers of the state. The first kind he says is worthless—the second not suitable for commonwealths, because it contains certain things, the knowledge of which is prejudicial to the people. What then are those things which are prejudicial to the multitude? "These," he says, "that Hercules, Esculapius, Castor, Pollux, are not gods, but were men who departed human life.—*Augustin de Civit. Dei, lib. iv. cap.* 27.

It hath been shown, that the Grecian and Asiatic Mysteries came originally from Egypt. Now, of the Egyptian, St. Austin giveth us this remarkable account. "Of the same nature, too, are those things which Alexander of Macedon wrote to his mother, as revealed unto him by one Leo,* chief hierophant of the Egyptian mysteries, whereby it appeared, that not only such as Picus, and Faunus, and Eneas, and Romulus, nay Hercules, and Esculapius, and Bacchus the son of Semele, and Castor, and Pollux, and all others of the same rank, had been advanced, from the condition of mortality, into gods, but that even those deities of the higher order, the Dii majorum gentium, those whom Cicero without naming seems to carp at, in his Tusculans, such as Jupiter, Juno, Saturn, Neptune, Vulcan, Vesta, and many others, whom Varro endeavors to allegorize into the elements or parts of the world, were, in truth, only mortal men. But the priest being under great fears and apprehensions, while he was telling this, as conscious he was betraying the secret of the mysteries, begged of Alexander, when he found that he intended to communicate it to his mother, that he would enjoin her to burn the letter, as soon as she had read it."†

To understand the concluding part, we are to know, that Cyprian, who has also preserved this curious anecdote, tells us, it was the dread of Alexander's power, which extorted the secret from the hierophant.‡ All this well illustrates a passage in Lucian's *council of the gods*; when after Momus had ridiculed the monstrous deities of Egypt, Jupiter replies, "it is true that these are abominable things, which you mention of the Egyptian worship. But then, consider, Momus, that

---

* It is not improbable but this might be a name of office. Porphyry in his fourth book of *abstinence*, informs us that the priests of the mysteries of Mithras were called *lions* the priestesses lionesses, and the inferior ministers ravens. For there was a great conformity, in the practices and ceremonies of the several mysteries, throughout the whole pagan world. And this conjecture is supported by a passage in Eunapius, which seems to say, that it was unlawful *to reveal the name of the hierophant.*

In the modern degree of masonry, called knight of the Eagle, and sovereign prince of Rose Cross de Heroden, the aspirant "solemnly promises on his honor, never to reveal the *place* where he was received, *who* received him, nor *those* who were present at his reception."

Also in the degree of "knight of Kadosh," "when a reception is made, the great commander remains alone in the chapter with the candidate, and must be so situated that the latter cannot see him, as he is not to know who initiates him." (Bernard.)—*Edit.*

† I suppose this communication to his mother, might be to let her understand, that he was no longer the dupe of her fine story of Jupiter's intrusion, and the intrigue of his divine original. For Erastosthenes, according to Plutarch, says, that Olympias, when she brought Alexander on his way to the army, in his first military expedition, acquainted him in private with the secret of his birth; and exhorted him to behave himself as became the son of Jupiter Hammon. This, I suppose, Alexander might tell to the priest and so the murder came out.

‡ But this is a mistake, at least it is expressed inaccurately. What was extorted by the dread of Alexander's power, was not the secret, which the initiated had a right to, but the priest's consent that he should communicate the secret to another, which was contrary to the laws of the mysteries.

much of it is enigmatical; and so, consequently, a very unfit subject for the buffoonry of the profane and uninitiated." To which the other answers with much spirit, " Yes, indeed, we have great occasion for the mysteries, to know that gods are gods, and monsters, monsters."

But Tully brings the matter home to the Eleusinian mysteries themselves, " What, says he, is not almost all heaven, not to carry on this detail any further, filled with the human race? But if I should search and examine antiquity, and from those things which the Grecian writers have delivered, go to the bottom of this affair, it would be found, that even those very gods themselves who are deemed the Dii majorum gentium, had their original here below ; and ascended from hence into heaven. Inquire, to whom those sepulchers belong, which are so commonly shown in Greece. *Remember, for you are initiated, what you have been taught in the mysteries; you will then at length understand how far this matter may be carried.—(Tusc. Disp, lib. i. cap.* 13.

He carries it further himself, for he tells us in another place, that not only the Eleusinian Mysteries, but the Samothracian likewise, and the Lemnian taught the error of polytheism, agreeably to this system, which supposes all the mysteries derived from the same original, and constituted for the same ends. " What think you, says he, of those who assert, that valiant, or famous, or powerful men, have obtained divine honors after death, and that these are the *very gods,* now become the *object of our worship, our prayers and adoration?* Euhemerus tells us, *when these gods died, and where they lie buried.* I forbear to speak of the sacred and august rights of Eleusis—I pass by Samothrace, and the mysteries of Lemnos, whose hidden rites are celebrated in darkness, and amidst the thick shades of groves and forests."

Here the author comments at considerable length on an equivocal passage of Cicero, immediately following that here quoted, " which, he says, M. Pluche, in his *Histoire du Ciel,* brings to prove, that the purpose of the mysteries was not to explain the nature of the gods." His criticism goes to show the absurdity of this inference. He thus concludes his remarks:

"It had hardly been worth while to take this notice of M. Pluche's interpretation of Cicero, had it not been evident, that his purpose in it was to disguise the liberty he took of transcribing the general explanation of the mysteries, as delivered in the first edition of this volume, printed in 1738, into the second edition of his book, called *Histoire du Ciel,* printed in 1741, without the least notice or acknowledgment."

That Mr. Pluche may have taken some of his ideas on the mysteries from the bishop's book, is highly probable, but his work certainly possesses sufficient originality to prove the laborious investigations of the author, upon ground not previously occupied, to establish his fame as an ingenious acute writer. In the disagreement of these authors in regard to the purport of the mysteries, the bishop has undoubtedly the advantage: he had evidently paid more attention to the subject than his cotemporary. The abbé was deceived by Cicero, in whom he appeared to place implicit confidence; but he should have remembered, that Cicero had been initiated into the Eleusinian mysteries, and, therefore, no doubt, felt under restraint when speaking of them. Besides, he had four characters to sustain; that of a philosopher, a statesman, a lawyer, and an augur or priest; in the due support of which, his popularity was, more or less, involved. A striking instance of the incompatibility with each other of the first and last mentioned of these characters, is exhibited by him, in the passage just quoted above and that before cited, in which he says, "Let the gods, and those who *were ever reckoned* in the *number* of the *celestials*, be worshipped: and those likewise, whom their *merits* have *raised* to *heaven*; such as Hercules, Bacchus, Esculapius, Pollux, and Romulus." Here the augur and the philosopher are at complete issue. Two sentiments more directly in opposition could not be entertained; and it is surprising the bishop did not notice their total contrariety.

What hath been said, will let us into the meaning of Plutarch's hint, in the following words of his tract concerning the ceasing of oracles. "As to the mysteries, in whose representations the true *nature of demons* is clearly and accurately held forth, a sacred silence, to use an expression of Herodotus, is to be observed."

Thus far in detection of polytheism. With regard to the doctrine of the unity, Clemens Alexandrinus informs us, that the Egyptian mystagogues taught it amongst their greater secrets. "The Egyptians," says he, "did not use to reveal their mysteries indiscriminately to all, nor expose their truths concerning their gods to the profane, but to those only who were to succeed to the administration of the state: and to such of the priests as were most approved, by their education, learning, and quality."

But, to come to the Grecian mysteries. Chrysippus, as quoted by the author of the Etymol. magnum, speaks to this purpose. "And Chrysippus says, that the secret doctrines concerning divine matters, are rightly called *Teletai*, for that these are the last things the initiated should be informed of: the soul having gained an able support; and, being possessed of her desires, (that is, the mistress of herself,) can keep silent before the uninitiated and profane." To the same purpose, Clemens: "The doctrines delivered in the greater mysteries, are concerning the universe. Here all instruction *ends*. *Things are seen as they are*; and nature, and the things of nature, are given to be comprehended."

Strabo having said, that nature dictated to men the institution of the mysteries, as well as the other rites of religion, gives this remarkable reason for his assertion, "that the secret celebration of the mysteries preserves the majesty due to the divinity, and, at the same time, *imitates its nature*, which hides itself from our senses."* A plain intimation of the nature of the secret. And had there been any ambiguity, he presently removes it, where, speaking of the different faculties exercised in the different rites of religion, he makes philosophy to be the object of the mysteries. Plutarch expressly says, that *the first cause of all things is communicated to those who approach the temple of Isis with prudence and sanctity.* By which words he means, the necessary qualifications for initiation.

We find Galen intimating, not obscurely, that the doctrine of the divine nature was taught in those very mysteries. In his excellent tract Of the use of the parts of the human body, he has these words: "The study, therefore, of the use of the parts, is not only of service to the mere physician, but of much greater to him who joins philosophy to the art of healing; and, in order to perfect himself in this mystery, labors to investigate the *universal nature*. They who *initiate* themselves here, whether private men or bodies, will find, in my opinion, nobler instruction than in the rites either of Eleusis or Samothrace. A clear implication, that to lead men thither was their special business.

But this seems to have been so well known to the learned in the time of Eusebius, that where this writer takes occasion to observe, that the Hebrews were the only people whose object, in their public and national worship, was the god of the universe, he suits his whole expression, by one continued metaphor, to the usuages of the mysteries. "For the Hebrew people alone," says he, " was reserved the honor of being initiated into the knowledge of God the creator of all things, and of being instructed in the practice of true piety towards him. Where, Epopteia, which signifies the inspection of the secret; Theopia, the contemplation of it; and Demiourgos, the creator, the subject of it, are all words appropriated to the secret of the greater mysteries. I am persuaded this learned writer had his eye on some particular passage of scripture; probably on the 45th chapter of Isaiah, where the prophet, foretelling the conquests of Cyrus, and the exaltation of his empire, apostrophises the God of Israel in this manner, "Verily thou art a God that hidest thyself, O God of Israel the Saviour." This was said with great propriety of the creator of all things, the subject of the *Aporreta* or *secret*,

---

* Here Strabo takes in all that is said, both of the gods, and of nature, in the two preceding passages from Crysippus and Clemens; and shows that by nature is not meant the *cosmical* but *theological* nature.

in all the *mysteries* throughout the Gentile world; and particularly of of those of *Mithras*, in the country which was the scene of the prophecy. That this is the true sense of this obscure passage, appears from the following words of the same chapter, where God himself addresseth the Jewish people: "I have not spoken in secret, in a dark place of the earth: I said not unto the seed of Jacob, seek ye me in vain." This was said, to show that he was taught amongst them in a different way from that participation of his nature to a *few select Gentiles*, in their *mysteries;* celebrated in *secret*, and in *dark subterraneous places;* which not being done in order to give him glory, by promoting his public and general worship, was done *in vain*.

This naturally leads us to the explanation of those oracles of *Apollo*, quoted by Eusebius from Porphyry; the sense of which neither those ancient writers, nor our Sir John Marsham seem rightly to have understood. The first is in these words, "The way to the knowledge of the *divine nature is extremely rugged, and of difficult ascent*. The entrance is secured by *brazen gates*, opening to the adventurer; and the *roads* to be passed through, *impossible to be described*. These, to the *vast benefit* of mankind, were first *marked out* by the Egyptians."

The second is as follows:—

"True wisdom was the lot only of the Chaldeans and Hebrews, who worship the governor of the world, the *self-existent deity*, with pure and holy rites."

Marsham, supposing after Eusebius, that the same thing was spoken of in both the oracles, says, " Certainly there can be no controversy, that, as the religious belief of the Hebrews in One Supreme Being, was esteemed very correct, the same belief by the Egyptians was equally estimable." And again,—" The truth is, Apollo was little consistent with himself; because in the one oracle, the Egyptians are said to be the first; and in the other, the Chaldeans and Hebrews the only people who knew the true God." But they are perfectly consistent; they treat of different things: the first, of the *knowledge* of the true God; and the second of his *public worship*.

I will only observe, that the *frights* and *terrors* to which the initiated were exposed, gave birth to all those metaphorical terms of *difficulty* and *danger* so constantly employed by the Greek writers, whenever they speak of the communication of the true God.

Thomas Taylor, in a note to his translation of Jamblichus on the mysteries of the Egyptians, Chaldeans, and Assyrians, has rendered the foregoing oracle in verse, agreeable to the original; which he introduces as follows:

THE ANCIENT MYSTERIES. 117

Most historians give the palm of antiquity to the Egyptians. And Lucian, in lib. De Dea, says, "That the Egyptians are said to be the first among men that had a conception of the gods, and a knowledge of sacred concerns. They were also the first that had a knowledge of *sacred names*." Conformably to this also, an oracle of Apollo, quoted by Eusebius, says that the Egyptians were the first that disclosed by *infinite actions* the *path* that *leads to the gods*. The oracle is as follows:

> "The path by which to deity we climb,
> Is *arduous, rough*, ineffable, sublime;
> And the strong *massy gates*, through which we pass
> In our first course, are bound with chains of brass.
> Those men the first who of Egyptian birth
> Drank the fair water of Nilotic earth,
> Disclosed by actions infinite *this road*,
> And many *paths to God* Phenicians showed.
> This *road* the Assyrians pointed out to view,
> And this the Lydians and Chaldeans knew."—(p. 295.)

Mr. Taylor has substituted *Lydians* for *Hebrews*, under a suspicion, as he says, that either Aristobulus, well known for interpolating the writings of the Heathens, or Eusebius, had fraudulently inserted the latter.

Means are taken to produce a like *terror* as spoken of above, in candidates for royal arch masonry. They are advised, that "It will be necessary for them to pass through many *trials*, and to travel in *rough* and *rugged* ways, to prove their fidelity." The *gates* alluded to in the oracle of Apollo, which *secure* the *entrance* to the knowledge of the *divine nature*, are actually represented in the scenery of this degree. The *true name* of the Supreme Being is affected to be communicated; and in an address to him are the following expressions: "Teach us, we pray thee, the true reverence of thy great, mighty and *terrible name*."

In a German work, by C. L. Reinhold, entitled *The Hebrew mysteries, or the oldest religious Freemasonry*, it is affirmed, "That the whole Mosaic religion was an initiation into mysteries, the principal forms and regulations of which were borrowed by Moses from the secrets of the old Egyptians."

Josephus, to the same purpose, says that, "That *high and sublime knowledge*, which the Gentiles with difficulty attained, in the rare and temporary celebration of their mysteries, was habitually taught to the Jews, at all times. So that the body politic seems, as it were, one great assembly, constantly kept together, for the celebration of some *sacred mysteries*."

The two great mysterious secrets of the Egyptians, it has been seen, were the existence of one Supreme Being, implying the error of polytheism; and a future state of rewards and punishments for acts committed in this life. The former of which only, it appears, was taught to the Jews. This is likewise communicated to the masons of the royal arch degree, and is the only secret of the order.

It is true, it was formerly enjoined upon the Jews to observe certain rites and ceremonies, which were then adapted to their peculiar circumstances; but which by the coming of Christ were rendered vain and useless, and were accordingly abrogated by the new dispensation.* For instance, they were taught that a person became defiled by touching a human corpse, and their priests were absolutely prohibited from doing it. So, at interments of their dead, those who enter the cemetery wash their hands on retiring, bowls of water and napkins being furnished for the purpose.

---

* "But notwithstanding he (Christ) obtained a more excellent ministry, by how much also he is the mediator of a better covenant, which was established upon better promises. For if that first covenant had been faultless, then should no place have been sought for the second." (Hebrews viii. 6-7.

The idea of defilement by touching human dead bodies, was also a pagan doctrine, for which Jamblichus gives the following reasons:

"It is not lawful to touch human dead bodies when the soul has left them, since a *vestige, image, or representation of divine life* is extinguished in the body by death. But it is no longer *unholy* to touch other dead bodies, because they did not *participate* of a more *divine life*. To other gods, therefore, who are *pure from matter*, our not touching dead bodies is adapted; but to those gods who preside over animals, and are proximately connected with them, invocation through animals is properly made."—(Taylor's Trans. p. 275.)

As to the mystery of obtaining remission of sins, by the performance of certain mystic rites, as is customary with the Jews at this time, on what are called atonement days, the secret is fully known to Roman Catholic priests, and practised upon by them with equal success.

In "A brief Examination of the Rev. Mr. Warburton's Divine Legation of Moses:" London, 1742, are the following remarks:

"We have no profane records that can reach, by many hundred years, so high as the ancient state and constitution of the religion and priesthood of Egypt, in and before the days of Moses. But as the Mosaic constitution itself was accommodated to the natural temper and bias of a people perfectly *Egyptianized*, and who knew nothing but the *language, religion, laws*, and *customs* of Egypt; and as this people could never be brought off from the religon and customs to which they had been naturalized, the history of Moses and the prophets gives one almost as just and adequate a notion of the religion, priesthood, and worship of Egypt, as if their own history had been handed down to us. Of this we need no other, or more authentic authority than our learned author's own concessions, who has granted as much in this respect as could have been desired. And though Moses attempted, in his law, to reform the religion of Egypt, with regard to their symbolical polytheism, or siderial worship by images; yet this could never be effected, but the gross of the people still continued in the symbolical worship of Egypt, except when restrained from it by force and compulsion under some of their kings. But they immediately fell back again to the same sort of religion and worship, as soon as that restriction and legal persecution were relaxed or taken off."

Thus, I think it appears, that the Aporreta, in the greater mysteries, were the detection of the origin of vulgar polytheism;* and the discovery of the doctrine of the unity.

I will venture to go further; and give the very history repeated, and the very hymn sung, on these occasions to the initiated: in the first of which was delivered the true origin and progress of vulgar polytheism; and in the other, the unity of the deity.

---

* What hath been said will give light to a strange story told by Thucydides, Plutarch, and others, of a debauch and night ramble of Alcibiades, just before his expedition to Syracuse. In which, they say, he revealed to, and acted over with his companions, the mysteries of Ceres: that he assumed the office of the hierophant, and called some of those he initiated Mystai, and others Epoptai: and that, lastly, they broke all the statues of Hermes. These are mentioned as distinct actions, and unconnected with one another. But now we see their relation, and how one arose from the other: for Alcibiades having revealed the origin of polytheism, and the doctrine of the unity, to his companions; nothing was more natural than for men, heated with wine, to run forth in a kind of religious fury, and break the statues of their idols. For, what he acted over, was the greater mysteries, as appears from Plutarch's calling them the mysteries of Ceres, and from Alcibiades' calling some Epoptai, the name of those who participated of the greater mysteries.

For it appears to me, that the celebrated fragment of Sanchoniatho, the Phenician, translated by Philo Byblius, and preserved by Eusebius, containing a genealogical account of the first ages, is that history, as it was wont to be read to the initiated, in the celebration of the Egyptian and Phenician mysteries. The purpose of it being to inform us, that their popular gods (whose chronicle is there given according to their generations) were only dead men deified.

And as this curious and authentic record (for such we shall find it was) not only serves to illustrate the subject we are now upon, but will be of use to support what is said hereafter of the rise, progress, and order of the several species of ancient idolatry, it may not be improper to give a short extract of it in this place.

He tells us, then, that, "of the two first mortals, Protogonus and Æon, (the latter of whom was the author of seeking and procuring food from forest-trees) were begotten Genos and Genea. These, in the time of great droughts, stretched their hands upwards to the sun, whom they regarded as a god, and sole ruler of the heavens. From these, after two or three generations, came Upsouranios and his brother Ousous. One of them invented the art of building cottages of reeds and rushes; the other the art of making garments of the skins of wild beasts. In their time, violent tempests of wind and rain having rubbed the large branches of the forest-trees against one another, they took fire, and burnt up the woods. Of the bare trunks of trees, they first made vessels to pass the waters; they *consecrated two pillars to fire and wind*, and then offered bloody sacrifices to them as to gods." And here let it be observed, that this worship of the elements and heavenly bodies is truly represented as the first species of idolatry.

"After many generations, came Chrysor; and he likewise invented many things useful to civil life; for which, after his decease, he was worshipped as a god. Then flourished Ouranos and his sister Ge; who deified and offered sacrifices to their father Upsistos, when he had been torn in pieces by wild beasts. Afterwards Cronos consecrated Muth his son, and was himself consecrated by his subjects." And this is as truly represented to be the second species of idolatry; the worship of dead men.

He goes on, and says, that " Ouranos was the inventor of the Bætylia, a kind of animated stones, framed with great art. And that Taautus formed allegoric figures, characters, and images of the celestial gods and elements." In which is delivered the third species of idolatry, statue and brute worship. For by the animated stones, is meant stones cut into human shape; brute, unformed stones being before this invention consecrated and adored. As by Taautus's invention of allegoric figures, is insinuated (what was truly the fact) the origin of brute worship from the use of hieroglyphics.

This is a very short and imperfect extract of the fragment; many particulars, to avoid tediousness, are omitted, which would much support what we are upon, particularly a *minute detail of the principal arts invented for the use of civil life*. But what has been selected on this head, will afford a good comment to a celebrated passage of Cicero, quoted, in this section, on another occasion.—As the two important doctrines, taught in secret, were the detection of polytheism, and the discovery of the unity; so, the two capital doctrines taught more openly, were the origin of society with the arts of life, and the existence of the soul after death in a state of reward or punishments.

The fragment explains what Tully meant by men's being drawn by the mysteries from an irrational and savage life, and tamed, as it were, and broken to humanity. It was, we see, by the information given them, concerning the origin of society, and the inventors of the arts of life, and the rewards they received from grateful posterity, for making themselves benefactors to mankind.

The reasons which induce me to think this fragment the very history narrated to the Epoptai, in the celebration of the greater mysteries, are these:

First, it bears an exact conformity with what the ancients tell us that history contained in general, namely, an instruction that all the national gods, as well those majorum, such as Hypsistus, Ouranos, and Cronos, as those minorum gentium, were only dead men deified: together with a recommendation of the advantages of civil life above the state of nature, and an excitement to the most considerable of the initiated (the summatibus viris, as Macrobius calls them) to procure it. And these two ends are served together, in the history of the rise and progress of idolatry as delivered in this fragment.

Again, in order to recommend civil life, and to excite men to promote its advantages, a lively picture is given of his miserable condition, and how obnoxious he was, in that state, to the rage of all the elements, and how imperfectly, while he continued in it, he could, with all his industry, fence against them by *food of acorns*, by *cottages of reeds*, and by *coats of skins:* a matter the mysteries thought so necessary to be impressed, that we find, by Diodorus Siculus, there was a *scenical* *representation* of this state exhibited in their shows.* And what stronger excitement had heroic minds, than to be taught, as they are in this fragment, that public benefits to their fellow creatures were reward with immortality.

My second reason for supposing it to be that very history, is our being told, that Sanchoniatho transcribed the account from secret records, kept in the penetralia of the temples, and written in a sacred sacerdotal character, called the Ammonean, from the place where they were first deposited; which, as Marsham reasonably supposes, was Ammon-no, or Thebes, in Egypt: a kind of writing employed, (as we have shown elsewhere) by the hierophants of the mysteries.

But, lastly, we are told, that when this genealogical history came into the hands of a certain son of Thabion, the first hierophant on record amongst the Phenicans, he, after having corrupted it with allegories, and intermixed physical and cosmical affections with historical, that is, made the one significative of the other, delivered it to the prophets of the orgies, and the hierophants of the mysteries; who left it to their successors. So that now we have an express testimony for the fact here advanced, that this was the very history read to the Epoptai in the celebration of the greater mysteries.

But one thing is too remarkable to pass by unobserved: and that is, Sanchoniatho's account of the corruption of this history with allegories and physical affections, by one of his own countrymen; and of its delivery, in that state, to the Egyptians, for Isiris is the same as Osiris, who corrupted it still more. That the pagan mythology was, indeed, thus corrupted, I have shown at large, in several parts of this work: but I believe, not so early as is here pretended: which makes me suspect that Sanchoniatho lived in a later age than his interpretor, Philo, assigns to him. And what confirms me in this suspicion, is that mark of national vanity and partiality, common to after-times, in making the mysteries of his own country original, and conveyed from Phenicia to Egypt. Whereas it is very certain, they came first from Egypt. But of this, elsewhere. However, let the reader take notice, that the question concerning the antiquity of Sanchoniatho does not at all affect our inference concerning the nature and use of this history.

* We here see the origin of the forlorn condition in which the candidate for masonic honors is placed, when prepared for initiation; who, "neither naked, nor clothed, bare-foot, nor shod; deprived of all metals; hoodwinked, with a cable-tow about his neck, is led to the door of the lodge, in *a halting moving posture.*"

His being hoodwinked is emblematical of the uninformed state of those not initiated into the mysteries; and the rope about his neck is in token of his submission to the divine will, as will hereafter be shown from the customs of the Druids.—Edit.

A criticism of that very knowing and sagacious writer, father Simon of the Oratory, will show the reader how groundless the suspicions of learned men are concerning the genuineness of this fragment. Father Simon imagines that Porphyry forged the history of Sanchoniatho, under the name of a translation by Philo Byblius; and conjectures, his purpose in so doing was to support paganism; by taking from it, its mythology and allegories, which the Christian writers perpetually objected to it. "He would make it appear, to answer the objections that were made on all sides upon this, that their theology was a pure mythology—they go back to the times which had preceded the allegories and the fictions of the sacrificers." (Bib. Crit. v. i. p. 140.) But this learned man totally mistakes the case. The Christians objected to vulgar paganism, that the stories told of their gods, were immoral. To this their priests and philosophers replied, that these stories were only mythological allegories, which veiled all the great truths of theology, ethics, and physics. The christians said, this could not be; for that the stories of the gods had a substantial foundation in fact, these gods being only dead men deified, who in life, had like passions and infirmities with others. For the truth of which they appealed to such writers as Sanchoniatho, who had given the history both of their mortal and immortal stations and conditions. How then could so acute an adversary as Porphyry, deeply engaged in this controversy, so far mistake the state of the question, and grounds of his defence, as to forge a book in support of his cause, which totally overthrew it?

The Rev. James Anderson, D. D. published, in 1723, the first book on masonry with the sanction of the grand lodge of England. The commencement of his work bears a strong resemblance to the foregoing fragment. Instead, however, of permitting the first inhabitants of the world to gain knowledge gradually by the aid of experience, he makes them finished artizans from the beginning. This was necessary for his purpose, which was to show the original establishment of the freemason society. As his account throws much light upon the early history of man, and the amasing progress of the arts and sciences in the first stages of human existence, and is, moreover, greatly relied upon by masons I will here give a short abstract of it.

"The Almighty Architect," says the Dr. "having created all things according to *geometry*, last of all formed Adam, and *engraved on his heart* the same noble science; which Adam soon discovered by *survey-*

ing his earthly paradise, and fabricating an arbor as a convenient shelter from heat, etc. When expelled from his lovely arbor, he resided in the most convenient abodes of the land of Eden, where he could be best secured from cold, heat, winds, rains, tempests, and wild beasts, till his sons grew up to *form a lodge;* whom he taught *geometry* and the great use of it in *architecture;* without which the children of men must have lived like brutes, in woods, dens, caves, etc.; or at best in poor huts of mud, or arbors made of branches of trees, etc. * * * Tubal Kain wrought in metals, Jubal elevated music, and Jabal extended his tents.

Adam was succeeded in the *grand direction* of the *craft* by Seth, Enock, Kainan, Mahalaleel, and Jared, whose son Enoch was *expert* and *bright*, both in the *science* and in the *art*, and *being a prophet*, he foretold the destruction of the earth for sin, first by water, and afterwards by fire. Therefore Enoch erected *two large pillars*, the one of *stone* and the other of *brick*, whereon *he engraved the abridgment of the arts and sciences, principally geometry and masonry.*

At last, when the world's destruction drew nigh, God commanded Noah to build the great ark or *floating castle,* and his three sons assisted, like a *deputy* and two *wardens.* That edifice, though of wood only, was fabricated by *geometry* as *nicely* as any stone-building, like true ship-building at this day, a curious and large piece of architecture, and finished when Noah entered into his *six hundredth year.* Aboard which he and his three sons and their four wives passed, and having received the cargo of animals by God's direction, they were saved in the ark, while the rest perished in the flood for their immorality and unbelief. And so from these *masons*, or four *grand officers*, the whole present race of mankind are descended.

After the flood, Noah and his three sons, having preserved the knowledge of the *arts* and *sciences,* communicated it to their growing offspring. And it came to pass, as they journeyed from the East towards the West, they found a plain in the land of Shinar, and dwelt there together, as *Noachidæ*, or sons of Noah, which was the first name of masons, according to some old traditions. When *Peleg* was born there to Heber, after the flood one hundred and one years, father Noah partitioned the earth, ordering them to disperse and take possession; but from a fear of the consequences of separation, they resolved to keep together.

Nimrod, the son of Cush, the eldest son of Ham, was at the head of those that would not disperse; or if they must seperate, they resolved to transmit their memorial illustrious to all future ages; and so employed themselves under *grand master* Nimrod,* in the large and fertile vale of Shinar along the banks of the Tygris, in building a stately tower and city, *the largest work that ever the world saw*, and soon filled the vale with splendid edifices. But they *over built* it, and knew not when to desist till their vanity provoked their Maker to confound their grand design, by confounding their speech. Hence the city was called *Babel, confusion*.

Thus they were forced to disperse, about fifty-three years after they began to build, or after the flood one hundred and fifty-four years, when the general migration from Shinar commenced. They went off at various times, and travelled North, South, East, and West, with their *mighty skill*, and found the good use of it in settling their colonies.

But Nimrod went forth no farther than into the land of Assyria, and founded the first great empire at his capital Nineveh, where he long reigned. Under him flourished many learned mathematicians, whose successors were long afterwards called Chaldees and Magians: and though many of them turned *image-worshippers*, yet even that idolatry occasioned an improvement in the arts of designing: for Ninus, king of Nineveh or Assyria ordered his best artists to frame the statue of Baal, that was worshipped in a gorgeous temple.

This history of Dr. Anderson is the only authority that masonry can produce to substantiate the extraordinary antiquity which it claims. The specimen I have given of it, is sufficient for the reader to form an opinion of its authenticity, as well as its resemblance to the fragment of Sanchoniatho. Nimrod, Bel, Baal, and Belus are supposed by mythologists to be the same person. We will turn to Warburton.

We now come to the hymn celebrating the unity of the godhead, which was sung in the Eleusian mysteries by the hierophant, habited like the *Creator*.† And this I take to be the little orphic poem quoted by Clemens Alexandrinus and Eusebius; which begins thus; " I will declare a *secret* to the Initiated ; *but let the doors be shut against the profane*. But thou, O Musæus, the offspring of bright Selene, attend carefully to my song ; for I shall deliver the truth without disguise. Suffer not, therefore, thy former prejudices to debar thee of that happy

---

* Nimrod signifies rebel, the name that the Israelites gave him ; but his friends called him Belus, lord.
† A Passage in Porphyry shows what kind of personage the *creator* was represented by ; and that it was, like all the rest, of Egyptian original ; and introduced into these secret mysteries, for the reason above explained.

life, which the knowledge of these sublime truths will procure unto thee; but carefully contemplate this divine oracle, and preserve it in purity of mind and heart. Go on, in the right way, and see the sole governor of the world;[*] he is one, and of himself alone; and to that one all things owe their being. He operates through all, was never seen by mortal eyes, but does himself see every one."

The reasons which support my conjecture are these: 1. We learn from the scholiast on Aristophanes and others, that hymns were sung in the mysteries. 2. Orpheus, as we have said, first brought the mysteries from Egypt into Thrace, and even religion itself; hence it was called Thresceia, as being supposed the invention of the Thracian. 3. The verses, which go under the name of Orpheus, are, at least, more ancient than Plato and Herodotus; though since interpolated. It was the common opinion, that they were genuine; and those who doubted of that, yet gave them to the earliest Pythagoreans. (Laertius in *Vita Pythag.* and Suidas.) 4. The subject of them are the mysteries, under the several titles of *Thronismoi metrooi, teletai, ieros, logos, and is ado Katabasis.* 5. Pausanias tells us, that Orpheus's hymns were sung in the rites of Ceres, in preference to Homer's, though more elegant, for the reasons given above. 6. This hymn is addressed to Musæus, his disciple, who was said, though falsely, to institute the mysteries at Athens, as his master had done in Thrace; and begins with the formula used by the mystagogue on that occasion warning the profane to keep at distance; and in the fourth line mentions that *new life* or *regeneration*, to which the initiated were taught to aspire. 7. No other original, than the singing the hymns of Orpheus in the Eleusinian mysteries, can be well imagined of that popular opinion, mentioned by Theodoret, that Orpheus instituted those mysteries, when the Athenians had such certain records of another founder. 8. We are told that one article of the Athenians' charge against Diagoras for revealing the mysteries, was his making the Orphic speech, or hymn, the subject of his common conversation. 9. But lastly, the account, which Clemens gives of this hymn, seems to put the matter out of question: his words are these: " But the Thracian mystagogue, who was at the same time a poet, Orpheus, the son of Oeager, after he had opened the mysteries, and sung the whole theology of idols, recants all he had said, and introduceth truth. The sacreds then truly begin, though late, and thus he enters upon the

---

[*] That is, his representative; but how he could be *habited like the Creator*, who was *never seen by mortal eyes*, it is difficult to imagine.—Edit.

matter." To understand the force of this passage, we are to know; that the mystagogue explained the representations in the mysteries; where, as we learn from Apuleius, the supernal and infernal gods passed in review. To each of these they sung a hymn; which Clemens calls the theology of images, or idols. These are yet to be seen amongst the works ascribed to Orpheus. When all this was over, then came the Aporreta, delivered in the hymn in question. And, after that, the assembly was dismissed, with these two barbarous words, *kogx omphax*, which shows the mysteries not to have been originally Greek. The learned Mr. Le Clerc well observes, that this seems to be only an ill pronunciation of *kots* and *omphets* which, he tells us, signify in the Phenician tongue, *watch and abstain from evil*.*

Thus the reader sees the end and use both of the *greater* and *less mysteries*; and that, as well in what they hid as what they divulged, all aimed at the benefit of the state. To this end, they were to draw in as many as they could to their general participation; which they did by spreading abroad the doctrine of a providence, and a future state; and how much happier the initiated would be, and what superior felicities they were entitled to in another life. It was on this account that antiquity is so full and express in this part. But then, they were to make those they had got in as virtuous as they could; which they provided for, by discovering, to such as were capable of the secret, the whole delusion of polytheism. Now this being supposed the shaking foundations, was to be done with all possible circumspection, and under the *most tremendous seal of secrecy*. (See cap. xx. of Meursius' Eleusinia.) For they taught, the gods themselves punished the revealers of the *secret*; and not them only, but the hearers of it too. (Apul. Met. lib. xi.) Nor did they altogether trust to that neither; for more effectually to curb an ungovernable curiosity, the state decreed capital punishments against the betrayers of the mysteries, and inflicted them with merciless severity. (Si quis arcanæ mysteria Cereris sacra vulgasset, lege morti addicebatur.)

The case of Diagoras, the Melian, is too remarkable to be omited This man had revealed the Orphic and Elusinian mysteries; and so passed with the people for an atheist; which at once confirms what hath been said of the object of the secret doctrines, and of the mischief that would attend an indiscreet communication of them. He likewise,

---

* In closing a royal arch chapter, the high priest says, " may we invariably practice all those duties out of the chapter, which are inculcated in it. Responce; so mote it be, Amen." (Bernard.)—Edit.

dissuaded his friends from being initiated into these rites ; the consequence of which was, that the city of Athens proscribed him, and set a price upon his head. While Socrates, who preached up the latter part of this doctrine (and was likewise a reputed atheist,) and Epicurus, who taught the former (and was a real one) were suffered, because they delivered their opinions only as points of philosophic speculation, amongst their followers, to live a long time unmolested. And this, perhaps, was the reason why Socrates declined being initiated.* Which, as it appeared a singular affectation, exposed him to much censure. But it was foreborn with his usual prudence. He remembered, that Eschylus, on a mere imagination of his having given a hint in his scenes of something in the mysteries, had like to have been torn in pieces on the stage by the people ; and only escaped by an appeal to the areopagus ; which venerable court acquited him of that dangerous imputation, on his proving that he had never been initiated. The famous Euhemerus, who assumed the same office of hierophant to the people at large, with more boldness than Socrates, and more temperance than Epicurus, employed another expedient to screen himself from the laws, though he fell, and perhaps deservedly, under the same imputation of atheism. He gave a fabulous relation of a voyage to the imaginary island of Panchæa, a kind of ancient Utopia ; where, in a temple of Jupiter, he found a genealogical record, which discovered to him the births and deaths of the greater gods ; and, in short, every thing that the hierophant revealed to the initated on this subject. Thus he too avoided the suspicion of a betrayer of the mysteries.

This, therefore, is the reason why so little is to be met with concerning the Aporreta. Varro and Cicero, the two most inquisitive persons in antiquity, affording but a glimmering light. The first giving us a short account of the *cause* only of the *secret*, without mentioning the *doctrine ;* and the other, a hint of the *doctrine*, without mentioning the *cause*.

But now a remarkable exception to all we have been saying concerning the secrecy of the mysteries, obtrudes itself upon us, in the case of the Creatans ; who, as Diodorus Siculus assures us, celebrated

---

* " Some enlightened persons did not believe that to be virtuous there was any necessity for such an association. Diogenes was once advised to contract his sacred engagement ; but he answered ; " Pataecion, the notorious robber, obtained initiation ; Epaminondas and Agesilaus never solicited it; is it possible I should believe that the former will enjoy the bliss of the *Elysian fields*, while the latter shall be *dragged through the mire of the infernal shades.*" (Travels of Anachar.)—Edit.

their mysteries *openly*, and taught their aporreta without reserve. His words are these: " At Cnossus in Crete, it was provided for, by an ancient law, that these mysteries should be shown openly to all ; and that those things, which in other places were delivered in secret, should be hid from none who were desirous of knowing them." But, as contrary as this seems to the principles delivered above, it will be found, on attentive reflection, altogether to confirm them. We have shown, that the great *secret* was the detection of polytheism ; which was done by teaching the original of the gods ; their birth from mortals ; and their advancement to divine honor, for benefits done to their country, or mankind. But it is to be observed, that the Cretans proclaimed this to all the world, by showing, and boasting of the tomb of Jupiter himself, the *Father of gods and men*. How then could they tell that as a secret in their mysteries, which they told to every one out of them ? Nor is it less remarkable that the Cretans themselves, as Diodorus, in the same place, tells us, gave this very circumstance of their celebrating the mysteries openly as a proof of their being the first who had consecrated dead mortals. " These are the old stories which the Cretans tell of their gods, who, they pretend to say, were born amongst them. And they urge this as an invincible reason to prove that the adoration, the worship, and the mysteries of these gods were first derived from Crete to the rest of the world, for, whereas, amongst the Athenians, those most illustrious mysteries of all, called the Eleusinian, those of Samothrace, and those of the Ciconians in Thrace, of Orpheus's institution, are all celebrated in *secret* ; yet in Crete"—and so on as above. For it seems the Cretans were proud of their invention ; and used this method to proclaim and perpetuate the notice of it. So when Pythagoras, as Porphyry informs us, had been initiated into the *Cretian* mysteries, and had continued in the Idean cave three times nine days, he wrote this epigram on the tomb of Jupiter, *Zan, whom men call Jupiter, lies here deceased.*

It was this which so much exasperated the other Grecians against them ; and gave birth to the common proverb of *Kretes aei pseystai, the Cretans are eternal liars.* For nothing could more affront these superstitious idolaters than asserting the fact, or more displease the politic protectors of the mysteries than the divulging it.

The mysteries then being of so great service to the state, we shall not be surprised to hear the wisest of the ancients speaking highly in their commendation ; and their best lawgivers, and reformers, providing carefully for their support. " Ceres (says Isocrates) hath made the Athenians two presents of the greatest consequence ; corn, which brought us out of a state of brutality ; and the mysteries, which teach the initiated to entertain the most agreeable expectations touching death and eternity." And Plato introduceth Socrates speaking after this manner: " In my opinion, those who established the mysteries, whoever they were, were well skilled in human nature. For in these rites it was of old signified to the aspirant, that those who died without being initiated, stuck fast in mire and filth ; but that he who was purified and initiated at his death should have his habitation " with the Gods." And Tully thought them of such use to society, for preserving and propagating the doctrine of a future state of rewards and punishments, that in the law where he forbids nocturnal sacrifices offered by women, he makes an express exception for the Mysteries of Ceres, as well as for the sacrifices to the *good goddess.*

Aristides said, the welfare of Greece was secured by the Eleusinian mysteries alone ! Indeed the Greeks seemed to place their chief happiness in them ; so Euripides makes Hercules say, " I was blest, when I got a sight of the mysteries ;" and it was a proverbial speech, when any one thought himself in the highest degree happy, to say, I seem as if I had been initiated in the higher mysteries.

But now, such is the fate of human things, these mysteries, venerable as they were, in their first institution, did, it must be owned, in course of time, degenerate ; and those very provisions made by the State, to enable the mysteries to obtain the end of their establishment, became the very means of defeating it. For we can assign no surer cause of the horrid abuses and corruptions of the mysteries (besides time, which naturally and fatally depraves and vitiates all things) than the season in which they were represented ; and the profound silence in which they were buried. For night gave opportunity to wicked men to attempt evil actions ; and secrecy, encouragement to repeat them ; and the inviolable nature of that secrecy, which encouraged abuses, kept them from the magistrate's knowledge so long till it was too late to reform them. In a word, we must own, that these mysteries, so powerful in their first institution for the promotion of virtue and knowledge, became, in time, horribly subservient to the gratification of lust and revenge. (Wisdom of Sol. xiv. 23. 24.) Nor will this appear at all strange after what hath been said above. A like corruption, from the same cause, crept even into the church, during the purest ages of it. The primitive Christians, in imitation, perhaps, of these pagan rites, or from the same kind of spirit, had a custom of celebrating vigils in the night; which, at first, were performed with all becoming sanctity; but, in a little time, they were so overrun with abuses, that it was necessary to abolish them.

And the same remedy, Cicero, tells us, Diagondas the Theban was forced to apply to the disorders of the mysteries.

However, this was not the only, though the most powerful cause of the depravation of the mysteries. Another doubtless was their being sometimes under the patronage of those deities, who were supposed to inspire and preside over sensual passions, such as Bacchus, Venus, and Cupid; for these had all their mysteries; and where was the wonder, if the initiated should be sometimes inclined to give a loose to vices, in which the patron god was supposed to delight? And in this case, the hidden doctrine came too late to put a stop to the disorder. However, it is remarkable, and confirms what hath been said concerning the origin of the Mysteries, and of their being invented to perpetuate the doctrine of a future state, that the doctrine continued to be taught even in the most debauched celebrations of the Mysteries of Cupid and Bacchus. Nay, even that very flagitious part of the mysterious rites when at worst, the carrying the *kteis and phallos*, in procession, was introduced but under pretence of their being *emblems* of the *mystical regeneration and new life*, into which the initiated had engaged themselves to enter.

The last cause to which one may ascribe their corruption, was the Hierophant's withdrawing the mysteries from the care and inspection of the civil Magistrate; whose original institution they were. But in aftertimes it would happen, that a little priest, who had borne an inferior share in these rites, would leave his society and country, and set up for himself; and in a clandestine manner, without the allowance or knowledge of the magistrate, institute and celebrate the mysteries in private conventicles. From rites so managed, it is easy to believe, many enormities would arise. This was the original of those horrid impieties commited in the mysteries of Bacchus at Rome; of which the historian Livy has given so circumstantial an account; for in the beginning of his story, he tells us, the mischief was occasioned by one of these priest's bringing the mysteries into Etruria, on his own head, uncommissioned by his superiors in Greece, from whom he learnt them; and unauthorized by the State, into which he had introduced them. The words of Livy show that the mysteries were, in their own nature, a very different affair; and invented for the improvement of knowledge and virtue. " A Greek of mean extraction, (says he,) a little priest and soothsayer, came first into Etruria, without any skill, or wisdom in mysterious rites, many sorts of which, that most improved people have brought in amongst us, for the culture and perfection both of mind and body."

What Livy means by the culture of the body, will be seen hereafter when we come to speak of the probationary and toilsome trials undergone by those aspirants to the mysteries, called the *soldiers of Mithras*.

However, it is very true, that in Greece itself the Mysteries became abominably abused ; a proof of which we have even in the conduct of their comic writers, who frequently lay the scene of their subject, such as the rape of a young girl, and the like, at the celebration of a religious mystery ; and from that mystery denominate the comedy. And in the time of Cicero, the terms, mysteries and abominations, were almost synonymous. The Academic having said they had secrets and mysteries, Lucullus replies, " Quæ funt tandem ista *myteria ?* aut cur celatis, quasi *turpe* aliquid, vestram sententiam ?" What, after all, are these *mysteries* ? or why conceal your purpose as if it included something *base*. However, in spite of all occasions and opportunities, some of the mysteries, as particularly the Eleusinian, continued, for many ages, pure and undefiled. The two capital corruptions of the mysteries were magic and impurities. Yet, so late as the age of Apollonius Tyan, the Elusinian kept so clear of the first imputation, that the hierophant refused to initiate that impostor because he was a magician. And, indeed, their long-continued immunity, both from one and the other corruption, will not appear extraordinary, if we consider, that, by a law of Solon, the Senate was always to meet the day after the celebration of these mysteries, to see that nothing had been done amiss during the performance. (Andoc. Orat.) So that these were the very last that submitted to the common fate of all human institutions.

And here the fathers will hardly escape the censure of those who will not allow high provocation to be an excuse for an unfair representation of an adversary. They will hardly escape censure, for accustoming themselves to speak of the mysteries as gross impieties and immoralities, in their very original.* Clemens Alexandrinus, in a heat

---

* What hath been said above, shows that M. Le Clerc hath gone into the other extreme, when he contends, (*Bibl. Univ.* tom. vi. p. 73.) that the mysteries were not corrupted at all. I can conceive no reason for his paradox, but as it favored an accusation against the fathers, who have much insisted on the corruption of them.—" The fathers have said that all kinds of lewdness were committed in the mysteries ; but whatever they may say, it is not credible that all Greece, however corrupt it may have been, has ever consented that the women and girls should prostitute themselves in the mysteries. But some Christian authors have found no difficulty in saying a thousand things little conformable to truth, to defame paganism ; as though there were none but pagans against whom they could discharge their calumnies."—*Bibl. Univ.* tom. vi. p. 120.

of zeal, breaks out, " Let him be accursed, who first infected the world with these impostures, whether it was Dardanus — or — etc. These I make no scruple to call wicked authors of impious fables; the fathers of an execrable superstition, who, by this institution, sowed in human life the seeds of vice and corruption." But the wisest and best of the pagan world invariably hold, that the mysteries were instituted pure; and proposed the noblest end, by the worthiest means.

The truth of the matter was this: the fathers bore a secret grudge to the mysteries for their injurious treatment of Christianity on its first appearance in the world. We are to observe, that atheism, by which was meant a contempt of the gods, was reckoned, in the mysteries, amongst the greatest crimes. So, in the sixth book of the Eneid, (of which more hereafter,) the hottest seats in Tartarus are allotted to the atheist, such as Salmoneus, Tityus, and the Titans, etc. Now the Christians, for their contempt of the national gods, were, on their first appearance, deemed atheists by the people; and so branded by the mystagogue, as we find in Lucian, and exposed amongst the rest in Tartarus, in their solemn shows and representations. This may be gathered from a remarkable passage in Origen, where Celsus thus addresses his adversary:

"But now, as you, good man, believe eternal punishments, even so do the interpreters of these holy mysteries, the mystagogues and initiators: you threaten others with them; *these*, on the contrary, *threaten you.*"

This, without doubt, was what sharpened the fathers against the mysteries; and they were not always tender in loading what they did not approve. But here comes in the strange part of the story; that after this, they should so studiously and formally transfer the *terms, phrases, rites, ceremonies* and *discipline* of these *odious mysteries* into our holy religion; and, thereby, very early vitiate and deprave what a pagan writer (Marcellinus) could see, and acknowledge to be absoluta and simplex, [perfect and pure] as it came out of the hands of its author. Sure then it was some more than ordinary veneration the people had for these mysteries, that could incline the fathers of the church to so fatal a counsel: however, the thing is notorious, and the effects have been severely felt.

The reader will not be displeased to find here an exact account of this whole matter, extracted from a very curious dissertation of a great and unexceptionable writer, Is. Casaubon, in his sixteenth Exer. on the Annals of Baronius.—[Bishop W. has given the remarks of Casaubon in the original Latin, of which the following is a translation:]

"When the fathers found it to be an easier way of bringing over minds corrupted by superstition to the love of the truth, they first adopted many terms used in their rites; and after thus treating of several heads of the true doctrines, they further adopted some of their ceremonies; that they might seem to be saying, as Paul said to the Gentiles,—'Whom ye ignorantly worship the same do I declare unto you!' Thence it came that the fathers *called* the sacraments by the same names as were used to describe the (pagan) mysteries, as *muescis, teletas, teleiosei, epopteias,* or *epopseias, telesteria,* and sometimes, but more rarely, *orgies.* The Eucharist they emphatically denominated the mystery of mysteries; and also, by antonomy, *the* mystery, or in the plural, *the* mysteries. And you may every where read in the writings of the fathers, when treating of the holy communion, the words *phrieta mysteria,* or *aporreton mysterion,* referring to those that were to be divulged and those that were not. So the Greek verb *myesthai* in the ancient writing is often employed to signify the becoming a partaker of the Lord's Supper; and the term *myesin* for the act itself, and *mystes* for the priest, who is also called *mystagogon,* and *hierotelestes.* In the Greek liturgies and elsewhere *hieratelete,* and *cryphia hai epiphobos telete* (the hidden and awful mystery) means the Eucharist.

"And as certain degrees were used in the pagan rites, so in like manner Dionysius divides the whole tradition of the sacraments into three acts, distinguished by their seasons and ceremonies. The first was *Catharsis,* the purgation, or purification, the second the *myestis* or initiation, and the third, *teleosis* or the consummation, which they also frequently called *epopsian,* or the *revered.* Tully had before affirmed that the Athenian mysteries brought to the dying better hopes. On their part, the fathers maintained, that the mysteries of Christ brought certain salvation and eternal life to those who worthily partook of them; and that for those who contemned them there was no salvation : and they did not scruple to say that the end and ultimate fruit of the sacraments was deification, when they knew that the authors of those vain superstitions had dared to promise the same honor to their initiates. And therefore you may read in the fathers that the end of the holy *mystagogies* was deification and that those who faithfully received them should in the life to come be gods. Athanasias has used the verb *theopoiesthai* (to deity) in the same sense, and subsequently confirmed it by saying, 'that by partaking of the spirit we are united to the God-head.' Of the symbols of the sacraments by which those ceremonies are celebrated, it is not here the place to treat : but that which is called a *symbol* of *faith* is various in its kinds, and they *serve* as *tokens* or *tests* by which the *faithful* may *recognize each other.* And we show that the same were used in the pagan mysteries. The formula pronounced by the deacons, 'Depart hence all ye catachumens, all ye possessed and uninitiated,' corresponds with the '*procul este profani*' of the pagans. Many rites of the pagans were performed in the night, and Guadentius has the expression '*splendidissima nox vigiliarum*,' the brightest night of the vigils. And as to what we have said of the *silence* observed by the pagans in their secret devotions, the ancient Christians so far approved, that they exceeded all their mysteries in that observance. And as Seneca has observed, the most holy of the sacred rites were only known to the initiated; and Jamblichus on the philosophy of the Pythagoreans has distinguished between the *aporreta* which could not be carried abroad, and the *exphora*, which might; so the ancient Christians distinguished their whole doctrines into those which might be divulged to all (the *exphora*) and the *aporreta*, or *arcana*, which were not rashly to be disclosed. Their dogmas, says Basilius, they kept secret, their preaching was public. And Chrisostom, treating of those who were baptized for the dead, says, 'I verily desire to relate the matter fully, but I dare not be particular, because of the uninitiated.' They make a difficulty for us in the interpretation, and oblige us either to speak without precision, or else to disclose what they should not be informed of: and as the pagans used the terms *exorcheisthai ta mysteria*, touching those who divulged the mysteries, so Dionysius says, 'See that you do not disclose, nor slightly reverence the mysteries, and every where in *Augustinus*, you will read of the sacrament known to the faithful.' And thus (in Johannem, tract. xvi) 'all the catachumens already believe in Christ, but Christ does not trust them:' and if we should ask one of them whether he eat the flesh of the Son of man, he would not understand what we meant; and again, 'The catachumens are ignorant of what the Christians receive.' Let them blush that they are ignorant"

We have observed above, that the fathers gave very easy credit to what was reported of the abominations in the mysteries; and the easier, perhaps, on account of the secrecy with which they were celebrated. The same affectation of secrecy in the Christian rites, and the same language in speaking of them, without doubt procured as easy credit to those calumnies of murder and incest, charged upon them by the pagans. Nay, what is still more remarkable, those very specific enormities in which their own mysteries were then known to offend, they objected to in the Christians.

"A catachumen is a candidate for baptism, or a person who prepares himself for receiving it. Towards the end of the first century, Christians were divided into two orders, distinguished by the names of *believers* and *catachumens*. The latter as contradistinguished from the former, were such as had not yet been dedicated to God and Christ by baptism, and were, therefore, admitted neither to the public prayers, nor to the holy communion, nor to the ecclesiastical assemblies. As they were not allowed to assist at the celebration of the *eucharist*, the deacon dismissed them, after sermon, with this formula, proclaimed three times, "*Ite catachumeni missa est.*" (Rees.) "Missa is derived from *mitto* to send. Missa has been used for *missio*. *Ite missa est* or *missio est*. You may all return home." (Bailey.)

"*Quod norunt fideles*, what the faithful know. These words, or, as expressed in Greek, *isasin oi pistuemenoi*, formes what may be called the watch-word of the *secret*, and occur constantly in the fathers. Thus St. Chrysostom, for instance,—in whose writings Casaubon remarked the recurrence of this phrase, at least fifty times, in speaking of the tongue (comment. in Psalm 153,) says, 'Reflect that this is the member with which we receive the *tremendous* sacrifice,—*the faithful know what I speak of.*' Hardly less frequent is the occurrence of the same phrase in St. Augustin, who seldom ventures to intimate the *eucharist* in any other way than by the words *Quod norunt fideles*."—(Travels in search of a Religion, Phila. ed. p. 82.)

This precaution needs no apology when referring to religious rites, which if exposed, would subject 'its votaries to punishment.—"It was," says the same writer, "in the third century, when the followers of Christ were most severely tried by the fires of persecution, that the discipline of secrecy, with respect to this (the Eucharist) and the other mysteries, was most strictly observed." "A faithful concealment (says Tertullian) is due to all mysteries from the very *nature* and *constitution* of them. How much more must it be due to *such mysteries* as, if they were once discovered, could not escape immediate punishment from the hands of man."—(*Ibid.* p. 73.)

The persecuted, when they obtained the majority, became the persecutors, and the Druids of England were under the same necessity of concealing their dogmas and rites, as the Christians formerly had been. But what excuse have the masons of the present day for making a mystery of the same rites when not in danger of persecution?

There can be no pretext for retaining *a secret*, when the cause that gave it birth no longer exists. Besides, the masons do not profess the doctrines of paganism, they merely repeat the ceremonies, parrot-like, without any regard to or knowledge of the original intention.

That the mysteries were invented, established, and supported by lawgivers, may be seen,

From the place of their original; which was Egypt. This Herodotus, Diodorus, and Plutarch, who collect from ancient testimonies, expressly affirm; and in this, all antiquity concurs; the Elusinian mysteries, particularly, retaining the very Egyptian gods, in whose honor they were celebrated; *Ceres and Triptolemus being only two other names for Isis and Osiris.**

---

* Mr. Le Clerc owns, that Plutarch, Diodorus, and Theodoret have all said this; yet, the better to support his scheme in the interpretation of the history of Ceres, he has thought fit to contradict them. Yet he in another place, could see that Astarte was certainly Isis, as Adonis was Osiris; and this, merely from the identity of their ceremonies.

Hence it is, that the universal nature, or the first cause, the object of all the mysteries, yet disguised under diverse names, speaking of herself in Apuleius, concludes the ennumeration of her various mystic rites, in these words—" The Egyptians skilled in ancient learning, worshipping me by ceremonies perefectly appropriate, call me by my true name, *queen Isis.*"

But the similitude between the rites practised, and the doctrines taught in the Grecian and Egyptian mysteries, would be alone sufficient to point up to their original: such as the secrecy required of the initiated; which, as we shall see hereafter, peculiarly characterized the Egyptian teaching; such as the doctrines taught of a metempsychosis, and a future state of rewards and punishments, which the Greek writers agree to have been first set abroach by the Egyptians;* such as abstinence enjoined from domestic fowl, fish, and beans, (see Porphyrius De Abstin,) the peculiar superstition of the Egyptians; such as the Ritual composed in hieroglyphics, an invention of the Egyptians. But it would be endless to reckon up all the particulars in which the Egyptian and Grecian mysteries agree: it shall suffice to say, that they were in all things the same.

Again; nothing but the supposition of this common original to all the Grecian mysteries can clear up and reconcile the disputes which arose amongst the Grecian states and cities concerning the first rise of the mysteries; every one claiming to be original to the rest. Thus Thrace pretended that they came first from thence; Crete contested the honor with those barbarians; and Athens claimed it from both. And at that time, when they had forgotten the true original, it was impossible to settle and adjust their differences: for each could prove that he did not borrow from others; and, at the same time, seeing a similitude in the rites, would conclude, that they had borrowed from him. But the owning Egypt for their common parent, clears up all difficulties: by accounting for that general likeness which gave birth to every one's pretensions.

Now, in Egypt, all religious worship being planned and established by statesmen, and directed to the ends of policy, we must conclude, that the mysteries were originally invented by legislators.

The sages who brought them out of Egypt, and propagated them in Asia, in Greece, and Britain, were all kings or lawgivers; such as

---

* Timæus the Locrain, in his book of the soul of the world, speaking of the necessity of inculcating the doctrine of future punishments, calls them Timoριαι ξεναι, foreign torments; by which name both Latin and Greek writers generally mean Egyptian, where the subject is religion.

Zoroaster, Inachus, Orpheus,* Melampus, Trophonius, Minos, Cinyras, Erectheus, and the Druids.

They were under the superintendence of the State. A magistrate, intitled Basileus, or *king, presided* in the Eleusinian mysteries. Lysias informs us, that *this king* was to offer up the public prayers, according to their country rites; and to see that nothing impious or immoral crept into the celebration. (In Andoc.) This title given to the president of the mysteries, was, doubtless, in memory of the first founder.

Though it be now apparent that the mysteries were the invention of the civil magistrate, yet even some ancients, who have mentioned the mysteries, seemed not to be apprised of it, and their ignorance hath occasioned great embroilment in all they say on this subject. The reader may see by the second chapter of Meursius' Eleusinia, how much the ancients were at a loss for the true founder of those mysteries: some giving the institution to Ceres; some to Triptolemus; others to Eumolpus; others to Musæus; and some again to Erectheus. How then shall we disengage ourselves from this labyrinth, into which Meursius has led us, and in which, his guard of ancients keep us inclosed? This clue will easily conduct us through it. It appears, from what hath been said, that Erectheus, king of Athens, established the mysteries;† but that the people unluckily confounded the institutor, with the priests, Eumolpus and Musæus, who first officiated in the rites; and, with Ceres and Triptolemus, the deities, in whose honor they were celebrated. And these mistakes were natural enough: the poets would be apt, in the licence of their figurative style, to call the gods, in whose name the mysteries were performed, the founders of those mysteries; and the people, seeing only the ministry of the officiating priests, in good earnest believed those mystagogues to be the founders. And yet, if it were reasonable to expect from poets or people, attention to their own fancies and opinions, one would think they might have distinguished better, by the help of that mark, which *Erectheus left behind him, to ascertain his title; namely, the erection of the officer called Basileus, or king.*

But this original is still further seen from the qualities required in the aspirants to the mysteries. According to their original institution, neither slaves nor foreigners were to be admitted into them.‡ Now if

---

* Of whom Aristophanes says, "Orpheus taught us the mysteries, and to abstain from murder," that is, from a life of rapine and violence, such as men lived in the state of nature.

† And so says Diodorus Siculus, lib. i. Bibl.

‡ Schol. Hom. Il. —. It was the same in the Cabiric mysteries, as we learn from Diodorus Siculus, lib. v. who speaks of the-like innovation made there. As to slaves, hear Aristophanes in his *Thesmophoriaz*. "Begone, ye vulgar crew, it is not fitting that slaves should hear these words."

the mysteries were instituted, primarily for the sake of teaching religious truths, there can be no reason given why every man, with the proper moral qualities, should not be admitted: but supposing them instituted by the state for political purposes, a very good one may be assigned; for slaves and foreigners have there neither property nor country. When afterwards the Greeks, by frequent confederations against the Persian, the common enemy of their liberties, began to consider themselves as one people and community, the mysteries were extended to all who spoke the Greek language. Yet the ancients, not reflecting on the original and end of their institution, were much perplexed for the reasons of an exclusion so apparently capricious. Lucian tells us, in the life of his friend Demonax, that that great philosopher had the courage, one day, to ask the Athenians, why they excluded barbarians from their mysteries, when Eumolpus, a barbarous Thracian, had established them:* but he does not tell us their answer. One of the most judicious of the modern critics (Is. Casaubon) was as much at a loss; and therefore thinks the restraint ridiculous, as implying, that the institutors thought the speaking the Greek tongue contributed to the advancement of piety.

Another proof of this original may be deduced from what was taught, promiscuously to all the initiated; which was, the necessity of a virtuous and holy life, to obtain a happy immortality. Now this, we know, could not come from the sacerdotal warehouse: the priests could afford their elysium, at the easy expense of oblations and sacrifices: for, as our great philosopher (who, however, was not aware of this extraordinary institution for the support of virtue, and therefore concludes too generally) well observes, "the priests made it not their business to teach the people virtue: if they were diligent in their observances and ceremonies, punctual in their feasts and solemnities, and the tricks of religion, the holy tribe assured them that the gods were pleased, and they looked no further: few went to the schools of philosophers, to be instructed in their duty, and to know what was good and evil in their actions: the priests sold the better pennyworths, and therefore had all the custom: for lustrations and sacrifices were much easier than a clean conscience and a steady course of virtue; and an expiatory sacrifice, that atoned for the want of it, much more conveniant than a strict and holy life.—(Locke's Reasonableness of Christianity.) Now we

---

* But the fact, their not being a Grecian but a foreign, that is, barbarous, invention, is proved by their very name, *mysteria*, from the eastern dialect, mistor, or mistur, res aut locus absconditus—(a thing or place hid.)

THE ANCIENT MYSTERIES.   139

may be assured, that an institution, which taught the necessity of a strict and holy life, could not but be the invention of lawgivers, to whose schemes virtue was so necessary.

It is now submitted to the reader, whether it be not fairly proved, that the mysteries were invented by the legislator, to affirm and establish the general doctrine of a providence, by inculcating the belief of a future state of rewards and punishments. Indeed, if we may believe a certain ancient, who appears to have been well versed in these matters, they gained their end, by clearing up all doubts concerning the righteous government of the gods. (Sopater in Divis. Quest.)

It seems of very little importance to determine whether the mysteries were the invention of civil legislators, or of the sacredotal order. And in fact, in Egypt where they were first established, the priesthood and the legislators formed but one body. This was also the case in Britain, where the Druids performed the offices of priests, and were at the same time the makers of the laws.

Tytler, in his Elements of general History in the chapter on Egypt, says, "The functions of the sovereign were partly civil, and partly religious. The king had the chief regulation of all that regarded the gods: and the priests, considered as his deputies, filled all the offices of state. They were both the *legislators* and the *civil* Judges; they imposed and levied the taxes, and regulated weights and measures."

The title of *Basileus* (*king*) given to one of the officers in the celebrations of the mysteries, who is decorated with a crown, has doubtless caused the supposition that this character was the representative of civil, temporal power. Whereas the crown was originally the ensign of divinity. "In the remotest antiquity, the crown was only given to *gods*. Leo, the Egyptian, says, it was Isis who first wore a crown, and that it consisted of ears of corn [grain] the use whereof she first taught men.

"In this most authors agree, that the crown originally was rather a religious than a civil ornament; rather one of the pontificalia, than the regalia; that it only became common to kings, as the ancient kings were priests as well as princes; and that the modern princes are entitled to it in their ecclesiastical capacity rather than their temporal."—(*Rees's Cycl.*)

The author cites no authority for his assertion that, "A magistrate, entitled *Basileus* or *king*, presided in the Eleusinian mysteries." But, he says, "Lysias informs us that *this king*, was to offer up the public prayers, according to their country rites; and to see that nothing impious or *immoral* crept into the celebration."

Lysias, it appears, was noticed by Cicero as an orator of some repute, but he is little known as an author; and he seems in this case, to have indulged his fancy in one of his popular orations, without possessing an absolute knowledge of the truth of his declaration; for there is no evidence of his having been initiated into the mysteries. He was no doubt, deceived by the title given to one of the officers in these celebrations, which was very likely to be generally known.

Besides, the bishop has shown above, that, "By a law of Solon, the Senate was always to meet the day after the celebration of these mysteries, to see that nothing had been done amiss during the performance." Now, if there were a magistrate appointed by the king, bearing his title, and presiding in these celebrations as his representative what need would there be for the meeting of the senate for the purpose here stated.

Jamblichus, who, by the by, was a Pagan priest, and appears to be thoroughly versed in the metaphysical science of the gods, has clearly intimated who this Basileus of the mysteries was. In speaking of the one Supreme, he says "prior to truly existing beings and total principles, there is one god, prior to the *first* god and *king*, immoveable, and abiding in the solitude of his own unity. Who is father of himself, is self-begotten, is father alone, and is truly good."—(*See Taylor's Trans.* p. 301.)

The original of that part of the passage particularly alluded to is *proton kai ton proton Theon kai Basileus*; which Gale properly translates, prior etiam primo Deo, et rege [sole.] That is, prior to the first god and king, the sun. For it is well known that the sun was the first object of adoration among all the ancient nations and he was styled the *king* or governor of the world.

The Supreme God, alluded to by Jamblichus, was called in Egypt, *Kneph*, of whom Plutarch says " the unbegotten Kneph was celebrated with an extraordinary degree of veneration by the Egyptian Thebans."

As a further proof of the erroneous opinion formed by our author on this subject, an appeal may be made to the practice of royal arch masonry, which I deem conclusive in this and similar cases. Here the hierophant or high priest is the presiding officer and the king holds the second rank, and presides only in the absence of the former. And the idea that this officer was ever the representative of an earthly monarch was never entertained by masons. No civil power has ever exercised any authority in the lodge; and although some of the royal family of England, and also of other countries have become members of the fraternity, they enter it like other men, on the ground of perfect equality. In short, the officer styled king, personates Osiris the sun, one of the divinities celebrated in the mysteries, the second person in the pagan trinity.

It is worthy of remark, and perhaps here is the most proper place to make it, that masonry conforms to the practice of the Egyptians, in prohibiting to slaves a participation of its mystic rites. It excludes also all those who possess any bodily defect. That a benevolent society, as the masonic institution is, should make a misfortune of this kind the cause of debaring admission to its social and friendly communion, admits of no justification; no mason can give a plausible reason for it.

It is an outrage against humanity. Any one who, in fighting the battles of liberty and his country, should have lost a leg or an arm in the conflict, would in vain apply for admission into this society. Every mason has sworn not to be present at the initiation of a person thus situated. He is bound down with the adamantine chains of precedent, which has often perverted the plainest principles of justice and common sense.

I do not believe there is a single mason who would not wish to get rid of this rule but the fraternity entertain a religious horror against defacing the "*old land marks*"— The oaths, therefore, engendered in days of darkness and superstition, must remain the same to the end of time.

This circumstance alone is a strong proof of the origin of the order. The practice arises from a stupid adherence to the religious customs and observances of the ancient Egyptians. The mysteries, it has been seen, were deemed a sacred institution, and the most rigid investigation of character, and the severest trials were imposed upon the aspirants to its benefits. " No person, says De Pauw (in his Phil. Diss. on the Egypt. and Chinese,) who was born with any remarkable *bodily imperfection*, could be consecrated in Egypt; and the very animals, when deformed, where never used either for sacrifice, or in symbolical worship."

The Levites among the Jews were subjected to the same rigid discipline; no one that had the least bodily blemish could be admitted into the sacerdotal order.

"As to the admittance of the Levites into the ministry, birth alone did not give it to them; they were likewise obliged to receive a sort of consecration. Take the Levites from among the children of Israel, says God to Moses, and cleanse them. And thus shalt thou do unto them, to cleanse them; sprinkle water of purifying upon them, and let them shave all their flesh, and let them wash their clothes, and so make themselves clean. Then let them take a young bullock, etc. *Numbers*, viii. v. 6.

Nor was any Levite permitted to exercise his functions till after he had served a sort of novitiate for five years, in which he carefully learned all that related to his ministry.

"From considering their order, we proceed to consider the manner in which the priests were chosen, and the defects which excluded them from the priesthood. Among the defects of body, which rendered them unworthy of the sacerdotal functions, the Jews reckon up *fifty* which are common to men and other animals, and *ninety* which are peculiar to men alone. The priest whose birth was polluted with any profaneness, was clothed in black, and sent without the verge of the priests' court, but he who was chosen by the judges appointed for that purpose, was clothed in white, and joined himself to the other priests. And I know not whether St. John does not allude to this custom when he says, "He that overcometh, the same shall be clothed in *white raiment*; and I will not blot his name out of the book of life." (*Rev.* iii. v. 5.) They whose birth was pure, but who had some defect of body, lived in those appartments of the temple wherein the stores of wood were kept, and were obliged to split, and prepare it for keeping up the fire of the altar." (Rev. Adam Clarke's Hist. Anc. Israelites. Burlington Edit —p. 273, 279.)

There is a remarkable similarity in the institutions of the Egyptians, Jews, and Freemasons. The probation of four years was required after initiation into the lesser mysteries, before the candidate could be admitted to a participation of the greater. An entered apprentice in the lodge of Freemasons had formerly to serve seven years in that grade before he could be advanced. This extra time, however, arose from the necessity of adapting the rules of the order to the craft of masonry; it being the usual period required for apprentices in that and other mechanical trades. The members of the masonic fraternity also "formerly wore *white* during lodge-hours but at present the white apron alone remains."—(*Smith*.)

CHAPTER III.

AN EXAMINATION OF VIRGIL'S SIXTH BOOK OF THE ENEID: IN WHICH IT IS SHOWN, THAT THE ALLEGORICAL DESCENT OF ENEAS INTO HELL, IS NO OTHER THAN AN ENIGMATICAL REPRESENTATION OF HIS INITIATION INTO THE MYSTERIES.

WE have seen in general, how fond and tenacious ancient paganism was of this extraordinary rite, as of an institution supremely useful both to society and religion. But this will be seen more fully in what I now proceed to lay before the reader; an examination of two celebrated pieces of antiquity, the famous *Sixth Book of Virgil's Eneid*, and the *Metamorphosis of Apuleius*. The first of which will show us of what use the mysteries were esteemed to society; and the second, of what use to religion.

An inquiry into Eneas' adventure to the shades, will have this farther advantage, the instructing us in the *shows and representations of the mysteries;* a part of their history, which the form of this discourse upon them hath not yet enabled us to give. So that nothing will be now wanting to a perfect knowledge of this most extraordinary and important institution.

For, the descent of Virgil's hero into the infernal regions, I presume, was no other than a figurative description of an *initiation;* and particularly, a very exact picture of the *spectacles* in the *Eleusinian* mysteries; where every thing was done in show and machinery; and where a representation of the history of Ceres afforded opportunity of bringing in the scenes of heaven, hell, elysium, purgatory, and whatever related to the future state of men and heroes.

As the Eneid is in the style of ancient legislation, it would be hard to think that so great a master in his art, should overlook a doctrine, which, we have shown, was the foundation and support of ancient politics; namely a future state of rewards and punishments. Accordingly he hath given us a complete system of it, in imitation of his models, which were Plato's vision of Erus, and Tully's dream of Scipio. Again, as the lawgiver took care to support this doctrine by a very extraordinary institution, and to commemorate it by a rite, which had all the allurement of spectacle; and afforded matter for the utmost embellishments of poetry, we cannot but confess a description of such a scene would add largely to the grace and elegance of his work; and must conclude he would be invited to attempt it. Accordingly, he hath done this likewise, in the allegorical descent of Eneas into hell; which is no other than an enigmatical representation of his initiation into the mysteries.

Virgil was to represent a perfect lawgiver, in the person of Eneas; now, initiation into the mysteries was what sanctified his character and enobled his function. Hence we find all the ancient heroes and lawgivers were, in fact, initiated.

Another reason for the hero's initiation, was the important instructions he received in matters that concerned his office.

A third reason for his initiation, was the custom of seeking support and inspiration from *the god who presided in the mysteries.*

A fourth reason for his initiation, was the circumstance in which the poet has placed him, unsettled in his affairs, and anxious about his future fortune. Now, amongst the uses of initiation, the advice and direction of the *oracle* was not the least. And an oracular bureau was so necessary an appendix to some of the mysteries, as particularly the Samothracian, that Plutarch, speaking of Lysander's initiation there expresses it by a word that signifies consulting the oracle: on this occount, Jason, Orpheus, Hercules, Castor, and (as Macrobius says) Tarquinius Priscus, were every one of them initiated into those mysteries.

All this the poet seems clearly to have intimated in the speech of Anchises to his son:

"Carry with you to Italy the choisest of the youths, the stoutest hearts. In Latium you have to subdue a hardy race, rugged in manners. But first, my son, visit Pluto's infernal mansions, and, in quest of an interview with me, cross the deep floods of Avernus."

A fifth reason was the conforming to the old popular tradition, which said, that several other heroes of the Trojan times, such as Agamemnon and Ulysses, had been initiated.

A sixth, and principal was, that Augustus, who was shadowed in the person of Eneas, had been initiated into the Eleusinian mysteries.— (Suet. Oct. cap. xciii.)

While the mysteries were confined to Egypt, their native country, and while the Grecian lawgivers went thither to be initiated, as a kind of designation to their office, the ceremony would be naturally described, in terms highly allegorical. This was, in part, owing to the genius of the Egyptian manners; in part, to the humor of travelers; but most of all, to the policy of lawgivers; who, returning home, to civilize a barbarous people, by laws and arts, found it useful and necessary (in order to support their own characters, and to establish the fundamental principle of a future state) to represent that initiation, in which, they saw the state of departed mortals in machinery, as an actual descent into hell. This way of speaking was used by Orpheus, Bacchus, and others; and continued even after the mysteries were introduced into Greece, as appears by the fables of Hercules, Castor, Pollux, and Theseus's descent into hell. But the allegory was generally so circumstanced, as to discover the truth concealed under it. So Orpheus is said to go to hell by the power of his harp: that is, in quality of lawgiver; the harp being the known symbol of his laws, by which he humanized a rude and barbarous people. So again, in the lives of Hercules and Bacchus, we have the true history, and the fable founded on it, blended and recorded together. For we are told, that they were in fact initiated into the Eleusinian mysteries; and that it was just before their descent into hell, as an aid and security in that desperate undertaking. Which, in plain speech, was no more, than that they could not safely see the shows, till they had been initiated. The same may be said of what is told us of Theseus's adventure. Near Eleusis there was a well, called Callichorus; and, adjoining to that, a stone, on which, as the tradition went, *Ceres sat down, sad and weary*, on her coming to Eleusis. Hence the stone was named Agelastus, the *melancholy stone*. On which account it was deemed unlawful for the initiated to sit thereon. "For Ceres, (says Clemens) wandering about, in search of her daughter Proserpine, when she came to Eleusis, grew weary, and sat down melancholy on the side of a well. So that, to this very day, it is unlawful for the initiated to sit down there, lest they, who are now become perfect, should seem to imitate her in her desolate condition." Now let us see what they tell us concerning Theseus's descent into hell. "There is also a stone," says the scholiast on Aristophanes, "called by the Athenians, Agelastus; on which, they say, Theseus sat when he was meditating his descent into hell. Hence the stone had its name. Or, perhaps, because Ceres sat there, weeping, when she sought Proserpine." All this seems plainly to intimate, that the descent of Theseus was his entrance into the Eleusinian mysteries. Which entrance, as we shall see hereafter, was a fraudulent intrusion.

Both Euripides and Aristophanes seem to confirm our interpretation of these descents into hell. Euripides, in his Hercules furens, brings the hero, just come from hell, to succor his family, and destroy the tyrant Lycus. Juno, in revenge, persecutes him with the furies; and he, in his transport, kills his wife and children, whom he mistakes for his enemies. When he comes to himself, he is comforted by his friend Theseus; who would excuse his excesses by the criminal examples of the gods: a consideration, which, as I have observed above, greatly encouraged the people in their irregularities; and was therefore obviated in the mysteries, by the detection of the vulgar errors of polytheism. Now Euripides seems plainly enough to have told us what he thought of the fabulous descents into hell, by making Hercules reply, like one just come from the celebration of the mysteries, and entrusted with the *aporreta*. "The examples," says he, " which you bring of the gods, are nothing to the purpose. I cannot think them guilty of the crimes imputed to them. I cannot apprehend, how one god can be the sovereign of another god. A god, who is truly so, stands in need of no one. Reject we then these idle fables, which the poets teach concerning them." A secret, which we must suppose, Theseus had not yet learnt.

The comic poet, in his *Frogs*, tells us as plainly what he too understood to be the ancient heroes' descent into hell, by the equipage, which he gives to Bacchus, when he brings him in, inquiring the way of Hercules. It was the custom, at the celebration of the Eleusinian mysteries, as we are told by the scholiast on the place, to have what was wanted in those rites, carried upon asses. Hence the proverb, *Asinus portat mysteria:* accordingly the poet introduces Bacchus, followed by his buffoon servant, Xanthius, bearing a bundle in like manner, and riding on an ass. And, lest the meaning of this should be mistaken, Xanthius, on Hercules's telling Bacchus, that the inhabitants of Elysium were *initiated*, puts in, and says, " And I am the ass carrying mysteries." This was so broad a hint, that it seems to have awakened the old scholiast; who, when he comes to that place, where the *chorus of the initiated** appears, tells us, we are not to understand this scene as really lying in the *Elysian fields*, but in the *Eleusinian mysteries*.

Here then, as was the case in many other of the ancient fables, the pomp of expression betrayed willing posterity into the marvellous. But

---

* The resemblance between the practices of masonry and those of the ancient mysteries, is too striking not to be noticed. Here we have the *chorus of the initiated* ; in masonry, we observe the apprentice's, the fellow craft's, and the master mason's *chorus* or *song* ; that is, songs adapted to each degree.—Edit.

why need we wonder at this in the genius of more ancient times, which delighted to tell the commonest things in a highly figurative manner, when a writer of so late an age as Apuleius, either in imitation of antiquity, or perhaps in compliance to the received phraseology of the mysteries, describes his initiation in the same manner. "I approached to the confines of death, and having trod on the threshold of Proserpine, I returned from it, being carried through all the elements. At midnight I saw the sun shining with a splended light; and I manifestly drew near to the gods beneath, and the gods above, and proximately adored them."

Eneas could not have described his night's journey to his companions, after he had been let out of the ivory gate, in properer terms, had it been indeed to be understood as a journey into hell.

Thus, we see, Virgil was obliged to have his hero initiated; and that he had the authority of fabulous antiquity to call his initiation a descent into hell. And surely he made use of his advantages with great judgment; for such a fiction animates the relation, which, delivered out of allegory, had been too cold and flat for epic poetry.

Had an old poem, under the name of Orpheus, entitled, "*A descent into hell*," been now extant, it would, perhaps, have shown us, that no more was meant than Orpheus's initiation; and that the idea of this sixth book was taken from thence.

But further, it was customary for the poets of the Augustan age to exercise themselves on the subject of the mysteries, as appears from Cicero, who desires Atticus, then at Athens, and initiated, to send to Chilius, a poet of eminence, an account of the Eleusinian mysteries; in order, as it would seem, to insert into some poem he was then writing. Thus it appears, that both the ancient and modern poets afforded Virgil a pattern for this famous episode.

Even Servius saw thus far into Virgil's design, as to say, that many things were delivered according to the profound learning of the Egyptian theology. And we have shown that the doctrines taught in the mysteries, were invented by that people. But though I say this was our poet's general design, I would not be supposed to think he followed no other guides. Several of the circumstances are borrowed from Homer; and several of the philosophic notions from Plato: some of which will be taken notice of, in their place.

The great manager in this affair is the sibyl; and, as a virgin, she sustains two principal and distinct parts: that of the inspired *priestess*, to pronounce the oracle; and that of hierophant, to *conduct the initiated through the whole celebration.**

For as we have observed, the initiated had a guide or conductor, called *Hierophantes, Mystagogos*, indifferently of either sex, who was to instruct him in the preparatory ceremonies, and lead him through and explain to him, all the shows and representations of the mysteries Hence Virgil calls the sibyl *Magna Sacerdos*, and *Docta Comes*, words of equivalent signification. And as the female mystagogue, as well as the male, was devoted to a single life, so was the Cumæan Sibyl, whom he calls *Casta Sibylla.* Another reason why a priestess is given to conduct him, is, because Proserpine presides in this whole affair. And the name of the priestess in the Eleusinian mysteries shows that she properly belonged to Proserpine, though she was called the priestess o Ceres. "The ancients," says Porphyrius, "called the priestesses of Ceres, *Melissai*, (*bees*,) as being the ministers or hierophants of the subterraneous goddess; and Proserpine herself, *Melitodes.*

It was for this reason that these female hierophants were called Melissai, as is well observed by the Schol. on Pind. in Pyth. the bee being, among the ancients, the *symbol of chastity.*†

Quod nec concubitu indulgent, nec corpora segnes
In Venerem solvunt.

The first instruction the priestess gives Eneas, is to search for the *golden bough*, sacred to Proserpine.

Under this branch is concealed the *wreath of myrtle*, with which the initiated were *crowned*, at the celebration of the mysteries—(Schol. Aristoph. Ranis.)

The golden bough is said to be sacred to Proserpine, and so we are told was the myrtle; Proserpine only is mentioned all the way; partly, because the initiation is described as an actual descent into hell; but principally, because, when the rites of the mysteries were performed, Ceres and Proserpine were equally invoked; but when the *shows* were represented, then Proserpine alone presided: now this book is a representation of the shows of the mysteries. The quality of this golden bough, with its *lento nimine*, admirably describes the tender branches of myrtle. But the reader may ask, why is this myrtle-branch represented to be of gold? not merely for the sake of the marvellous, he may be

---

* This remark can apply only to the *shows* and *representations* of the *lesser* mysteries; at the conclusion of which the office of female hierophant ends, if we can judge by the duty imposed upon the sibyl by Virgil, as will appear further on.—Edit.

† The *bee*, or rather *bee-hive*, among the masonic symbols, is considered an emblem of *industry:* for which there is probably some authority in antiquity.—Edit.

assured. A golden bough was literally part of the sacred equipage in the shows of the mysteries. For, the branch which was sometimes *wreathed into a crown*, and *worn on the head*, was, at other times, carried in the hand. Clemens Alexandrinus tells us, from Dionysius Thrax the grammarian, that it was an Egyptian custom to hold a branch in the act of adoration. And of what kind these branches were, Apuleius tells us, in his description of a procession of the initiated in the mysteries of Isis: "A third advanced bearing a palm branch of thin *guilt leaves*, and also the *Mecurial Caduceus*." The golden branch, then, and the caduceus were related. And accordingly Virgil makes the former do the usual office of the latter, in affording a free passage into the regions of the dead. Again, Apuleius, describing the fifth person in the procession, says, "A fifth (bearing) a golden van full of golden boughs." So that a golden bough, we see, was an important implement, and of a very complicated intention in the shows of the mysteries.

Eneas having now possessed himself of the golden bough, a passport as necessary to his descent as a myrtle crown to initiation.

He is then led to the opening of the descent:

"Here stood a cave profound and hideous, with a wide yawning mouth, stony, fenced by a black lake and gloomy woods."

And his reception is thus described:

"The ground beneath their feet began to rumble, the mountain tops to quake, and dogs were seen to howl through the shade of the woods at the approach of the goddess."

How similar is all this to the fine description of the poet Claudian, where, professedly and without disguise, he speaks of the tremendous entry into these mystic rites:

"Now I see the shrines shake upon their tottering bases, and lightnings, announcing the deity's approach, shed a vivid glare around. Now a loud warring is heard from the depths of the earth, and the *Cecropian temple re-echoes;* and *Eleusis raises her holy torches; the snakes of Triptolemus hiss,* and lift their scaly necks rubbed by their curved yokes. So afar, the three-fold Hecate bursts forth."—(De raptu Proserpinæ.)

Both these descriptions agree exactly with the relations of the ancient Greek writers on this subject. Dion Crysostom, speaking of initiation into the mysteries, gives us this general idea of it: "Just so it is, as when one leads a Greek or barbarian to be initiated in a certain mystic dome, excelling in beauty and magnificence; where he sees many mystic sights, and hears in the same manner a multitude of voices; where darkness and light alternately affect his senses; and a thousand other uncommon things present themselves before him.

"The ritual of initiation was read aloud, and *hymns were sung* in honor of Ceres.— Soon after a hollow sound was heard, and the earth seemed to groan beneath our feet: we heard thunder; and perceived by the glare of the lightning, phantoms and specters wandering in darkness, and filling the holy places with howlings that chilled us with terror, and groans that rent our hearts."—(Travels of Anacharsis.)

"This happy moment (de l'autopsia) was introduced, says Dupuis, by frightful scenes, by alternate fear and joy, by light and darkness, by the glimmerings of light, by the terrible noise of thunder, which was imitated, and by the apparitions of specters, of magical illusions, which struck the eyes and ears all at once." (See Moore's Epicurean.)

De Pauw, in his Philosophical Dissertation on the Egyptian and Chinese, observes "Were it true, as some have pretended, that certain mysteries were celebrated in apartments of the labyrinth, it would not have been difficult to produce noise there as violent as thunder. Pliny assures us, that the re-percussion of the air in that edifice, merely on opening the doors, which probably acting as suckers caused others to shut. According to the common report thunder was imitated in Greece, by rolling stones in vessels of copper. The initiated were to be terrified, and this was done effectually in the mysteries of Mithra." (Vol. 1. p. 305.)

If Virgil copied solely from initiations in the Eleusinian mysteries, the temples of Ceres would seem to have been constructed on a plan similar to that of the Egyptian labyrinth; for in the sixth book of the Eneid, v. 136, are the following lines:

> Now, with a furious blast, the hundred doors
> Ope of themselves; a rushing wirlwind roars
> Within the cave, and Sibyl's voice restores.

Similar delusions are practised in royal arch masonry, where thunder is imitated by rolling cannon balls, etc.

The poet next relates the fanatic agitation of the mystagogue, on this occasion.

"Procul, O procul, este, profani, etc. Hence, far hence, O ye profane, exclaims the prophetess, and begone from all the grove.* This said, she furiously plunged into the open cave."

So again, Claudian, where he counterfeits, in his own person, the raptures and astonishment of the initiated, and throws himself, as it were, like the sibyl, in the middle of the scene.

"Away, ye profane,—now fury has expelled human feelings from my breast." The affectation of fury or madness, as we are told by Strabo, (lib. x.) was an inseparable circumstance of the mysteries.

The procul, O procul este, profani of the sibyl, is a literal transla-

---

* When about to open a chapter of royal arch masons, the high priest says, "If there be any person present, who is not a royal arch mason, he is requested to retire." Bernard. Edit.

tion of the formula used by the mystagogue, at the opening of the mysteries:

Ekas, ekas este, bebeloi.

But now the poet, intending to accompany his hero through all the mysterious rites of his initiation, and conscious of the imputed impiety in bringing them out to open day, stops short in his narration, and breaks out into this solemn apology.

Dii, quibus in imperium est animarum, etc.

"Ye gods, to whom the empire of ghosts belongs, and ye silent shades, and Chaos, and Phlegethon, places where silence reigns around in the realms of night! permit me to utter the secrets I have heard; may I have your divine permission to disclose things buried in deep earth and darkness."

Claudian, who, as we have observed, professes openly to treat of the Eleusinian mysteries, at a time when they were in little veneration: yet, in compliance to old custom, excuses his undertaking in the same maner:

Dii, quibus in numerum, etc.

Had the revealing the mysteries been as penal at Rome, as it was in Greece, Virgil had never ventured on this part of his poem. But yet it was esteemed impious.

He therefore does it covertly; and makes this apology to such as saw into his meaning.

The hero and his guide now enter on their journey:

"They advanced under the solitary night through the shade, and through the desolate halls and empty realms of Pluto; their progress resembling a journey in woods by the precarious glimmering moon under a faint malignant light, when Jupiter hath wrapped up the heavens in shade, and sable night hath stripped objects of color."

This description will receive much light from a passage in Lucian's dialogue of the tyrant. As a company made up of every condition of life, are voyaging together to the other world, Mycillus breaks out, and says: "Bless us! how dark it is! where is the fair Megillus? who can tell in this situation, whether Simmiche or Phryna be the handsomer? every thing is alike, and of the same color; there is no room for rivalling of beauties. My old cloak, which but now presented to your eyes so irregular a figure, is become as honorable a garb as his majesty's purple. They are, indeed, both vanished,[*] and retired

---

[*] The original has a peculiar elegance. Haphano gar ampho, etc. alludes to the ancient Greek notions concerning the first matter, which they called aphanes, invisible, as being without the qualities of form and color. The investing matter with these qualities,

together under the same cover. 'But my friend, the Cynic, where are you? give me your hand: *you are initiated in the Eleusinian mysteries. Tell me now, do you not think this very like the blind march they make there? Oh extremely: and see, here comes one of the Furies as I guess by her equipage; her torch, and her terrible looks.*"

The Sibyl, on their approach to the mouth of the cave, had advised Eneas to call up all his courage, as being to undergo the serverest trials.

"Do you, Eneas, boldly march forward, and snatch your sword from its sheath; now is the time for fortitude, now for firmness of resolution."

These trials were of two sorts: the encountering real labors and difficulties; and the being exposed to imaginary and false terrors. This latter was submitted to by all the initiated in general; the other was reserved for chiefs and leaders. On which account, Virgil describes them both in their order; as they were both to be undergone by his hero. The first in these words,—

"Before the very courts and in the opening jaws of hell, grief and tormenting cares have fixed their couches; and pale diseases, repining age, fear, and famine, forms terrible to view, (terribiles visuformæ) and death and toil; then sleep that is akin to death, and criminal joys of the mind; and in the opposite threshold murderous war, the iron bed chambers of the furies, and frantic discord."

To understand the force of this description, it will be necessary to transcribe the account the ancients have left us of the probationary trials in the mysteries of Mithras, whose participation was more particularly aspired to, by chiefs and leaders of armies; whence those initiated were commonly called the soldiers of Mithras. "No one," says Nonnus, "could be initiated into these mysteries till he had passed gradually through the probationary labors, by which he was to acquire a certain *apathe* and sanctity. There were eighty degrees of these labors, from less to greater; and when the aspirant has gone through them all, he is initiated. These labors are,—to pass through fire, to endure cold, hunger, and thirst, to undergo much journeyings; and, in a word, every toil of this nature."

---

was the production of bodies, the ta Phainomena: their dissolution, a return to a state of invisibility.—eis Ha phanes chorei ta dialuomena, as the pretended Merc. Trismag. has it, cap. xi. Matter, in this state of invisibility, was, by the earlier Greeks, called Hades. Afterwards, the state itself was so called; and at length it came to signify the abode of departed spirits: hence some of the Orphic odes, which were sung in the mysteries, bore the title of e eis Adoy Katabasis, a descent into the regions of the dead, a little equivalent to Teaetai and Hieros Logos.

They exercised the candidates, says Dupuis, in his Recherches sur les Initiations, many days, to cross by swimming, a large extent of water; they threw them into it, and it was with great difficulty that they extricated themselves. They applied a sword and fire to their bodies: they made them pass over flames. The aspirants were often in considerable danger, and Pythagoras, we are told, nearly lost his life in the trials.

In tracing the early connections of spectacles with the ceremonies of religion, Voltaire says, "The truly grand tragedies, the imposing and terrible representations, were the sacred mysteries, which were celebrated in the greatest temples in the world, in presence of the initiated only; it was there that the habits, the decorations, the machinery were proper to the subject, and the subject was the present and future life."—*Ibid.*

Volney, shows the origin of these ceremonies. "The Egyptians, says Porphery, employ every year a talisman in remembrance of the world; at the summer solstice, they mark their houses, flocks, and trees with red, supposing that on that day the whole world had been set on fire. It was also at the same period that they celebrated the pyrrhic or fire dance." And this illustrates the origin of purification by fire and water, for having denominated the tropic of cancer, *gate* of heaven and of heat or celestial fire, and that of Capricorn, *gate* of deluge or of water, it was imagined that the spirits or souls who passed through these gates in their way to and from heaven, were scorched or bathed; hence the baptism of Mithra, and the passage through the flames, observed throughout the east long before Moses. Ruins, p. 238.

Ancient masonry has slightly imitated these trials, particularly in the third and royal arch degrees. The Druids who established it, were, perhaps, fearful that by carrying the joke too far, their practices might come to the knowledge of the government, which would probably have led to the destruction of the order. For, formen, whose professed object was merely to teach the mechanical art of masonry, to be engaged in the performance of such extravagances as were practised in the ancient mysteries, would certainly have alarmed even the initiated themselves; a great portion of whom, who were carried no farther than the third degree, doubtless retained their attachment to the Christian religion. They knew not what was meant by the ceremonies; they were pleased, however, with the shows.

But the inventors of modern degrees of the order, without any regard to religion, keeping, however, for the most part, within the pale of Christianity, have indulged their imaginations to an unbounded extent. They could have been influenced by no other motives than the pleasure of exercising their wit in experiments upon human credulity.

The following specimens will show that the ancient models have served as the ground work upon which the new superstructure has been reared; which, by the by, already extends fifty stories above the old fabric.

In the degree, called Chevalier de l' Orient, or knight of the East, the master says to the junior *general,* cause Zerubbabel to undergo the seventy trials, which I reduce to *three,* namely, first that of the body; second,' that of his *courage*; third, that of his *mind.* After which, perhaps, he may merit the favor which he demands.—(*Bernard.*)

The following is taken from the Abbé Barruel, but whose book, being replete with falsehoods against masonry, renders the account justly entitled to suspicion. It relates to initiations in the degree of Knight of Kadosh, or as (he says) the regenerated Man."

"Adepts have told me, that, no physical art is spared; that there is no machinery, specters, terrors, etc. which are not employed, to try the constancy of the candidate. We are told by Mr. Monjoy, that the duke of Orleans was obliged to ascend, and then throw himself off a ladder. A deep cave, or rather precipice, whence a narrow tower rises to the summit of the lodge, having no avenue to it but by subterraneous passages replete with horror, is the place where the candidate is abandoned to himself, tied hand and foot. In this situation he finds himself raised from the ground by machines making the most frightful noise. He slowly ascends this dark vault, and then suddenly falls, as if he were not supported by any thing. Thus mounting and falling alternately he must carefully avoid showing any sign of fear."

Perhaps, on account of the high rank of the duke of Orleans, he was thought entitled to greater perils and trials than common men. Bernard gives this degree, and, although a ladder is required to be ascended, and the candidate is prohibited to return the same way, yet no such hazards as here related, are spoken of.

The description of the ceremonies in the degree of *knights* of the *White Eagle* or *Pelican*, as reported to Carlile, exceeds, in terrors and awfulness, even Barruel's account of those in the knight of Kadosh. It must have been got up by persons intimately acquainted with the practices of the holy *Inquisition*, particularly in regard to *Auto-da-fée*. I will give a short extract from it.

Second Point of Reception.

The apartment for the preparation, and for this reception, is made as terrifying as possible, to resemble the torments of hell. It has *seven* chandeliers, with grey burning flambeaus, whose mouths represent death's heads with cross bones. The walls are hung with tapestry, painted with flames and figures of the damned.

The door is opened by a brother appointed to guard it, to whom each gives the report of a perfect mason and the pass word *Emanuel*. The candidate is instructed to say, " I am one of the brothers, who seek the *word lost*, by the aid of the new law, and the three columns of masonry." At these words, the guard takes his sash and apron from him, saying these marks of decoration are not humble enough to qualify him to find it, and that he must pass through much more vigorous trials. He then covers him with a black cloth, so that he can see nothing, telling him that he must be conducted to the darkest of places, from which the word must come forth *triumphant*, to the glory of masonry, and that he must abandon all self-confidence. In this condition, he is conducted into an apartment, in which there is a steep descent, up and down which he is directed to *travel*. After which, he is conducted to the door, and the black cloth is removed. Before him stand *three* figures dressed as devils. He is then ordered to parade the room *three* times, in memory of the mysterious descent into the dark places, which lasted *three days*. He is then led to the door of the apartment, covered with the black cloth, and told, that the horrors through which he has passed are as nothing, in comparison with those through which he has to pass: therefore he is cautioned to summon all his fortitude, to meet the *dreadful* scene. After farther manœuvering of this sort, the candidate is reported to the master, by the deacon, as a knight of the Eagle, who, after penetrating the deepest places, hopes to procure the *lost word*, as the fruit of his research and to become a *perfect mason, etc.*

On turning to Bernard's description of this degree, I find he agrees in substance with Carlile. He says, " On the hangings of the third apartment must be represented, in transparent paintings, all the *horrors* which we attach to the *idea of hell*; such as human figures and monsters with convulsed muscles, engulfed in flames, etc. etc. On each side of the door is a human skeleton, with an arrow in his hand, etc."

Virgil has made the sufferings in the other world, preparatory to admission into Elysium, as related by Anchises to Eneas, to correspond with the trials to which candidates were subjected in the mysteries. Bishop Warburton refers to that part of the poem which describes the nature and end of purgatory, but does not quote the passage.

Anchises, says:—"Even when with the last beams of light their life is gone, yet not every ill, nor all corporeal stains, are quite removed from the unhappy beings, and it is absolutely unavoidable that many *vicious habits*, which have long grown up with the soul, should be strangely confirmed and riveted therein. Therefore are they afflicted with pains, and pay the penalties of their former ills. Some, hung on high, are spread out to whiten in the empty winds: in others the guilt not done away is washed out in a vast watery abyss, or burned away in fire. We have each of us a Demon, from whom we suffer, till length of time, after the fixed period is elapsed, hath done away the inherent stains, and hath left celestial reason pure from all irregular passions, and the *soul* that spark of *heavenly fire*, in its *original* purity and brightness, simple and unmixed : then are we conveyed into Elysium, and we, who are the happy few, possess the fields of bliss."—(*Davidson's Trans.*)

The second sort of trial were the imaginary terrors of the mysteries ; and these, Virgil describes next. And to distinguish them from the real labors preceding, he separates the two accounts by that fine circumstance of the *tree of dreams* which introduces the latter.

" In the midst a gloomy elm displays its boughs and aged arms ; which seat vain dreams are said to haunt, and under every leaf they dwell. Besides many monstrous spectres of various forms ; in the gate Centaurs, and double-formed Scylas, Briareus with his hundred hands, and the enormous snake of Lerna hissing dreadful, and Chimæra armed with flames ; Gorgons, Harpes and the form of Geryon's three-bodied ghost."

These terribiles visu formæ are the same which Pletho, in the place quoted above, calls *allokota tas morphas phasmata*, as seen in the entrance of the mysteries ; and which Celsus tells us, were likewise presented in the Bacchic rites.

But it is reasonable to suppose, that though these things had the use here assigned to them, it was some circumstance in the recondite physiology of the East, which preferred them to this station. We are to consider then this dark entrance into the mysteries, as a representation of the *Chaos*, thus characterised.

" They advanced under the solitary night through the desolate halls and empty realms of Pluto."

And amongst the several powers invoked by the poet, at his entrance on this scene, Chaos is one.

Now a fragment of Berosus, preserved by George Syncellus describes the ancient Chaos, according to the physiology of the Chaldeans, in this manner :—" There was a time, they say, when all was water and darkness. And these gave birth and habitation to monstrous animals of mixed forms and species. For there were men with two wings, others with four, and some again with double faces. Some had the horns of goats, some their legs, and some the legs of horses; others had the hind-parts of horses, and the fore-parts of men, like the hippocentaurs. There were bulls with human heads, dogs with four bodies ending in fishes, horses with dogs heads; and men, and other creatures with the heads and bodies of horses, and with the tails of fishes. And a number of animals, whose bodies were a monstrous compound of the dissimilar parts of beasts of various kinds. Together with these, were fishes, reptiles, serpents, and other creatures, which, by a reciprocal translation of the parts to one another, became all portentously deformed : the pictures and representations of which were hung up in the temple of Belus. A woman ruled over the whole whose name was Omoroca, in the Chaldee tongue Thalath, which signifies the sea ; and, in the course of connexion, the moon." This account seems to have been exactly copied in the mysteries, as appears from the description of the poet.

The canine figures have a considerable station in this region of monsters : And he tells us, " And dogs were seen to howl through the shade of the woods," which Pletho explains in his scholia on the magic oracles of Zoroaster. " It is the custom, in the celebration of the mysteries, to present before many of the initiated, phantasms of a canine figure, and other monstrous shapes and appearances."

The woman, whose name coincides with that of the moon, was the Hecate of the Greeks, who is invoked by Eneas on this occasion.

" By mistic sounds invoking Hecate, powerful both in heaven and hell." Hence terrifying visions were called Hecatea.

The ancients called Hecate, *diva triformis*. And Scaliger observes that the word *thalath*, which Syncellus, or Berosus, says, was equivalent to the moon, signifies *tria*.

And now we soon find the hero in a fright, " Here Eneas, disconcerted with sudden fear, grasps his sword, and presents the naked point to each approaching shade."

With these affections the ancients represent the initiated as possessed on his first entrance into these holy rites. " Entering now into the mystic dome (says Themistius) he is filled with horror and amazement. He is seized with solicitude, and a total perplexity ; he is unable to move a step forward, and at a loss to find the entrance to that road which is to lead him to the place he aspires to—till the prophet or conductor, laying open the vestibule of the temple"—To the same purpose Proclus; " As in the most holy mysteries, before the scene of the mystic visions, there is a terror infused over the minds of the initiated, so," etc.

The adventurers come now to the banks of Cocytus. Eneas is surprized at the crowd of ghosts which hover round it, and appear impatient for a passage. His guide tells him they are those who have not had the rites of sepulture performed to their manes, and so are doomed to wander up and down for a hundred years, before they be permitted to cross the river.

We are not to think this old notion took its rise from the vulgar superstition. It was one of the wisest contrivances of ancient politics; and came originally from Egypt, the fountain-head of legislation. Those profound masters of wisdom, in projecting for the common good, found nothing would more contribute to the safety of their fellow citizens than the public and solemn interment of the dead; as without this provision, private murders might be easily and securely committed. They therefore introduced the custom of pompous funeral rites; and, as Herodotus and Diodorus tell us, were of all people the most circumstantially ceremonious in the observance of them. To secure these by the force of religion, as well as civil custom, they taught, that the deceased could not retire to a place of rest, till they were performed. The notion spread so wide, and fixed its roots so deep that the substance of the superstition remains, even to this day, in most civilized countries. By so effectual a method did the legislature gain its end, the security of the citizen.

Mr. Bayle cries out, " What injustice is this! was it the fault of these souls, that their bodies were not interred?" But not knowing the origin of this opinion, nor seeing its use, he ascribes that to the blindness of religion, which was the issue of wise policy.

The next thing observable is the ferryman, Charon; and he, the learned well know, was a substantial Egyptian; and, as an ingenious writer says, fairly existing in this world.—(*Blackwell's life of Homer.*) The case was plainly thus; the Egyptians, like the rest of mankind, *in their descriptions of the other world, used to copy from something they were well acquainted with in this.* In their funeral rites, which, as we observed, was a matter of greater moment with them than with any other people, they used to carry their dead over the Nile, and through the marsh of Acherusia, and there put them into subterraneous caverns; the ferryman employed in this business being, in their language, called Charon. Now in their mysteries, the description of the passage into the other world was borrowed, as was natural, from the circumstances of their funeral rites. And it might be easily proved, if there were occasion, that they, themselves transferred these realities into the *mythos*, and not the Greeks, as later writers generally imagine.

Eneas having crossed the river, and come into the proper regions of the dead, the first apparition that occurs is the dog Cerberus; "Huge Cerberus makes those realms resound with barking from his triple jaws, stretched at his enormous length in a den that fronts the gate."

This is plainly one of the phantoms of the mysteries, which Pletho tells above, was in the shape of a dog *kunode tina*. And in the fable of Hercules's descent into hell, which, we have shown, signified no more than his initiation into the mysteries, it is said to have been, amongst other things, for fetching up the dog Cerberus.

The prophetess, to appease his rage, gives him a medicated cake, which casts him into a slumber; "Flings to him a soporific cake of honey and medicated grains"—(*medicatis frugibus.*)

In the mysteries of Trophonius (who was said to be nursed by Ceres, that is to derive his rites from the Eleusinian,) the initiated carried the same fort of medicated cakes to appease the serpents he met with in his passage. Tertullian, who gives all mysteries to the devil, and makes *him* the author of what is done there, mentions the offering up of these cakes, *celebrat et panis oblationem*. This in question was of poppy-seed, made up with honey; and so I understand medicatis frugibus, here, on the authority of the poet himself, who, in the fourth book, makes the priestess of Venus prepare the same treat for the dragon who guarded the Hesperian fruit.

But without doubt, the images, which the juice of poppy presents to the fancy, was one reason why this drug had a place in the ceremonial of the shows; not improbably, it was given to some at least of the initiated, to aid the impression of those mystic visions which passed before them.* For that something like this was done, that is, giving medicated drugs to the aspirants, we are informed by Plutarch; who speaks of a shrub called Leucophyllus used in the celebration of the mysteries of Hecate, which drives men into a kind of frenzy, and makes them confess all the wickedness they had done or intended. And *confession* was one necessary preparative for initiation.†

---

* This practice obtains in a modern degree of masonry, denominated *Le Petit Architect*. A potion is given to the candidate, which, he is told is a part of the *heart* of *master Hiram*, preserved ever since his assassination; which every *faithful* mason may receive, but that it cannot remain in the body of one who is *perjured*. After the candidate has swallowed the dose, the master thus addresses him, brother, one thing you came here to learn is, that you ought never to refuse to *confess your faults*; obstinacy ought to be banished from the heart of every good mason.—*Edit.*

† What were called the secret ceremonies of the gods, says Fontenelle, were without

The regions, according to Virgil's geography, are divided into three parts, Purgatory, Tartarus, and Elysium.

The mysteries divided them in the same manner. So Plato, where he speaks of what was taught in the mysteries, talks of souls sticking fast in mire and filth, and remaining in darkness, till a long series of years had purged and purified them; and Celsus, in Origen, says, that the mysteries taught the doctrine of eternal punishments.

Of all the three states this of *Tartarus*, only was *eternal*. There was, indeed, another, in the ancient pagan theology, which had the same relation to Elysium, that Tartarus had to Purgatory, the extreme of reward, as Tartarus of punishment. But then this state was not in the infernal regions, but in Heaven. Neither was it the lot of common humanity, but reserved for heroes and dæmons; Beings, of an order superior to men, such as Hercules, Bacchus, etc. who became Gods on their admission into that state, where the *eternity* was in consequence of their deification.

And here it is to our purpose to observe, that the virtues and vices, which stock these three divisions, with inhabitants, are such as more immediately affect society. A plain proof that the poet followed the views of the legislator, the institutor of the mysteries.

Purgatory, the first division, is inhabited by suicides, extravagant lovers, and ambitious warriors: and in a word, by all those who had indulged the violence of the passions; which made them rather miserable than wicked. It is remarkable that amongst these we find one of the initiated : "Polybetes devoted to Ceres." This was agreeable to the public doctrine of the mysteries, which taught that initiation with *virtue* procured men great advantages over others, in a future state; but that *without virtue*, it was of no service.

Of all these disorders, the poet hath more distinctly marked out the misery of suicide.

---

doubt the best artifices the priests could invent to keep people in the dark; and yet they could not so well hide the juggle, but that the cheat would be suspected by many persons: and therefore they contrived among themselves to establish certain mysteries which should engage those who were initiated into them to an inviolable secrecy. Those who were initiated also gave further security for their discretion ; for they were obliged to make a confession to their priests of all the most private actions of their lives ; so that by this means they became slaves to their priests, that *their own secrets might be kept.*

It was upon this sort of confession that a Lacedemonian, who was going to be initiated into the mysteries of Samothrace, spoke roundly thus to the priest; if I have committed any crimes, *surely the Gods are not ignorant of them.*

Another answered almost after the same manner ; *is to you or to God we ought to confess our crimes ? It is to God,* says the priest. Well then retire thou, answered the Lacedemonian, and *I will confess them to God.* These Lacedemonians were not very full of the spirit of devotion.—(*Hist. of Oracles, p.* 114, *London,* 1688).—*Edit.*

Here he keeps close to the mysteries; which not only forbade suicide, but taught on what account it was criminal. "That which is said in the mysteries (says Plato) concerning these matters of man's being placed in a certain watch or station, which it is unlawful to fly from, or forsake, is a profound doctrine, and not easily fathomed."—(Phæd. p. 62. Ser. ed. tom. 1.)

Hitherto all goes well. But what must we say to the poet's putting new-born infants, and men falsely condemned into his purgatory? For though the *faith and inquisition* of modern Rome send many of both sorts into a place of punishment, yet the genius of ancient paganism had a gentler aspect. It is, indeed, difficult to tell what these inmates have to do here. Let us consider the case of the infants; and if we find it can only be cleared up by the general view of things here offered, this will be considered as another argument for the truth of our interpretation.

" Forthwith are heard voices, loud wailings, and weeping ghosts of infants, in the first opening of the gate: whom, bereaved of sweet life out of the course of nature, and snatched from the breast, in a black unjoyous day cut off, and buried in an untimely grave."

These appear to have been the cries and lamentings that, Proclus tells us, were heard in the mysteries. So that we only want to know the original of so extraordinary a circumstance. Which, I take, to have been just such another provision of the lawgiver for the security of infancy, as that about funeral rites was for the adult. For nothing could more engage parents in the care and preservation of their young, than so terrible a doctrine. Nor are we to imagine, that their natural fondness needed no inforcement, or support; for that most degenerate and horrid practice among the ancients, of *exposing* infants, was universal;* and had almost erased morality and instinct. St. Paul seems to have had this in his eye, when he accused the pagan world of being without natural affection. It needed therefore the strongest and severest check; and I am well persuaded it occasioned this counterplot of the magistrate, in order to give instinct fair play, and call back banished

---

* We may well judge it to be so, when we find it amongst the Chinese (see M. Polo lib. ii. cap. 26.) and the Arabians, the two people least corrupted by foreign manners, and the vicious customs of more civilized nations. The Arabians, particularly, living much in a state of nature, where men's wants are few, and consequently where there is small temptation to this unnatural crime, yet were become so prone to it, that their lawgiver Mahomet found it necessary to exact an oath of the Arabian women, not to destroy their children. The form of this oath is given us by Gagnier, in his notes on Abel-feda's Life of Mahomet, and it is in these words;—" You will associate nothing with God; nor indulge anger; nor destroy your children; nor be disobedient to the Apostle of God, in that which is just."

nature. Nothing, indeed, could be more worthy of his care: for the destruction of children, as Pericles finely observed of youth, is like cutting off the spring from the year. Accordingly we are told by Diodorus, that the Egyptians had a law against this unnatural practice, which law he numbers amongst the singularities of that people. "They are obliged says he, to bring up all their children, in order to render the country populous, this being esteemed the best means of making states flourishing and happy." And Tacitus speaks of the prohibition as no less singular amongst the Jews.

Here again Mr. Bayle is much scandalized: "The first thing which occurred, on the entrance into the other world, was the station assigned to infants, who cried and lamented without ceasing; and next to that, the station of men unjustly condemned to death. Now what could be more shocking or scandalous than the punishment of those little creatures, who had yet committed no sin, or those persons whose innocence had been oppressed by calumny?" The first difficulty is already cleared up: the second shall be considered by and by. But it is no wonder Mr. Bayle could not digest this doctrine of the *infants;* for I am much mistaken, if it did not stick with Plato himself; who, relating the Vision of Erus, the Pamphylian, concerning the distribution of rewards and punishments in another life, when he comes to the condition of infants, passes it over in in these words:—"But of children who died in their infancy, he reported certain other things *not worthy to be remembered.* Erus's account of what he saw in another world, was a summary of what the Egyptians taught in their mysteries concerning that matter. And I make no doubt but the thing not worthy to be remembered, was the doctrine of *infants in purgatory:* which appears to have given Plato much scandal, who did not, at that time at least, reflect upon its original and use.

But now, as to the falsely condemned, we must seek another solution:

"Next to those are such as had been condemned to death by false accusation. Nor yet were these seats assigned them without destination and appointment, or without the sentence of a judge. Minos, as inquisitor, shakes their urn: he convokes the council of the silent shades, and examins their lives and crimes."

This designment appears both iniquitous and absurd. The falsely accused are not only in a place of punishment, but, being first delivered under this single predicament, they are afterwards distinguished into two sorts.; some as blameable, others as innocent. To clear up this confusion, it will be necessary to transcribe an old story, told by Plato in his Gorgias: "This law, concerning mortals, was enacted in the time of Saturn, and is yet, and ever will be in force amongst the gods; that he who had lived a just and pious life, should at his death be carried into the islands of the blessed, and there possess all kinds of happiness, untainted with the evils of mortality: but that he who had lived unjustly and impiously, should be thrust into a place of punishment, the prison of divine justice, called Tartarus. Now the judges, with whom the execution of this law was intrusted, were, in the time of Saturn, and under the infancy of Jove's government, living men, sitting in judgment on the living; and passing sentence on them, upon the day of their decease. This gave occasion to unjust judgments: on which account, Pluto, and those to whom the care of the happy islands was committed, went to Jupiter, and told him, that men came to them wrongfully judged, both when acquitted and when condemned. To which the father of the gods thus replied: I will put a stop to this evil. These wrong judgments are partly occasioned by the corporeal covering of the persons judged; for they are tried while living: now many have their corrupt minds hid under a fair outside, adorned with birth and riches; and, when they come to their trial, have witnesses at hand, to testify for their good life and conversation; this perverts the process, and blinds the eyes of justice. Besides, the judges themselves are encumbered with the same corporeal covering: and eyes and ears, and an impenetrable tegument of flesh, hinder the mind from a free exertion of its faculties. All these, as well their own covering, as the covering of those they judge, are bars and obstacles to right judgment. In the first place then, says he, we are to provide that the fore-knowledge which they now have of the day of death, be taken away: and this shall be given in charge to Prometheus; and then provide, that they who come to judgment be quite naked: for from henceforth they shall not be tried, till they come into the other world. And as they are to be thus stripped, it is but fit their judges should await them there in the same condition; that, at the arrival of every inhabitant, soul may look on soul, and all family relation, and every worldly ornament being dropt and left behind, righteous judgment may at length take place. I, therefore, who foresaw all these things, before you felt them, have taken care to constitute my own sons, the judges: two of them Minos and Rhadamanthus, are Asiatics; the third, Eacus, an European. These, when they die, shall have their tribunal erected in the shades, just in that part of the highway, where the two roads divide, the one leading to the happy islands, the other to Tartarus.

Rhadamanthus shall judge the Asiatics, and Eacus the Europeans; but to Minos I give the superior authority of hearing appeals, when any thing obscure or difficult shall perplex the others' judgments: that every one may have his abode assigned him with the utmost equity."

The matter now begins to clear up; and we see plainly, that the circumstance of the falsely condemned, alludes to this old fable: so that by *falso damnati crimine mortis*, if it be the true reading, Virgil did not mean, as one would suppose, men falsely condemned, but wrongfully judged, whether to acquittal or conviction; but condemnation being oftenest the sentence of justice, the greater part is put figuratively for the whole.

One difficulty remains; and that, to confess the truth, hath arisen rather from a mistake of Virgil, than of his reader. We find these people yet unjudged, already fixed with other criminals in the assigned district of purgatory. But they are misplaced, through an oversight of the poet; which, had he lived to perfect the Eneid, he would probably have corrected: for the fable tells us they should be stationed on the borders of the three divisions, in that part of the high road that divides itself in two, which lead to Tartarus and Elysium, thus described by the poet:

"This is the place where the path divides in two: the right is that which leads to great Pluto's walls, by this our way to Elysium lies; but the left carries on the punishments of the wicked, and conveys to cursed Tartarus."

It only remains to consider the origin or moral of the fable; which, I think, was this: it was an Egyptian custom, as we are told by Diodorus Siculus, for judges to sit on every man's life, at his interment; to examine his past actions, and to condemn and acquit according to the evidence before them. These judges were of the priesthood; and so, it is probable, taught, like the priests of the church of Rome, that their decrees were ratified in the other world. Partiality and corruption would, in time, pervert their sentence; and spite and favor prevail over justice. As this might scandalize the people, it would be found necessary to teach, that the sentence which influenced every one's final doom, was reserved for a future judicature. However, the priest took care that all should not go out of his hands; and when he could be no longer *judge*, he contrived to find his account in turning *evidence*; as may be seen by the singular cast of this ancient inscription: "I Sextus Anicius pontiff certify that this man has lived honestly: may his soul rest in peace." (Fabius Celsus Inscript. Antiq. lib. iii.)

Eneas, having passed this first division, comes now on the confines of *Tartarus;* and is instructed in what relates to the crimes and punishments of the inhabitants.

It is remarkable, that Eneas is led through the regions of Purgatory and Elysium; but he only sees the sights of Tartarus at a distance, and this could not be otherwise in the shows of the mysteries, for very obvious reasons.

Among the criminals destined to eternal punishment, in this division, are, those who had sinned so secretly as to escape the animadversion of the magistrate.

And it was principally on account of such crimes that the legislator enforced the doctrine of a future state of punishment.

The infringers of the duties of *imperfect obligation, which civil laws cannot reach:* such as those without natural affection to brothers, duty to parents, protection to clients, or charity to the poor.*

The *invaders and violators of the holy mysteries*, held out in the person of Theseus, make the last class of offenders.

"There sits, and to eternity shall sit, the unhappy Theseus; and Phlegyas most wretched is a monitor to all, and with loud voice proclaims through the shade: *warned by my example, learn righteousness, and not to contemn the gods.*"

The fable says, that Theseus and his friend Pirithous formed a design to steal Proserpine from hell; but being taken in the fact, Pirithous was thrown to the dog Cerberus, and Theseus kept in chains, till he was delivered by Hercules: which without doubt means the death of one, and the imprisonment of the other, for their clandestine intrusion into the mysteries. We have already offered several reasons, to show that the descent of Theseus into hell, was a violation of the mysteries: to which we may add what the ancients tell us of the duration of his imprisonment, which was four years; the interim between the celebrations of the greater mysteries.

But when Virgil comes to describe these shows, which were supposed to be a true representation of what was done and suffered in hell, Theseus is put among the damned, that being his station in the other world.

This will remind the learned reader of a story told by Livy. "The Athenians, says he, drew upon themselves a war with Philip, on a very slight occasion; and at a time when nothing remained of their ancient fortune, but their high spirit. Two young Acarnanians, during the

---

* So the law of the *Twelve Tables: Patronus si clienti fraudem fecerit, sacer esto.*

days of initiation, themselves uninitiated, and ignorant of all that related to that secret worship, entered the temple of Ceres along with the crowd. Their discourse soon betrayed them; as making some absurd inquiries into what they saw; so being brought before the president of the mysteries, although it was evident they had entered ignorantly and without design, they were put to death, as guilty of a most abominable crime."

The office Theseus is put upon, of admonishing his hearers against impiety, could not, sure, be discharged in these shows by any one so well, as by him who represented the violator of them. But the critics, unconscious of any such design, considered the task the poet has imposed on Theseus, of perpetually sounding in the ears of the damned, this admonition:

"Warned by my example, learn righteousness, and not to contemn the gods," as a very impertinent employment. For though it was a sentence of great truth and dignity, it was preached to very little purpose amongst those, to whom there was no room for pardon or remission.

Even Scarron hath not neglected to urge this objection against it:* and it must be owned, that, according to the common ideas of Eneas's descent into hell, the objection is not easily got over.

But, suppose Virgil to be here relating the admonitory maxims delivered during the celebration of these *mystic shows*, and nothing could be more just or useful: for then the discourse was addressed to the vast multitude of living spectators. Nor is it a mere supposition that such discourses made part of these representations. Aristides expressly says, that in no place were more astonishing words pronounced or sung, than in these mysteries; the reason, he tells us, was, that the *sounds* and the *sights* might mutually assist each other in making an impression on the minds of the initiated. But, from a passage in Pindar, I conclude, that in these shows, *from whence men took their ideas of the infernal regions*, it was customary for each offender as he passed by, in machinery, to make an admonition against his own crime. " It is reported, says, Pindar, that Ixion, by the decrees of the gods, while he is incessantly turning round his rapid wheel, calls out upon mortals to this effect: that they should be always at hand to repay a benefactor for the kindness he had done them." Where the word *Brotoi*, living men, seems plainly to show that the speech was at first made before men in this world.

---

* Cette sentence est bonne & belle,
Mais en Enfer de quoi sert-elle!

The poet closes his catalogue of the damned with these words:

Ausi omnes immane nefas, ausoque potiti.

For the ancients thought that an action was sanctified by the success; which they esteemed a mark of the favor and approbation of heaven. As this was a very pernicious opinion, it was necessary to teach, that the imperial villain who trampled on his country, and the baffled plotter who expired on a gibbet, were equally the objects of divine vengeance.

Eneas has now passed through *Tartarus;* and here end the *lesser mysteries.*

The hero advances to the borders of Elysium, and here he undergoes the lustration:

"Eneas springs forward to the entry, *sprinkles his body with fresh water*, and fixes the bough in the fronting portal."

"Being now about to undergo the lustration, says Sopater, which immediately precede initiation into the greater mysteries, they called me happy."

Accordingly, Eneas now enters on the greater mysteries, and comes to the abodes of the blessed:

"They came at length to the regions of eternal joy, delightful green retreats, and blessed abodes in groves where happiness abounds. Here the air they breathe is more free and enlarged, and clothes the fields with radiant light: here the happy inhabitants know their own sun and their own stars."

These two so different scenes explain what Aristides meant, when he called the shows of the Eleusinian mysteries, that most shocking, and at the same time, most ravishing representation.

The initiated, who till now only bore the name of Mystai, are called Epoptai, and this new vision, Autopsia. "The Autopsia, or the *seeing with their own eyes*, says Psellus, is when he who is initiated beholds the *divine lights.*"

In these very circumstances Themistius describes the initiated, when just entered upon this scene. "It being thoroughly purified, he now discloses to the initiated, a region all over illuminated, and shining with a divine splendor. This which was *all over illuminated*, and which the priest had *thoroughly purified*, was *agalma*, an image. The reason of transferring what is said of the illumination of the *image*, to the illumination of the *region*, is, because this image represented the appearances of the divine Being, in one large, uniform, extensive light. This, Jamblichus says, was *without figure.* To this image, the following lines in the oracles of Zoroaster allude:

"Invoke not the self-conspicuous image of nature, for thou must not behold these things before thy body be purified by initiation." This *autopton agalma* was only a diffusive shining light, as the name partly declares; and the *sight* of this divine *splendor* was what the mysteries called *autopsia*.

The cloud and thick darkness are dispersed; and the mind emerges, as it were, into day, full of light and chearfulness, as before, of disconsolate obscurity.

Pletho tells us with what these clouds were accompanied, namely, *thunder* and *lightning*, and other meteoric appearances. He says, they were symbols, but not of the nature of the deity : and this was true; for the symbol of that was the autopton agalma which followed: hence, as we see above, it was *without figure*.

Let me observe, that the lines, "Here the air they breathe is more free and enlarged, and clothes the fields with radient *light*: here the happy inhabitants know their own *sun*, and their own stars," are in the very language of those who profess to tell us what they saw at their *initiation into the greater mysteries*. "At midnight I saw the sun shining with a splendid light," says Apuleius on that occasion.

Dupuis, speaking of the mysteries, says, "They discovered the origin of the soul, its fall to the earth through the spheres and the elements, and it's return to the place of its origin : here was the most metaphysical part and which could not be understood by the generality of the initiated, but of which they gave them the sight by figures and allegorical specters."—(See Moore's Epic.)

Thomas Taylor, a modern writer, and I believe still living, in a Dissertation on the Eleusinian and Bacchic Mysteries, contends for the reality of the descent of the gods through magical evocation ; and he quotes the authority of ancient authors in proof of the fact.

Mr. Taylor possesses great erudition; has translated the commentaries of Proclus, and the works of Jamblichus and Apuleius; is a thorough convert to the Platonic philosophy, and an enthusiastic admirer of the rites of Ceres and Bacchus; "In the composition of which he says we may discern the traces of *exalted wisdom, and recondite theology*; of a theology the most *venerable* for its antiquity, and the most admirable for its excellence and *reality*.

Plato, says he, in the Phœdrus, thus describes the felicity of the virtuous soul prior to its descent, in a beautiful allusion to the *arcane* vision of the mysteries :

"But it was then lawful to survey the most splendid beauty, when we obtained together with that blessed choir, this happy vision and contemplation. And we indeed enjoyed this blessed spectacle together with Jupiter, but others, in conjunction with some other god ; at the same time being initiated in those mysteries, which it is lawful to call the most blessed of all mysteries. And these divine Orgies were celebrated by us, while we possessed the proper integrity of our nature, and were freed from the molestations of evil which awaited us in a succeeding period of time. Likewise in consequence of this divine initiation, we became spectators of entire, simple, immoveable, and blessed visions, resident in a pure light; and were ourselves pure and immaculate

SIXTH BOOK OF VIRGIL'S ENEID.

and liberated from this surrounding vestment, which we denominate body, and to which we are now bound like an oyster to its shell." Upon this beautiful passage Proclus observes, in Theol. Plat. lib. 4. p. 193. "That initiation and inspection are symbols of ineffable silence, and of union with mystical natures, through intelligible visions!"

Now, from all this, it may be inferred, that the most sublime part of epoptia or inspection, consisted in beholding the gods themselves invested with a resplendent light; and that this was symbolical of those transporting visions, which the virtuous soul will constantly enjoy in a future state, and of which it is able to gain some ravishing glimpses, even while connected with the cumbrous vestment of the body.

But that this was actually the case, is evident from the following unequivocal testimony of Proclus in Plat. Repub. p. 380.

"In all initiations and mysteries, the gods exhibit many forms of themselves, and appear in a variety of shapes; and sometimes indeed, an *unfigured light of themselves* is held forth to the view, sometimes *this light is figured according to a human form, and sometimes it proceeds into a different shape.*" This doctrine, too, of divine appearances in the mysteries, is clearly confirmed by Plotinus, Ennead i. lib. 6. p. 55. and Ennead 9. lib. .6 p. 700. And in short, that *magical evocation* formed a part of the *sacerdotal office* in the mysteries, and that this was universally believed by all antiquity, long before the era of the latter Platonists, is plain from the testimony of Hippocrates, or at least Democritus, in his treatise de Morbo. Sacro. p. 86. For speaking of those who attempt to cure this disease by magic, he observes:

"If they profess themselves able to draw down the moon, to obscure the sun, to produce stormy and pleasant weather, as likewise showers of rain, and heats, and to render the sea and the earth barren, and to accomplish every thing else of this kind, whether they derive this knowledge from the mysteries, or from some other institution or meditation, they appear to me to be impious, from the study of such concerns." From all which it is easy to see, how *egregiously* Dr. Warburton was *mistaken*, when in his Divine Legation, he asserts, "that the light beheld in the mysteries, was nothing more than an illuminated image which the priests had thoroughly purified."

But he is likewise no less mistaken, in transferring the injunction given in one of the magic oracles of Zoroaster, to the business of the Eleusinian mysteries, and in perverting the meaning of the Oracle's admonition. For thus the Oracle speaks:

"Invoke not the self conspicuous image of nature, for you must not behold these things before your body has received the purification necessary to initiation." Upon which he observes, "that the self conspicuous image was only a diffusive shining light, as the name partly declares." But this is a piece of gross ignorance, from which he might have been freed by an attentive perusal of Proclus on the Timæus of Plato, for in these truly divine commentaries we learn, "that the moon is the self conspicuous image of fontal nature."—In Tim. p. 260.

Theurgic magic is still adhered to by the church of Rome, and *forms a part of the sacerdotal office.* By which means, it is believed, that the *real presence* of the Saviour is manifested in the eucharist.

Masonry adopts the same principle. In the royal arch degree, the *autopton agalma* is exhibited in an *illuminated bush*: the candidate for initiation is ordered to put off his shoes, being told that the place where he stands is holy ground. In fact one of the characters personates the deity, and announces his actual appearance.

The more we examine the pagan system of religion, the more shall we be convinced that the rites and ceremonies of masonry, as well as those of the Catholic church, are derived from that ancient institution.

Virgil, by leaving his master, and copying the amiable paintings of Elysium, as they were represented in the mysteries, hath artfully avoided a fault too justly objected to Homer, of giving so dark and joyless a landscape of the *fortunata nemora*, as could raise no desire or appetite for them: his favorite hero, himself, who possessed them, telling Ulisses, that he had rather be a day laborer above, than command in the regions of the dead. Such a representation defeats the very intent of the law giver, in propagating the doctrines of a future state. Nay, to mortify every excitement to noble actions, the Greek poet makes reputation, fame, and glory, the great spur to virtue in the pagan system, to be visionary and impertinent. On the contrary, Virgil, whose aim, in this poem, was the good of society, makes the love of glory so strong a passion in the other world, that the Sibyl's promise to Palinurus, that his name should only be affixed to a promontory, rejoices his shade even in the regions of the unhappy.

It was this ungracious description of Elysium, and the licentious stories of the gods, both so pernicious to society, that made Plato banish Homer out of his republic.

But to return. The poet having described the climate of the happy regions, speaks next of the amusement of its inhabitants.

'Some exercise their limbs on the grassy plains, in sports contend, and wrestle on the yellow sand.'

Besides the obvious allusion in these lines to the philosophy of Plato concerning the duration of the passions, it seems to have a more secret one to what he had all the way in his eye, the Eleusinian Mysteries, whose celebration was accompanied by the Grecian games. On which account too, perhaps it was that, in the disposition of his work, his fifth book is employed in the games, as a prelude to the descent in the sixth.

The first place in these happy regions, is assigned to the lawgivers, and those who brought mankind from a state of nature into society.

At the head of these is Orpheus, the most renowned of the European lawgivers; but better known under the character of poet: for the first laws being written in measure, to allure men to learn them, and when learnt, to retain them, the fable would have it, that by the force of harmony, Orpheus softened the savage inhabitants of Thrace.

But he has the first place; because he was not only a legislator but the bringer of the mysteries into that part of Europe.

The next is allotted to patriots, and those who died for the service of their country.

The third to virtuous and pious priests. For it was of principal use to society, that religious men should lead holy lives; and that they should teach nothing of the gods but what was agreeable to the divine nature.

The last place is given to the inventors of arts mechanical and liberal. The order is exact and beautiful. The first class is of those who founded society, heroes and lawgivers: the second, of those who supported it, patriots and holy priests: and the third, of those who adorned it, the inventors of the arts of life, and the recorders of worthy actions.

Virgil has all along closely followed the doctrine of the mysteries, which carefully taught that *virtue only could entitle men to happiness;* and that rites, ceremonies, lustrations, and sacrifices would not supply the want of it.

Nor has he been less studious in copying their shows and representations; in which the figures of those heroes and heroines, who were most celebrated in the writings of the ancient Greek authors, passed in procession.—(Aristid.)

But notwithstanding this entire conformity between the poet's scenes and those represented in the mysteries, something is still wanting to complete the identification: and that is, the famous *secret* of the mysteries, *the unity of the godhead*, of which so much hath been said above. Had Virgil neglected to give us this characteristic mark, though, even then, we could not but say, his intention was to represent an initiation; yet we must have been forced to own he had not done it with the utmost art. But he was too good a painter, to leave any thing ambiguous; and hath therefore concluded his hero's initiation, as was the custom, with instructing him in the Aporreta, or the doctrine of the unity. Till this was done, the initiated was not arrived to the highest stage of perfection; nor, in the fullest sense, intitled to the appellation of Epoptes.

Musæus, therefore, who had been *hierophant* at Athens, takes the place of the Sibyl, *as it was the custom to have different guides in different parts of the celebration*, and is made to conduct him to the recess where his father's shade opens to him the hidden doctrine of perfection, in these sublime words:

"First then, the divine *spirit* within sustains the heavens, the earth, and watery plains, the moon's enlightened orb, and shining stars; and the *eternal mind*, defused through all the parts of nature, actuates the whole stupendous frame and mingles with the vast body of the universe. Thence proceed the race of men and beats, the vital principles of the flying kind, and the monsters which the ocean breeds under its smooth crystal plain."

This was no other than the doctrine of the old Egyptians, as we are assured by Plato; who says they taught that Jupiter was the *spirit which pervadeth all things*.

We have shown how easily the Greek philosophy corrupted this principle into what is now called Spinozism. Here Virgil has proved his judgment to great advantage. Nothing was more abhorrent from the mysteries, than Spinozism, as it overturned the doctrine of a future state of rewards and punishments, which the mysteries so carefully inculcated; and yet the principle itself, of which Spinozism was the abuse, was cherished there, as it was the consequence of the doctrine of the *unity*, the *grand secret* of the *mysteries*. Virgil, therefore, delivers the principle, with great caution, and pure and free of the abuse; though he understood the nature of Spinozism, and in his fourth Georgic, where he delivers it, appears to have been infected with it.

The doctrine of the *unity* of the *godhead*, here contended by the author to be taught by Virgil, and as being the doctrine of the *old Egyptians*, must not be understood as opposed to the belief in the *triplicity* of the Supreme Being, an opinion universally held by the ancient world. Different nations expressed this triplicity by various names, to which they also assigned different attributes.

"The philosophers of all nations (says Ramsey, in a Dissertation on the Theory and Mythology of the Pagans) seem to have had some idea, more or less confused, of the *triplicity of the Supreme Unity*. Plato speaks of the three forms of the Divinity, which he calls *Agathos, Logos*, and *Psyche*; the *sovereign good*, which is the principle of deity; the *intelligence*, which drew the plan of the world; and the *energy*, which executed it."

An erroneous assignment is here made, by Ramsey, of the attributes or powers of the persons composing this trinity. Agathos, the sovereign good, is the *intelligence*, which drew the plan of the world; Logos or Word is the *energy* which executed it; and Psyche, is but another name for Isis, indicating the productions of the earth, which gives a finish and beauty to the whole creation. This is agreeable to the masonic trinity, which is denominated *Wisdom, Strength*, and *Beauty*.

Fontenelle gives the following curious anecdote of a responce from the Oracle of Serapis:

"Thulis, a king of Egypt, who, as is said, gave the name of *Thule* to the isle now called Iceland; his empire reaching thither was of large extent; and, being puffed up with pride, he went to the oracle of Serapis, and thus spake to it: 'Thou that art the god of fire, and who governest the *course* of the *heavens*, tell me *the truth*; was there ever, or will there ever be, one so puissant as myself?' The oracle answered him thus: 'First *God*, then the *Word* and *Spirit*, all united in one, whose power can never end. Go hence immediately, O mortal! whose life is always uncertain.' And Thulis at his going thence, had his throat cut." (Suidas.) History Oracles, p. 9, London, 1689.

The Greek inscription on the great obelisk at Rome, says Chateaubrian, was to this effect: "The Mighty God; Begotten of God; and the All-resplendent Apollo, the Spirit."—(See Knapp's Spirit. Mas. p. 102.)

The idea of the pagan trinity, according to Volney's opinion, was founded on the **three modes of action of the sun**, in the three seasons of the year. The sun thus characterized, "Is, says he, no other than the *three-eyed* Jupiter, *eye* and *sun* being expressed by the same word in most of the ancient languages of Asia. This is the origin of all the trinitary system subtilised by Pythagoras and Plato, and totally disfigured by their interpreters."—(*Ruins*, p. 159.)

Although innovations appear to have been introduced in the administration of the rites of the lesser mysteries, in Greece and Rome, particularly in the latter, still it does not appear that women, as our author supposes, were even admitted to participate in the celebrations of the greater mysteries; much less to act as hierophants, to expound what were called the *sacred secrets* therein contained. This would have been too great a departure from the original, and, moreover, exposed the secrets to too great hazard. "In Egypt the office of the priesthood is in every instance confined to the men; there are no priestesses in the service of male or female deities."—(See Bedoe's Herodotus.) And here it may be worthy of remark, that the freemasons have adhered closely to their prototype, by the total exclusion of females from their order.

Women and children, as we have seen, were freely admitted to the trifling shows and representations of the lesser mysteries, and here, it seems, women sometimes took the lead, and presided at the celebrations.

Virgil has made this distinction as pointed as possible, in the duties he assigns to the Sibyl. When she arrives in sight of Elysium, where the greater mysteries commence, her command ceases, and she resigns her office to Musæus. She was an utter stranger to the country, and applies to him for instruction. Eneas, while under her guidance, could only view at a distance, like Moses upon Mount Pisgah, the happy regions of the blessed:

> The chief beheld their chariots *from afar*,
> Their shining arms, and coursers trained to war.
> Their lances fix'd in earth—their steeds around,
> Free from their harness, graze the flow'ry ground.
> The love of horses which they had, alive,
> And care of chariots, after death survive.
> Some cheerful souls were feasting on the plain;
> Some did the song, and some the choir, maintain,
> Beneath a laurel shade, where mighty Po
> Mounts up to woods above, and hides his head below.
> To these the Sibyl thus her speech address'd,
> And first to him surrounded by the rest—
> (Tow'ring his height, and ample was his breast)—
> "Say, happy souls! divine Musæus! say,
> Where lives Anchises, and *where lies our way*
> To find the hero, for whose only sake
> We sought the dark abodes, and cross'd the bitter lake?"
> To this the sacred poet thus reply'd:
> "In no fix'd place the happy souls reside.
> In groves we live, and lie on mossy beds,
> By crystal streams, that murmur through the meads:
> But pass yon easy hills, and thence descend;
> The path conducts you to your journey's end."
> This said, *he led them* up the mountain's brow,
> And shows them all the shining fields below;
> They wind the hill, and thro' the blissful meadows go.
>
> (*Dryden's Trans.*)

The mysteries did not teach the doctrine of the unity for mere speculation; but, as we said before, to obviate certain mischiefs of polytheism, and to support the believe of a providence. Now, as a future state of rewards and punishments did not quite remove the objections to its inequalities here, they added to it the doctrine of the *metempsychosis*, or the believe of a *prior state*. (Vid Porph. de Abst. 1. iv. sect. 16. et Cic Fragm. ex lib. de Philosophia.) And this, likewise, our poet has been careful to record. For after having revealed the great *secret* of the *unity*, he goes on to speak of the metempsychosis, or transmigration, in this manner;

"All these souls whom you see, after they have rolled away a thousand years, are summoned forth by the god, in a great body to the river Lethe; to the intent that, losing memory of the past, they may reviset the upper regions, and again become willing to return into bodies."

And thence takes occasion to explain the nature and use of purgatory, which, in his hero's passage through that region, had not been done: this affords him too an opportunity for that noble episode, the procession of the hero's posterity, which passes in review before him: And with this the scene closes.

In attending the hero's progress through the three estates of the dead, we have shown, from some ancient author, at almost every step, the exact conformity of his adventures to those of the initiated in the mysteries. We shall now collect these scattered lights to a point; which will, I am persuaded, throw such a lustre on this interpretation, as to make the truth of it irresistible. To this purpose, I shall have nothing to do, but to transcribe a passage from an ancient writer, preserved by Stobæus; which professes to explain the exact conformity between death, or a real descent to the infernal regions, and initiation, where the representation of those regions was exhibited. His words are these: "The mind is affected and agitated in death, just as it is in initiation into the grand mysteries. And word answers to word as well as thing to thing: for *Teleytan* is to die; and *Teleisthai*, to be initiated. The first stage is nothing but errors and uncertainties; *laborious wanderings; a rude and fearful march through night and darkness.* And now arrived on the verge of death and initiation, every thing wears a dreadful *aspect*: it is all *horror, trembling*, and affrightment. But this scene once over, a *miraculous* and *divine light* displays itself; and shining plains and flowery meadows open on all hands before them. Here they are entertained with hymns, and dances, with the sublime doctrines of sacred knowledge, and with reverend and holy visions. And now become perfect and initiated, they are free and no longer under restraints; but *crowned*, and *triumphant*, they walk up and down the regions of the blessed; converse with pure and holy men; and *celebrate the sacred mysteries at pleasure.*"

The Son of Sirach, who was full of Grecian ideas, and hath embellished his admirable work of Ecclesiasticus with a great deal of Gentile learning, hath plainly alluded, though in few words, to these circumstances of initiation, where encouraging men to seek after *wisdom*, he says:—" At first she will walk with him by *crooked* ways, and bring *fear* and *dread* upon him, and *torment him with her discipline*, until she may trust his soul, and *try* him by her laws. Then will she return the *straight* way unto him, and *comfort* him, and show him her *secrets.*"—(Chap. iv. 17, 18.)

The conjecture of the author, that an allusion is here made to circumstances attending initiations into the mysteries, is corroborated, or, I might say, confirmed by masonry; for a known practice in the one renders it pretty certain that the same existed in the other.

In the royal arch degree, after the candidates have taken the required oath, they are told, that hey were now obligated and received as royal arch masons, but as this degree was *infinitely* more important than any of the preceeding, it was necessary for them (as before noticed) to *pass through many trials, and travel in rough and rugged ways to prove their fidelity*, before they could be *entrusted* with the more important *secrets* of this degree. They are futher told, that though they could not discover the path they were to travel, they were under the direction of a *faithful guide*, who would "bring the *blind* by a way they know not, and led them in *paths* they had not known; who would make *darkness light* before them, and *crooked things straight*; who would do these things, and not forsake them." (Isaiah 42, v. 16.)—Bernard.

The progress finished, and every thing over, Eneas and his guide are let out again to the upper regions, through the ivory gate of *dreams.* A circumstance borrowed from Homer, and very happily applied to this subject; for, as Euripides elegantly expresses it,

"A dream is the lesser mysteries of death."

But, besides this of ivory, there was another of horn. Through the fisrt issued fasle visions; and through the latter, true.

Servius, with the spirit of a rank grammarian, who seldom finds any thing to stop at but a solecism in expression, says very readily, "Vult autem intelligi, falsa esse omnia quæ dixit. He would have you understand by this, that all he has been saying is false and groundless." Other critics give the same solution. Ruæus, one of the best, may speak for them all; "When, therefore, Virgil sends Eneas forth through the ivory gate, he clearly indicates that whatever he has said in regard to the infernal regions, is to be reckoned among the fables."

This interpretation is strengthened by Virgil's being an Epicurean; and making the same conclusion in his second Georgic:

"Felix, qui potuit cognoscere causas,
Atque metus omnes et inexorabile fatum
Subjecit pedibus, strepitumque Acherontis avari!"

"Happy is he who can know the causes of things, and tread under foot all fear, inexorable fate, and the noise of greedy Acheron."

But Virgil wrote, not for the amusement of women and children over a winter's fire, in the taste of the Milesian fables; but for the use of men and citizens; to instruct them in the duties of humanity and society. The purpose, therefore, of such a writer when he treats of a future state, must be to make the doctrine interesting to his reader, and useful in civil life: Virgil hath done the first, by bringing his Hero to it through the most perilous achievement; and the second, by appropriating the rewards and punishments of that state to *virtue* and to *vice* only.

The truth is, the difficulty can never be gotten over, but by supposing the desent to signify an initiation into the mysteries. This will unriddle the enigma, and restore the poet to himself. And if this was Virgil's meaning, it is to be presumed, he would give some private mark to ascertain it: for which no place was so proper as the conclusion. He has, therefore, with a beauty of invention peculiar to himself, made this fine improvement on Homer's story of the two gates; and imagining that of horn for true visions, and that of ivory for false, insinuates by the first the reality of another state; and by the second, the shadowy representations of it in the shows of the mysteries: so that, not the things objected to Eneas, but the scenes of them only, were false; as they lay not in *hell* but in the *temple* of *Ceres*.

But though the visions which issued from the ivory gate were unsubstantial, as being only representative; yet I make no question, but the ivory gate itself was real. It appears, indeed, to be no other than that sumptuous door of the temple, through which the initiated came out, when the celebration was over. This temple was of an immense bigness.*

---

* Ancient authors inform us that the festivals of Ceres sometimes brought to Eleusis thirty thousand of the initiated, without including those who came only from motives of curiosity. These were not present at all the ceremonies. To the more secret, no doubt, were only admitted the small number of novices who every year received the last seal of initiation, and some of those who had received it long before.

Behind the temple, on the western side, is still to be seen a terrace, cut in the rock itself, and raised eight or nine feet above the floor of the temple. Its length is

And now, having occasionally, and by parts only, said so much of these things, it will not be amiss, in conlusion to give one general and concise idea of the whole. I suppose the substance of the celebration to be a kind of drama of the history of Ceres, which afforded opportunity to represent the three particulars, about which the mysteries were principally concerned. The rise and establishment of civil society. The doctrine of a future state of rewards and punishments. The error of polytheism, and the principle of the unity.

But here let it be observed, that the *secrets* of the mysteries were unfolded both by *words* and *actions:* of which Aristides, quoted above, gives the reason; "That so the *sounds* and *sights* might mutually assist each other in making an impression on the minds of the initiated." The *error of polytheism* therefore was as well exposed by the *dark wanderings* in the subterraneous passages through which the initiated began his course, as by the information given him by the hierophant: and the *truth of the unity* as strongly illustrated by ths *autopton agalma* the *self seen image*, the diffusive *shining light*, as by the *hymn of Orpheus*, or the *speech of Anchises*.

On the whole, if I be not greatly decieved, the view in which I place this famous episode, not only clears up a number of difficulties inexplicable on any other scheme; but likewise ennobles, and gives a graceful finishing to the whole poem; for now the episode is seen to be an assential part of the main subject, which is the erection of a civil policy and a religion. For custom had made initiation into the mysteries a necessary preparative to that arduous undertaking.

To conclude, the principles here assumed, in explaining this famous poetical fiction, are, I presume, such as give solidity, as well as light, to what is deduced from them; and are, perhaps, the only principles from which any thing reasonable can be deduced in a piece of criticism of this nature. For from what I have shown was taught and represented in the mysteries, I infer that Eneas's *descent into hell* signifies an *initiation;* because of the exact conformity, in all circumstances, between what Virgil relates of his hero's adventure, and what antiquity delivers

---

about 270 feet, and its breadth in some places 44. At the northern end is to be seen the remains of a chapel, to go up into which there were several steps.

I conjecture that on this terrace was exhibited the scenery; that it was divided lengthwise into three great galleries, the two first of which represented the region of trial, and that of the infernal shades; and the third, covered with earth, presented groves and meadows to the view of the initiated, who from thence went up into the chapel, where their eyes were dazzled by the splendor of the statue of the goddess. (Travels of Anacharsis.)—Edit.

concerning the shows and doctrines of those mysteries, into which heroes were wont to be initiated.

The view taken by bishop Warburton of the purport of the sixth book of the Eneid, was new, and caluculated to excite the deep attention of the learned world. Accordingly various opinions were entertained for and against the correctness of the position assumed by him. Among the critics who entered the lists in opposition to the author, was the celebrated historian Gibbon. And this, he says, was his first publication in English. His remarks on the subject are contained in the third volume of his miscellaneous work; which he introduces as follows:

"The allegorical interpretation which the bishop of Gloucester has given of the sixth book of the Eneid, seems to have been very favorably received by the public. Many writers, both at home and abroad, have mentioned it with approbation, or at least with esteem; and I have more than once heard it alleged, in the conversation of scholars, as an ingenious improvement on the plain and obvious sense of Virgil. As such, it is not undeserving the notice of a candid critic; nor can the inquiry be void of entertainment, whilst Virgil is our constant theme.

"I shall readily allow, what I believe may in general be true, that the mysteries exhibited a theatrical representation of all that was believed or imagined of the lower world; that the aspirant was conducted through the mimic scenes of Erebus, Tartarus, and Elysium; and that a warm enthusiast, in describing these awful spectacles, might express himself as if he had actually visited the infernal regions. It is not surprising that the *copy* was like the *original;* but it still remains undetermined, whether Virgil intended to describe the *original* or the *copy.*"

If the copy was a true representation of the original, of what consequence is it which the poet took as his sampler? But, as it was more easy to procure a correct description of the spectacles exhibited in the temple of the Eleusinian Ceres, than of what takes place in the regions below, it is most probable Virgil chose the former. Besides, it may be remarked, that the description of the infernal regions was doubtless first matured in the mysteries. No author, it is presumed, had before their establishment, ever given any thing like a detailed account of such place. They therefore, properly speaking, are the *original*, and the *parallel* is to be found in Virgils description of Eneas's descent.

Mr. Voltaire showed great fickleness in his opinion on this subject; sometimes giving it in favor of Warburton's hypothesis, and at others, the contrary. Speaking of the Eleusinian mysteries, (tome. xvi, p. 162) he says,—

"The mysterious ceremonies of Ceres were an imitation of those of Isis. Those who had committed crimes confessed and expiated them: they fasted, they purified themselves, and gave alms. All the ceremonies were held secret, under the religious sanction of an oath, to render them more venerable. The mysteries were celebrated in the night, to inspire a holy horror. They represented a kind of tragedy in which the spectacle exposed to view the happiness of the just and the torments of the wicked. The greatest men of antiquity, the Platos, the Ciceros have eulogized these mysteries, which had not then degenerated from their primative purity.

"Very learned men have supposed that the sixth book of the Eneid was a description of what passed in these secret and celebrated shows." Again, he says, "The sixth book of the Eneid is only a description of the mysteries of Isis and the Eleusinian Ceres."

He afterwards recants this opinion, and says, "I think I see a description of the Eleusinian Ceres, in Claudian's poem on the *Rape of Proserpine much clearer* than I can see any in the sixth book of the Eneid. Virgil lived under a prince who joined to all his other bad qualities that of wishing to pass for a religious character; who was probably initiated in these mysteries himself, the better thereby to impose upon the people: and who would not have tolerated what would have been pretended to be such decided profanation."

Why, Augustus was the hero of the poem; it was for his honor and glory that the poet labored. He was, says our author, *shadowed in the person of Eneas;* and would not, therefore, probably have been very scrupulous about a vague exposition of the mysteries, while it tended to his own glorification.

"Claudian, (says Warburton,) professes openly to treat of the Eleusinian mysteries, at a time when they were in little veneration." It is not strange, therefore, that Mr. Voltaire should *see a description of the Eleusinian Ceres, in Claudian's poem, much clearer than in the sixth book of the Eneid;* the author of which evidently not intending that his object should be generally known.

Voltaire seems frequently to have written off hand, without subjecting himself to the trouble of rigid scrutiny; and, indeed, he wrote so much, and upon such a variety of topics, that it would appear impossible that he should bestow strict attention to them all. In the present case, his first impressions appear to have been founded on the opinions of the *learned men* he alludes to, and he probably adopted a contrary belief in like manner, without an attentive examination of the subject.

Bishop Warburton was probably occupied many years in the composition of his learned work; he had thoroughly studied the subject, and it is confidently believed that this application of the sixth book of the Eneid to the mysteries will stand the test of the most severe criticism.

The Abbé Barthelemi, in an article on the mysteries, in his "Travels of Anacharsis," quotes the Eneid in a description of them, as if no question then existed in regard to Virgil's views.

CHAPTER IV.

THE METAMORPHOSIS OF APULEIUS: AND THE AMOUR OF CUPID AND PSYCHE.

Thus far concerning the use of the mysteries to society. How essential they were esteemed to religion, we may understand by the *Metamorphosis of Apuleius;* a book, indeed, which from its very first appearance hath passed for a trivial fable. Capitolinus, in the life of Clodius Albinus, where he speaks of that kind of tales which disconcert the gravity of philosophers, tells us that Severus could not bear with patience the honors the Senate had conferred on Albinus; especially their distinguishing him with the title of *learned*, who was grown old in the study of old-wives-fables, such as the Milesian-Punic tales of his countryman and favorite, Apuleius.

The writer of the Metamorphosis, however, was one of the gravest and most virtuous, as well as most learned philosophers of his age. Albinus appears to have gone further into the true character of this work, than his rival Severus. And if we may believe Marcus Aurelius, who calls Albinus, "A man of experience, of demure life, and grave morals," he was not a man to be taken with such trifling amusements as Milesian fables. His fondness therefore for the Metamorphosis of Apuleius shows that he considered it in another light. And who so likely to be let into the author's true design, as Albinus, who lived very near his time, and was of Adrumetum in the neighborhood of Carthage, where Apuleius sojourned and studied, and was distinguished with public honors? The work is indeed of a different character from what some ancients have represented it; and even from what modern critics have pretended to discover of it. Those ancients, who stuck in the outside, considered it, without refinement, as an idle fable; the moderns, who could not reconcile a work of that nature to the gravity of the author's character, have supposed it a thing of more importance, and no less than a general satire on the vices of those times.

But this is far short of the matter. The author's main purpose was not to satirize the specific vices of his age, though to enliven his fable, and for the better carrying on his story, he hath employed many circumstances of this kind, but to recommend *Pagan religion*, as the only cure for *all vices whatsoever*.

To give what we have to say its proper force, we must consider the real character of the writer. Apuleius, of Madaura in Africa, was a devoted Platonist; and, like the Platonists of that age, an inveterate enemy to Christianity. His zeal for the honor of *philosophy* is seen in that solemn affirmation, when convened before a court of justice, "I have never derogated ought from the honor of philosophy, which is more precious to me than life." His superstitious attachment to the religion of his country is seen in his immoderate fondness for the mysteries. He was initiated, as he tells us, into almost all of them; and in some, bore the most distinguished offices. In his Apology before the proconsul of Africa, he says, "Will you have me relate what kind of things those were, which wrapped up in a napkin, I confided to the house of Pontianus? You shall be allowed. I have been initiated in Greece into many mysteries. I carefully guard certain of their signs and tokens which have been committed to me by the priests. I say nothing unusual, nothing unknown. Ye who are present know what thing it is of father Bacchus Symmistæ which you keep concealed at home, and silently venerate apart from the profane. But I, as I have said, through love of truth, and duty to the gods, have learnt numerous mysteries, and very many rites, and various ceremonies. Nor do I make up this for the occasion: but it is about three years ago that shortly after my arrival at Oea, in a public discourse on the majesty of Æsculapius I made some declaration, and enumerated whatever mysteries I knew. That discourse is very celebrated; is generally read; is in the hands of every body,—commended to the pious people of Oea, not so much by my eloquence, as by the mention of Æsculapius. Can it then appear strange to any body who has any knowledge of religion, that a man versed in so many mysteries of the gods should keep certain holy trifles in his house? I am accustomed wherever I go to take with me the image of some god packed up among my books, and on festivals to worship it with incense and wine, and sometimes with sacrifices."

His great devotion to Paganism, therefore, must needs have been attended with an equal aversion to Christianity; and it is more than probable, that the oration he speaks of as made in honor of Æsculapius, was in the number of those invectives, at that time so well received by the enemies of our holy faith. For, not to insist on the success of his oration, which, he tells us, was in every body's hands, a thing common to discourses on subjects that engage the public attention, but rarely the fortune of such stale ware as panegyrics on a God long worn into an establishment; not, I say, to insist upon this, we may observe that

Æsculapius was one of those ancient heroes, who were employed, by the defenders of Paganism, to oppose to Jesus; and the circumstances of Æsculapius's story made him the fittest of any in fabulous antiquity, for that purpose.

Having seen what there was in the common passion of his sect, and in his own fond mode of superstition, to indispose Apuleius to Christianity, let us inquire what private provocation he might have to prejudice him against it: for, a private provocation, I am persuaded, he had; occasioned by a personal injury done him by one of this profession; which, I suppose, did not a little contribute to exasperate his bigotry. He had married a rich widow, against the will of her first husband's relations; who endeavored to set aside the marriage on pretence of his employing sorcery and enchantments to engage her affections. Of this, he was judicially accused by his wife's brother-in-law, Licinius Æmilianus, before the Proconsul of Africa. Now his accuser, if I am not much mistaken, was a Christian, though this interesting circumstance hath escaped his commentators.

Now irreligion and atheism, we know, was the name Christianity at that time went by, for having dared to renounce the whole family of the gentile gods in a lump. Æmilianus had made such clear work, that there was not so much as an anointed stone, or a tree adorned with consecrated garlands, to be found throughout his whole Farm. That the Atheism of Æmilianus was of this sort, and no *courtley or philosophic* impiety, appears from his character and station. He was neither a fine gentleman or a profound inquirer into nature; characters indeed which are sometimes found to be above religion; but a mere rustic in his life and manners. Now plain unpolished men in such a station are never without some religion or other; when we find Æmilianus, therefore, not of the *established*, we must needs conclude him to be a *sectary* and a *Christian*. His neglect of his country gods was not a mere negative affront; of forgetfulness. He gloried in being their despiser; and took kindly to the name of Mezentius, as a title of honor,—(alterum, quod libentius audit, ob deorum contemptum, Mezentius,) which I would consider as a further mark of a Christian convict. He even held it an abomination so much as to put his hand to his lips, (according to the mode of adoration in those times,) when he passed by a heathen temple; (nefas habet adorandi gratia manum labris admovere,) the most characteristic mark of a *primitive confessor*, by which he could never be mistaken; nor, one would think, so long overlooked.

The aversion therfore, which Apuleius had contracted to his Christian accuser, and we see, by his apology, it was in no ordinary degree, would without doubt increase his prejudice to that religion. I am persuaded he gave the character of the Baker's wife, in his golden ass for no other reason than to outrage our holy faith. He draws her stained with all the vices that could fall to the share of a woman; and then, to finish all, he makes her a Christian.

Let us see now how this would influence his writings. There was nothing the Philosophers of that time had more at heart, especially the Platonists and Pythagoreans, than the support of sinking Paganism. This service, as hath been occasionally remarked they performed in various ways and manners: some by allegorizing their theology; some by spiritualizing their philosophy; and some as Jamblicus and Philostratus, by writing the lives of their Heroes, to oppose to that of Christ; others again, as Porphyry, with this view, collected their oracles; or as Melanthius, Menander, Hicesius, and Sotades wrote descriptive encomiums on their Mysteries. Which last, as we shall now show, was the province undertaken by Apuleius; his Metamorphosis being nothing else but one continued recommendation of them.

But let us enquire into the motives our author might have for entering at all into the defence of Paganism: His reasons for choosing this topic of defence, the recommendation of the mysteries.

As to his defence of paganism in general, we may observe, that works of this kind were very much in fashion, especially amongst the philosophers of our author's sect. He was, as we have seen, most superstitiously devoted to pagan worship: and, he bore a personal spite and prejudice to the Christian profession.

As to his making the defence of the mysteries his chioce, still stronger reasons may be assigned. These were the rites to which he was so peculiarly devoted, that he had contrived to be initiated into all the mysteries of note, in the Roman world; and in several of them had borne the most distinguished offices. The mysteries being at this time become extremely corrupt, and consequently, in discredit, needed an able and zealous apologist: both of which qualities met eminently in Apuleius. The corruptions were of two kinds, debaucheries and magic. Their debaucheries we have taken notice of, above: their magic will be considered hereafter. But, our author's close attachment to mysterious rites was, without question, the very thing that occasioned all those suspicions and reports, which ended in an accusation of magic: and considering what hath been said of the corrupt state of the mysteries, the reader will not wonder at it.

Such then being the general character of the mysteries, and of this their great devotee, nothing was more natural than his projecting their defence; which at the same time, that it concurred to the support of paganism in general, would vindicate his own credit, together with an institution of which he was so immoderately fond. And the following considerations are sufficient to show, that the Metamorphosis was written after his Apology: for, his accusers never once mention the fable of the *golden ass* to support their charge of magic, though they were in great want of proofs, and this lay so ready for their purpose. He positively asserts before the tribunal of Maximus Claudius that he had never given the least occasion to suspect him of magic: "Nusquam passus sum vel exiguam suspicionem magiæ consistere."

Now antiquity considered initiation into the *mysteries as a delivery from a living death of vice, brutality, and misery, and the beginning of a new life of virtue, reason, and happiness.* This therefore, was the very circumstance which our author chose for the subject of his recommendation.

And as in the mysteries, their moral and divine truths were represented in *shows* and *allegories*, so in order to comply with this method of instruction, and in imitation of the ancient masters of wisdom, who borrowed their manner of teaching from thence, he hath artfully insinuated his doctrine in an agreeable fable; and the fittest one could conceive for his purpose, as will be seen when we come to examine it.

The foundation of this allegory was a Milesian fable, a species of polite trifling then much in vogue, and not very unlike the modern *Arabian tales*. To allure his readers, therefore, with the promise of a fashionable work, he introduces his Metamorphosis in this manner: "And I too will deliver to you various fables in this Milesian style, and delight your ears in a gentle whisper;" plainly intimating that there was someting of more consequence at bottom. But they took him at his word: and, never troubled their heads about a further meaning. The outside engaged all their attention, and sufficiently delighted them; as we may gather from the early title it bore of *Asinus Aureus*:[*]

---

[*] From the beginning of one of Pliny's epistles, I suspect that *Aureæ* was the common title given to the *Milesian*, and such like tales as strollers used to tell for a piece of money to the rabble in a circle. Pliny's words are these—assem para et accipe *auream* fabulam. l. ii, Ep. 20.

unless we will rather suppose it to have been bestowed by the few intelligent readers in the secret; for, in spite of the author, a secret it was, and so all along continued.

Upon one of these popular fables, he chose to ingraft his instruction; taking a celebrated tale from the collections of one Lucius of Patræ; who relates his transformation into an Ass, and his adventures under that shape. Lucian has epitomised this story, as Apuleius seems to have paraphrased it: and the subject being a metamorphosis, it admirably fitted his purpose; as the metempsychosis to which that superstition belongs, was one of the fundamental doctrines of the mysteries.

The fable opens with the representation of a young man, personated by himself, sensible of the advantages of *virtue* and *piety*, but immoderately fond of *pleasure*, and as curious of *magic*. He gives a loose to his vicious appetite, and the crimes and follies into which they lead him soon ends in his transformation to a brute.

This contrivance of the introductory part is artful; and finely insinuates the great moral of the piece, that brutality attends vice as its punishment: and punishment by actual transformation was keeping up to the popular opinion.

St. Austin permitted himself to doubt whether Apuleius's account of his change into an ass was not a true relation. I shall say nothing to this extravagant doubt, but only observe, that it appears from hence, that St. Austin esteemed Apuleius a profligate in his manners, and addicted to the superstitions of magic.

But to proceed with his plan. Having now shown himself thoroughly brutalized by his crimes; he goes on to represent at large the miseries of that condition, in a long detail of his misadventures; in the course of which he fell, by turns, under the dominion of every vicious passion; though the incidents are chiefly confined to the mischiefs of unlawful love: and this, with much judgement, as one of the principal ends of the mysteries was to curb and subdue this inordinance, which brings more general and lasting misery upon mankind than all the other. And as it was the great moral of his piece to show that *pure religion*, such as a Platonic philosopher esteemed pure, was the only remedy for human corruption; so, to prevent the abuse or mistake of this capital principle, he takes care to inform us, that an attachment to superstitious and corrupt religion does but plunge the wretched victim into still greater miseries. This he finely illustrates, in the history of his adventures with the *begging priests of Cybele*; whose enormities are related in the eighth and ninth books; and whose corrupt mysteties are intended as a contrast to the pure rites of Isis; with which in a very studied description and encomium he concludes the Fable.

In the mean time, matters growing from bad to worse, and Lucius plunged deeper and deeper in the sink of vice, his affairs come to a crisis. For this is one great beauty in the conduct of the fable, that every change of station, while he remains a brute, makes his condition still more wretched and deplorable. And being now about to perpetrate one of the most shocking enormities; Nature, though so deeply brutalized, *revolts;* he abhors the idea of his projected crime; he evades his keepers; he flies to the sea-shore; and, in this solitude, begins to reflect more seriously on his lost condition. This is finely imagined, for we often see men, even after a whole life of horrors, come suddenly to themselves on the hideous aspect of some monster-vice too frightful even for an hardened conscience to endure. Nor is it with less judgment that the author makes these beginnings of reformation confirmed by solitude; when the unhappy victim of pleasure hath broken loose from the companions and partakers of his follies.

And now, a more intimate acquaintace of his hopeless state obliges him to fly to heaven for relief. The moon is in full splendor, and the awful silence of the night inspires him with sentiments of religion.

He then purifies himself in the manner prescribed by Pythagoras, the philosopher most addicted to initiations of all the early sages; as Apuleius, of all the later; and so makes his prayer to the moon or *Isis,* invoking her by her several names of the *Eleusinian Ceres,* the *celestial Venus, Diana and Proserpine,* when betaking himself to repose, she appears to him in a dream, under that shining image so much spoken of by the *mystics,* as representing the divine nature in general.*

These several symbolic attributes, [as described by Apuleius, but here omitted,] the *lucid round,* the *snakes,* the *ears of corn,* and the *sistrum,* represent the tutelar Deities of the Hecatæan, Bacchic, Eleusinian and Isiac mysteries. That is, the mystic rites in general: for whose sake the allegory was invented. As the black Palla in which she is wrapped, embroidered with a *silver moon,* and *stars,* denotes the *time,* in which the mysteries were celebrated, namely

---

* Artemidorus says, that for a man to dream that *Ceres Proserpine,* or *Bacchus* appears to him, betokens some extraordinary good fortune to happen to him. This popular divination by dreams was apparently founded on the common opinion of the advantages attending initiation into the mysteries. The ancient *Onirocritics* were not founded on the arbitary fancies of the impostors who professed that art, but on the customs and superstitions of the times, and with a principal reference to the *Egyptian Hieroglyphics* and *mysteries.*

in the dead of *night*; which was so constant and inseparable a circumstance, that the author calls initiation, *noctis societas*.*

"Behold, Lucius, I, moved by thy prayers, am present with thee; I, who am Nature, the parent of things, the queen of all the elements, the primordial progeny of ages, the Supreme of Divinities, the sovereign of the spirits of the dead, the first of the celestials, and the uniform resemblance of gods and goddesses. I who rule by my nod the luminous summits of the heavens, the salubrious breezes of the sea, and the deplorable silences of the realms beneath: and whose one divinity the whole orb of the earth venerates under a manifold form, by different rites, and a variety of appalletions. Hence the primogenial Phrygians call me Pessinuntica, the mother of the gods; the Attic Aborigines, Cecropian Minerva; the floating Cyprians, Paphian Venus; the arrow-bearing Cretans, Diana Dictynna; the three tongued Sicilians, Stygian Proserpine; and the Eleusinians, the ancient goddess Ceres. Some also call me Juno, others Bellona, others Hecate, and others Rhamnusia. And those who are illuminated by the incipient rays of that divinity, the sun, when he rises, viz. the Ethiopians, the Arii, and Egyptians skilled in ancient learning, worshipping me by ceremonies perfectly appropriate, call me by my true name *queen Isis*." This was exactly adapted to the *design* of the mysteries; and preparatory to the communication of the *aporreta*. It had likewise this further use, to patch up and recommend the pagan religions; by showing that their *Polytheism* consisted in nothing else than in giving the *Supreme God* various *names*, merely expressive of his various *attributes*. This was the fashionable coloring, which, after the appearance of Christianity, the advocates of paganism employed to blanch their Idolatry. I will only observe further that the words *the Egyptians worshipping me with ceremonies perfectly appropriate*, insinuate what was true, that all *mysterious* worship came *first* from *Egypt*; this people having penetrated furthest into the nature of the gods: as the calling *her* who represents the mysteries in general *rerum natura parens*, shows plainly what were the *aporreta* of them all.

Parent *Nature* then reveals to Lucius the means of his recovery. Her *festival* was on the following day; when there was to be a *pro-*

---

* Masonic meetings are nocturnal, and the aprons of the fraternity are generally ornamented with figures of the *sun*, *moon*, and *seven stars*, or *planets*; which shows that the principal design of the institution was something very different from the mechanical occupation of masonry. They show, indeed, that it was founded on *Sabeism*, the worship of the stars.—Edit.

cession of her *votaries*. The priest who led it up, would have a chaplet of roses in his hand, which had the virtue to restore him to his former shape. But as breaking through a habit of vice is, of all things, the most difficult; she adds encouragements to her promises, "Nor should you fear any thing pertaining to my concerns as difficult. For in this very same moment of time in which I come to you, being there also present, I order my priest in a dream to do those things which are to be done hereafter." Alluding, to what was taught in the mysteries, that, the assistance of Heaven was always present to second the efforts of virtue. But in return for the favor of releasing him from his brutal shape, that is of reforming his manners by initiation, she tells him she expected the service of his whole life; and this, the mysteries required. Nor should his service go unrewarded, for he should have a place in *Elysium* hereafter; and this, too, the mysteries promised.

Lucius is at lenght confirmed in his resolution of aspiring to a life of virtue. And on this change of his dispositions, and entire conquest of his passions, the author finely represents all nature as putting on a new face of cheerfulness and gaiety. "All things likewise, independent of my peculiar joy, seemed to me to exult with such great hilarity that I might have thought that cattle of every kind, every house, and even the day itself, rejoiced with a serene countenance." And to enjoy Nature, in these her best conditions, was the boasted privilege of the *Initiated*, as we may see from a Chorus in the *Frogs* of Aristophanes.

And now the *procession*, in honor of Isis, begins. Where by the way, we must observe, that the two first days of the celebration of the Eleusinian mysteries are plainly described: the one called *agyrmos*, from the multitude assembled; the other *alase mystai*, from the procession made to the sea-shore. "Then there was an influx of a crowd of those who had been initiated in the *sacred rites* of the goddess, respledent with the *pure whiteness of linen garments*. In the next place, the images of the gods, carried by the priests of Isis, proceeded, not disdaining to walk with the feet of men; *this* terriffically raising a *canine* head; but *that* being the messenger of the infernal gods, and of those in the realms beneath, with an erect face, partly black, and partly of a golden color, bearing in his left hand a *caduceus*, and shaking in his right hand branches of the flourishing palm tree; whose footsteps, a *crow*, in an erect position, immediately followed. This crow was the prolific resemblance of the all-parent goddess, and was carried on the sholders of one of the *blessed* servants of this divinity and who acted the part of a mimic as he walked; another carried a *cista* or *chest*, containing *arcana*, and *perfectly concealing* the *mystic symbols* of a magnificent religion. And another bore in his *happy bosom* the venerable effigies of the *Supreme Divinity*, which was not similar to any cattle, bird or wild beast, nor even to man; but being venerable for the subtilty by which it was invented, and also for its novelty, was an ineffable indication of a more *sublime religion*, and which was to be *concealed* with the *greatest silence.*"* The priest or hierophant of the rites leads up the train of the initiated with a garland of roses in his hand. Lucius approaches, devours the roses, and is according to the promise of the goddess, restored to his natural form, by which, as we have said, no more was meant than a change of manners from vice to virtue. And this the author plainly intimates by making the goddess thus address him under his brutal form, "Immediately divest yourself of the hide of that worst of beasts, and which for *some time since* has been to me detestable." For an Ass was so far from being detestable, that it was employed in the celebration of her rites; and was ever found in the retinue of Osiris or Bacchus. The garland plainly represents that which the aspirants were *crowned* with at their initiation; just as the *virtue* of the *roses* designs the mysteries. At his transformation he had been told, that *roses* were to restore him to humanity † so that amidst all his adventures, he had still this remedy in view.

Our author proceeds to tell us, that the people wondered at this instantaneous metamorphosis. "The people admire, and the religious venerate so evident an indication of the power of the Supreme Divinity, and the magnificence and facility of my restoration." For

---

* I have given a more full account of this procession, from the work of Apuleius, than is copied by Warburton. In the processions of the London masons, before noticed, at laying the foundation stone, and the dedication, of freemasons' hall, in 1775, and 1776, among other things, were carried, three pitchers, containing corn, wine, and oil; the bible; *wand* or *caduceus*; a *cista* or *chest*, here called the *lodge* &c. After the ceremony of laying the foundation stone, "the brethren proceeded through the city in procession, without *exposing* any of the *ensignia* of the order." Smith.—Edit.

† The modern masomic degree of Rose-Cross seems to allude to this ridiculous conceit regarding the virtue of roses. The following dialogue takes place between the master and senior warden:—"Do you know the *Pelican?*—I do.—What does it signify?—*Among us* it is a symbol of the *Saviour* of the world, and of his *perfect humanity*. What is the object of the degree of Knights of the Rose-Cross?—To lead us to respect the decrees of the Most High, who is able to *reinstamp* his image on us." To reinstamp is here intended to signify the restoration to a former state; which is exactly what occurred to Lucius, when in his *asinine* condition, by the *eating* of *roses*. The Pelican is a Roman Catholic symbol of the Saviour, arising from the fable that this bird perforates its breast, and suffers its young to feed upon the blood issuing therefrom.

The Saviour, in the ritual of the Catholic Church, is thus addressed: "*O Pelican Jesus! cleanse us with thy blood, one drop of which is sufficient to purify a world.*"

The degree of Rose-Cross was invented in France, a Roman Catholic country.—*Edit.*

the mysteries boasted the power of giving a sudden and entire change to the mind and affections. And the advocates of paganism against Christianity used to oppose this boast to the real and miraculous efficacy of grace.

As soon as Lucius had recovered the integrity of his nature by initiation, the priest covers him, naked as he was, with a *linen* garment. A habit always bestowed upon the aspirant, on his admission to the mysteries; the *rationale* of which, Apuleius himself gives us in his apology.* When all was over, the priest accosts his penitent in the following manner. "O Lucius! you have at length arrived at the port of quiet, and the altar of pity, having endured many and various labors, and great tempests of fortune, and been tossed about by mighty waves of calamity. Assume now a more joyful countenance, and more adapted to that *white garment* which you wear. Attend the pomp of your *saviour goddess* with triumphant steps. *Let the irreligious see, let them see and acknowledge their error.* Behold Lucius, rejoicing in the providence of the great Isis, and freed from his pristine miseries, triumphs in his own fortune."†

Here the moral of the fable is delivered in plain terms; and, in this moral, all we have advanced, concerning the purpose of the work, fully confirmed. It is expressly declared, that vice and inordinate curiosity were the causes of Lucius's disasters; from which the only relief was *initiation* into the *mysteries*. Whereby the author would insinuate that nothing was more abhorrent from those holy rites than *debauchery* and *magic;* the two enormities they were then commonly suspected to encourage.

It hath been observed above, that, by Lucius's return to his proper form, was meant his initiation; and accordingly, that return is called, as initiation was, *the being born again,—ut renatus* quodammodo,

---

* "Wool, the excretion of the most sluggish body belonging to the herd, was for that reason, pronounced by Orpheus and Pythagoras, to be a *profane* raiment. But flax, truly the most cleanly of the best production of the earth, not only cloathed and vailed the most holy priests of Egypt, but was used also to cover the sacred utensils." Apul. p. 64.

† "Whilst the *apron* with which we [masons] are *cloathed indicates* a disposition of *innocence*, and belies not the wearer's heart, let the ignorant deride and scoff on: superior to the ridicule and malice of the *wicked*, we will enfold ourselves in the garb of our own virtue; and safe in our self-approving conscience, stand unmoved against the persecutions of adversity.

"The raiment which *truly implies* the innocence of the heart, is a badge more honorable than ever was devised by kings; the Roman eagle, with all the orders of knighthood, are thereunto inferior." Smith.

"Formerly masons used to be cloathed in *white* during Lodge hours, which practice is still followed in many lodges in Germany, France, and Holland: but in England, the *white apron* is only remaining." Ibid.—Edit.

and—*sua providentia quodammodo renatos;* but this was only to the *lesser,* not the *greater mysteries.* The first was to *purify* the mind: hence it was called by the ancients, kakias aphairesin, *a separation from evil:* the second was to *enlighten* it, when purified, and to bring it to the knowledge of *divine secrets.* Hence they named the one Katharsin, and the other Teleiothta, *purification* and *perfection.** The first is here represented in the incident of Lucius's being restored to humanity by the use of *roses:* The second, as the matter of chief importance, the author treats more circumstantially.

He begins with making the priest take occasion, from the benefit already received, to press Lucius to enter into the *greater* mysteries of Isis.

But at the same time makes him inform the candidate, that nothing was to be precipitated: for that not only many previous rites and ceremonies, concerning religious diet, and abstinence from profane food, were to be observed; but that the aspirants to these higher mysteries were to wait for a *call.*

The author, by the doubts and apprehensions which retarded his initiation, first gives us to understand, that the highest degree of sanctity was required of those who entered into the mysteries.

These difficulties being surmounted, he is initiated with the accustomed ceremonies. He then makes his prayer, in which the grand aporreta of the mysteries is still more plainly referred to.

"Thou, O holy and perpetual *saviour* of the human race, being always munificent in cherishing mortals, dost employ the sweet affection of a mother in the misfortunes of the miserable. Nor is there any day or night, or even a slender moment of time, which passes unattended by thy benevolent interpositions. Thou protectest men both by sea and land, and dispersing the storms of life, dost extend thy salutary right hand, by which thou drawest back the enextricably twisted thread of the Fates, and dost mitigate the tempests of inclement fortune, and restrain the noxious courses of the stars. The supernal gods reverence thee, and those in the realms beneath attentively observe thy nod. Thou rollest the sphere of the universe round the steady poles, dost illuminate the sun, govern the world, and tread on the dark realms of Tartarus. The stars move responsive to thy command,† the gods rejoice in thy

---

* The masonic "Degree of *Perfection,* or the *grand elect, perfect,* and *sublime* mason," it may be presumed, is entitled to the appellation of *Teleiothta.*—Edit.

† *Respondent cidera.* This, I suppose, relates to the *music* of the *spheres.* The image is noble and sublime. It is taken from the *consent* in the lyre, to answer to, and obey the hand of the master who had put them into tune.

divinity, the hours and seasons return by thy appointment, and the elements reverence thy decree. By thy nod blasts of wind blow, the clouds are nourished, seeds germinate, and blossoms increase. Birds swiftly pass through the tracks of the air, wild beasts wandering on the mountains, serpents concealed in the ground, and the enormous monsters that swim in the sea, are terrified at the majesty which invests thy divinity, etc."

The affair thus over, the author, in the next place, takes occasion, agreeably to his real practice and opinions, to recommend a *multiplicity of initiations.* He tells us how Isis counseled him to enter into the mysteries of Osiris: how, after that she invited him to a *third* initiation: and then rewarded him for his *accumulated piety* with an abundance of temporal blessings.

All this considered, we can no longer doubt but that the true design of his work was to recommend initiation into the mysteries, in opposition to the new religion. We see the catastrophe of the piece, the whole Eleventh Book, entirely taken up with it; and composed with the greatest seriousness and superstition.

And, surely, nothing could be better conceived, to recommend the mysteries, than the idea of such a plan; or better contrived than his execution of it. In which, he omits no circumstance that might be plausibly opposed to Christianity; or that might be recommended, with advantage, to the magistrate's favor: as where he tells us, that in these rites, they prayed for the prosperity of all orders in the State,—" For the great Emperor, the senate, the equestrian order, and for all the Roman people."

This interpretation will throw new light on every part of the *golden ass.* But I have been so long upon the subject, that I have only time to give one instance; and this, chiefly because it reflects it back again on the general interpretation of the fable.

The Amour of Cupid and Psyche.

In the fifth and sixth books is the long episode of *Cupid and Psyche,*[*] visibly allegorical throughout; and entirely foreign to all the rest of the

---

[*] In order to a due understanding of the Fable, it is necessary to know the nature of the characters upon which it is founded.

"Psyche, (Greek, the soul or life) a goddess by which the ancients seem to mean the human soul. She was represented with the wings of a butterfly on her shoulders, to intimate by the nimbleness of that creature, the activity, nature and properties of the soul."—(Bailey.)

According to ancient mythology, there were two cupids, one, born of Venus, and begotten by Jupiter, the inciter of celestial love; the other, the son of Erebus and Nox, the author of *terrestial amours.*—(Edit.)

work, considered as a mere Milesian fable; but very applicable to the writer's purpose, if he had that moral to inculcate which we have here assigned him.

There was no man, though he regarded the golden ass as a thing of mere amusement, but saw that the story of Cupid and Psyche was a philosophic allegory of the progress of the soul to perfection, in the possession of divine love and the reward of immortality.* Now we have shown at large, that the professed end of the mysteries was to restore the soul to its *original rectitude*, and to encourage good men with the promises of happiness in another life. The fable, therefore, of Cupid and Psyche, in the fifth and sixth books, was the finest and most artful preparative for the subject of the eleventh, which treats of the mysteries.

But if we look more nearly into this beautiful fable, we shall find that, besides its general purpose, it has one more particular. We have observed that the corrupt state of the mysteries, in the time of Apuleius, was one principal reason of his undertaking their apology. These corruptions were of two kinds, *debaucheries* and *magic*. Their debaucheries have been taken notice of above. Their *magic* was of three sorts: The magic of invocation or *necromancy*; the magic of transformation or *metamorphosis*; and the magic of divine communication under a visible appearance or *theürgy*. The shows of the mysteries seem to have given birth to the first, the doctrine of the metempsychosis taught therein to the second, and the *Aporreta* concerning the divine nature, to the third. The abomination of the two first sorts was seen, by all, and frankly given up as criminal: but the fanatic *Platonists* and *Pythagoreans* of the latter ages, espousing the third, occasioned it to be held in credit and reverence. So that, as Heliodorus tells us, the Egyptian priests, (between whose Philosophy and fanatic Platonism, there was at this time a kind of coalition,) affected to distinguish between the magic of *necromancy* and the magic of *theürgy*, accounting the first infamous and wicked; but the last very fair, and even commendable. For now both those fanatics had their *philosophic mysteries:* the rites of which consisted in the practice of this *theürgic magic*. These were the mysteries, to observe it by the way, of which the emperor Julian was so fond, that he placed his principal felicity, as the Christians did his principal

---

* The Amour of Cupid and Psyche was a subject which lay in common amongst the Platonic writers. And every one fashioned this agreeable fiction according to the doctrines he had to convey under it. By this means it could not but become famous. The remaining monuments of ancient sculpture convince us that it was very famous; in which, nothing is so common as the figures of Cupid and Psyche in the various circumstances of their adventures.

crime, in their celebration. But our author who had imbibed his Platonism, not at the muddy streams of those late enthusiasts, but at the pure fountain-head of the Academy itself, well understood how much this superstition, with all its plausible pretences, had polluted the mysteries; and, therefore, as in the course of the adventures of his *golden ass*, he had stigmatized the two other kinds of *magic*, he composed this celebrated tale, hitherto so little understood, to expose the magic of *theürgy*. It is, as we said, a philosophic allegory, delivered in the adventures of Psyche, or the soul: whose various labours and traverses in this progress, are all represented as the affects of her indiscreet passion for that species of magic called Theürgy.

To understand this, we must observe, that the enthusiastic Platonists, in their pursuit of the Supreme Good, the *union with the Deity*, made the completion and perfection of it to consist in the theurgic vision of the Autopton Agalma or the self seen image, that is, seen by the splendor of its own light. Now the story tells us, there were three sisters, the youngest of whom was called Psyche; by which we are to understand, the *three peripatetic souls*, the *sensitive*, the *animal*, and the *rational*: or, in other words, *sense*, *appetite*, and *reason*: that the beauty of Psyche was so divine, that men forsook the altars of the gods to follow and worship her, according to the ancient aphorism:

Nullum Numen abest, si sit Prudentia.

No Deity is wanting, if Prudence is consulted.

She is contracted to, and possesses the celestial Cupid or *divine love*, invisibly. In the mean time her sisters, envious of her superior enjoyments, take advantage of the god's *invisibility* to perplex her with a thousand doubts and scruples, which end in exciting her *curiosity* to get a *sight* of her lover. By which the author seems to insinuate that they are the irregular passions and appetites which stir up men's curiosity to this species of magic, the *theürgic vision*. Psyche is deluded by them, and against the express injunction of the god, who calls it *sacrilega curiositas*, attempts this *fobidden sight*. She succeeds, and is undone. Divine love forsakes her: the scenes of pleasure vanish: and she finds herself forlorn and abandoned; surrounded by miseries, and pursued with the vengeance of Heaven. In this distress she comes to the temples of Ceres and Juno, and seeks protection of those deities; by which is meant, the having recourse to their mysteries, against the evils and disasters of life; as is plainly marked by the reason given for her application:—" Not willing to omit any even doubtful means of bettering my condition." They both deny admittance to her; intimating that the *purer mysteries* discouraged all kind of *magic*, even the most specious. In a word, after a long and severe repentance and penance, in which the author seems to have shadowed the trials and labors undergone by the aspirants to the mysteries, she is pardoned and restored to the favor of Heaven. She is put again into possession of Divine Love, and rewarded with the prerogative of immortality.

There are many other circumstances in this fine allegory equally serving to the end here explained: as there are others which allude to divers beautiful platonic notions, foreign to the present discourse. It is enough that we have pointed to its chief and peculiar purpose; which it was impossible to see while the nature and design of the whole fable lay undiscovered.

Before I totally dismiss this matter it may not be improper to observe, that both Virgil and Apuleius have represented the genuine mysteries, as Rites of perfect sanctity and purity; and recommended only such to their countrymen; while they expose impure and impious rites to the public aversion; for it was their purpose to stigmatize the reigning corruptions and to recommend the ancient sanctity. On the contrary, a man attached by his office to the recommendation of the mysteries, as then practised, was to do the best he could, when deprived of the benefit of this distinction; and was to endeavor to give fair colors to the foulest things. This was the case of Jamblichus. His friend Porphyry had some scruples on this head. He doubts whether those rites could come from the gods, which admitted such a mixture of lewdness and impurity. Such a mixture Jamblichus confesses; but at the same time, endeavors to account for their divine original, by showing, that they are only the emblems of natural truths; or a kind of moral purgation of the inordinate passions.

Hitherto we have considered the legislator's care in perpetuating the doctrine of a future state. And if I have been longer than ordinary on this head, my excuse is, that the topic was new, and the doctrine itself, which is the main subject of the present inquiry, much interested in it.

Theürgy.

Theürgy is compounded of Theos, God, and ergon, work, and signifies *magic* operating by divine or celestial means, or the power of doing extraordinary and supernatural things by lawful means, as prayer, invocation of God, etc., called by some *white magic*.—Bailey.

The wisest of the pagan world, and their greatest philosophers held Theürgic magic in the highest esteem. Theürgy was, according to them, a divine art, which served only to advance the mind of man to the highest perfection, and render the soul more pure; and they, who by means of this magic had the happiness to arrive at what they called *Autopsia*, or *Intuition*, a state wherein they enjoyed intimate intercourse with the gods, believed themselves invested with all their power, and were persuaded that nothing to them was impossible. Towards this state of perfection all those aspired, who made profession of that sort of magic; but then it laid them under severe regulations. None could be priest of this order but a man of unblemished morals, and all who joined with him in his operations, were bound to strict purity; they were not allowed to have any commerce with women; to eat any kind of animal food, nor to defile themselves by the *touch* of a *dead body*. The philosophers, and persons of the greatest virtue, thought it their honor to be initiated into the mysteries of this sort of magic."—Mayo's Myth. v. 1, p 277.

Thomas Taylor, in a note to his translation of Jamblichus, observes:—"This art of *divine works* is called *theürgy*, in which Pythagoras was mitiated among the Syrians, as we are informed by Jamblichus in his life of that philosopher. Proclus was also skilled in this art, as may be seen in his life by Marinus. Psellas, in his MS. treatise on Demons, says, 'that magic formed the last part of the *sacerdotal science*:' in which place by magic he doubtless means that kind of it which is denominated theürgy. And that theürgy was employed by the ancients in their mysteries, I have fully proved in my treatise on the Eleusinian and Bacchic mysteries. This theürgy, is doubtless the same as the magic of Zoroaster, which Plato in his first Alcibiades says, consisted in the worship of the gods."

"The emperor Julian alludes to this theürgical art, in the following extract from his Arguments against the Christians, preserved by Cyril:

'For the inspiration which arrives to men from the gods is rare, and exists but in a few. Nor is it easy for every man to partake of this, nor at every time. It has ceased among the Hebrews, nor is it preserved to the present time among the Egyptians. Spontaneous oracles, also, are seen to yield to temporal periods. This, however, our philanthropic lord and father Jupiter understanding, that we might not be entirely deprived of communion with the gods, has given us observation through *sacred arts*, by which we have at hand sufficient assistance.' "—(p. 343, 347

This art was professed by the early masons, as appears by an examination of one of the brotherhood by King Henry VI. It is, as before observed, a fundamental doctrine of the Roman Catholic church.

"The priests of Egypt, Persia, India, etc. pretended to bind the gods to their idols, and *to make them descend from heaven at their pleasure;* they threatened the sun and moon to reveal the *secret mysteries, to shake the heavens*, etc." (Eusebius Prep. Evang. p. 198, and Jamb. do Myst. Egypt.—See Ruins, p. 235.)

CHAPTER IV.

A SKETCH OF THE LIFE AND DOCTRINES OF PYTHAGORAS, THE FOUNDER OF THE SECT OF ANCIENT PAILOSOPHERS THAT BORE HIS NAME. ALSO THE DOCTRINES AND CUSTOMS OF THE DRUIDS, THE PRIESTS OF THE ANCIENT BRITONS.

Notwithstanding Pythagoras died, at least fifteen hundred years before the institution of the Freemasons' society, he is hailed by the fraternity as a *brother mason*. Both Cross and Webb, in treating of masonic emblems, among which they include a diagram of the forty-seventh problem of Euclid, hold the following language:

"This was an invention of *our ancient friend and brother*, the great Pythagoras, who in his travels through Asia, Africa and Europe, was initiated into several orders of priesthood, and *raised to the sublime degree of master-mason*. This wise philosopher, enriched his mind abundantly in a general knowedge of things, and more especially in geometry *or masonry*; on this subject he drew out many problems and theorems." etc.

The appellation of grandfather of freemasons would perhaps apply much more appropriately to Pythagoras, than that of *brother* ; for he probably was the father of Druidism, and this was the father of the masonic society; which it made use of as a mere cloak to cover its religious observances, with no special regard to the improvement of the craft. The idea however of a connection between Pythagoras and masonry, must have been handed down in tradition by the old Druidical masons; which is a strong evidence, that the secrets and ceremonies of masonry, are derived from the ancient Egyptian mysteries through the Pythagorian school.

Upon this supposition, of the truth of which I have no doubt, it becomes important to give some account of this celebrated philosopher, whose memory is so deservedly venerated by the masonic order.

The best arranged account of his life and doctrines, that I have met with, is contained in Rees's Cyclopedia; I therefore make the following abstract from that work.

Pithagoras was of Samos, the son of a lapidary, and the pupil of Pherecydes, and flourished, says Bayle, about five hundred years before Christ, in the time of Tarquin, the last king of Rome, and not in Numa's time, as many authors have supposed.—(*See Cicero Tus. Ques. lib. iv. cap.* 1.

Posterity has been very liberal to this philosopher, in bestowing upon him all such inventions as others had neglected to claim, particularly in music ; for there is scarcely any part of it, as a science, with which he has not been invested by his generous followers in biography.

Musical ratios have been assigned to him, with the method of determining the gravity or acuteness of sounds by the greater or less degree of velocity in the vibration of strings ; the addition of an eighth to the lyre, (Pliny. lib. ii cap. 2.) the harmony of the spheres (Plato,) and the Greek musical notation (Boethius). His right, indeed, to some of these discoveries has been disputed by several authors, who have given them to others with as little reason, perhaps, as they have been before bestowed upon him.

After musical ratios were discovered and reduced to numbers, they were made by Pithagoras and his followers, the type of order and just proportion in all things; hence virtue, friendship, good government, celestial motion, the human soul, and God himself were harmony.

This discovery gave birth to various species of music, far more strange and inconceivable than chromatic and enharmonic; such as *divine* music, *mundane* music, *elementery* music, and many other divisions and subdivisions, upon which Zarlino, Kircher, and almost all the old writers, never fail to expatiate with wonderful complacence.* It is perhaps, equally to the credit and advantage of music and philosophy, that they have long descended from these heights, and taken their proper and separate stations upon earth; that we no longer admit of music that cannot be heard, or of philosophy that cannot be understood.

Master Thomas Mace, author of a most delectable book, called "Music's Monument," would have been an excellent Pythagorean; for he maintains that the mystery of the Trinity is perspicuously made plain by the connection of the three harmonical concords, 1, 3, 5; that music and divinity are nearly allied; and that the contemplation of concord and discord, of the nature of the octave and unison, will so strengthen a man's faith, "that he shall never after degenerate into that gross sub-beastical sin of atheism."

Pythagoras is said by the writers of his life, to have regarded music as something celestial and divine, and to have had such an opinion of its power over the human affections, that according to the Egyptian system, he ordered his deciples to be waked every morning, and lulled to sleep every night, by sweet sounds. He likewise considered it as greatly conducive to health, and made use of it in disorders of the body, as well as in those of the mind. His biographers pretend to tell us what kind of music he applied upon these occasions.

---

* The terms *sacred* and *profane* music, are still retained, appropriating grave and plain ive tones to the former, and gay and lively to the latter. On this account, it is reported, that Wesley, the founder of the Methodist sect, declared that the Devil should not have all the best tunes, and accordingly, he introduced into his church service the most sprightly airs, which are still in use among his followers, having, it is said, the most happy effect.— *Edit*.

Grave and solemn, we may be certain; and vocal, say they, was preferred to instrumental, and the lyre to the flute, not only for its decency and gravity, but because instruction could be conveyed to the mind, by means of articulation in singing, at the same time as the ear was delighted by sweet sounds.

In perusing the list of illustrious men, who have sprung from the school of Pythagoras, it appears that the love and cultivation of music was so much a part of their discipline, that almost every one of them left a treatise behind him upon the subject.

The first journey of Pythagoras from the Grecian islands was probably into Egypt, which were celebrated in his time for that kind of wisdom which best suited his genius and temper. In his way thither, Jamblichus asserts that he visited Phœnecia, and conversed with the prophets and philosophers that were the successors of Mochus the Physiologist.

While he was in Egypt, he was introduced by the recommendation of Polycrates, tyrant* of Samos, to Amasia, king of Egypt, a distinguished patron of literary men, and thus obtained access to the colleges of the priests. Having found it difficult to gain this privilege, he performed many severe and troublesome preliminary ceremonies, and even submitted to circumcision, a prescribed condition of his admission. He passed twenty-two years in Egypt, availing himself of all possible means of information with regard to the recondite doctrines of the Egyptian priests, as well as their astronomy and geometry, and Egyptian learning in its most unlimited extent.

After his return from Egypt to his native island, he wished to communicate the benefit of his researches and studies to his fellow-citizens, and with this view he attempted to institute a school for their instruction in the elements of science; proposing to adopt the Egyptian mode of teaching, and to communicate his doctrines under a symbolical form. But the Samians were either too stupid or too indolent to profit by his instructions. Although he was obliged to relinquish his design, he did not altogether abandon it. In order to engage the attention of his countrymen by some other means, he repaired to Delos; and after presenting an offering of cakes to Apollo, he there received, or pretended to receive, moral dogmas from the priestess, which he afterwards delivered to his deciples under the character of divine precepts. With

---

† The name tyrant, as at first used, merely designated the chief magistrate of a place: the Greeks in old time, called the supreme governor of every city a tyrant or king. Bailey.—*Edit.*

the same views he also visited the island of Crete, so celebrated in mythological history; where he was conducted by the Corybantes, or priests of Cybele, into the cave of mount Ida, in which Jupiter is said to have been buried. Here he conversed with Epimenides, an eminent pretender to prophetic powers, and was by him initiated into the most sacred mysteries of Greece. About the same time he visited Sparta and Elis, and was present during the celebration of the Olympic games, where he is said to have exhibited a golden thigh to Abaris, in order to convince him that he was Apollo. Besides other places which he visited during his stay in Greece, he repaired to Phlius, where he first assumed the appellation of philosopher. Having thus added to the stores of learning which he had previously accumulated, and acquired a kind of authority which was calculated to command respect, he returned to Samos, and made a second attempt, more successful than his first, to establish a school of philosophy. In a semicircular kind of building, which the Simians had used as a place of resort for public business, he delivered, with an assumed authority of a sacred nature, popular precepts of morality; and he also provided himself with a secret cave, into which he retired with his intimate friends and professed deciples, and here he gave his followers daily instructions, accompanied with a considerable parade of mystery, in the more abstruse parts of philosophy. His fame, and the multitude of his followers, increased. What he failed to accomplish by mere force of learning and ability, he effected by concealing his doctrines under the veil of mysterious symbols, and issuing forth his precepts as responses from a divine oracle. About the beginning of the fifty-ninth Olympiad, Pythagoras, desirous of escaping the tyranical government exercised in his native island, by Syloson, the brother of Polycrates, left Samos, and, as we have already hinted, passed over into Italy, and attempted to establish his school among the colonies of Magna Græcia. It is probable, that, in order to obtain credit with the populace, he about this time pretended to possess a power of performing miracles, and practised many arts of imposture. The first place at which he arrived in Italy was Crotona, a city in the bay of Tarentum, the inhabitants of which were very corrupt in their manners. But such were his reputation and influence, that he was treated with great respect, and people of all classes assembled to hear his discourses; insomuch that the manners of the citizens were soon totally changed from great luxury and licentiousness to strict sobriety and frugality. It is said that six hundred, (some say two thousand,) persons were prevailed upon to submit to the strict discipline which he required and to throw their effects into a common stock for the benefit of the whole fraternity. The influence of his philosophy extended from Crotona to many other cities of Magna Græcia, and obtained for Pythagoras from his followers a degree of respect little short of adoration. If he had contented himself with delivering doctrines of philosophy and precepts of practical wisdom, he might probably have continued his labors, without molestation, to the end of his life. But he manifested a strong propensity towards political innovations; and he employed his influence in urging the people to the strenuous assertion of their rights, against the encroachment of their tyrranical governors. This course of conduct raised against him a very powerful opposition which he was unable to resist and contend against, and which obliged him to retire to Metapontum. Here he found himself still surrounded with enemies, and was under a necessity of seeking an assylum in the temple of the Muses, where not being supplied by his friends with sufficient food, he perished with hunger.* The time of his death is uncertain; but according to the Chronicon of Eusebius, he died in the third year of the sixty-eighth Olympiad, B. C. 506, after having lived according to the most probable statement of his birth, to the age of eighty years. After his death his followers paid a superstitious respect to his memory. They erected statues in honor of him, converted his house at Crotona into a temple of Ceres, the street in which it stood was called the Museum, and appealed to him as a divinity, swearing by his name.

It appears, from the history of this philosopher, that with all his talents and learning, he owed much of his celebrity and authority to imposture. His whole manner of life confirms this opinion. Clothed in a long white robe with a flowing beard, and, as some say, with a golden crown on his head, he preserved among the people, and in the presence of his desciples, a commanding gravity, and majesty of aspect. He recurred to music for promoting the tranquility of his mind, frequently singing, for this purpose, hymns of Thales, Hesiod, and Homer. He had such an entire command over himself, that he was never seen to express, in his countenance, grief, joy, or anger. He refrained from animal food, and confined himself to a frugal vegetable diet, excluding from his simple bill of fare, for mystical reasons, pulse

---

* Anobius affirms that Pythagoras was buried alive in a temple; others state that he was slain in attempting to make his escape. It can hardly be doubted that his death was violent, and that, with all his caution to preserve himself, he fell a martyr to his generous efforts to undeceive mankind. An ill construction was put upon the union of the Pythagoreans, and it proved very fatal to them. That society of students being looked upon as a faction which conspired against the state, sixty of them were destroyed, and the rest went into banishment.—Diegesis, by the Rev. R. Taylor.—*Edit.*

or beans. By this artificial demeanor, Pythagoras appeared among the vulgar as a being of an order superior to the common condition of humanity, and persuaded them that he had received his doctrine from heaven. Pythagoras married Theano of Crotona, or, as some say, of Crete, by whom he had two sons, Telaugus and Mnesarchus, who, after his death took the charge of his school. Whether this philosopher left behind him any writings has been a subject of dispute. Many works have been enumerated under his name by Leartius, Jamblichus, and Pliny: but it is the declared opinion of Plutarch, Josephus, Lucian, and others, that there were no genuine works of Pythagoras extant; and it appears highly probable, from the pains which he took to confine his doctrine to his own school during his life, that he never committed his philosophical system to writing, and that the pieces to which his name was affixed at an early period, were written by some of his followers, upon the principles imbibed in his school. The famous golden verses attributed to Pythagoras, and illustrated with a commentary by Hierocles, were not written by our philosopher, but are to be ascribed to Epicharmus, or Empedocles. They may, however, be considered as a brief summary of his popular doctrines.

His method of instruction, formed upon the Egyptian model, was "exoteric," and "esoteric," that is, public and private. Those auditors, who attended his public lectures, did not properly belong to his school, but followed their usual mode of living. His select deciples called his *companions* and friends, were such as submitted to a peculiar plan of discipline, and were admitted by *a long course of instruction, into all the mysteries of his esoteric doctrine.*[*]

---

[*] Masons, who have taken only the three first degrees of the order, are taught only what may be called the exoteric doctrine of masonry, and this in an obscure symbolical manner, not intended to be fully understood. In this grade, they call each other *brother*. They were formerly, that is, in the time of the Druids, not permitted to advance further, until they had convinced their superiors that confidence might be placed in them, and that they were worthy of receiving the *esoteric* principles of the order. When raised to the sublime degree of royal arch, they address one another by the appellation of *companion*. And then, no doubt, in ancient times, the whole secret of masonry, that is, the doctrine of Druidism was clearly exposed.

Dermott, after making some remarks on the conduct of certain persons, who, it seems, were dissatisfied at not having been admitted to the royal arch degree, says, "To this I will add the opinion our *worshipful* brother, Dr. Fifield D'Assigney, printed in the year 1744. 'Some of the fraternity, says he, have expressed an uneasiness at this matter's being kept a secret from them, since they had already passed through the usual degrees of probation; but I cannot help being of opinion that they have no right to any such benefit until they make a proper application, and are received with due formality; and as it is an organized body of men, who have passed the chair, and given *undeniable proofs of their skill in architecture*, it cannot be treated with too much *reverence*.''

Now, Dr. Fifield must have been sensible, that architecture was not taught in the lodge in his day. This ridiculous parade, therefore, about *skill* in this *art*, is a mere excuse for the observance of an ancient custom, the reason for which was unknown. *Edit.*

OF PYTHAGORAS.

Previously to the admission of any person into this fraternity, Pythagoras examined his features and external appearance; inquired how he had been accustomed to behave towards his parents and friends; marked his manner of laughing, conversing, and keeping silence; and observed what passions he was most inclined to indulge; with what kind of company he chose to associate; how he passed his leisure moments; and what incidents appeared to excite in him the strongest emotions of joy or sorrow. Nor after this examination was any one admitted into his society, till he was fully persuaded of the docility of his disposition, the gentleness of his manners, his power of retaining in silence what he was taught, and, in fine, his capacity of becoming a true philosopher. After the first probationary admission, the fortitude and self-command of the candidate were put to the trial by a long course of severe abstinence and rigorous exercise. The course of abstinence and self-denial comprehended food and drink, and clothing, all which were of the most plain and simple kind, and the exercises prescribed were such as could not be performed without pain and fatigue. To teach them humility and industry, he exposed them, for three years, to a continued course of *contradiction, ridicule and contempt*, among their fellows.* In order to restrain the powerful passion of avarice, he required his disciples to submit to voluntary poverty : he deprived them of all command over their own property, by casting the possessions of each individual into a common stock, to be distributed by proper officers as occasion required. After this sequestration of their goods, they lived together on a footing of perfect equality, and sat down together daily at a common table. If any one afterwards repented of the connection, he was at liberty to depart, and might reclaim, from the general fund, his whole contribution. That his disciples might acquire a habit of entire docility, Pythagoras enjoined upon them, from their first admission, a

---

* This is imitated in the *past master's degree* of masonry. The newly initiated member, perfectly ignorant of the mode of proceedings in a lodge, is, against his will, placed in the chair of the master as presiding officer; and "the installed worshipful is made the butt for every worthy brother to exercise his wit upon."

This custom, it would appear, has descended from the Druids, the ancient schoolmasters of England, to the universities and colleges, even of America; where those of the freshmen, or newly entered class, are made the butt and ridicule of the higher classes for twelve months. The latter are empowered to direct the former to perform any errand they wish; can order them to repair to their rooms, and there lecture them for their awkwardness, ignorance, etc. This practice was doubtless introduced upon the principle of Pithagoras, to inculcate *humility*; but when exercised upon a raw, diffident, country boy, it must prove extremely discouraging and oppressive. The custom however, it is said has gone into disuse. Gen. Erastus Root of Delhi, in this State, by a resolute refusal to submit to this discipline, has the honor, as I am informed by a graduate of Dartmouth college, of putting an end to this vile practice in that institution.—*Edit.*

long term of silence, called *echemythia*. This initiatory silence, which probably consisted in refraining from speech, not only during the hours of instruction, but through the whole term of initiation, continued from two to five years, according to the propensity discovered by the pupil towards conceit and loquacity. With regard to himself, this was a judicious expedient, as it checked impertinent curiosity, and prevented every inconvenience of contradiction. Accordingly his disciples silenced all doubts and refuted all objections, by appealing to his authority *Autos epha, ipse dixit*, decided every dispute. Moreover, during the years of initiation, the disciples were prohibited from seeing their master, or hearing his lectures, except from behind a curtain,[*] or receiving instructions from some inferior preceptor.

To the members of thee soteric school (who were called *gyesioi emiletai* genuine disciples) belonged the peculiar privilege of receiving a full explanation of the whole doctrine of Pythagoras, which was delivered to others in brief precepts and dogmas, under the concealment of symbols. Disciples of this class were permitted to take minutes of their master's lectures in writing, as well as to propose questions, and offer remarks, upon every subject of discourse. These were particularly distinguished by the appellation of the "Pythagoreans," they were also called "Mathematicians," from the studies upon which they entered immediately after their initiation. After having made a sufficient progress in geometrical science, they proceeded to the study of nature, the investigation of primary principles, and the knowledge of God. Those who pursued these sublime speculations were called "Theorists," and those who devoted themselves more particularly to Theology, were styled *sebastikoi,*, religious. Others, according to their abilities and inclinations, were engaged in the study of morals, economics, and policy; and were afterwards employed in managing the affairs of the fraternity, or sent into the cities of Greece, to instruct them in the principles of government, or assist them in the institution of laws.

The brethren of the Pythagorean college at Crotona, called *coniobion*, coenobium, about six hundred in number, lived together as in one family, with their wives and children, and the whole business of the society was conducted with the most perfect regularity. Every day commenced with a deliberation upon the manner in which it should be spent, and concluded with a retrospect of the events which had occurred,

---

[*] There is an affectation of this sort, as before observed, in the masonic degrees of "Knight of the Eagle," and "Knight of Kadosh," in which the candidate is not permitted to see the person who initiates him.—*Edit.*

and of the business that had been transacted. They rose before the sun that they might do him homage; after which they repeated select verses from Homer and other poets, and made use of music, both vocal and instrumental, to enliven their spirits and fit them for the business of the day. They then employed several hours in the study of science. These were succeeded by an interval of leisure, which was commonly spent in a solitary walk for the purpose of contemplation. The next portion of the day was allotted to conversation. The hour immediately before dinner was filled up with various kinds of athletic exercises. Their dinner consisted chiefly of bread, honey, and water; for after they were perfectly initiated, they wholly denied themselves the use of wine. The remainder of the day was devoted to civil and domestic affairs, conversation, bathing and religious ceremonies.

The "exoteric" disciples of Pythagoras were taught after the Egyptian manner, by images and symbols, obscure and almost unintelligible to those who were not initiated into the mysteries of the school; and those who were admitted to this privilege were under the strictest obligation of silence with regard to the recondite doctrines of their master. The wisdom of Pythagoras, that it might not pass into the ears of the vulgar, was committed chiefly to memory; and when they found it necessary to make use of writing, they took care not to suffer their minutes to pass beyond the limits of the school.*

Clemens observes, that the two orders above described corresponded very exactly to those among the Hebrews; for in the schools of the prophets there were two classes, viz: the sons of the prophets, who were the scholars; and the doctors or masters, who were also called perfecti; and among the Levites, the novices or tyros, who had their quinquenial exercises, by way of preparation. Lastly, even among the proselytes there were two orders: exoterici, or proselytes of the gate;

---

* The principal and and most efficacious of their doctrines, the Pythagoreans committed to memory, and communicated them to their successors as *mysteries* from the gods; and if at any time there were any *extraneous*, or, as I may say, *profane* persons among them, they signified their meaning by symbols.

Hence Lysis reproving Hipparchus for communicating the *discourse* to uninitiated persons, void of *mathematics* and *theory*, saith, it is reported that you teach philosophy in public to all that come, which Pythagoras would not do. If you are changed, I shall rejoice; if not, you are dead to me: for we ought to remember that it is *pious*, according to the direction of *divine* and *human* exertations, that the *goods of wisdom* ought not to be communicated to those whose *soul is not purified* so much as in dream. It is not lawful to bestow on every one that which was acquired with so much labor, nor to reveal the mysteries of the Eleusinian goddess to profane persons. They who do both these, are alike unjust and irreligious. It is good to consider within ourselves how much time was employed in taking away the *spots* that were in our breasts, that after five years we might be made capable of his [Pythagoras's] discourses.—Jamblichus. Quoted in T. Stanley's History of Philosophy. London, 1666, p. 376.—*Edit.*

and intrinseci, or perfecti, proselytes of the covenant. He adds, it is highly probable, that Pythagoras himself had been a proselyte of the gate, if not of the covenant.

After the dissolution of the assembly of Pythagoras's disciples by the faction of Cylo, a man of wealth and distinction at Crotona, it was thought necessary by Lysis and Archippus, in order to preserve the Pythagorean doctrine from oblivion, to reduce it to a systematic summary; at the same time, however, strongly enjoining their children to preserve these memoirs secret, and to transmit them in confidence to their posterity. From this time books began to multiply among the followers of Pythagoras, till at length, in the time of Plato, Philolaus exposed the Pythagorean records to sale, and Archytas of Tarentum gave Plato a copy of his commentaries upon the aphorisms and precepts of his master. Of the imperfect records of the Pythagorean philosophy left by Lysis, Archytas, and others, nothing has escaped the wreck of time, except perhaps sundry fragments collected by the diligence of Stobæus, concerning the authenticity of which there are some grounds for suspicion; and which, if admtted as genuine, will only exhibit an imperfect view of the moral and political doctrine of Pythagoras under the disguise of symbolical and enigmatical language. The strict injunction of secrecy, which was given by oath to the initiated, Pythagoreans has effectually prevented any original records of their doctrine concerning Nature and God from passing down to posterity. On this head we are to rely entirely for information, and indeed concerning the whole doctrine of Pythagoras, upon Plato and his followers. Plato himself, while he enriched his system with stores from the magazine of Pythagoras, accommodated the Pythagorean doctrines, as he also did those of his master Socrates, to his own system, and thus gave an imperfect, and, we may suppose, in many particulars, a false representation of the doctrines of the Samian philosopher. It was farther corrupted by the followers of Plato, even in the old academy, and afterwards in the Alexandrian school. To which we may add, that the doctrine of Phythagoras itself, probably in its original state, and certainly in every form under which it has been transmitted to us, was observed, not only by symbolical, but by mathematical language, which is rather adapted to perplex than to illustrate metaphysical conceptions. In this fault Pythagoras was afterwards imitated by Plato, Aristotle, and others.*

---

* Moderatus saith, that the Pythagoric philosophy came at last to be extinguished; first, because it was enigmatical; next, because the writings were in the Doric dialect, which is obscure, by which means the doctrines delivered in it were not understood;

We extract from Brucker the following faint delineation of the Pythagorean philosophy: The end of philosophy is to free the mind from those incumbrances, which hinder its progress towards perfection, and to raise it to the contemplation of immutable truth, and the knowledge of divine and spiritual objects. This effect must be produced by easy steps, lest the mind, hitherto conversant only with sensible things, should revolt at the change. The first step towards wisdom is the study of mathematics, a science which contemplates objects that lie in the middle way between corporeal and incorporeal beings, and as it were on the confines of both, and which most advantageously inures the mind to contemplation.

The monad, or unity, is that quantity, which, being deprived of all number, remains fixed; whence called monad from *to meneia*. It is the fountain of all number. The duad is imperfect and passive, and the cause of increase and division. The triad, composed of the monad and duad, partakes of the nature of both. The tetrad, tetractys, or quaternion number, is the most perfect. The decad, which is the sum of the four former, comprehends all arithmetical and musical proportions.

According to some writers, the monad denotes the active principle in nature, or God; the duad, the passive principle, or matter; the triad, the word formed by the union of the two former; and the tetractys, the perfection of nature. Some have understood by this mysterious number the four elements; others, the four faculties of the human mind; others, the four cardinal virtues; and others have been so absurd as to suppose that Pythagoras made use of this number to express the name of God, in reference to the word —— [Gehovah,] by which that name is expressed in the Hebrew language. But every attempt to unfold this mystery has hitherto been unsuccessful.

Next to numbers, music had the chief place in the preparatory exercises of the Pythagorean school, by means of which the mind was to be raised above the dominion of the passions, and inured to contemplation. Pythagoras considered music, not only as an art to be judged of by the ear, but as a science to be reduced to mathematical principles and proportions.

---

and, moreover, because they who published them were not Pythagoreans. Besides, Plato, Aristotle, and others, as the Pythagoreans affirm, vended the best of them as their own, changing only some few things in them, but the more vulgar and trivial, and whatsoever was afterwards *invented by curious and calumnious persons*, to cast a contempt upon the Pythagorean school, they collected and delivered as proper to that sect.—(Porphyry, p. 36; Stanley, p. 363.)—*Edit.*

It was said of Pythagoras by his followers, who hesitated at no assertion, however improbable, which might seem to exalt their master's fame, that he was the only mortal so far favored by the gods as to be permitted to hear the celestial music of the spheres. Pythagoras applied music to the cure of diseases both bodily and mental. It was, as we have seen, the custom of his school, to compose their minds for rest in the evening, and to prepare themselves for action in the morning, by suitable airs, which they performed upon the lute, or other stringed instruments. The music was, however, always accompanied with verse, so that it may be doubted, whether the effect was to be ascribed more to the musician or to the poet. It is said of Clinius, a Pythagorean, that whenever he perceived himself inclined to anger, spleen, or other restless passions, he took up his lute, and that it never failed to restore the tranquility of his mind. Of Pythagoras himself, it is related, that he checked a young man, who, in the midst of his revels, was meditating some act of Bacchanalian madness, by ordering the musician, who had inflamed his passions by Phrygian airs, to change the music on a sudden into the slow and solemn Doric mood. If the stories which are related by the ancients concerning the wonderful effects of their music are to be credited, we must acknowledge we are strangers to the method by which these effects were produced.

Besides arithmetic and music, Pythagoras cultivated geometry, which he had learned in Egypt; but he greatly improved it, by investigating many new theorems, and by digesting its principles, in an order more perfectly systematical than had before been done. Several Grecians, about the time of Pythagoras, applied themselves to mathematical learning, particularly Thales in Ionia. But Pythagoras seems to have done more than any other philosopher of this period towards reducing geometry to a regular science. His definition of a point is a monad or unity with position. He taught that a geometrical point corresponds to unity in arithmetic, a line to two, a superficies to three, a solid to four. Of the geometrical theorems ascribed to Pythagoras, the following are the principal: that the interior angles of every triangle are together equal to two right angles; that the only polygons which fill up the whole space about a given point, are the equilateral triangle, the square, and the hexagon; the first to be taken six times, the second four times, and the third three times; and that, in rectangular triangles, the square of the side which subtends the right angle is equal to the two squares of the sides which contain the right angle. Upon the invention of this later proposition (Euclid, l. i. prop. 47,) Plutarch says, that Pythagoras offered an ox, others, an hecatomb, to the gods. But this story is thought by Cicero inconsistent with the institutions of Pythagoras, which, as he supposes, did not admit of animal sacrifices.

Theoretical philosophy, which treats of nature and its origin, was the highest object of study of the Pythagorean school, and included all those profound mysteries, which those, who have been ambitious to report what Pythagoras said behind the curtain, have endeavored to unfold. Upon this subject, nothing can be advanced with certainty, especially respecting theology, the doctrine of which, Pythagoras, after the manner of the Egyptian priests, was peculiarly careful to hide under the vail of symbols, probably through fear of disturbing the popular superstitions. The ancients have not, however, left us without some grounds of conjecture.

With respect to God, Pythagoras appears to have taught, that he is the Universal Mind, diffused through all things, the source of all animal life, the proper and intrinsic cause of all motion, in substance similar to light, in nature like truth, the first principle of the universe, incapable of pain, invisible, incorruptible, and only to be comprehended by the mind.

The region of the air was supposed by the Pythagoreans to be full of spirits, demons, or heroes, who cause sickness or health to man or beast, and communicate, at their pleasure, by means of dreams, and other instruments of divination, the knowledge of future events. That Pythagoras himself held this opinion cannot be doubted, if it be true, as his biographers relate, that he professed to cure diseases by incantations. It is probable that he derived it from the Egyptians, among whom it was believed that many diseases were caused by *demoniacal possessions*.

The doctrine of the Pythagoreans, respecting the nature of brute animals, and *metempsychosis*, the transmigration of souls, were the foundation of their abstinence from animal food, and of the exclusion of animal sacrifices from their religious ceremonies.

This doctrine Pythagoras probably learned in Egypt, where it was commonly taught. Nor is there any sufficient reason for understanding it, as some have done, symbolically.

The precept prohibiting the use of beans, is one of the mysteries which the ancient Pythagoreans never disclosed, and which modern ingenuity has in vain attempted to discover. Pythagorean precepts of more value are such as these: Discourse not of Pythagorean doctrines without light. Above all things govern your tongue. Quit not your station without the command of your general. Remember that the paths of virtue and of vice resemble the letter Y. To this symbol Persius refers, when he says,

> "There has the Samian Y's instructive make
> Pointed the road thy doubtful foot should take;
> There warn'd thy raw and yet unpractis'd youth,
> To tread the rising right-hand path of truth."

(*Brucker's Hist. Philos. by Enfield, vol.* i. b. c. 12.)

After the death of Pythagoras, the care and education of his children, and the charge of his school, devolved upon Aristæus of Crotona, who, having taught the doctrine of Pythagoras thirty-nine years, was succeeded by Mnesarchus, the son of Pythagoras. Pythagorean schools were afterwards conducted in Heraclia by Clinias and Philolaus; at Metapontum by Theorides and Eurytus; and at Tarentum by Archytas, who is said to have been the eighth in succession from Pythagoras. The first person who divulged the Pythagorean doctrine was Philolaus.

The symbolical use of the letter Y has reference to the old fable, before noticed, of the *trivia* or triple path, that is, where the road to the infernal regions divides into two, the one leading to Elysium, and the other to Tartarus. This letter was a very appropriate symbol to mark out these roads; the disproportion of the two strokes which form it, being indicative of the comparative numbers to be accommodated in the two courses; that is, of the righteous and the wicked. St. Matthew, no doubt, makes allusion to the common idea entertained upon this subject, when he says,

"Enter ye in at the straight gate: for wide is the gate, and broad is the way, that leadeth to destruction, and many there be which go in thereat: because straight is the gate, and narrow is the way, which leadeth unto life; and few there be that find it." (vii. 13.)

"It is surprising, says Bayle, that a philosopher so skillful as Pythagoras in astronomy, in geometry, and in other parts of the mathematics, should be pleased to deliver his most beautiful precepts under the vail of enigmas. This vail was so thick, that the interpreters have found in it ample matter for conjecture. This symbolic method was very much used in the East, and in Egypt. It is from thence without doubt Pythagoras has derived it. He returned from his travels laden with the spoils of the erudition of all the countries he had visited. It is pretended that his *tetractys* is the same thing as the name *tetragrammaton*, a name ineffable and full of mystery, according to the Rabbins. Others will have it, that this *tetractys*, this grand object of *veneration* and of *oaths*, is nothing more than a mysterious manner of dogmatising by numbers. But let us not forget, that Pythagoras and his successors had two ways of teaching, one for the initiated, and the other for strangers and the profane. The first was clear and unvailed, the second was symbolic and enigmatical."—(Dict.)

It is somewhat remarkable, that a difference of opinion should exist among the learned in regard to the meaning which Pythagoras intended to convey to his pupils of the *esoteric* class, by the word *Tetractys*: for it appears pretty evident, that he used it enigamatically as synonymous with geometry. And so Bailey, who seems to have known more of antiquity than any other of his day, defines it. He says, "Tetractys, in *ancient* geometry, signified a point, a line, a surface, and a solid." Hutchinson, in his 'Spirits of Masonry,' gives the same definition. He says, "The Pythagoric tetractics [tetractys] were a point," etc. as above.

The ancient Druidical Freemasons were taught, as reported by Prichard, that there are four principles in masonry, which are specified agreeably to the above definition of tetractys.

These four principles contained in the tetractys or geometry, comprehend the entire of physical nature, and on this account the enigma of the perfection of the number four has been erected.

A writer on masonry (see Carlile. p. 99) observes, "That the Pythagoreans affirmed the tetractys, or number four to be the sum and completion of all things, as comprising the four, great principles both of arithmetic and geometry. In the center of a masonic lodge, within an irradiation or blazing star, is inscribed the letter G, denoting the *great* and *glorious* science of geometry, as cultivated by our ancient and *venerable masters*." And adds, "Whilst each of those our symbols reciprocally serves to illustrate the rest, there is one sense, in which they yield to the decided preëminence of the great central emblem, whose *sacred initial character*, surrounded by a blaze of glory, recalls our minds from the work to the *architect*, from the science to its mystery."

The Egyptians invented geometry, and they found it of such infinite importance, that they in a manner deified the science. Hence the great respect paid to its initial in masonry. It is, in fact, made to indicate the Supreme Being, who, according to the Pythagorean doctrine, was mysteriously involved in the physical principles of nature. Geometry is painted as a lady, with a sallow face, clad in a green mantle, fringed with silver, and holding a silver *wand* [the Nilometer] in her right hand.—*Bailey*.

The Eleusinian mysteries were regularly celebrated every fifth year, that is, after a revolution of four years. The Olympic games took place at the same time, the name of which originated from their being first celebrated near the city of Olympia. Hence the olympiad, an epoch of four years; all arising, evidently, from the perfection attributed to the number four.

The Customs and Religious Dogmas, of the Druids of England, extracted from the History of Great Britain, by Robert Henry, D. D.

When the Romans first invaded Britain, under Julius Cæsar, the inhabitants of it were famous, even among foreign nations, for their superior knowledge of the principles, and the great zeal for the rites of their religion.

To say nothing here of the profits which the Druids derived from the administration of justice, the practice of physic, and teaching the sciences, (which were all in their hands,) they certainly received great emoluments from those whom they instructed in the principles, and *initiated* into the *mysteries* of their theology; especially from such of them as were of high rank, and came from foreign countries.

Nothing can be affirmed with certainty, concerning the precise number of the British Druids, though, in general, we have reason to believe, that they were very numerous. Both the Gauls and the Britons of these times were much addicted to superstition; and among a superstitious people, there will always be many priests. Besides this, they entertained an opinion, as we are told by Strabo, which was highly favorable to the increase of the priestly order. They were fully persuaded, that the greater number of Druids they had in their country, they would obtain the more plentiful harvests, and the greater abundance of all things. Nay, we are directly informed by Cæsar, that great numbers of people, allured by the honors and privileges which they enjoyed, embraced the discipline of the Druids of their own accord, and that many more were dedicated to it by their parents. Upon the whole, therefore, we shall probably not be very much mistaken, if we suppose that the British Druids bore as great a proportion in number to the rest of the people, as the clergy in popish countries, bear to the laity, in the present age.

The Druids, as well as the Gymnosophists of India, the Magi of Persia, the Chaldeans of Assyria, and all the other priests of antiquity, had two sets of religious doctrines and opinions, which were very different from one another. The one of these systems they communicated only to the *initiated*, who were *admitted into their own order*, and at their admission were *solemnly sworn* to keep that system of doctrines a *profound secret* from all the rest of mankind. Besides this, they took several other precautions to prevent these secret doctrines from transpiring. They taught their disciples, as we are told by Mela, in the most private places, such as *caves* of the earth, or the *deepest recesses* of the *thickest forests*, that they might not be overheard by any who were not initiated. They never committed any of these doctrines to writing, for fear they should thereby become public. Nay, so jealous were some orders of these ancient priests on this head, that they made it an inviolable rule never to communicate any of these secret doctrines to *women*, lest they should blab them. The other system of religious doctrines and opinions was made public, being adapted to the capacities and superstitious humors of the people, and calculated to promote the honor and opulence of the priesthood.

It cannot be expected, that we should be able to give a minute detail of the secret doctrines of the Druids. The Greeks and Roman writers, from whom alone we can receive information, were not perfectly acquainted with them, and therefore they have left us only some general hints, and probable conjectures about them, with which we must be contented. The secret doctrines of our Druids were much the same with those of the Gymnosophists and Brachmans of India, the Magi of Persia, the Chaldeans of Assyria, the priests of Egypt, and of all the other priests of antiquity. All these are frequently joined together by ancient authors, as entertaining the same opinions in religion and philosophy, which might be easily confirmed by an induction of particulars. The truth is, there is hardly anything more surprising in the history of mankind, than the similitude, or rather identity, of the opinions, institutions, and manners of all these orders of ancient priests, though they lived under such different climates, and at so great a distance from one another, without intercourse or communication. This amounts to a demonstration, that all these opinions and institutions flowed originally from one fountain. The secret doctrines of the Druids, and of all these different orders of priests, were more agreeable to primitive tradition and right reason, than their public doctrines; as they were not under any temptation, in their private schools, to conceal or disguise the truth. It is not improbable that they still retained, in secret, the great doctrine of one God, the creator and governor of the universe. This, which was originally the belief of all the orders of priests which we have mentioned, was retained by some of them long after the period we are now considering, [that is from the first invasion of England by the Romans under Julius Cæsar, fifty-five years before the Christian era, to the arrival of the Saxons, A. D. 449,] and might therefore be known to the Druids at this period. This is one of the doctrines which the Brachmans of India are sworn to keep secret: "That there is one God, the creator of heaven and earth." Cæsar acquaints us, that they taught their disciples many things about the nature and perfections of God. Some writers are of opinion, and have taken much learned pains to prove, that our Druids, as well as the other orders of ancient priests, taught their disciples many things concerning the creation of the world —the formation of man—his primitive innocence and felicity—and his fall into guilt and misery—the creation of angels—their rebellion and expulsion out of Heaven—the universal deluge, and the final destruction of this world by fire; and that their doctrines on all these subjects were not very different from those which are contained in the writings of Moses, and other parts of Scripture. There is abundant evidence that the Druids taught the doctrine of the immortality of the souls of men; and Mela tells us, that this was one of their doctrines which they were permitted to publish, for political rather than religious reasons. "There is one thing which they teach their disciples, which hath been made known to the common people, in order to render them more brave and fearless; viz: "that souls are immortal, and that there is another life after the present." Cæsar and Diodorus say, that the Druids taught the Pythagorean doctrine of the transmigration of souls into other bodies. This was perhaps their public doctrine on this subject, as being most level to the gross conceptions of the vulgar. But others represent them as teaching that the soul after death ascended into some higher orb, and enjoyed a more sublime felicity. This was probably their private doctrine, and real sentiments.*

But however agreeable to truth and reason, the secret doctrines of the Druids might be, they were of no benefit to the bulk of mankind, from whom they were carefully concealed. For these artful priests, for their own mercenary ends, had embraced a maxim, which hath unhappily survived them, that ignorance was the mother of devotion, and that the common people were incapable of comprehending rational principles, or of being influenced by rational motives; and that they were therefore to be fed with the coarser food of superstitious fables. This is the reason assigned by Strabo, for the fabulous theology of the ancients. "It is not possible to bring women, and the common herd of mankind to religion, piety, and virtue, by the pure and simple dictates of reason. It is necessary to call in the aids of superstition, which must be nourished by fables and portents of various kinds. With this view therefore were all the fables of ancient theology invented, to awaken superstitious terrors in the minds of the ignorant multitude." As the Druids had the same ends in view with the other priests of antiquity, it is highly probable that their public theology was of the same complexion with theirs; consisting of a thousand mythological fables, concerning the genealogies, attributes, offices, and actions of their gods; the various superstitious methods of appeasing their anger, gaining their favor, and discovering their will. This farrago of fables was couched in verse full of figures and metaphors, and was delivered by the Druids from *little eminences* (of which there are many still remaining) to the surround-

---

* Man is placed, according to their [the Druids'] doctrine, says Dr. Lingard, in his history of England, in the circle of *courses:* good and evil are placed before him for his selection. If he prefer the former, death transmits him from the earth into the circle of *felicity;* but if he prefer the latter, death returns him to the circle of *courses:* he is made to do penance for a time in the body of a beast or reptile; and then permitted to re-assume the form of man. According to the predominance of vice or virtue in his disposition, a repetition of his probation may be necessary; but after a certain number of transmigrations his offences will be expiated, his passions subdued, and the circle of felicity will receive him among its inhabitants.—Edit.

ing multitudes. With this fabulous divinity, these poetical declaimers intermixed moral precepts, for the regulation of the lives and manners of their hearers; and were peculiarly warm in exhorting them to abstain from doing any hurt or injury to one another; and to fight valiantly in defence of their country. These pathetic declamations are said to have made great impression on the minds of the people, inspiring them with a supreme veneration for their gods, an ardent love to their country, an undaunted courage and sovereign contempt of death. The secret and public theology of the Druids, together with their system of morals and philosophy, had swelled to such an enormous size, in the beginning of this period, that their disciples employed no less than twenty years in making themselves masters of all their different branches, and in getting by heart, that infinite multitude of verses in which they were contained.

The sun seems to have been both the most ancient and most universal object of idolatrous worship; insomuch, that perhaps there never was any nation of idolators, which did not pay some homage to this glorious luminary. He was worshipped by the ancient Britons with great devotion, in many places, under the various names of Bel, Belinus, Belatucardus, Apollo, Grannius, etc., all which names in their language were expressive of the nature and properties of that visible fountain of light and heat. To this illustrious object of idolatrous worship, those famous circles of stones, of which there are not a few still remaining, seem to have been chiefly dedicated: where the Druids kept the *sacred fire*,* the *symbol* of this *divinity*, and from whence, as being situated on eminences, they had a full view of the heavenly bodies.

As the moon appeared next in lustre and utility to the sun, there can be no doubt, that this radient queen of heaven obtained a very early and very large share in the idolatrous veneration of mankind. The Gauls and Britons seem to have paid the same kind of worship to the moon, as to the sun; and it hath been observed, that the circular temples dedicated to these two luminaries were of the same construction, and commonly contiguous. But a great number of the gods of Gaul and Britain, as well as of Greece and Rome, had been men, victorious princes, wise legislators, inventors of useful arts, etc.

---

* Like the ancient Jews and Persians, the Druids had a sacred, inextinguishable fire, which was preserved with the greatest care. At Kildare, (Ireland,) it was guarded from the most remote antiquity, by an order of Druidesses, who were succeeded in later times by an order of Christian Nuns."—(Higgins's Celtic Druids, p. 263.)—*Edit.*

They worshipped also several female divinities or goddesses; as Andraste, who is supposed to have been the same with Venus or Diana; Minerva, Ceres, Proserpine, etc. Nay, into such an abyss of superstition and idolatry were they sunk, that according to Gildas, they had a greater number of gods than the Egyptians; and there was hardly a river, lake, mountain, or wood, which was not supposed to have some divinities, or genii residing in them.

As it hath always been one end of religious worship, to obtain certain favors from the objects of it, so prayers and suplications for these favors, have always made a part of the religious worship of all nations, and in particular of that of the ancient Britons. When in danger, they implored the protection of their gods; prayers were intermixed with their praises, accompanied their sacrifices, and attended every act of their religion. It seems, indeed, to have been the constant, invariable practice of all nations, the Jews not excepted, whenever they presented any offerings or sacrifices to their gods, to put up prayers to them to be propitious to the persons by whom and for whom the offerings or sacrifices were presented; and to grant them such particular favors as they desired. Offerings of various kinds constituted an important part of the religion of the ancient Britons. This was a mode of worship, which the Druids very much encouraged, and their sacred places were crowded with those pious gifts.

Mankind in all ages, and in every country, have betrayed a consciousness of guilt, and dread of punishment from *superior beings*, on that occount. In consequence of this, they have employed various means to expiate the guilt of which they were conscious, and to escape the punishment of which they were afraid. The means which have been most universally employed by mankind for these ends, were sacrifices of living creatures to their offended gods; which constituted a very essential part of the religion of the ancient Britons, and of almost all other ancient nations. The animals which were sacrificed by them, as well as by other nations, were such as they used for their own food; which being very palatable and nourishing to themselves, they imagined would be no less agreeable to their gods. These victims were examined by the Druids with great care, to see that they were the most perfect and beautiful in their several kinds; after which they were killed, with various ceremonies, by priests appointed for that purpose. On some occasions the victims were consumed entirely by fire upon the altar; but more commonly they were divided into three parts, one of which was consumed upon the altar, another fell to the *share* of the *priests* who officiated; and on the third, the person who bought the sacrifice, feasted with his friends.

It had been well, if our British ancestors had confined themselves to the sacrificing of oxen, sheep, goats, and other animals; but we have undoubted evidence, that they proceeded to the most horrid lengths of cruelty in their superstition, and offered human victims to their gods. It had unhappily become an article in the Druidical creed, " That nothing but the life of man could atone for the life of man." In consequence of this maxim, their altars streamed with human blood, and great numbers of wretched men fell a sacrifice to their barbarous superstition. They are said indeed to have preferred such as had been guilty of thieft, robbery, and other crimes, as most acceptable to their gods; but when there was a scarcity of criminals, they made no scruple to supply their place with innocent persons. These dreadful sacrifices were offered by the Druids for the public, at the eve of a dangerous war, or in the time of any national calamity; and for particular persons of high rank, when they were afflicted with any dangerous disease. By such acts of cruelty did the ancient Britons endeavor to avert the displeasure, and gain the favor of their gods.

It seems to have been one article in the creed of the ancient Britons and of all the other nations of antiquity, that the gods whom they worshipped had the government of the world, and the direction of future events in their hands; and that they were not unwilling upon proper application, to discover these events to their pious worshippers. " The gods (says Amianus,) either from the benignity of their own natures, and their love to mankind, or because men have merited this favor from them, take a pleasure in discovering impending events by various indications." This belief gave rise to astrology, augury, magic, lots, and an infinite multitude of religious rites and ceremonies; by which deluded mortals hoped to discover the counsels of Heaven, with regard to themselves and their undertakings. We learn from Pliny, that the ancient Britons were greatly addicted to divinition, and excelled so much in the practice of all its arts, that they might have given a lesson to the Persians themselves.

The British sovereigns of this period had not much authority either in the making or executing the laws, which are the principal acts of government in peaceful times. In that great relaxation of political union and civil government which prevailed in times of peace, their religion seems to have been the chief bond of union among the British tribes and nations; and the Druids, who were the ministers of that religion, appear to have professed the sole authority of making, explaining, and executing the laws; an authority to which the clergy of the church of Rome long and eagerly aspired, but never fully obtained. One great reason of the superior success of the Druids in their ambitious schemes was this: the laws among the ancient Britons, and some other ancient nations, were not considered as the decrees of their princes, but as the commands of their gods; and the Druids were supposed to be the only persons to whom the gods communicated the knowledge of their commands, and consequently the only persons who could declare and explain them to the people. The violations of the laws were not considered as crimes against the prince or state, but as sins against Heaven; for which the Druids, as the ministers of Heaven, had alone the right of taking vengeance. All these important prerogatives of declaring, explaining, and executing the laws, the Druids enjoyed and exercised in their full extent. "All controversies, says Cæsar, both public and private are determined by the Druids. If any crime is committed, or any murder perpetrated; if any disputes arise about the division of inheritances, or the boundaries of estates, they alone have the right to pronounce sentence; and they are the only dispensers both of rewards and punishments. These ghostly judges had one engine which contributed much to procure submission to their decisions. This was the sentence of excommunication or interdict, which they pronounced against particular persons, or whole tribes, when they refused to submit to their decrees. The interdicts of the Druids were no less dreadful than those of the Popes, when their power was at its greatest height. The unhappy persons against whom they were fulminated, were not only excluded from all sacrifices and religious rites; but they were held in universal detestation, as impious and abominable; their company was avoided as dangerous and contaminating; they were declared incapable of any trust or honor, put out of the protection of the laws, and exposed to injuries of every kind.* A condition which must have rendered life intolerable, and have brought the most refractory spirits to submission.

The first day of May was a great annual festival, in honor of Bel-

---

* Here doubtless is the source of the severity said to be enjoined upon the masonic brotherhood towards backsliding or contumacious members; but the tolerant spirit of the age has, no doubt, left the threats held out in this case, a mere dead letter. Masons expel their members for immoral conduct, and so do all other religious societies. They have a practice, however, in this regard, that appears reprehensible, which is, to publish in their registers, the names of all those who have had the misfortune to be expelled from the order. This tends to fix an indelible stigma upon the character of an offending brother, prejudicial not only to himself, but to his family connections. The list containing names of delinquents, should never be permitted to go beyond the walls of the lodge room.—Edit.

inus, or the sun. On this day prodigious fires were kindled in all their sacred places, and on the tops of all their cairns, and many sacrifices were offered to that glorious luminary, which now began to shine upon them with great warmth and lustre. Of this festival there are still some vestiges remaining, both in Ireland and in the Highlands of Scotland, where the first of May is called Beltain, that is, the fire of Bel, or Belinus.* Midsummer-day and the first of November, were likewise annual festivals; the one to implore the friendly influences of heaven upon their fields, and the other to return thanks for the favorable seasons and the fruits of the earth; as well as to pay their yearly contributions to the ministers of their religion. Nay, it is even probable, that all their gods and goddesses, their sacred groves, their hallowed hills, lakes, and fountains, had their several anniversary festivals; so that the Druidish calendar was perhaps as much crowded with holidays as the popish one is at present. On these festivals, after the appointed sacrifices and other acts of devotion were finished, the rest of the time was spent in feasting, singing, dancing and all kinds of diversions.

It was an article in the Druidical creed, "That it was unlawful to build temples to the gods: or to worship them within walls and under roofs." All their places of worship therefore were in the open air, and generally on *eminences*, from whence they had a full view of the heavenly bodies, to whom much of their adoration was directed. But that they might not be too much incommoded by the winds and rains, distracted by the view of external objects, or disturbed by the intrusion of unhallowed feet, when they were instructing their disciples, or performing their religious rites, they made choice of the deepest recesses of groves and woods for their sacred places. These groves were planted, for that purpose, in the most proper situations, and with those trees in which they most delighted. The chief of these was the strong and spreading oak, for which tree the Druids had a very high and superstitious veneration. These sacred groves were watered by some consecrated fountain or river, and surrounded by a ditch or mound, to prevent the intrusion of improper persons.† In the centre of the grove was a

---

* I am inclined to think the author has mistaken the cause of these illuminations, and that they were originally signals for a general purification, mentioned by Pluche, in which every thing subject to decay, for the benefit of health, was consumed by fire, on the first of February in Egypt. They were called the festival of the *fire-brands;* which name probably became changed, in consequence of the origin and intention of the custom having been lost.—Edit.

† Where (says masonry) did our ancient brethren meet, before lodges were erected? Answer. Upon *holy ground*, or the *highest hill*, or lowest vale, or any other secret place; the better to guard against cowans and enemies."—Edit.

circular area, inclosed with one or two rows of large stones set perpendicular in the earth; which constituted the temple, within which the altar stood, on which the sacrifices were offered. In some of their most magnificent temples, as particularly in that of Stone-henge, they had laid stones of prodigious weight on the tops of the standing pillars, which formed a kind of circle aloft in the air, and added much to the grandeur of the whole.

The British Druids were in the zenith of their power and glory at this period; enjoying an almost absolute authority over the minds and persons of their own countrymen; and being greatly admired and resorted to by strangers. But as the Romans gained ground in this island, the power of the Druids gradually declined, until it was quite destroyed. For that victorious people, contrary to their usual policy, discovered every where a very great animosity against the persons and religion of the Druids. They deprived the Druids of all authority in civil matters, and showed them no mercy when they found them trangressing the laws, or concerned in any revolt.

Such of the Druids as did not think fit to submit to the Roman government, and comply with the Roman rites, fled into Caledonia, Ireland, and the lesser British isles, where they supported their authority for some time longer. Many of them retired into the isle of Anglesey, which was a kind of little world of their own; and where the Arch Druid of Britain is thought to have had his stated residence. But they did not long remain undisturbed in this retirement. For Suetonius Paulinus, who was governor of Britain under Nero, A. D. 61, observing that the isle of Anglesey was the great seat of disaffection to the Roman government, and the asylum of all who were forming plots against it, determined to subdue it. Having conducted his army to the island, and defeated the Britons, who attempted to defend it, though they were animated by the presence, the prayers, and the exhortations of a great multitude of Druids and Druidesses, he made a very cruel use of his victory. Not content with cutting down their sacred groves, demolishing their temples, overturning their altars, he burned many of them in the fires, which they had kindled for sacrifising the Roman prisoners, if the Britons had gained the victory. So many of the Druids perished on this occasion, and the unfortunate revolt under Boadicia, queen of the Iceni, which happened soon after, that they were never able to make any considerable figure after this period.

But though the dominion of the Druids in South Britain was destroyed at this time, many of their superstitious practices continued much longer. Nay so deeply rooted were these principles in the minds of the people both of Gaul and Britain, that they not only bafled all the power of the Romans, but they even resisted the superior power and divine light of the gospel for a long time after they had embraced the Christian religion. This is the reason that we meet with so many edicts of emperors, and canons of councils, in the sixth, seventh, and eight centuries, against the worship of the sun, moon, mountains, rivers, lakes, and trees. This superstition continued even longer in Britain than in some other countries, having been revived first by the Saxons, and afterwards by the Danes. It is a sufficient proof of this, that so late as the eleventh century, in the reign of Canute, it was found necessary to make the following law against those heathenish superstitions: "We strictly *discharge* and forbid all our subjects to worship the gods of the gentiles; that is to say, the sun, moon, fires, rivers, fountains, hills or trees, and wood of any kind."

Extract from Dr. Lingard's History of England.

To the veneration which the British Druids derived from their sacerdotal character, must be added the respect which the reputation of knowledge never fails to extort from the ignorant. They professed to be the repositories of a *sacred science*, far above the comprehension of the vulgar: and their schools were opened to none but the sons of illustrious families. Such was their fame, that the Druids of Gaul, to attain the perfection of the institute, did not disdain to study under their British brethren. They professed to be acquainted with the nature, the power, and the providence of the divinity; with the figure, size, formation, and final destruction of the earth; with the stars, their position and motions, and their supposed influence over human affairs. They practiced the art of *divination* and magic. Three of their ancient astrologers were able, it is said, to foretel whatever should happen before the day of doom. To medicine also they had pretensions: but their knowledge was principally confined to the use of the miseltoe, vervain, savin, and trefoil; and even the efficacy of these simples was attributed not the nature of the plants, but to the influence of *prayers* and *incantations*.

From the Edinburgh Encyclopedia.

The garments of the Druids were remarkably long; and, when employed in religious ceremonies, they always wore a *white* surplice.

They generally carried a *wand* in their hands; and wore a kind of ornament enchased in gold about their necks, called the *Druid's egg*. Their necks were likewise decorated with gold chains, and their hands and arms with bracelets: they wore their hair very short, and their beards remarkably long.

The Druids had one chief, or Arch-druid, in every nation, who acted as high-priest, or *pontifex maximus*. They had absolute authority over the rest: and commanded, decreed, punished, etc. at pleasure. He was elected from amongst the most eminent Druids, by a plurality of votes.

They worshipped the Supreme Being under the name of *Esus*, or *Hesus*,* and the symbol of the oak; and had no other temple than a wood or a grove, where all their religious rites were performed. Nor was any person admitted to enter that *sacred recess*, unless he carried with him a *chain*, in token of his absolute dependence on the Deity.

The *consecrated groves*, in which they performed their religious rites, were fenced round with stones, to prevent any persons entering except through the passages left open for that purpose, and which were *guarded* by some *inferior Druids*, to prevent any *stranger* from intruding into their *mysteries*. These groves were of different forms; some quite circular, others oblong, and more or less capacious as the votaries in the districts to which they belonged were more or less numerous.

In the *chain* carried by the ancient Britons, in the performance of their religious rites, is to be seen the archetype of the cable-tow, or tow-rope, worn about the neck of the aspirant to masonic secrets; which is the subject of much ridicule among the uninitiated *profane*, and, indeed, the fraternity themselves do not seem to be aware of its true import. They are not conscious that this humble badge is a testimony of their belief in God, their dependence on him, and their solemn obligations to devote themselves to his will and service.

The candidate for masonic instruction should be looked upon as an untutored, wild man of the woods: a mere child of nature, unregenerated and destitute of any knowledge of the true God, as well as the conveniences and comforts of civilized life. For

---

* "Horus, says Pluche, assumed the casque and buckler, when levies or recruits were intended. He was then called *Harits*, that is, *the mighty, the formidable*, (violentes. Job xv. 20.) The Syrians softened this word and pronounced *Hazis*. We find the same word *hazis* or *hesus*, used to signify *the terrible in war*. "The Lord strong and mighty, the Lord *mighty in battle*." Ps. xxiv. 8. Others pronounced it without aspiration, and said *Ares*; others with a very harsh and rough aspiration, and pronounced *Warets*. This figure of Horus in a warlike dress, became the god of combats. He evidently is the *Asis* of the inhabitants of Edesse, the *Hezus*, of the Gauls, the *Ares* of the Greeks, the *Warts* or *Mars* of the Sabines and Latins."—*Edit.*

this reason, he is exhibited blindfolded, "Neither naked nor clothed," but about halfway between both.

Here also may be seen the type of the masonic Tiler, an *inferior officer*, with a drawn sword, to guard the lodge from the impertinent intrusion of cowans, or rather covins, and eavesdroppers. It will not be pretended that a sword is needed in this case; it is a mere ensign of office, in conformity to the Druidical custom.

The following extracts from Hume's History of England, will account for the slow introduction of Christianity among the ancient Britons.

The most memorable event which distinguished the reign of this great prince [Ethelbert,] was the introduction of the Christian religion among the English Saxons. The superstition of the Germans, particularly that of the Saxons, was of the grossest and most barbarous kind, and being founded on traditionary tales received from their ancestors, not reduced to any system, nor supported by political institutions like that of the Druids, it seems to have made little impression on its votaries, and to have easily resigned its place to the new doctrine promulgated to them.

On the contrary, the constant hostilities which the Saxons maintained against the Britons, would naturally indispose them for receiving the Christian faith, when preached to them by such inveterate enemies.

The Saxons, though they had been long settled in the island, seem not as yet, [early part of the ninth century,] to have been much improved beyond their German ancestors, either in arts, civility, knowledge, humanity, justice, or obedience to the laws. Even Christianity though it opened the way to connections between them and the more polished states of Europe, had not hitherto been very effectual in banishing their ignorance, or softening their barbarous manners. As they received that doctrine through the corrupted channels of Rome, it carried along with it a great mixture of credulity and superstition, equally destructive to the understanding and to morals. The reverence toward saints and reliques, seems to have almost supplanted the adoration of the Supreme Being. Monastic observances were esteemed more meritorious than the active virtues; the knowledge of natural causes was neglected, from the universal belief of *miraculous interposition* and *judgments*; bounty to the church atoned for every violence against society; and the remorses for cruelty, murder, treachery, assassination, and the more robust vices, were appeased, not by amendment of life, but by penances, servility to the monks, and an abject and illiberal devotion. * * * The ecclesiastics, in those days of ignorance, [middle of the ninth century,] made rapid advances in the acquisition of power and grandeur; and in inculcating the most absurd and most interested doctrines. Not content with the donations of land made them by the Saxon Princes and nobles, they had cast a wishful eye on a vast revenue, which they claimed as belonging to them, by a sacred and indefeasible title. However little versed in the scriptures, they had been able to discover, that, under the Jewish law, a tenth of all the produce of land was conferred on the priesthood; and, forgetting what they themselves taught, that the moral part only was obligatory on Christians, they insisted that this donation *conveyed a perpetual property, inherent, by divine right*, in those who officiated at the altar. During some centuries, the whole scope of sermons and homilies was directed to this purpose; and one would have imagined, from the general tenor of these discourses, that all the practical parts of Christianity were comprised in the exact and fathful payment of the tithes to the clergy. Encouraged by their success in inculcating these doctrines, they ventured farther than they were warranted, even by the Levitical law, and pretended to draw the tenth of all industry, merchandize, wages of laborers, and pay of soldiers; nay, some canonists went so far as to affirm, that the clergy were entitled to the tithe of the profits made by courtesans in the exercise of their profession.

Slavery in England.

As slaves are not admitted into the society of Freemasons, it may be interesting to some of my readers, unacquainted with the fact, to know the vast extent of the evils of slavery in England at the time when this institution is supposed to have been established, and the great proportion of the inhabitants, particularly of the mechanical and laboring classes, that were consequently excluded from a participation in its charitable and benevolent purposes. I, therefore, give the following extract from Dr. Henry's History of the different ranks of people, in Britain, from the arrival of the Saxons, A. D. 449, to the landing of William, duke of Normandy, 1066.

The lowest order of people among the Anglo-Saxons, and the other nations of Britain, in this period, were slaves, who with their wives and children were the property of their masters. Besides those who were native slaves, or slaves by birth, others frequently fell into this wretched state, by various means; as, by an ill run at play,—by the fate of war, or by forfeiting their freedom by their crimes, or even by contracting debts which they were not able to pay. These unhappy people, who were very numerous, formed an article, both of internal and foreign trade; only if the slave was a Christian, he was not to be sold to a Jew or a Pagan; or if he belonged to the same nation with his master, he was not to be sold beyond the sea. Slaves were, however, of various kinds, among the Anglo-Saxons, employed in various works, and were not all in an equal state of thraldom. Some of them were called *villani*, or *villains*, because they dwelt at the villages belonging to their masters, and performed the servile labors of cultivating their lands, to which they were annexed, and transferred with these lands from one owner to another. Others were domestic slaves, and performed various offices about the houses and families of their masters. Some of these domestic slaves of the king and the nobility, were taught the mechanic arts, which they practised for the benefit of their owners; and the greatest number of the mechanics of those times seem to have been in a state of servitude. Slaves were not supposed to have any family or relations who sustained any loss by their death; and, therefore, when one of them was killed by his master, no mulct was paid, because the master was supposed to be the only loser; when slain by another, his price or manbote was paid to his master. In a word, slaves of the lowest order, were considered merely as animals of burden, and parts of their owners' living stock. In the laws of Wales it is expressly said: " That a master hath the same right to his slaves as to his cattle."

The horrors of this cruel servitude were gradually mitigated; and many of those unhappy wretches were raised from this abject state to the privileges of humanity. The introduction of Christianity contributed not a little, both to alleviate the weight of servitude, and diminish the number of slaves. By the canons of the church, which were in those times incorporated with the laws of the land, and of the same authority, Christians were commanded to allow their slaves certain portions of time to work for their own benefit, by which they acquired property,—the bishops had authority to regulate the quantity of work to be done by slaves,—and to take care that no man used his slave harshly but as a fellow-Christian. The bishops and clergy recommended the manumission of slaves as a most charitable and meritorious action; and in order to set the example, they procured a law to be made, that all English slaves of every bishop should be set at liberty at his death, and that every other bishop and abbot in the kingdom should set three slaves at liberty. But after all these mitigations of the severities of slavery, and diminuitons of the number of slaves, the yoke of servitude was still very heavy, and the greatest part of the laborers, mechanics, and common people, groaned under that yoke at the conclusion of this period.

The next class or rank of people in Britain, in this period, was composed of those who were called *frilazin;* who had been slaves, but had either purchased, or by some other means obtained their liberty. Though these were in reality free-men, they were not considered as of the same rank and dignity with those who had been *born* free; but were still in a more ignoble and dependent condition, either on their former masters, or on some new patrons. This custom, the Anglo-Saxons seemed to have derived from their ancestors in Germany, among whom those who had been made free did not differ much in point of dignity or importance in the state, from those who continued in servitude. This distinction, between those who had been made free, and those who enjoy freedom by descent from a long race of freemen, still prevails in many parts of Germany; and particularly in the original seasts of the Anglo-Saxons. Many of the inhabitants of towns and cities in England, in this period, seem to have been of this class of men, who were in a kind of middle state, between slaves and freemen.

The third class, or rank of people in Britain, in the period we are now considering, consisted of those who were completely free, and descended from a long race of freemen. This numerous and respectable body of men, who were called *ceorls* constituted a middle class, between the laborers and mechanics, who were generally slaves, or descended from slaves on the one hand, and the nobility on the other. They might go where they pleased, and pursue any way of life that was most agreeable to their humor.—vol. iii. p. 320

In the time of the Anglo-Saxon rule, says Dr. Lingard, not less than two thirds of the population of Britain, existed in a state of slavery. And the sale and purchase of slaves publicly prevailed during the whole of this period. These unhappy men were sold like cattle in the market. The Northumbrians, like the savages of Africa, are said to have carried off, not only their own countrymen, but even their friends and relatives, and to have sold them as slaves in the ports of the continent. The men of Bristol were the last to abandon this nefarious traffic. Their agents travelled into every part of the country; they were instructed to give the highest price for females in a state of pregnancy; and the slave ships regularly sailed from that port to Ireland, where they were secure of a ready and profitable market.

CHAPTER V.

OPINIONS AND OBSERVATIONS OF LEARNED WRITERS ON FREEMASONRY, WHO ARE IN FULL COMMUNION WITH THE ORDER.

Most of those writers on masonry who belong to the craft, either through ignorance or design, have mystified the subject in such a manner as to render it, not only unintelligible, but absolutely forbidding. The opinions, therefore, of those of the order who have written with candor, and with a view of eliciting the truth, so far as they deemed consistent with their obligations, are entitled to great consideration. Such are the writings from which the following extracts are made, or, at least, the passages selected generally bear that character.

From "The Spirit of Masonry," by William Hutchinson. Carlisle, (England,) 1802.

I am induced to believe the name of *mason* has its derivation from a language, in which it implies some strong indication, or distinction, of the nature of the society; and that it has no relation to architects.

The titles of masons and masonry most probably were derived from the Greek language, as the Greek idiom is adopted by the Druids, as is shown in many instances in the course of this work. When they committed any thing to writing, they used the Greek alphabet—and I am bold to assert the most perfect remains of the Druidical rites and ceremonies are preserved in the ceremonials of masons, that are to be found existing among mankind. My brethren may be able to trace them with greater exactness than I am at liberty to explain to the public. The original names may probably be derived from or corrupted of *Mysterion, res arcana,* mysteries, and *Mystes, sacris initiatus mystis*— those initiated to sacred mysteries.*

There is no doubt that our ceremonies and mysteries were derived from the rites, ceremonies, and institutions of the ancients, and some of them from the remotest ages.

---

* The English word mason has a very simple origin; it comes from *maçon,* French; "From *mas,* an old word which signifies house; thus a mason is a person who makes houses."—(French Enc.) The awkard connection which architecture is made to bear towards the mysteries involved in freemasonry, is easily accounted for on the supposition, which is undoubtedly a fact, that the Druids made use of the craft of masonry merely as a cover to their mystic worship.

The ancient masonic record, [the examination of a freemason by Henry VI.] says, that masons knew the way of gaining an understanding of Abrac. On this word all commentators (which I have yet read) on the subject of masonry, have confessed themselves at a loss.

Abrac, or Abracar, was a name which Basilides, a religious of the second century, gave to God, who he said was the author of three hundred and sixty-five.

The author of this superstition is said to have lived in the time of Adrian, and that it had its name after *Abrasan*, or *Arbaxas*, the denomination which Basilides gave to the Deity —— He called him the *Supreme God*, and ascribed to him seven subordinate powers or angels, who presided over the heavens:—and also, according to the number of the days in the year, he held that three hundred and sixty-five virtues, powers, or intelligences, existed as the emanations of God: the value, or numerical distinctions of the letters in the word, according to the ancient Greek numerals, made 365—— A B P A X A Σ.
$$\phantom{\text{Greek numerals, made 365—— }}1\ \ 2\ 100\ 1\ 60\ 1\ 200.$$

With antiquaries, *Abraxas* is an antique gem or stone, with the word abraxas engraven on it. There are a great many kinds of them, of various figures and sizes, mostly as old as the third century. Persons professing the religious principles of Basilides, wore this gem with great veneration, as an amulet; from whose virtues, and the protection of the Deity, to whom it was consecrated, and with whose name it was inscribed, the wearer presumed he derived health, prosperity, and safety.

In the British museum is a beryl stone, the form of an egg. The head is in camio, and reversed in taglio. The head is supposed to represent the image of the Creator, under the denomination of Jupiter Ammon:—the sun and moon on the reverse, the *Osiris and Isis* of the Egyptians; and were used hieroglyphically to represent the omnipotence, omnipresence, and eternity of God. The star seems to be used as a point only, but is an emblem of *prudence*, the third emanation of the Basilidian divine person.

In church history, *Abrax* is noted as a mystical term, expressing the Supreme God; under whom the Basilidians supposed three hundred and sixty-five dependent deities; it was the principle of the gnostic hierarchy; whence sprang their multitudes of Thæons. From *Abraxas* proceeded their *primogænial mind*; from the primogænial mind, the *logos* or word; from the logos, the *Phronæsis* or prudence: from phronæsis, *Sophia* and *Dynamis*, or wisdom and strength; from these two proceeded *principalities, powers, and angels ;* and from these other angels, of the number of three hundred and sixty-five, who were supposed to have the government of so many celestial orbs committed to their care. The Gnostics were a sect of Christians having particular tenets of faith ; they assumed their name to express that new knowledge and extraordinary light to which they made pretensions ; the word *gnostic* implying an enlightened person.

Jupiter Ammon, was worshipped under the symbol of the *sun*. He was painted with *horns*, because with the astronomers the sign *Aries* in the zodiac is the beginning of the year : when the sun enters into the house of Aries, he commences his annual course. Heat, in the Hebrew tongue is *Hammah*, and in the prophet Isaiah *Hammamin* is given as a name of such images. The error of depicting him with horns, grew from the doubtful signification of the Hebrew word, which at once expresses *heat*, splendor, or brightness, and also *horns*.

" The sun was also worshipped by the house of Judah, under the name of *Tamuz*, for Tamuz, saith Hierom, was *Adonis*, and Adonis is generally interpreted the sun, from the Hebrew word *Adan* signifying *dominus*, the same as Baal or Moloch, formerly did the *lord or prince of the planets*. The month which we call June, was by the Hebrews called Tamuz ; and the entrance of the sun into the sign cancer, was in Jews' astronomy termed *Tekupha Tamuz*, the revolution of Tamuz.— About the time of our Saviour, the Jews held it unlawful to pronounce that essential name of God, Jehovah ; and instead thereof, read Adonai, to prevent the heathen blaspheming that holy name, by the adoption of the name of Jove, etc. to the idols. Concerning Adonis, whom some ancient authors call Osiris, there are two things remarkable : the death or loss of Adonis, and the finding of him again : as there was great lamentation at his loss, so was there great joy at his finding. By the death or loss of Adonis, we are to understand the departure of the sun ; by his finding again, the return of that luminary. Now he seemeth to depart twice in the year ; first, when he is in the tropic of cancer, in the farthest degree northward ; and, secondly, when he is in the tropic of capricorn, in the farthest degree southward. Hence we may note, that the Egyptians celebrated their Adonia in the month of November, when the sun began to be farthest southward, and the house of Judah theirs in the month of June, when the sun was farthest northward ; yet both were for the same reasons. Some authors say, that this lamentation was performed over an *image* in the night season ; and when they had sufficiently lamented, a candle was brought into the room, which ceremony might mystically denote the return of the sun, then the priest with a soft voice, muttered this form of words, "*Trust ye in God, for out of pains salvation is come unto us.*"—*Godwyn's Moses and Aaron.*

Our ancient record, which I have mentioned, brings us positive evidence of the Pythagorean doctrine, and Basilidian principles, making the foundation of our religious and moral rules.

As the servants of *one God*, our predecessors professed the temple, wherein the deity approved to be served, was not the work of men's hands. In this the Druids copied after them: the universe, they confessed, was filled with his presence, and he was not hidden from the most distant quarters of creation: they looked upwards to the heavens as his throne, and wheresoever under the sun, they worshipped, they regarded themselves as being in the dwelling place of the divinity, from whose eye nothing was concealed. The ancients not only refrained from building temples, but even held it utterly unlawful; because they thought no temple spacious enough for the sun, the great symbol of the deity. "*Mundus universus est templum solis**" was their maxim; they thought it profane to set limits to the infinity of the deity ; when, in later ages, they built temples, they left them open to the heavens, and unroofed.

As we derived many of our mysteries and moral principles from the doctrines of Pythagoras, who had acquired his learning in Egypt, and others from the Phœnicians, who had received the Egyptian theology in an early age, it is not to be wondered that we should adopt Egyptian symbols, to represent or express the attributes of the Divinity.

The third emanation of Abrax, in the Gnostic hierarchy, was Phronœsis, the emblem of Prudence, which is the first and most exalted object that demands our attention in the Lodge. It is placed in the centre, ever to be present to the eye of the mason, that his heart may be attentive to her dictates, and steadfast in her laws ;—for prudence is the rule of all virtues ;—prudence is the path which leads to every degree of propriety ;—prudence is the channel whence self-approbation flows for ever :—she leads us forth to worthy actions, and as a *Blazing Star*, enlighteneth us through the dreary and darksome paths of this life.†

---

* The maxim of the ancients, that "*The whole world was the temple of the sun*," does not indicate that they looked upon the sun as the symbol of the Deity, but as the Deity itself.

† It is a difficult task for masons to make out any thing respecting this *blazing star*, that has the least semblance of reason. They find it among the symbols, but are not aware how it came there, and endeavor to make the best of it they possibly can. The reader will recollect that it is Anubis the dog-star, who warned the Egyptians to retire from the plain with their produce, to avoid the destructive effects of the inundation.

That innocence should be the professed principle of a mason, occasions no astonishment, when we consider that the discovery of the Deity leads us to the knowledge of those maxims wherewith he may be well pleased. The very idea of a God, is succeeded with the belief, that he can approve of nothing that is evil; and when first our predecessors professed themselves servants of the Architect of the world, as an indispensable duty, they professed innocence, and put on white raiment, as a type and characteristic of their conviction, and of their being devoted to his will. The Druids were apparelled in white, at the time of their sacrifices and solemn offices. The Egyptian priests of Osiris wore snow-white cotton in the service of Ceres, [Isis] under whom was symbolized the gift of Providence in the fruits of the earth—and the Grecian priests also put on white.

Every degree of sin strikes the rational mind of man with some feelings of self-condemnation. Under such conviction, who could call upon, or claim the presence of a Divinity, whose demonstration is good works?—Hence are men naturally led to conceive, that such Divinity will accept only of works of righteousness. Standing forth for the approbation of heaven, the servants of the *first revealed God*, bound themselves to maxims of purity and virtue; and as masons, we regard the principles of those who were the first worshippers of the *true God*, we imitate their apparel, and assume the badge of *innocence*.

In this pretension of the author, that the predecessors of the freemasons were the first to discover the true God, an allusion is evidently made to the Egyptians, who seem to have been great boasters in this respect.

"The most ancient of the profane historians, and he who speaks in the most learned manner of the religion of the Egyptians, is Herodotus. The Egyptians, according to him, are the first people in the world who knew the names of the *twelve* great gods, and from them the Greeks had learnt them. They too are the first who erected altars to the gods, made representations of them, raised temples to them, and had priests for their service, excluding wholly the other sex from the priesthood. Never was any people, continues he, more religious. They even had two sorts of writing, the one common, and the other *sacred*; and this last is set apart solely for the mysteries of religion. Their priests *shave their whole body* every third day. Clothed in linen, with sandals made of the plant papirus, they are not allowed to wear other apparel, nor other covering for their feet. They are obliged to bathe themselves in cold water twice a day, and as often by night. So scrupulously exact must the priests be in the choice of the victims which they are to offer to their gods, that they are punished with death if they offer up any which have not the qualities requisite." Mayo's Myth. v. 11. p. 27.

The color of *white's* being made a symbol of purity and innocence probably owes its origin to the following absurd notions of the ancients:

"As the *constellations* of summer accompanied the season of long, warm and unclouded days, and that of fruits, and harvests, they were considered as the powers of light, fecundity and creation, and by a transition from a physical to a moral sense, they became genii, angels of science, of benificence, of purity and virtue: and as the constellations of winter were connected with long nights and polar fogs, they were the genii of darkness, of destruction, of death, and, by transition, angels of ignorance, of wickedness, of sin and vice.

"Now, as the earthly states, the greater part despotic, had already their monarchs, and as the sun was apparently the monarch of the skies, the summer hemisphere, empire of light, and its constellations, a people of *white* angels, had for king an enlightened God, a creator intelligent and good. And as every rebel faction must have its chief, the heaven of winter, the subterraneous empire of darkness and woe, and its stars, a people of *black* angels, giants or demons, had for their chief a malignant genius, whose character was applied by different people to the constellation which to them was the most remarkable.—Ruins p. 144–5.

"The priests, says Dupuis, clothe themselves in white, a color assigned to Aromaze or the god of light."

The superstition, or rather affectation in regard to this color, is still retained among some Christian sects, whose priests cover themselves with this pagan, outward show of purity.

It is somewhat remarkable that *white* as an emblem of purity and innocence should have descended to the aborigines of America. The *prophet*, who accompanied Black Hawk and other chiefs to Washington as hostages for the faithful performance of the treaty made with their nation, (1833) thus addressed the President of the United States:

"Father I have come this day *clothed in white* (pointing to his leather doublet) in order to *prove* that my intentions are of the most pacific nature, and (raising his hands to heaven) I call upon the great spirit of myself and forefathers to witness the purity of my heart on this occasion."

In this country, [England] under the Druids, the first principles of our profession most assuredly were taught and exercised.

We are bold to say, that if we trace the antiquity of masonry on operative principles, and derive such principles from the building of Solomon's Temple, we may as well claim all the professions which Hiram excelled in.

Assuredly the secrets revealed to us were for other uses than what relate to labouring up masses of stone; and our society, as it now stands, is an association on religious and charitable principles; which principles were instituted and arose upon the knowledge of God.

We ground a judgment of the nature of our profession on our ceremonials, and flatter ourselves every mason will be convinced that they have no relation to building and architecture, but are emblematical, and imply moral, and spiritual, and religious tenets. It appears self-evident, that the situation of the Lodge, and its several parts, are copied after the Tabernacle and Temple, and are representative of the universe implying that the universe is the temple in which the Deity is every where present;* our mode of teaching the principles of our profession, is derived from the Druids; our maxims of morality, from Phythagoras; our chief emblems, orignally from Egypt; to Basilides we owe the science of Abrax, and the characters of those emanations of the Deity which we have adopted, and which are so necessary for the maintenance of a moral society.

Our Lodges are not now appropriated to worship and religions ceremonies; we meet as a social society, inclined to acts of benevolence, and suffer the more sacred offices to rest unperformed. Whether this neglect is to our honor, we presume not to determine; in our present state professing ourselves free and accepted masons, we are totally severed from architects, and are become a set of men working in the duties of charity, good offices, and brotherly love.

From the ancient rites and ceremonies which we have laid before you, it will be easy for you to trace the origin of our own rites, and to discover the foundations on which our society is formed.

We have explained to you, that the structure of the Lodge is a pattern of the universe, and that the first entry of a mason represents the first worship of the true God. We have retained the Egyptian symbols of the sun and moon, as the emblems of God's power, eternity, omnipresence, and benevolence; and thereby we signify, that we are the children of light, and that the first foundation of our profession, is the knowledge and adoration of almighty *Mesouraneo*, who seateth himself in the centre of the heavens:—we derive from the Druids many of the Amonian rites; and have saved from oblivion, many of their religious rites, in our initiation to the first degree of masonry, which otherwise would have slept in eternity. These we seem to have mixed and tempered with the principles of the Essenes, who are a sect as ancient as the departure of the children of Israel out of Egypt. The philosophy of the Egyptians, and the manners, principles, and customs of the Hebrews, were introduced to this land by the Phœnicians, and make a part of our profession, so far as they are adapted to the worship of Nature's great Author, unpolluted by idolatry.

We hold our grand festival on the day of St. John, which is midsummer day; in which we celebrate that season when the sun is in its

---

* This was a pagan principle, according to the author's own showing above. The fact is, the tabernacle, as well as the temple of Solomon, appear to have been constructed upon the same plan as the temples of the ancients.

greatest altitude, and in the midst of its prolific powers: the great type of the omnipotence of the Deity.

We are not to search for our antiquity in the mythology of Greece or Rome, we advance into remoter ages. Religion was the original and constituent principle; a recognition of the Deity first distinguished us from the rest of mankind ; our predecessors searched for the divine essence in the wonders displayed on the face of nature—they discovered supreme wisdom in the order of the universe—in the stellary system they traced the power, in the seasons and their changes the bounty, and in animal life the benevolence of God; every argument brought with it conviction, and every object confirmation, that all the wonders displayed to the eye of man, were only to be produced by some superlative being, and maintained by his superintendency. It was from such conviction, that men began to class themselves in religious societies.

I may venture to assert, it was the only consequence which could ensue, whilst men, were looking up to the Divinity through his works, that they would conclude the sun was the region, where, in celestial glory, the Deity reposed.

We discover in the Amonian and Egyptian rites, the most perfect remains of those originals, to whom our society refers. We are told they esteemed the soul of man to be an emanation of the Supreme, and a spirit detached from the seraphic bands, which filled the solar mansions, and surrounded the throne of majesty. They looked up to this grand luminary, as the native realm from whence they were sent on this earthly pilgrimage, and to which they should, in the end, return ; the figure of the sun was at once a memorial of their divine origin, a badge of the religious faith they professed, and a monitor of those principles, which should conduct and ensure their restoration. How soon, or to what extreme, superstition and bigotry debased this emblem, is a research painful and unprofitable.

We masons have adopted three particular characteristics, secrecy, charity, and brotherly love. Our sense of these great duties has been explained, and of what especial import they are to masons ; or to men who have separated themselves from the rest of mankind, and professed they are servants of *Him who ruleth in the midst of heaven.*

If our ceremonies mean not the matter which has been expressed ; if they imply not the moral and religious principles which we have endeavored to unvail; it may be asked of you, masons, what they do imply, import, or indicate ?

Genius of Masonry.

Samuel L. Knapp, Esq., in a work entitled "The Genius of Masonry, or a Defence of the Order," in taking notice of the late discoveries made by Champollion and others, of the hidden wisdom of the Egyptians, by ascertaing a clue to the understanding of their hieroglyphics, observes:

"These distinguished men who have embarked with so much of that zeal which is necessary for the accomplishment of any great object, will, we trust, be permitted to entirely draw the veil of Isis which has covered her mysteries so long that the world began to despair of ever seeing the glories it concealed. Behind this veil of Isis I have long thought was concealed our masonic birth. I now fully believe it. There was the *cradle* of masonry: no matter by what *name* it was called: no matter by whom it was enjoyed."—p. 99.

An Ahiman Rezon;*

By brother Frederick Dalcho, M. D., Charleston, S. C., 1807. Containing extracts from an Oration delivered by him, before the grand lodge of South Carolina, 1801 : from which the following is taken.

In the earliest age of man, when the human mind, untainted by the vices and prejudices of later times, unshackled by the terrors and anathemas of contending sectaries, and the machinations of biggotted priests, the God of nature received the homage of the world, and the worship of his adorable name constituted the principal employment of him, to whom the mysteries of nature were first revealed. After the deluge, the worship of the Most High was obscured by clouds of imagery, and defiled by idolatry.

In many of the ancient nations of the east, their religious rights were enveloped by the priests, in allegories, emblems, hieroglyphics, and mystic devices, which none could understand, but those of their own order. From these ancient examples, the mysteries of the craft have been wisely concealed from the vulgar ; and under cover of various well adapted symbols, is conveyed to the enlightened freemason an uniform and well connected system of morality.

I am of opinion that the ancient society of free and accepted masons was never a body of architects; that is, they were not, origi-

---

* The book of constitution is usually denominated, *Ahiman Rezon:* which is a corruption of three Hebrew words, *achi man ratzon*, which signifie the thoughts, or opinions, of a true and faithful brother.

nally, embodied for the purposes of building, but were associated for moral and religious purposes. It must be evident to every freemason, that the situation of the lodge, and its several parts, are copied after the tabernacle and temple; and represent the universe as the temple in which the Deity is every where present. Our manner of teaching the principles of our mystic profession is derived from the Druids, who worshipped one supreme God, immense and infinite; our maxims of morality from Pythagoras, who taught the duties we owe to God as our creator, and to man as our fellow creature; many of our emblems are originally from Egypt; the science of Abrax, and the characters of those emanations of the Deity, which we have adopted, are derived from Basilides.

The word Mason is derived from the Greek, and, literally, means a member of a religious sect, or one who is professedly devoted to the worship of the Deity.*

As humanity ever springs from true religion, every religious sect, which acknowledges the Supreme Being, are equally respected by the order. Religious disputes are banished from our societies, as tending to sap the foundations of friendship, and to undermine the basis of the best institutions. The great book of nature is revealed to our eyes; and the universal religion of her God, is what we profess, as freemasons.

Dr. Dalcho published a second edition of his Ahiman Rezon, with *additions* and *explanatory notes*, in 1822. And it may not be improper to state, that previously to this period he had taken clerical orders: which perhaps caused him to examine the masonic institution more critically than he had done, to ascertain if it contained anything inconsistent with his sacerdotal functions. At any rate, a change in his opinions on some points, seems to have taken place; which are set forth in his explanatory notes, from which the following extracts are taken.

Origin of Freemasonry.

The principles of our order, are coeval with the creation. Founded upon the laws of nature, and the commands of God, nothing had precedence of them in time. The origin of the society, however, as an institution distinct from other associations, is involved in impenetrable obscurity. And notwithstanding the learning and zeal of many industrious masons, it will, I fear, forever remain unknown. Various

---

* The author here adopts Hutchinson's conjecture, upon trust, which has been shown to be erroneous.

indeed, have been the speculations on this subject; and great has been the labor expended by many "good men and true," to prove that every man of note, from Adam down to the present day, were freemasons. But such round assertions are beneath the dignity of the order, and would not be urged by men of letters. Neither Adam, nor Noah, nor Nimrod, nor Moses, nor Joshua, nor David, nor Solomon, nor Hiram, nor St. John the Baptist, nor St. John the Evangelist, belonged to the masonic order, however congenial their principles may have been. It is unwise to assert more than we can prove, and to argue against probability. Hypothesis in history is absurd. There is no record, sacred or profane, to induce us to believe that these holy and distinguished men, were freemasons, and our traditions do not go back to their days. To assert that they were freemasons, may "make the vulgar stare," but will rather excite the contempt, than the admiration of the wise. If St. John was a freemason, then it is impossible that Solomon should have been one, because his lodges could not have been dedicated to St. John, who was not born until a thousand years after the first temple was built, therefore, there would have been in St. John's day, what there was not in Solomon's, which would be contrary to our known principles. And besides if both these personages were freemasons, then we have the evidence that Solomon was the greater mason of the two, and our lodges should be dedicated to him, instead of St. John. But if Solomon was a freemason, then there could not have been a freemason in the world, from the day of the creation, down to the building of the temple, as must be evident to every master-mason.

The excellence of our institution depends upon its usefullness, and not its antiquity. It is sufficient for us to know, that the origin of the institution is so remote, that the date is lost in the lapse of ages, and can now only be indistinctly traced by occasional records, and the traditions of the order.

Dr. Priestly, in his remarks on Mr. Dupuis' Origin of all Religions, classes the freemasons and Gypsies together. He affirms that, "they have formed themselves into a body, though of a very heterogeneous kind, but are not able to give any rational account of their origin." (Institutes of Moses page 336.) The philosopher has certainly placed us in bad company, by classing us with these vagrants; but his inference is nevertheless true. The purposes for which our institution was originally organized, are now as unknown as the date of its origin. Whether it was designed for architectural purposes, for the improvement of the arts and sciences, or for the preservation of revealed religion, by significant symbols and impressive rights, in an idolatrous and barbarous age cannot now be ascertained. Perhaps all these objects gave rise or perfection to the institution.

When the Hindoos claim for their Shastras an antiquity of more than two millions of years; when the Chaldeans boast of observations of the stars for more than four hundred and seventy thousand years, and Manetho Sebennyta, the high priest of Heliopolis, claims for the Egyptians, a national existence of near fifty-four thousand years, who would hesitate to pronounce them all fabulous? Let freemasons, then, give up the vain boastings, which ignorance has foisted into the order, and relinquish a fabulous antiquity rather than sacrifice common sense. Let us trace our principles to Adam, or even to God himself, with reverence be it spoken, but let us not excite the pity of the wise, by calling Adam a freemason. This will not lessen the dignity or importance of the institution, but rather add to its celebrity by giving it a reasonable origin.

Mr. Clinch supposes freemasonry was introduced into Europe by means of the Gypsies. (See Anthologia Hibernica, for April, 1794, p. 280.)

Although this is a very ridiculous supposition, it is highly probable that the leaders of the first emigrants of this tribe from Egypt, had been initiated into the lesser mysteries; and perhaps copied in part from them the forms of the oath which they administer to their initiates.

"Every person who was not guilty of some public crime, could obtain admission to the lesser mysteries. Those vagabonds called Egyptian priests in Greece and Italy, required considerable sums for initiations; and the Gypsies practise similar mummeries to obtain money."—(De Pauw's Egypt, vol. 2. p. 42.)

The customs of the latter, and the oath which they impose upon each other, has been preserved by Bailey; from which, as a curious antique, I make the following extract.

The Gypsies derive their origin and name from the Egyptians, a people heretofore very famous for astronomy, natural magic, the art of divination, etc., and therefore, are great pretenders to *fortune-telling*.

It is the custom of these vagrants to swear all that are admitted into their fraternity, by a form and articles annexed to it, administered by the principal Maunder or roguish Strowler, and which they generally observe inviolably. The manner of admitting a new member, together with the said oath and articles, are as follows:

The name of the person is first demanded, and a nick-name is then given him in its stead, by which he is ever after called, and in time, his other name is quite forgotten. Then standing up in the middle of the fraternity, and directing his face to the Dimber-Damber, or prince of the gang, he swears in this manner, as is dictated to him by one of the most experienced.

"I, Crank-Cuffin, do swear to be a true brother, and will in all things obey the commands of the great Tawney Prince, and keep his counsel, and not divulge the secrets of my brethren.

I will never leave nor forsake this company, but observe and keep all the times of appointments, either by day, or by night, in any place whatsoever.

I will not teach any one to cant; nor will I disclose ought of our *mysteries* to them, although they flog me to death.

I will take my Prince's part against all that shall oppose him, or any of us, according to the utmost of my ability; nor will I suffer him, or any belonging to us, to be abused by any strange Abrams, Rufflers, Hookers, etc., but will defend him or them as much as I can against all other outlyers whatever.

I will not conceal ought I win out of Libkins, or from the Ruffmans; but will preserve it for the use of the company."

The canters have, it seems a tradition, that from the three first articles of this oath, the first founders of a certain boastful, worshipful fraternity, who pretend to derive their origin from the earliest times, borrowed of them, both the hint and form of their establishment. And that their pretended derivation from the first Adam, is a forgery, it being only from the first Adam-Tiler.

The same author has given the meaning of the cant terms here used as follows:

Abrams; shabby beggars. Rufflers; notorious rogues. Hookers; petty thieves. Libkin; a house to lie in. Ruffmans; the woods or bushes. Adam-Tiler; the comrade of a pick-pocket, who receives stolen goods or money, and scours off with them.

Festival of St. John the Evangelist.

In every country where freemasonry is encouraged, their anniversary festival is celebrated with great ceremony. It is a day set apart by the brotherhood, to worship the Supreme Architect of heaven and earth; to implore his blessings upon the great family of mankind; and to partake of the feast of brotherly affection. All who can spare a day from their necessary avocations, should join in this celebration. The freemasons of South Carolina have chosen St. John the Evangelist's day, as their anniversary.

The annual festival of the order, is celebrated in some places on St. John the Baptist's day, (June 24.) and in others on St. John the Evangelist's day, (Dec. 27.) The latter has been preferred in South Carolina, on account of the heat of our climate. But why either of them should be chosen in preference to any other day, is, perhaps, difficult to explain. I know of no connection between these eminent " Saints and Servants" of God, and the lodge of freemasons. *I now write* as a minister of that God, to whose honor and glory, my life is devoted, and to whom I must, ere long, give an account of my stewardship. I think I run no hazard of contradiction in saying that if either of these most holy men, were now permitted to revisit the earth, they would greatly wonder at finding their names enrolled as patrons of an institution, of which they had never heard. And there can be no question of the fact, that if they were now to apply for admission into any of our lodges, they would be utterly incapable of " working their way in."

The annual masonic festival in England, is held " on the anniversary of the feast of St. John the Baptist, or of St. George, or on such other day as the grand master may appoint." Their reasons for selecting these days, are sufficiently expressive of their opinions. The feast of St. John the Baptist, occurs on the 24th June, when, in that climate, the weather is not too warm for a public procession; and St. George, whose anniversary is held April 23d, is the patron Saint of England. This, to me, is clear evidence, that the anniversary of St. John was not selected, because they deem him to have been a freemason.

I am, however, of opinion, that we act wisely in taking St. John the Evangelist, for the patron of our order. He is worthy of imitation, both in his principles and conduct. But, as it has been well said of old *Amicus Plato, Amicus Socrates, sed magis amica veritas;* so I may truly say, that I highly venerate the masonic institution, under the fullest persuasion, that where its principles are acknowledged, and its laws and precepts obeyed, it comes nearest to the Christian religion, in its moral effects and influence, than any institution with which I am acquainted. At the same time, I hold truth to be too sacredly connected with my office and character, to allow me to approve of the custom, now generally adopted, of dedicating our lodges "to God and the holy St. John," as joint patrons of the society. I hold it to be irreverent, to unite the name of any created being, with the uncreated Godhead. The name of God is surely sufficiently honorable and powerful as the patron of our institution, without the addition of any other. If the lodge be dedicated to God, let it be dedicated to him alone. He can bless all our " work begun, continued, and ending" in Him, without the assistance of St. John. But, if it be necessary to have St. John, let us take him alone, as our tutelary head, or unite with him any of the old worthies, usually considered as masons.

It is a well known fact, as before observed, that the early Christians very judiciously adopted, not only the festival days of the pagans, but even their manner of celebrating them. This was doubtless done with the view of rendering the change in the new religion less perceptible, and consequently less shocking to the prejudices of those who adhered to the ancient instition. Among the principal festivals of the pagans were those of the solstices and equinoxes.

De Pauw, in his Philos. Diss. on the Egyptians and Chinese, observes, that "Besides the Sabbath, which the Egyptians seem to have observed very regularly, they had a fixed festival at each new moon; one at the summer and one at the winter solstice, as well as the vernal and autumnal equinoxes. All others except that at the rising of Sirius were changeable, and dependent on certain combinations known to the priests only, who transferred them arbitrarily, whenever they occurred on the neomenia, the equinox, or the solstice."—Vol. 2. p. 159.

"The festival of the 25th of December, (says Higgins, in his Celtic Druids, p. 165.) was celebrated by the Druids in Britain and Ireland, with great *fires* lighted on the tops of the hills. This festival was repeated on the twelfth day, or on what we call the Epiphany. In some parts the fires are still continued. The *evergreens*, and particularly the missletoe, which are used all over the country, and even in London, in this festival, betray its Druidical origin.

"On the 25th of December, at the first moment of the day throughout all the ancient world, the birth day of the *god Sol* was celebrated. This was the moment, when, after the supposed winter solstice, and the lowest point of his degradation below our hemisphere, he began to increase, and gradually to ascend. At this moment, in all the ancient regions, his birth day was kept; from India to the ultima Thule, these ceremonies partook of the same character: every where the god was feigned to be born, and his festival was celebrated with great rejoicings."

The fires on the hills are emblematical of the power and ardor of the sun, when he should have ascended to the upper regions, which he was then approaching; and the evergreens are typical of the effect that would be produced in the vegetable kingdom by that event.

What possible allusion can the display of evergreens at Christmas have, unless that here suggested? The custom is undoubtedly borrowed from the Druids, and is continued without the least applicability to the Christian religion. Masonic lodges, moreover, are decorated in this manner on the 27th of December, which is corroborative of the opinion here advanced.

The Roman and Episcopal churches still retain an astronomical cast, as is apparent both in their *fixed and moveable feasts*. "The principal of the moveable feasts is *Easter*, which governs the rest. Easter was an idol or goddess of the Saxons, in honor of whom, sacrifices were offered about the time of the year which is now observed by the church in commemoration of our Saviour's resurrection. It is kept on the first Sunday after the *full moon*, succeeding the *vernal equinox*." (Bailey.

The *birth days* of the two St. Johns, it appears, are fixed by the framers of the church ritual, at the periods of the solstices. These of course were observed as festival days by the Druidical masons; and as they were celebrated openly with pompous processions, etc., it became necessary for them to use every precaution to prevent a discovery of the real cause of these demonstrations of joy. With this view they appropriated the names of the feasts or festivals that had been assumed for them by the Catholic Church. But while they ostensibly honored the two St. Johns, they were mentally paying homage to their favorite divinity, the sun.

Signs and Symbols,

Illustrated and explained, in a course of Lectures on Freemasonry. By George Oliver Vicar of Clee, etc.—*Grimsby*, 1826.

Under what denomination soever our Science has been known in the world; under what form soever it may have been practised; it has always been understood to have a distinct reference to the worship of God, and the moral culture of man.

The characteristic propensities of a people, the state of their progress from barbarism to civilization; their intellectual attainments, the character of their government, or their intercourse with other nations, might and did create some distinction in the ceremonial, but the great essentials, broadly struck out by the Cabiric priests, did never vary.

In a word, the mysteries were the only vehicles of religion throughout the whole idolatrous world; and it is probable that the very name of religion might have been obliterated from amongst them, but for the support it received by the periodical celebrations, which preserved all the forms and ceremonies, rites and practices of divine worship; and the varieties of custom in this particular, constituted the sole difference betwixt the masonry (shall I so call it?) of different nations. Wheresoever the mysteries were introduced, they retained their primitive form, adapted to the customs and usages of the national religion: and if varied in some unimportant points, it was to commemorate certain extraordinary performances of the tutelary deities, or to perpetuate some remarkable circumstance attending their first institution in a particular country. Hence the same, or similar ceremonies, which were applied to Osiris and Isis in Egypt, the great source of secret and mysterious rites, (Lucian de Dea Syr,) were celebrated in Greece, in honor of Bacchus and Rhea; at Eleusis, they were applied to Ceres and Proserpine; in Tyre and Cyprus, to Adonis and Venus; in Persia, to Mithras and Mithra; in India, to Maha Deva and Sita; in Britain, to Hu and Ceridwen; in Scandinavia, to Odiñ and Frea; and in Mexico, to Tlaloc and the Great Mother; for these appear to be but different names for the same deities, and most probably referred to Noah and the Ark. They were all originally the same system.

They used as most significant emblems, the Theological Ladder —the triple support of the universal lodge, called by masons, wisdom, strength, and beauty; the point within a circle, and many other legitimate emblems of masonry; they used the same form of government —the same system of secrecy, allegory, and symbolical instruction; all tending to the same point, the practice of moral virtue. None were admitted without previous probation and initiation; the candidates were bound by solemn oaths; united by invisible ties; taught by symbols; distinguished by signs and tokens; and, impelled by a conscientious adherence to the rules of the order, they professed to practice the most rigid morality; justice towards men, and piety to the gods.

If primitive masonry was a system of light, the initiated heathen equally paid divine honors to the sun, as the source of light, by circumambulating *in the course of that luminary*, during the ceremony of initiation.

Did the initiated refer to the four elements? They were portrayed by certain prismatic colors. *White* represented the air; *Blue* the water; *Purple* the earth; and *Crimson* the fire.

The Zodiac was considered as the great assembly of the *twelve gods*; the sun being supreme, and the planets his attendants.

The emblems which masons now make use of as the secret repositories of their treasures of morality, were adopted by the ancients in very early times, as signs and symbols; and were even substituted for alphabetical characters.

The triangle, now called a trowel, was an emblem of very extensive application, and was much revered by ancient nations as containing the greatest and most abstruce mysteries. It signified equally the Deity, Creation, and Fire.

On the name of the Deity.

The great name of the Deity, which is termed by Josephus, incommunicable, is said to be preserved in the system of freemasonry. Calmet observes, "when we pronounce Jehovah, we follow the crowd; for we do not know distinctly the manner wherein this proper and incommunicable name of God should be pronounced, which is written with Iod, Hi, Vau, Hi, and comes from the verb haiah, he has been. The ancients have expressed it differently. Sanchoniathon writes Jevo; Diodorus the Sicilian, Macrobius, St. Clemens Alexandrinus, St. Jerom, and Origen, pronounce Iao," etc.

The Tetragrammaton was preserved and transmitted by the Essenes. It was always communicated in a whisper, (R. Tarphon, apud. Ten. Idol. page 395,) and under such a disguised form, that while its component parts were universally known, the connected whole was an incommunicable mystery. They used, in common with the whole Jewish nation, the ancient and significant symbol by which this name was designated, viz. three jods, with the point kametz placed underneath them, thus, (⸫) to express the equality of the three persons of which they believe the godhead to be composed. This holy name they held in the utmost veneration. Calmet, says, they believe the name of God to include all things. "He who pronounces it, say they, shakes heaven and earth, and inspires the very angels with astonishment and terror. There is a sovereign authority in this name; it governs the world by its power."

The letter schin, ש, was adopted as a mysterious emblem to designate the Tetragrammaton; and hence this letter was supposed to comprehend many valuable qualities. It was, therefore, deeply engraven by the Jews on their phylacteries, both before and behind, to induce the protection of the omnipresent deity it represented. Another symbol was an equilateral triangle illuminated with a single jod. △ This initial letter jod, "denotes the thought, the idea of God. It is a Ray of Light, say the enraptured cabbalists, which darts a lustre too transcendent to be contemplated by mortal eye; it is a point at which thought pauses, and imagination itself grows giddy and confounded. Man, says M. Basnage, citing the rabbies, may lawfully roll his thoughts from one end of heaven to the other; but they cannot approach that inaccessible Light, that primitive existence contained in the letter Jod." (Maur. Ind. Ant. vol. iv.)

The chief varieties of this sacred name amongst the inhabitants of different nations, were Jah, and Bel or Baal, and On or Om. The first of these, as we have just seen, had many fluctuations. Jupiter, Jove, Evohe, etc. were but corruptions of Jah or Jehovah. Iao, was pronounced by the oracle of Apollo, to be the first and greatest of the deities. (Macrob. Saturn. 1. 18.)

The compounds of the second name Bel, are of great variety. Belus, was used by the Chaldeans; and the deity known amongst the ancient Celtæ, by the name of Bel or Bel-enus, which title, by the modern authors, is identified with Apollo.

The third variation was On. Under this appellation the deity was worshipped by the Egyptians; and they professed to believe that he was eternal, and the fountain of light and life; but, according to their gross conceptions, being necessarily visible, the sun was adored as his representative, and was, most probably the same as Osiris. They knew the general purport of the name and little more. If they believed On to be the living and eternal God, they allowed the same attributes to the sun, which they undoubtedly worshipped as the Lord of the creation. Oannes was the god of the Chaldeans; and Dag-On of the Philistines, both of which are derivations of the same name. On, was evidently the same deity as the Hebrew Jehovah; and was introduced amongst the Greeks by Plato, who acknowledges his eternity and incomprehensibility in these remarkable words; "Tell me of the god ON; which IS, and never knew beginning." (In Timœo. v. iii. p. 27.) And the same name was used by the early Christians for the true God; for St. John in the Apocalypse, (Chap. 1. v. 4.) has this expression—*On, kai ó en, kai ó erchomenos*, which is translated in our authorized version of the Scriptures, by, "HIM, which is, and which was, and which is to come."

The same word with a small variation, was one of the names of the supreme deity in India; and a devout meditation on it was considered capable of conveying the highest degree of perfection.* In the ordinances of Menu, we are informed how this sacred word was produced. "Brahma milked out, as it were, from the three Vedas, the letter A, the letter U, and the letter M; which form, by their coalition, the triliteral monosyllable, together with three mysterious words, bhur, bhuvah, swer; or, earth, sky, heaven." (S. W. Jones. Works, vol. iii. p. 93.) These three letters, which are pronounced OM, refer to the deity in his triple capacity of creator, preserver, and destroyer. The method of using it is given in the same code. "Three suppressions of breath, made according to the divine rule, accompanied with the triverbal phrase, bhurbhuvahswah and the triliteral syllable OM, may be considered as the highest devotion of a Brahmin." (Ibid. p. 235.) Mr. Colebrooke informs us that "a Brahmana, beginning and ending a lecture of the Veda, or the recital of any holy strain, must always pronounce to himself the syllable OM; for unless the syllable Om precede, his learning will slip away from him; and unless it follow, nothing will be retained; or that syllable being prefixed to the several names of worlds, denotes that the seven worlds are manifestations of the power, signified by that syllable." (Asiat. Res. vol. v. p. 352.)

On the Cherubim.

Every branch of science is progressive. In the first degree of masonry, we are *taught* the several duties of our station, whether to

---

* Seneca, the stoic, says, "It is of little consequence by what name you call *the first nature*, and the *divine reason* that presides over the universe, and fills all the parts of it —he is still the same God. You may give him as many names as you please, provided you allow *but one sole principle*, every where present."—*Edit.*

God, our neighbor, or ourselves;—the practice of the *Theological* and *Cardinal Virtues*, and every moral and social work. In the second degree, we are admitted to a participation in the *mysteries of human science;* and catch a *glimpse of celestial glory.* But in the third degree, the vail is removed; we are admitted to the *holy of holies*—we view the *Cherubim* in all their brightness; and are blessed with a *foretaste of heaven,* through the *resurrection of the dead.* And if we pass on to the royal arch, we receive a wonderful accession of knowledge, *and find every thing made perfect;* for this is the *ne plus ultra* of masonry, and can never be exceeded by any human institution.

In the peculiar lectures of masonry, much importance is attached to that great symbol of the glory of God, the cherubim. It is a subject which adds much to the *dignity* and *authority* of our science; inasmuch as its illustration has formed an important part of speculative masonry.

When the true invisible God was renounced and forgotten, this symbol furnished mankind with plausible substitutes; and hence in almost all the heathen nations of which we have any account, the Supreme Being was worshipped under the corporeal form of one or other of its component parts; and they all ultimately referred to the sun; and hence this luminary, in connection with the cherubic animals, became a chief object of Gentile worship throughout the world.

The ox was adored in Egypt, India and Britain; China and Japan; Persia, Greece, and Peru. (Plin. Nat. Hist. 1. viii. c. 46.—Asiat. Research. vol. i. p. 250.—Dav. Druids. p. 128.)

As the ox was the predominating figure in the cherubim, so it was the most universal symbol of idolatry, and was frequently worshipped in a compound form.

He was an emblem of the great father or Noah; and the ark was called *Ken-Tauros,* the stimulator of the bull. (Bryant. Anal. vol. ii. p. 440.) He was worshipped with splendid rites, at that season of the year particularly when the sun was in Taurus.

In India, the bull was held in high veneration; and honored with diurnal worship in conjunction with the Linga or Phallus, as an emblem of justice and prolific power.

A bull was also the well known symbol of Bacchus; who is styled in the Orphic hymns, "the deity with two horns, having the head of a bull." (Hymn 29.)

The Lion was adored in the east and the west, by the Egyptians and the Mexicans as a most powerful divinity. (Diod. Sic. Bibl. 1. i. c. 6.)

The same animal was emblematical of the sun in Tartary and Persia; (Hesych.) and hence, on the national banner of Persia, a lion was emblazoned with the sun rising from his back. "The sovereigns of Persia have for many centuries preserved as the peculiar arms of their country, the sign or figure of Sol in the constellation Leo; and this device, which exhibits a lion couchant and the sun rising at his back, has not only been sculptured upon their palaces, and embroidered upon their banners, but has been converted into an order, which in the form of gold and silver medals, has been given to those who have distinguished themselves against the enemies of their country." (Sir John Malcom's Hist. of Pers. c. xxv.)

The Egyptian astronomers taught that the creation of the world took place at the precise period of time when the sun rose in Leo; which sign was hence esteemed the peculiar habitation of the sun; and this belief gave an additional stimulus to the veneration which mankind entertained for the king of animals. Mr. Bryant observes in reference to this superstition; "as the chief increase of the Nile was when the sun was passing through Leo, the Egyptians made the lion a type of an innundation. All effusions of water were specified by this characteristic. And from hence has been the custom of making the water which proceeds from cisterns and reservoirs, as well as spouts from the roofs of buildings, come through the mouth of a lion." (Bryant's Plagues of Egypt, p. 86. note.)

The eagle was sacred to the sun in many countries, particularly in some parts of Egypt, Greece and Persia. In our Scriptures the king of Babylon is termed an Eagle. It was reputed to have fed Jupiter with nectar in the Cretan cave, and was certainly an emblem of his dominion. With the British Druids it formed a symbol of their supreme god; it was embroidered on the consecrated standard of the Mexican princes; and the common ensign of the Roman legions was a golden eagle. Indeed the peculiar property which this noble bird possesses of beholding with impunity the undiminished vigor of the sun's meridian rays, would naturally procure for it an emblematical distinction.

The man, or idol in human shape, was worshipped all over the world; for which custom this reason has been assigned by Porphiry, when charged with worshipping God under the figure of a man. He allowed the deity to be invisible, but thought him well represented in that form: not because he is like him in external shape, but because that which is divine is rational. (Porph. In Euseb. de præp. evan, l iii. c. 7.)

The Cherubim, according to the author, consist of the figures of a man, an ox, a lion, and an eagle: which combination he represents as awfully sacred and sublime, evidently with the view of heightning the mystical importance of royal arch masonry, whose *armorial ensigns* it composes.

Dr. Rees remarks, that "Cherub, or Cherubim, in Hebrew, is sometimes taken for a cralf or on ox. In Syriac and Caldee, the word cherub signifies to till or plough, which is the work of oxen. According to Grotius, the Cherubim were figures resembling a calf. Bochart and Spencer think they were similar to an ox. The figure of the Cherubim was not always uniform, since they are differently described in the shapes of men, eagles, oxen, lions, and a composition of all these figures put together.* After all the suggestions and conjectures of learned persons, it still remains to be determined, what these emblematic figures were intended to represent."

They form a part of the machinery of pagan worship, each figure being symbolical of the great object of adoration, the sun. This Mr. Oliver himself has fully shown.

Thus it appears that the masonic Cherubim, composing its arms, consists of representations of the sun under various figures, conformible to the fanciful superstitious notions of ancient nations.

"Ye inhabitants of India ! in vain you cover yourselves with the vail of mystery : the hawk of your god Vichenou is but one of the thousand emblems of the sun in Egypt ; and your incarnations of a god in the fish, the boar, the lion, the tortoise, and all his monstrous adventures, are only the metamorphoses of the sun, who, passing through the signs of the twelve animals, was supposed to assume their figures, and perform their astronomical functions. People of Japan ! your bull which breaks the mundane egg, is only the bull of the zodiac, which in former times opened the seasons, the age of creation, the vernal equinox. It is the same bull Apis which Egypt adored, and which your ancestors, O Jewish rabbins ! worshipped in the golden calf. This is still your bull, followers of Zoroaster ! which sacrificed in the symbolical mysteries of Mythra, poured out his blood which fertalized the earth." Ruins, p 138.

The supporters of the armorial ensigns of royal arch masonry, according to Cross's chart, are two figures representing the god Pan ; who may be considered as one of the most ancient divinities of paganism.

"Orpheus says that Pan signifies universal nature, proceeding from the divine mind, of which the heaven, earth, sea, and the eternal fire, are so many members. He was generally represented with the body and head of a man, and the lower parts were those of a goat." Bailey.

On the mysterious darkness of the Third Degree.

In the ancient mysteries, the Epoptes, or perfectly initiated aspirants, were reputed to have attained a state of pure and ineffable *Light*, and

---

* At the end of the planetary system, the mystagogue presents us with a picture of the fixed heavens, and the four celestial figures which were placed at the four corners of heaven, according to the astrological scheme.

These four figures were the lion, the bull, the man (Aquarius,) and the eagle, which divide the whole zodiac into four parts of three signs each, in the points of the sphere called fixed and solid. The stars which correspond to these are called the four *royal stars*.—(Dupuis, p. 557.)—*Edit.*

pronounced safe under the protection of the celestial gods; (Diod. Sic. Bibl, 1. v. c. 3.) while the unhappy multitude who had not undergone the purifying ceremonies, were declared reprobate; said to wander in all the obscurity of darkness, to be deprived of the divine favor, and doomed to a perpetual residence in the infernal regions, amidst a cheerless and overwhelming contamination. (Plato Phædone.—Arist. Eleusinia et apud Stobæum. Serm. 189, etc. Schol. Arist. Ranis.)

During the Persian initiations, this doctrine was enforced *ex cathedra*, (from the desk or pulpit.) The Archimagus informed the candidate at the moment of illumination, that the *divine lights* were displayed before him; (Psell. in Schol. in Orac. Zoroast.) and after explaining the nature and purport of the mysteries in general, he taught that the universe was governed by a good and evil power who were perpetually engaged in contest with each other, and as each in turn prevailed, the world was characterized by a corresponding succession of happiness and misery; that uninitiated and immoral men were votaries of the evil power, and the virtuous initiated of the good; and that at the end of the world, each, with his followers will go into a separate abode; the latter with *Yazdan* shall ascend by means of a *ladder* to a state of eternal *light*, where exists unalloyed happiness and the purest pleasures; the former with *Ahriman*, shall be plunged into an abode of *darkness*, where they shall suffer an eternity of disquietude and misery, in a desolate place of punishment situated on the shore of a stinking river, the waters of which are black as pitch and cold as ice. Here the souls of the uninitiated eternally float. Dark columns of smoke ascend from this stream, the inside of which is full of serpents, scorpions, and venomous reptiles. (Hyde. de relig. vet. Pers. p. 399.)

The multitude, being thus amused with fables, and terrified with denunciations, were effectually involved in uncertainty, and directed to paths where error only could be found; for every proceeding was mysterious, and every mythological doctrine shrouded under a corresponding symbol. These allegorical fables becoming popular, the simple rites of primitive worship soon assumed a new and more imposing form, and religion was at length envelloped in a veil so thick and impervious as to render the interpretation of their symbolical imagery extremely difficult and uncertain. The slender thread of truth being intimately blended and confused with an incongruous mass of error, the elucidation was a task so complicated and forbidding, that few had the courage to undertake it; and men were rather inclined to bow implicitly to popular tradition, than be at the pains to reconcile truth with itself, and separate, with a nice and delicate hand, the particles of genuine knowledge from the cumbrous web of allegory and superstition, in which they were interwoven.

It is an extraordinary fact, that there is scarcely a single ceremony in freemasonry, but we find its corresponding rite in one or other of the idolatrous mysteries; and the coincidence can only be accounted for by supposing that these mysteries were derived from masonry. Yet however they might assimilate in ceremonial observances, an essential difference existed in the fundamental principles of the respective institutions.*

In all the ancient mysteries, before an aspirant could claim to participate in the higher secrets of the institution, he was placed within the *Pastos*, or *Bed*, or *Coffin ;* or in other words, was subjected to a solitary confinement for a prescribed period of time, that he might reflect seriously, in seclusion and *darkness*, on what he was about to undertake; and be reduced to a proper state of mind for the reception of great and important truths, by a course of fasting and mortification. *This was the symbolical death of the mysteries*, and his deliverance from confinement was the act of regeneration, or being born again ; or, as it was also termed, *being raised from the dead*. " Clement of Alexandria tells us, that in the formulary used by one who had been initiated, he was taught to say, I have descended into the bed chamber. The ceremony here alluded to was doubtless the same as the descent, into Hades ; and I am inclined to think, that when the aspirant entered into the mystic cell, *he was directed to lay himself down upon the bed, which shadowed out the tomb or coffin of the Great Father*. This pro-

---

* The author, in the commencement of his work, says:—" One important question which appears to have been almost wholly neglected, by masonic writers, is, whether freemasonry be a servile imitation of certain ceremonies in the ancient idolatrous mysteries, as is asserted by some writers; or whether it be the *great original* from which the mysteries themselves were derived. On this inquiry, I have bestowed much deliberate consideration; for I found it impossible to be satisfied with practising a science derived from the *polluted dregs* of idolatry." And, he comes to the conclusion, that freemasonry is, "in reality, the original institution from which all the mysteries were derived." And adds, "We have ample testimony to establish the fact, that the mysteries of all nations were originally the same, and diversified only by the accidental circumstances of local situation and political economy."

That *an essential difference exists* between the ancient mysteries and freemasonry, wants evidence. The whole of bishop Warburton's dissertation on the subject of the former, goes to disprove the assertion. However erroneous both may be in a theological point of view, they agree in moral principles, and are unexceptionable. And that any institution called freemasonry, or having a relation thereto, existed anterior to that which is termed *the mysteries*, is a gratuitous assumption, without a shadow of proof. The mysteries, under the name of freemasonry, were first introduced in the eleventh century of the Christian era.

The Reverend author, it is evident, instead of having any qualms of conscience on the subject, was endeavoring to satisfy the scruples which might arise in the minds of some of his less liberal parishioners.

cess was equivalent to his entering into the infernal ship; and while stretched upon the holy couch, *in imitation of his figurative deceased prototype*, he was said to be wrapped in the deep sleep of death. *His resurrection from the bed was his restoration to life*, or his regeneration into a new world; and it was virtually the same as his return from Hades, or his emerging from the gloomy cavern, or his liberation from the womb of the ship-goddess.* (Fab. Pag. Idol. b. v. c. 7.)

The candidate was made to undergo these changes in scenic representation; and was placed under the Pastos in perfect darkness, generally for the space of *three days and nights*. The time of this solitary confinement however varied in different nations. In Britain *nine* days and nights was the specified period; (W. Arch. Tri. 50 apud Dav. Druids. p. 404.) in Greece, three times nine days; (Porph. vit. Pyth.) while in Persia it extended to *fifty* days and nights of darkness, want of rest, and fasting! (Porph. de abstin. c. vi. s. 18.) To explain the nature of these places of penance and mortification, I need not carry you to distant shores; the remains in our own country are both numerous and open to public inspection; for I have no doubt but the British Cromlech was the identical vehicle of preparation for the Druidical mysteries.

A celebrated piece of antiquity was recently standing near Maidstone, called Kit's Cotti House. This was a dark chamber of probation; for Kit is no other than Ked, or Ceridwen, the British Ceres; and Cotti or Cetti meant an Ark or Chest; hence the compound word referred to the Ark of the diluvian god Noah, whose mysterious rites were celebrated in Britain; and Ceridwen was either the consort of Noah, or the Ark itself; symbolically the great mother of mankind.

---

* This is exactly imitated in the third degree of masonry; where the candidate personates *his figurative deceased prototype*, Hiram. Of this Mr. Oliver is fully aware, yet with all this pitiful mummery before him, he, as we have seen above, says:

"In the third degree, the *veil is removed*; we are admitted to the *holy of holies*; we view the *cherubim*, [the ox, the lion, etc.] in all their brightness; and are blessed with *a foretaste of heaven, through the resurrection of the dead.*"

Voltaire, in speaking of the Eleusinian mysteries, says, "This pure religion consisted in the acknowledgment of one Supreme God, of his providence, and of his justice. That which *disfigured* these mysteries was, if we can believe Tertullien, the ceremony of *regeneration*. It was necessary that the initiated should appear to be *resuscitated*; it was the symbol of the new life he was about to embrace. The hierophant raised over him the sacred knife: they feign to strike him, and he also feigns to fall dead; after which he appears to be resuscitated. There is still among the freemasons, a remnant of this ancient ceremony."—(Oeuvres, tome 16, p. 166.)

The whole of this nonsense grows out of the fabled death of the sun. "It is he, [the sun] that, under the name of Osiris, persecuted by Typhon and by the tyrants of the air, was *put to death, shut up in a dark tomb, emblem of the hemisphere of winter*; and afterwards, ascending from the inferior zone towards the zenith of heaven, *arose again from the dead,* triumphant over the giants and the angels of destruction."—(Ruins, p 139.)

The Phallus was the gross Symbol under which Noah, or the great father of the mysteries was worshipped; and it was usually represented by a pyramidal stone.

Coincidences like these are too striking to be overlooked; particularly when we consider that the initiations formed a most important and essential part of religious worship; and no person could hold any dignified appointment as a priest, or legislator, without passing through these forms, which included, as an indispensable preliminary rite, *the solitary confinement of the darkened Pastos.*

On the three pillars, wisdom, strength, and beauty.

In the British and other mysteries, these three Pillars represented the great emblematical Triad of Deity, as with us they refer to the three principal officers of the lodge. We shall find however that the symbolical meaning was the same in both. It is a fact, that in Britain, the Adytum or lodge was actually supported by three stones or pillars, which were supposed to convey a regenerating purity to the aspirant, after having endured the ceremony of initiation in all its accustomed formalities. The delivery from between them was termed a new birth. (Hanes Taliesin, c. iii.—Dav. Druids, p. 230.) The corresponding pillars of the Hindu mythology were also known by the names of wisdom, strength, and beauty, and placed in the east, west, and south, crowned with three human heads. They jointly referred to the creator, who was said to have planned the great work by his infinite wisdom; executed it by his strength; and to have adorned it with all its beauty and usefulness for the benefit of man. These united powers were not overlooked in the mysteries, for we find them represented in the solemn ceremony of initiation, by the three presiding Brahmins or Hierophants. The chief Brahmin sat in the east, high exalted on a brilliant throne, clad in a flowing robe of azure, thickly sparkled with golden stars, and bearing in his hand a magical rod; thus symbolizing Brahma, the creator of the world. His two compeers, clad in robes of equal magnificence, occupied corresponding situations of distinction. The representative of Vishnu, the setting sun, was placed on an exalted throne in the west; and he who personated Siva, the meridian sun, occupied a splendid throne in the south. The masonic lodge, *bounded only by the extreme points of the compass, the highest heavens and the lowest depths of the central abyss,* is said to be sppported by three pillars, wisdom, strength, and beauty. In like manner the Persians, who termed their emblematical Mithratic cave or lodge, the Empyrean, feigned it to be supported by three intelligences, Ormisda, Mithra, and Mithras, who were usually denominated, from certain characteristics which they were suppored individually to possess, eternity, fecundity, and authority. (Vid. Ramsay's travels of Cyrus and dissertation thereto annexed.) Similar to this were the forms of the Egyptian Deity, designated by the attributes of wisdom, power, and goodness: (Plut. de Isid. and Osir. p. 373.) And the sovereign good, intellect, and energy of the Platonists, which were also regarded as the respective properties of the divine Triad. (Plat. in Timæo.)

It is remarkable that every mysterious system practised on the habitable globe, contained this Triad of deity. The oracle in Damascius asserts that "throughout the world a Triad shines forth, which resolves itself into a Monad;" and the uniform symbol of this three-fold Deity, was, an equilateral triangle; the precise form occupied by our pillars of wisdom, strength, and beauty. In the mysteries of India, Brahma—Vishnu—Siva, were considered as a tri-une god, distinguished by the significant appellation of Tri-murti.* Brahma was said to be the creator, Vishnu the preserver, and Siva, the judge or destroyer. In the east, as the pillar of wisdom, this deity was called Brahma; in the west, as the pillar of strength, Vishnu; and in the south as the pillar of beauty, Siva: and hence, in the Indian initiations, as we have just observed, the representative of Brahma was seated in the east; that of Vishnu in the west; and that of Siva in the south. A very remarkable coincidence in the practice of ancient masonry.

On the point within a Circle.

The tribes contiguous to Judea, placed a jod (,) in the center of a circle, as a symbol of the Deity surrounded by eternity, of which he was said to be the inscrutable author, the ornament and support. The Samothracians had a great veneration for the circle, which they considered as consecrated by the universal presence of the deity; and hence rings are distributed to the initiated,† as amulets possessed of the power of averting danger. (Plin. Nat. Hist. l. xxxiii. c. i.) The Chinese used a symbol which bore a great resemblance to that which

---

* "The word murti or form, is exactly synonymous with eidolon; and in a secondary sense means an image; but in its primary acceptation, it denotes any shape or appearance assumed by a celestial being." Wilford in Asiat. Res. vol. iii. p. 359.
† Rings are also presented to the initiated into the masonic degree of Noachidæ. Edit.

is the subject of this lecture. The circle was bounded north and south by two serpents, equivalent to the two perpendicular parallel lines of the masonic symbol; and was emblematical of the universe, protected and supported equally by the power and wisdom of the creator. The Hindus believed that the Supreme Being was correctly represented by a perfect sphere, without beginning and without end. (Holwel. Hist. Events.) The first settlers in Egypt transmitted to their posterity an exact copy of our point within a circle, expressed in emblematical language. The widely extended universe was represented as a circle of boundless light, in the center of which the deity was said to dwell; or in other words, the circle was symbolical of his eternity.

The point within the circle, afterwards became an universal emblem to denote the temple of the deity, and was referred to the planetary circle, in the center of which was fixed the sun, as the universal god and father of nature; for the whole circle of heaven was called God; (Cicero. de nat. deor. 1.) Pythagoras esteemed them the central fire, the supernal mansion of Jove; (Stob. Phys.—Aristot. de Cælo. 1. ii.) and he called it *Mesouraneo*, because the most excellent body ought to have the most excellent place: i. e. the center. (Plut. Simplic.) And Servius tells us it was believed that the center of a temple was the peculiar residence of the deity: the exterior decorations being merely ornamental. (Serv. Georg. 3.) Hence the astronomical character used to denote or represent the sun, is a point within a circle; because that figure is the symbol of perfection. The most perfect metal gold, is also designated in chymistry by the same character.

With this reference, the point within a circle was an emblem of great importance amongst the British Druids. Their temples were circular; many of them with a single stone erected in the center; their solemn processions were all arranged in the same form; their weapons of war, the circular shield with a central boss, the spear with a hollow globe at its end, etc. all partaking of this general principle: and without a circle it was thought impossible to obtain the favor of the gods. The rites of divination could not be securely and successfully performed unless the operator was protected within the consecrated periphery of a magical circle. The plant vervain was supposed to posses the virtue of preventing the effects of facination, if gathered ritually with an iron instrument, at the rising of the dog-star, accompanied with the essential ceremony of describing a circle on the turf, the circumference of which shall be equally distant from the plant, before it be taken up. (Borl. Ant. Corn. p. 91. from Pliny.)

Specimens of British temples founded on the principle of a point within a circle are still in existence to demonstrate the truth of the theory.

The body of the temple at Classerniss, in the island of Lewis, sacred to the sun and the elements, will illustrate the principle before us. This curious Celtic temple was constructed on geometrical and astronomical principles, in the form of a cross and a circle. The circle consisted of twelve upright stones, in allusion to the solar year, or the twelve signs of the Zodiac; the east, west, and south are marked by three stones each, placed without the circle, in direct lines, pointing to each of those quarters; and towards the north, is a double row of twice nineteen stones, forming two perpendicular parallel lines, with a single elevated stone at the entrance. In the center of the circle, stands, high exalted above the rest, the gigantic representative of the Deity, to which the adoration of his worshippers was peculiarly directed. (Olaus Magnus, apud Borl. Ant. of Corn. p. 193. Toland. Druids. Vol. 1. p. 90.

This extraordinary symbol was also used by the ancient inhabitants of Scandinavia; and had an undoubted reference to the hall of Odin, or the Zodiac; which, the Edda informs us, contained twelve seats disposed in the form of a circle, for the principle gods, besides an elevated throne in the centre for Odin, as the representative of the great father.

It is remarkable that in all the ancient systems of mythology, the Great Father, or the male generative principle was uniformly symbolized by a point within a circle. This emblem was placed by the Scandinavian priests and poets, on the central summit of a Rainbow, which was fabled to be a bridge leading from earth to heaven; the emblem therefore represented Valhall, or the supernal palace of the chief celestial deity. It is said in the Edda, that this bridge "is all on fire; for the giants of the mountains would climb up to heaven by it, if it were easy for any one to walk over it." The palace thus elevated, was no other than the celestial system, illuminated by a central sun, whose representative on earth was Thor, a god depicted by Verstegan with a crowned head placed in the center of twelve bright stars, expressive of the sun's annual course through the Zodiacal Signs. (Rest. of Dec. Int. p. 74.)

Circumambulation.

The author, in conclusion of his course of lectures, among other remarks, observes

"It was an ancient custom to use circumambulation during the performance of religious ceremonies. In Greece, while the sacrifice was in the act of consuming, the priests and people walked in procession round the altar *thrice, singing the sacred hymn*, which was divided into three parts, the Strophe, the Antistrophe, and the Epode. While the first part was chanted, they circumambulated in a direction from east to west, emblematical of the *apparent* motion of the heavenly bodies; at the commencement of the second part, they changed their course and proceeded from west to east, pointing out their *real* motion; and during the performance of Epode, they remained stationary around the altar, a symbol of the stability of the earth, waiting for some propitious omen which might announce the divine acceptance of the sacrifice.

In Britain, the devotional exercises of the insular sanctuary were conducted on a similar principle. Ceremonial processions moved round it, regulated by the mystical numbers, and observing the course of the sun; sometimes moving slowly and with solemn gravity, chanting the sacred hymn to Hu; at others, the devotees advanced with great rapidity, using impassioned gestures, and saluting each other with secret signs. This was termed, "*the mystical dance of the Druids.*" The circular movement was intended to symbolize the motion of the earth, and to give an idea of God's immensity which fills the universe.

The foundation stone of every magnificent edifice was usually laid in the *north-east;* which accounts in a *rational manner* for the general disposition of a newly initiated candidate when enlightened but uninstructed, he is accounted to be in the most superficial part of masonry. This stone, to which some portion of secret influence was formerly attributed, is directed in Alet's Ritual to be "solid, angular, of about a foot square, and laid in the north-east."

It was incumbent on the author, in the first place, to *account in a rational manner* for the origin of the custom of laying the foundation stone of buildings in the *north-east*. As the whole machinery of the religion from which masonry is derived, was founded on the movements of the heavenly bodies, there is doubtless an astronomical reason for this practice.

Now, we are told by Mr. Bryant, quoted by our author, that the "Egyptian astronomers taught that the creation of the world took place at the precise period of time when the sun rose in Leo." And admitting that this notion was got up when that constellation was situated in the north-east at the rising of the sun, this circumstance would naturally, in accordance with the Egyptian mode of worship, induce the custom of commencing magnificent edifices at the north-east corner, in imitation of that glorious luminary, believed by the Egyptians to be the Supreme Architect of the world. This, among a superstitious people, would be deemed a certain means of insuring their stability and usefulness.

Mr. Oliver has bestowed great labor in his researches into the original meaning and intention of the ancient pagan symbols, and shed much light upon the subject. But by endeavoring to place freemasonry, or something like it, before the pagan mysteries, he has thrown a veil of darkness over the investigation, tending to bewilder his readers who have any wish to arrive at truth in this inquiry. By this course he expects to clear freemasonry from the imputation of having descended from what he considers a vitiated source, and, on the contrary, to show it to be derived from a pure institution, of which in his opinion, the mysteries are a corruption.

In this way he thinks to connect Christianity with ancient masonry, and consequently show that he, as a minister of the gospel, may without impropriety ally himself to the order. There is no need of this fastidiousness. Ancient masonry is a pure moral institution, but has no connection or relation whatever with Christianity. Its original dogmas are totally different; but these at present are not regarded, nor even known to the craft, who perform the ceremonies for mere sociability and pastime.

The Secret Discipline,

Mentioned in ancient Ecclesiastical History explained.

A small, but learned work bearing this title has lately been issued from the press, in this city, under a fictitious signature, edited by Samuel L. Knapp, Esq.

This author adduces many authorities, in addition to those before cited in this volume, which go to prove that the fathers of the church adopted the terms and ceremonies used in the ancient mysteries.

The following are extracts from the work.

St. Cyril, Bishop of Alexandria, in 412, in his VIIth book against Julian, declares, "These mysteries are so profound and so exalted, that they can be comprehended by those only who are enlightened. I shall not therefore attempt to speak of what is most admirable in them, lest by discovering them to the uninitiated, I should offend against the injunction not to give what is holy to the impure, no' to cast pearls before such as cannot estimate their worth." And elsewhere, "I should say much more if I were not afraid of being heard by those who are uninitiated; because men are apt to deride what they do not understand; and the ignorant, not being aware of the weakness of their minds, condemn what they ought most to venerate."

Theodoret, Bishop of Cyzicus, in Syria, 420, in the first of his three dialogues, that entitled "The Immutable," introduces Orthodoxus, speaking thus—"answer me if you please in mystical and obscure terms, for, perhaps, there are persons present who are not initiated in the mysteries." And in his preface to Ezekiel, tracing up the secret discipline to the commencement of the Christian era, says, "these mysteries are so august, that we ought to keep them with the geatest caution."

To show that these *mysteries* were retained under ecclesiastial saction to a still later period, I refer to the *Seal of the ancient Abbey of Arbroath, in Scotland*, and to the explanation given of it by the Rev. Charles Cordinet, in his "Description of the Ruins of North Britain," 2 vols. 4to.

"The figures sculptured on the seal marked INITIATION, evidently reprerent (says he) some formidable ceremony in a sacred place where a pontiff presides in state; one hand on his breast expressive of seriousness, the other stretched out at a right angle holding a rod and cross, the badge of high office, while he makes some awful appeal respecting a suppliant, who, in a loose robe, blindfolded with seeming terror kneels before the steps of an altar, while several attendants with drawn swords brandished them over his head." Mr. Cordinet intimates the resemblance of these figures to an engraving which made the frontispiece to a book about freemasonry; and then adds, that both bring to remembrance a description which Plutarch, in his famous essay "De Osiris," gives of the engraving of a seal which the priests of Isis used in their solemnities,—namely, that of *a man kneeling with*

his hands bound, a knife at his throat, etc. "And (says he) it is not a little remarkable, which is more to the present purpose, in how many particulars the mysterious fate of *Osiris*, as recorded by the above celebrated author, corresponds with the account of *Hiram ;* a strong insinuation that the annals of the latter, however mutilated and defaced, have somehow or other been descended from the Eleusinian Mysteries, and that the *Masonic rites of initiation into a lodge*, are a faint sketch, an imperfect epitome of the august ceremonies which took place at initiation into the secrets which hallowed the *primeval fanes:* and this high origin, when discerned, may have been at the bottom of that general respect which men of learning have avowed for them.

This subject as an amusing research into antiquity, may be resumed; it only remains at present to specify that Hiram coming forth in hallowed dignity of character from within the veil of the sanctuary; violated in the open temple of the world by the ignorant and profane; concealed for a time in awful secrecy; the want of his presence pathetically deplored; the ardent solicitude with which he is sought for; the acclamation of joy at finding him again; and consequent discovery of the word, *almost of itself developes the secret which the personification had involved.*"

It does indeed develope the *secret*, that the Hiram of masonry is substituted for Osiris, one of the pagan gods of the mysteries. Mr. Cordinet understands what is meant by the lost *word*, which is declared in the royal arch degree, to be recovered, and proves to be the *Logos*, the second person of the ancient trinity, the lost sun.

" *The rod and cross, the badge of high office,*" held by the pontiff, is precisely a copy of the measure of the Nile, which was originally put into the hands of a figure of Anubis, to indicate the rise of the inundation, upon which mainly depended the subsistence, or temporal salvation of Egypt.

This pole or rod afterwards obtained, says Pluche, the name of *Caduceus*, or Mercury's *wand*, and was borne as *a sceptre or staff of honor, indicating a sacred person.* The figure (10), a cabalistic number, supposed, says Bailey, "to conjoin the *virtue* of all numbers," marked upon this copy, shows its original to have been a measure. Mr. Oliver observes, that "the amount of the points contained in a Pythagorean circle, is exactly ten, which is the consummation of all things."

CHAPTER VI.

AN INQUIRY INTO THE ORIGIN AND HISTORY OF FREEMASONRY.

"The spirit of innovation had seized all the Brethren. No man can give a tolerable account of the origin, history, or object of the Order, and it appeared to all as a lost or forgotten mystery. The symbols seemed to be eqally susceptible of every interpretation, and none of these seemed entitled to any decided preference."—*Professor Robison*.

Proofs of the existence of the society of freemasons at certain remote periods, added to the occurrence of events that would naturally tend to create it, will point out its origin with sufficient accuracy for the present inquiry. No regular history of the order is attainable at this time, nor is it essential to our purpose.

It is highly probable, as asserted by Dr. Anderson, that many valuable documents relating to the society, were destroyed at the revolution of the order in 1717, by some scrupulous brethren, for fear that an improper use might be made of them.

I shall endeavor to show that the British Druids instituted this society, and the first consideration will be to point out the period when they were in a condition that required a resort to such secret means for the preservation and continuance of their religious rites.

We have seen that their open worship was entirely prohibited by the edict of Canute, who reigned from 1015 to 1035. Within those periods, therefore, this edict was issued; by which the very existence of the Druids in England was put at hazard.* Cut off from their favorite devotional retreat, no means were left them but to devise some mode to evade the scrutinizing eye of the ministers of the law.

"About the beginning of the fifth century, (says Lawrie,) Theodosius the Great prohibited, and almost totally extinguished the pagan theology in the Roman empire, (Gibbon ;) and the mysteries of Eleusis, suffered in the general devastation. (Zosim. Hist.) It is probable, however, that these mysteries were *secretly celebrated*, in spite of the severe edicts of Theodosius; and that they were partly continued dur-

---

* It appears that paganism existed at this time, not only in England, but in most of the other states of Europe. Dr. Lingard, speaking of Olave, king of Norway, says, "That prince was a zealous Christian; but his religious innovations irritated the jealousy of the pagan priests; and he was murdered in an insurrection of his subjects," [in 1028.]

ing the dark ages, though stripped of their original purity and splendor: we are certain, at least, that many rites of the pagan religion were performed, under the dissembled names of *convivial meetings*, long after the publication of the emperor's edict. (Gibbon.) And Psellus, informs us, that the mysteries of Ceres subsisted in Athens till the eighth century of the Christian era, and were never totally suppressed." (p. 22.)

A similar course would naturally suggest itself to the Druids: that such a course was adopted, and that they fixed on the craft of masonry, as a cloak under which to screen their mystic ceremonies and dogmas will, it is believed, appear so evident in the sequel as to leave no room for doubt upon the subject.

During the reign of Canute, therefore, it may fairly be presumed, the famous freemason society was first established.

The conquest of England, by William, duke of Normandy, occurred in 1066, and it is highly probable that many of the artisans who were induced by him to emigrate from France into England, were initiated into the order of freemasons, and greatly contributed to raise its fame as an operative masonic institution. "King William, (says Dr. Anderson,) brought many expert masons from France. He died in Normandy, in 1087."

It is probable that many of these masons were attached to the Druidical religion, as the rites of Druidism are said to have been openly practiced in France, upwards of a hundred years after the edict of Canute prohibiting them in England.

The condition and character of the people of England, at the time of the conquest, is thus portrayed by Guthrie:

"With regard to the manners of the Anglo-Saxons, we can say little, but that they were in general, a rude, uncultivated people, ignorant of letters, *unskilful in the mechanical arts*, untamed to submission under law and government, addicted to intemperance, riot, and disorder. Even so late as the time of Canute, they sold their children and kindred into foreign parts.

Their best quality was their military courage, which yet was not supported by discipline or conduct. Even the Norman historians, notwithstanding the low state of the arts in their own country, speak of them as barbarous, when they mention the invasion of the duke of Normandy. Conquest placed the people in a situation to receive slowly from abroad the *rudiments* of science and cultivation, and to correct their rough and licentious manners.'

"He (William) introduced the Norman laws and language. He built the stone square tower at London; *bridled* the country with forts, and disarmed the old inhabitants; in short, he attempted every measure possible to obliterate even the traces of the Anglo-Saxon constitution; though, at his coronation, he took the same oath that had been taken by the ancient Saxon kings." Great advancement however in the art of building it seems, soon followed this event. Dr. Henry, in his "History of the necessary arts in Britain, from 1066 to 1216," says:

"Architecture, in all its branches, received as great improvements in this period as agriculture. The truth is, that the twelfth century may very properly be called the age of architecture, in which the rage for building was more violent in England than at any other time.

"The great and general improvements that were made in the frabrics of houses and churches in the *first years* of this century, are thus described by a cotemporary writer: 'The new cathedrals and innumerable churches that were built in all parts, together with the many magnificent cloisters and monasteries, and other apartments of monks, that were then erected, afford a sufficient proof of the great felicity of England in the reign of Henry I.'"

Henry I. was the third son of William, and ascended the throne in 1100; only thirty-four years after the conquest. To enable him to carry on such extensive works in architecture, required that his subjects should have been previously instructed by his predecessors. Under the patronage, therefore, of King William, there is the strongest reason to believe, the masonic society was fostered and protected. And although the principal purpose of the leading members of the institution was the preservation of their religious rites, yet attention was required to be given by them to the ostensible object of the establishment. Through this means, there is no reason to doubt, that architecture was improved to a greater extent in England, at this time, than it would have been but for this adventitious circumstance.

The mere craftsman, however, knew nothing of the secret views of his superiors. The symbols made use of in the lodge were unintelligible to him. But he was pleased with the tinsel show of the representations; and when he was found sufficiently intelligent, and was thought worthy to be trusted, he was raised to the *sublime* degree of *Holy Royal Arch*, and gained the honorary appellation of *companion*. Here, if duly attentive to the symbols and ceremonies, he might make some progress towards discovering the hidden scheme upon which free masonry was founded.

Lawrie observes, "The principles of the order were even imported into Scotland,* where they continued, for many ages, in their primitive simplicity, long after they had been extinguished in the continental kingdoms. What those causes were which continued the societies of freemasons longer in Britain than in other countries, it may not, perhaps, be easy to determine; but as the fact itself is unquestionably true, it must have arisen either from favorable circumstances in the political state of Britain, which did not exist in the other governments of Europe; or from the *superior policy*, by which the British masons eluded the suspicions of their enemies, and the superior prudence with which they maintained the primitive simplicity and respectability of the order. In this manner did freemasonry flourish in Britain when it was completely abolished in every part of the world."

"That freemasonry was introduced into Scotland by those architects who built the abbey of Kilwinning, is manifest, not only from those authentic documents, by which the existence of the Kilwinning lodge has been traced back as far as the end of the fifteenth century, but by other collateral arguments which amount almost to a demonstration.

"In every country where the temporal and spiritual jurisdiction of the Pope was acknowledged, there was a continual demand, particularly during the twelfth century, for religious structures, and consequently for operative masons, proportional to the piety of the inhabitants, and the opulence of their ecclesiastical establishments; and there was no kingdom in Europe where the zeal of the inhabitants for popery was more ardent, where the kings and nobles were more liberal to the clergy, and where, of consequence, the church was more richly endowed, than in Scotland.† The demand, therefore, for elegant cathedrals and ingenious artists, must have been proportionably greater than in other countries, and that demand could be supplied only from the trading associations on the continent. We are authorized, therefore, to conclude, that those numerous and elegant ruins which still adorn the villages of Scotland, were erected by foreign masons, who introduced into this island the customs of their order.

"It is a curious fact, that in one of those towns where there is an elegant abbey, which was built in the twelfth century, the author of this history has often heard that it was erected by a company of indus-

---

* A. D. 1140. Vid. Statistical account of Scotland, vol. xi. Parish of Kilwinning; or, Edinburgh Magazine for April, 1802, p. 234.
† The church possessed about one half of the property in the kingdom. Robertson's Hist. of Scotland.

trious men who spoke in a foreign language, and lived separately from the town's people. And stories are still told about their petty quarrels with the inhabitants.

"It was probably about this time, also, that freemasonry was introduced into England; but whether the English received it from the Scotch masons at Kilwinning, or from other brethren who had arrived from the continent, there is no method of determining. The fraternity in England, however, maintain that St. Alban was the first that brought masonry to Britain, about the end of the third century; that the brethren received a charter from King Athelstane, and that his brother Edwin summoned all the lodges to meet at York, which formed the first grand lodge of England, in 926. But these are merely assertions, not only incapable of proof from authentic history, but inconsistent, also, with several historical events which rest upon indubitable evidence.—(See Dr. Plot's Nat. Hist. of Staffordshire, chap. viii, pp. 316–318.) In support of these opinions, indeed, it is alleged, that no other lodge has laid claim to greater antiquity than that of York, and that its jurisdiction over the other lodges of England has been invariably acknowledged by the whole fraternity. But this argument only proves that York was the birth place of freemasonry in England. It brings no additional evidence in support of the improbable stories about St. Alban, Athelstane, and Edwin. If the antiquity of freemasonry in Britain can be defended only by the forgery of silly and uninteresting stories, it does not deserve to be defended at all. Those who invent and propagate such tales, do not surely consider that they bring discredit upon their order by the warmth of their zeal; and that by supporting what is false, they debar thinking men from believing what is true."

Mr. Lawrie has made it appear very probable that the churches erected in Scotland in the twelfth century, were built by foreign masons. Indeed, the want of skill in the natives is a sufficient evidence of the fact. But this is no proof that they belonged to the freemason society. And the dissolution of the *trading associations on the continent*, of which he speaks, as soon as the rage for church-building ceased, while freemasonry held its ground in England, is conclusive that there was no connection between them.

But even admitting that the foreign masons who built the abbey of Kilwinning, were freemasons, the presumption would be, that they had been initiated in England; and there is no evidence that the secrets of the society were communicated to the Scotch. They could be of no possible advantage to operative masons, and the people of Scotland appear to have been thoroughly imbued with popery to embrace them in a religious point of view. Besides, if these foreigners were freemasons, and had admitted into their society a portion of the inhabitants of the places where they were employed, it is not probable that the *petty quarrels* mentioned by Lawrie, would have occurred.

The case was different in England, where Druidism had been revived by the Danish emigrants, after its conquest by that nation.

Upon the whole, there is no conclusive evidence that freemasonry was established in Scotland, till after its reorganization in England, in 1717.—The mason-associations in that country before this period, appear to be no other than common trade-companies, such as those incorporated in London.

They had a chief or grand master, with deputies in the different counties; all appointed by the king; tho sometimes by consent of the craft. The master was styled the *patron, protector, judge,* or *master* of the masons of Scotland; and the craft styled themselves " free of the masons and hammermen." Lawrie cites the following:

" In the Privy Seal-book of Scotland there is a letter dated at Holyrood-house, 25th Sept. 1590, and granted by King James VI. 'to Patrick Copland of Udaught, for using and exercising the office of Wardanrie over the art and craft of masonrie, over all the boundis of Aberdeen, Baff, and Kincardine, to had warden and justice courts within the boundis, and there to minister justice.' " Lawrie also observes, that "In the year 1645, a particular jurisdiction for masons was established in France. All differences which related to the art of building, were decided by particular judges who were called overseers of the art of masonry; and several counsellors were appointed for pleading the causes which were refered to their decision. This institution has such a striking resemblance to the warden courts which existed in Scotland in the sixteenth century, that it must have derived its origin from these. In both of them, those causes only were decided which related to masonry, and overseers were chosen in both for bringing these causes to a decision."

There is nothing of freemasonry in all this; there is nothing of Druidism, the very spirit and soul of the order, to be seen in it.—There is every reason to believe that freemasonry was first established in England, and that there it remained till the famous meeting of the brotherhood, at the Apple Tree tavern, in 1717, when it took wing, and visited all parts of the civilized world.

In fact, there was no cause for its institution in any other country than England, where the edict of Canute had compelled the Druids to relinquish their religion altogether, or practise its rites and ceremonies covertly.

"As the Druids (says Hutchinson) were a sect of religious peculiar to Gaul and Britain, it may not be improper to cast our eyes on the ceremonies they used: their antiquity and peculiar station, render it probable some of their rites and institutions might be retained, in forming the ceremonies of our society. In so modern an era as 1140, they were reduced to a regular body of religious in France, and built a college in the city of Orleans. They were heretofore one of the two estates of France, to whom were committed the care of providing sacrifices, of prescribing laws for worship, and deciding controversies concerning rights and properties," etc.—(Spirit of Mas. p. 37.)

As, therefore, it does not appear that Druidism at any time, was under a positive legal restraint except in England, it may be reasonably inferred that its offspring freemasonry existed no where else, till the period above stated.

"All the brethren on the continent agree in saying, that freemasonry was imported from Great Britain about the beginning of this [the eighteenth] century, and in the form of a mystical society."—(Robison's Proofs, p. 393.)

Robison, in speaking of freemasonry in Germany, observes, "Tho no man could pretend that he understood the true meaning of freemasonry, its origin, its history, or its real aim, all saw that the interpretations of its hieroglyphics, and the rituals of the new degress imported from France, were quite gratuitous. It appears, therefore, that the safest thing for them was an appeal to the birth-place of masonry. They sent to London for instructions. There they learned, that nothing was acknowledged for genuine, unsophisticated masonry but the three degrees; and that the mother lodge of London alone, could, by her instructions, prevent the most dangerous schisms and innovations. Many lodges, therefore, applied for patents and instructions. Patents were easily made out, and most willingly sent to the zealous brethren; and these were thankfully received and paid for. But instruction was not so easy a matter.

"They afterwards sent a deputation to Old Aberdeen, Scotland, to inquire after the caves where their venerable mysteries were known, and their treasures were hid. They had, they thought, merited some confidence, for they had remitted annual contributions to their unknown superiors to the amount of some thousands of dollars. But alas! their ambassadors found the freemasons of Old Aberdeen ignorant of all this, and equally eager to learn from the ambassadors, what was the true origin and meaning of freemasonry, of which they knew nothing but the simple tale of old Hiram."

Mr. Ward, in his Anti-Masonic Review, v. 1, p. 345, quotes the following from a French work, entitled "Essais sur la Franche Maçonnerie," by J. L. Laurens, which shows very conclusively that the freemason society originated in England. Mr. Laurens says:

"Impossible as it is, to determine the precise era of the establishment of freemasonry in Europe, so easy it is, to show in what manner and by what means it spread and propagated itself. Many reasons concur to make us believe that the English brought it into Europe; and that they have given it the exterior form, and the different names by which we know it at this day. Independent of the historical monuments, which prove that long before the 14th century it was known in England, it appears indisputable that in that country of Europe it has been *furnished*, if I may so express myself, with the form in which it has come to us. There is not a doubt that the names *Franche-Maçonnerie* and *Francs-maçons* are purely of English origin. *Freemasonry—freemason;* that is to say, *maçonnerie libres, maçons lebres*, literally rendered into French, have produced those strange terms, a manner of speaking far enough removed both from our customs, and the genius of our language; for it is certain if what we understand by freemasonry and freemasons, had received in France, or in any other country besides England, any name whatever, that name could not have had so characteristic a mark of the English tongue. A slight knowledge of the principal languages of Europe, and especially to know, that in English the *adjective* commonly precedes the *noun*, is enough in order to become convinced that these names have been formed by the genius of the English tongue.'

"After criticising the masonic word *lodge* at some length, he goes on to say: 'I might further push the investigation of the terms of English etymology peculiar to freemasonry, did I not fear to enter upon details, which I am not permitted to publish. The usages and practices of the lodges in what concerns only the exterior of freemasonry, present some points of resemblance not less striking; and it is this intimate relation with the peculiar character of the English people, that I cite in support of my proposition.

'What is the origin of that wearisome quantity of healths, with which the masonic entertainments were formerly burdened, which have been the occasion of so much sarcasm against freemasonry, and which a good taste has now wisely reformed? Is not this immoderate use of a custom innocent in itself, an image of the too often repeated toast, which so much distinguishes English Clubs? The love of good cheer, the profusion, the lengthening out of the feast, the intemperate drinking, which are contrary to French sobriety, and which reason and decency have long since banished to the taverns of London, to which they legitimately belong, can these have any relation to the object of masonic fellowship, of which they are at best only a despicable parody? The grossness of these practices, introduced into France with freemasonry, is too nearly allied to the taste of the English nation, not to be attributed to their invention.

'The nature of the customs connected with freemasonry, its peculiar name, the most of the words that express the matters which make up its exterior form, are precisely conformed to the taste and peculiar genius of the English, and prove that in England it began to have being as a society.'

"After further argument from the geographical position, free institutions, and melancholy temperament of the English, Mons. Laurens adds: 'all these observations incline us to believe, that it is from England freemasonry comes to us, as it exists now; that is to say, dressed in this whimsical fashion, which almost entirely disguises it, and scarcely permits us to discover it in the precious allegory of the Egyptian philosophy.'"—p. 215.

The allegories of the Egyptian mysteries required to be disguised, to prevent the real purport of masonry's being discovered. The idea of the author, that the English first established freemasonry is very correct, but inaccurately expressed: they did not *bring* it into Europe; they manufactured it themselves at home, from what he calls "the precious allegory of the Egyptian philosophy."

I will now produce such proofs of the long standing of the society of freemasons in England, as have survived the wreck of time.

Examination of a Mason, by King Henry VI.

One of the documents referred to by freemasons in proof of their antiquity, and which is considered as more decisive than any other, is a paper said to have been found in the Bodleian library, in 1696, and supposed to have been written in about the year 1436. It purports to be an examination of one of the brotherhood by King Henry VI.

Altho there are suspicious circumstances attending this manuscript in regard to its authenticity, yet it appears to possess an internal evidence of genuineness. The objections to it are, that it was first printed at Frankfort, in Germany, as late as 1748, and is accompanied with annotations attributed to the learned John Locke, a most absurd supposition, tending to cast a doubt upon the original document itself. The annotations never eminated from the philosophical mind of Locke. They were written by a zealous mason superstitiously credulous in the mysteries of the craft, or intending to impose upon the credulity of others. Locke was not a mason, and if he had been, he would not have given countenance to the absurdities set forth in this manuscript.

It would seem, that the Frankfort editor had heard of the learned John Locke, and in order to give the greater respectability to the record, he singles him out as a proper person to write a commentary upon it. But not having a sufficient knowledge of English characters to select a suitable person to be addressed by Locke on the occasion, he directs his letter enclosing the record and comments, to the Rt. Hon. * * *, Earl of * * * *; and for fear of detection by what is technically called an *alibi*, he dates the letter, without giving the place from whence it was written, May 6, 1696. The address continued to be thus printed in copies issued in England as late as 1764, when Dermott first published his Ahiman Rezon. Since that period, some English editor, to rid the document of this awkward appearance, substituted for the blanks Thomas Pembroke. Hutchinson gives this amendment in 1772. Where did he obtain the information? The parties concerned, however, were all defunct, and there were no means of detecting the fraud. But, altho the connecting of the name of John Locke in this affair, is evidently a forgery, still that does not destroy the validity of the record, which accords in every respect with Druidical masonry.

This paper is said to have been found in the desk of a deceased brother at Frankfort, but how it came into his possession is not accounted for. If believed to be authentic, it would no doubt, be highly prized by a superstitious mason, and preserved with great care. Every thing, at the time of its supposed discovery in 1696, relating to the origin and purport of masonry, was kept a profound secret; and this document went to expose both. It is, therefore, not a little surprising that the fraternity should ever have acknowledged its authenticity. The pride of antiquity seems in this case to have prevailed over discretion, for all masonic writers claim it as genuine. The author of a work entitled, *Annales Maçonnique*, speaking of this document, says, " We ought to value this piece the more, because it is an historical monument of the dawn of the fifteenth century, a time when we march through a vast wilderness. So the thirsty traveler, finding an unexpected fountain in the desert, rests and refreshes himself, and quits it only with painful regret."—(See Anti-mas. Review, vol. 2d. p. 23.)

I shall give the whole of this curious document. In copying it, however, I have changed the ancient orthography to the present, and corrected, according to the annotations, the errors it contains in respect to persons and places.

The title of the paper is, Certain questions, with answers to the same, concerning the *mystery* of masonry, written by King Henry, the sixth, and faithfully copied by me, John Leylande, antiquarius, by command of his highness.

They are as follows:

What mote it be?—It is the knowledge of nature and the power of its various operations; particularly, the skill of reckoning, of weights and measures, of constructing dwellings and buildings of all kinds, and the true manner of forming all things for the use of man.

Where did it begin?—It began with the first men of the east, who were before the first men of the west, and coming westerly, it hath brought with it all comforts to the wild and comfortless.

Who brought it to the west?—The Phenicians, who being great merchants, came first from the east into Phenicia, for the convenience of commerce, both east and west, by the Red and Mediterranean seas.

How came it into England?—Pythagoras, a Grecian, traveled to acquire knowledge in Egypt and Syria, and in every other land where the Phenicians had planted masonry; and gaining admittance into all lodges of masons, he learned much, and returned and dwelt in Grecia Magna, growing and becoming mighty wise, and greatly renowned. Here he formed a great lodge at Crotona, and made many masons, some of whom traveled into France and there made many more, from whence, in process of time, the art passed into England.

Do masons discover their arts to others?—Pythagoras, when he traveled to gain knowledge, was first made [initiated] and then taught; this course should rightly be applied to all others.—Nevertheless masons have always, from time to time, communicated to mankind such of their secrets as might be generally useful; they have kept back such only as might be hurtful if taught to improper persons, or such as would not be beneficial without the necessary teaching joined thereto in the lodge; or such as do bind the brethren more strongly, by the profits and convenience accruing to the fraternity therefrom.

What arts have the masons taught mankind ?—The arts of agriculture, astronomy, arithmatic, music, poetry, chymistry,* government and religion.

How does it happen that masons are better teachers than other men ?—*They only* have the art of *finding new arts*, which the first masons *received from God;* by which they *discover what arts they please*, and the true way of teaching the same. What other men find out, is only by chance, and therefore but of little value, I tro.

What do the masons conceal and hide ?—They conceal the art of finding new arts, and that for their own profit and praise: they conceal the art of keeping secrets, that so the world may hide nothing from them. They conceal the art of *wonder-working* and *fortelling things to come*, that so the same art may not be used by the wicked to a bad end; they also conceal the art of *changing*, the way of obtaining the *faculty of Abrac*, the skill of becoming *good* and *perfect* without the aid of *hope* or *fear*, and the *universal language* of *masons*.

Will you teach me the same arts?—You shall be taught if you be worthy, and able to learn.

Do all masons know more than other men ?—Not so. They only have a right and opportunity to know more than other men, but many fail from want of capacity, and many more from want of industry, which is very necessary for gaining all knowledge.

Are masons better men than others?—Some masons are not so virtuous as some other men ; but for the most part, they are better than they would be if they were not masons.

Do masons love one another mightily, as is said ?—Yea verily, and that can not be otherwise: for the better men are the more they love one another.

" Our celebrated annotator, says Hutchinson, has taken no notice of the masons having the art of working miracles, and foresaying things to come." This circumstance alone, renders it sufficiently evident, that Locke was not the annotator ; for such a bold assumption would not have escaped his observation and severe animadversion. The annotator was doubtless fearful of involving the craft in difficulty by touching upon this subject; altho he might have cited the mysteries in support of the pretention.

The universal language of masons, so much vaunted of, extends no

---

* It has been objected, that the word *chymistry* was not in use in the time of Henry VI.—Its appearance, however, in this document may be accounted for, by supposing that the Frankford editor substituted it for *alchymy*.—Edit.

further than to a few words, signs, and grips, by which they can communicate to each other that they are masons, and have been initiated into certain degress. They may also learn a cypher that is given in the royal arch, but which not one in a thousand takes the pains to acquire, and if obtained, can be of no masonic use, that is, to communicate any secrets of the craft, for masons are prohibited from committing these to writing, printing, carving, or engraving.

John Guillim.

In a work entitled "The Display of Heraldry," by John Guillim, it is stated, that the company of masons, being otherwise termed *freemasons*, of ancient standing, and good reckoning, by means of affable and kind meetings, divers times did frequent this mutual assembly in the time of King Henry VI. in the twelfth year of his reign, 1434.

Elias Ashmole.

Ashmole, in his diary, p. 15, says, "I was made a freemason at Warington in Lancarshire, 16th of October, 1646.—On March the 10th, 1682, I received a summons to appear at a lodge, to be held the next day, at masons' hall, in London. March 11th, I accordingly attended, where I was the senior fellow among them, it being nearly 35 years since I had been admitted into the fraternity. We all dined at the half-moon tavern, where we partook of a sumptious dinner, at the expence of the new accepted mason.

Lawrie, in recording this anecdote, says, "This gentleman was the celebrated antiquary who founded the Ashmolean museum at Oxford. His attachment to the fraternity is evident from his diligent inquiries into its origin and history, and his long and frequent attendance upon its meetings.—See Diary, p. 66."

Robert Plott, L.L.D., keeper of the Ashmolean museum, etc. says, in his Natural History of Staffordshire, (1686) that " They have a custom in Staffordshire of admitting men into the society of freemasons ; that in the *moorelands* of this country seems to be of greater request than any where else, tho I find the custom spread more or less all over the nation ; for here I found persons of the most eminent quality, that did not disdain to be of this-fellowship; nor indeed need they, were it of that antiquity and honor that is pretended in a large parchment volume they have among them, containing the history and rules of the craft of masonry, which is there deduced not only from sacred writ, but pro-fame story," etc.—(Freemas. Poc. Comp. p. 192. Antimas. Review, vol. 2d. p. 334.

New Regulations.

According to a *copy* of the *old constitutions*, says Anderson, a general assembly and feast was held, on St. John's day, 27th December, 1663; when Henry Jermyn, earl of St. Albans, was elected grand master, who appointed Sir John Denham his deputy, and Mr. (afterwards Sir) Christopher Wren, and John Webb his wardens. At this assembly the following regulations, among others, were made:

"That no person of *what degree soever, be made* or *accepted* a free mason, unless in a *regular lodge*, whereof *one* to be a *master* or *warden* in that limit or division where such lodge is kept, and *another* to be a *craftsman* in the *trade* of *free* masonry."

This regulation shows clearly that the society was not confined to opperatives. It shows also, that it was at this time, in a very disorderly condition.

"That *for the future*, the fraternity of freemasons shall be regulated and governed by *one grand master*, and as many wardens as the society shall think fit to appoint at every annual general assembly.'

It appears by this, that at the period here spoken of, whatever may have been the case formerly, the freemasons had no grand master, and that each lodge regulated its own affairs.

"That no person shall be accepted, unless he be *twenty-one* years old, or more."

It is evident that this regulation was an innovation, and that previously apprentices were entered at the usual age in which they are taken in other trades.

Sir Christopher Wren, says Anderson, was chosen grand master, in 1698. He then enumerates the public buildings that were erected by freemasons under his superintendance, and adds, "some few years after this St. Christopher neglected the office of grand master; yet the old lodge near St. Paul's and a few others, continued their stated meetings."

Previously to this period, the government "enacted the building of fifty new churches in the suburbs of London," to supply the places of those consumed, at the great fire in London, in 1666; and Sir Christopher Wren, an eminent architect, was appointed one of the commissioners to superintend the construction of these edifices.

It is highly probable that Wren was at this time master or president of the company of operative masons of London, and may perhaps have been a member of the freemasons' society; but that the latter as a body, was employed to construct public works is not probable. It was not acknowledged by the government as a company of architects, and whatever may have been its standing in the time of the Druids, it was at this period, in little repute.

Anderson gives the following account of the revolution of the order which took place at this period. "In 1716, the few lodges in London, finding themselves neglected by Sir Christopher Wren, thought fit to cement under a *grand master* as the *center of union* and *harmony*." It here appears that the order made in 1663, in regard to a grand master, had become neglected. These lodges were those "that met, 1, at the Goose and Gridiron Ale-house, in St. Paul's church yard; 2. at the Crown Ale-house, in Parker's lane; 3. at the Apple-tree Tavern, in Charles-street, Covent Garden; 4. at the Rummer and Grapes tavern, in Channel Row, Westminster.

" The members of these lodges and some old brothers met at the said Apple-tree, and having put into the chair the *oldest master mason* they *constituted themselves a grand lodge, pro tempore in due form*, and forthwith *revived* the quarterly communication of the officers of lodges, called the *grand lodge*, and resolved to hold the *annual assembly and feast;* and then to choose a grand master from among themselves, till they should have the *honor* of a *noble brother* at their head.

"Accordingly, on St. John Baptist's day, [the 24th June, the summer solstice,] 1717, the assembly and feast of the *free* and *accepted* masons was held at the aforesaid Goose and Gridiron Ale-house."

The freemasons at this time, seem to have rummaged their old records, and found out what the society formerly was, and come to a determination to *revive* old Druidical, Hiram masonry.

At this assembly, "Mr. Anthony Sayre, gentleman, was elected grand master of masons, who being forthwith invested with the badges of office and power, and installed, was duly congratulated by the assembly, who payed him *the homage*. Capt. Joseph Elliot, and Mr. Jacob Lamball, carpenter, were appointed grand wardens."

The brethren did not wait long before a *noble brother condescended* to be placed at their head; for on the 24th of June, 1721, the duke of Montague was elected and accepted the office of grand master of masons. From that time to the present, a nobleman or a prince has constantly presided over the lodges of England. The society soon became fashionable. The brilliant processions and luxurious feasts now got up, which had for a long time been neglected, added to the sublime mysteries and secrets held out to the initiated, allured the young, the gay, and the inquisitive, to the standard of the order, which now assumed such an imposing appearance as caused it to spread, with astonishing rapidity, over Europe, Asia, and America. The year 1717 forms and important epoch in the history of freemasonry. It had till then been for some centuries, almost exclusively, in the hands of mere craftsmen who knew not what to make of it. Druidism being extinct, the religious cement which had bound them together, was dissolved; and the incorporated company of masons, no doubt, rendered its combination in respect to that profession inefficient.

As operative masons, the incorporated company would naturally take the lead of a society not sanctioned by the laws, and the utility of whose mystic rites could not be estimated, after the religion which gave them birth, was no longer known.

Dermott names eight persons, among whom is the Rev. Dr. Desaguliers, who was elected grand master in 1719, as the authors of this remarkable revolution. At this revival, the ostensible ground upon which the society was originally founded, the craft of masonry, as though in derision of the pretention, was utterly abandoned, and no longer considered as a recommendation for admission into the order.

The society, however, keeps up a show of respect to the craft by marching in processions, to lay the corner stone of masonic halls, and other public edifices. This, was an ancient religious custom, having no reference to the art of building.

Incorporation of Masons in London.

Masons No. 30.—By the arms granted this society by William Hanckestow, Clarencieux-king at arms,* in the year 1477, it appears to be of considerable antiquity; however, it was only incorporated by *Letters Patent* of the 29th, of Charles 2d, Sept. 17, anno 1677, by the name of the master, wardens, assistants and commonalty of the company of masons of the city of London.

"They consist of a master, two wardens, twenty-two assistants, and seventy livery men, whose fine of admission is five pounds. They have a small, but convenient hall in Mason-alley, Basing-hall street.

Their armorial ensigns are *azure* on a chevron between three cas-

---

* Kings at arms, are officers of great antiquity, and anciently of great authority; they direct the heralds, preside at their chapters, and have the jurisdiction of armory. There are three in number, Garter, Norroy, and Clarencieux. Bailey.

tles *argent*, a pair of compasses somewhat extended of the first. Crest a castle of the second."—(Maitland's History of London, from its foundation to 1756.)

This incorporation of course included the operatives of the freemasons, who in their society make use of the same armorial bearings, which it is very probable, originally belonged to them.

To what period the pagan rites, under the name of Druidism, were sustained in different parts of Europe, is uncertain: but that they were not concealed, under the title of freemasonry, in any other quarter than Britain, is evident from the charters of all lodges on the continent's emanating from either the grand lodge of England or that of Scotland. The latter, however, was not instituted till 1736.

The grand lodge of Ireland was formed in 1730. And in 1733, a charter for a lodge was obtained for Boston. So, it is seen, that America was not far behind in availing itself of the earliest opportunity to become a partaker in the advantages resulting from a knowledge of this *wonderful secret*.

To suppose, as some writers have done, that the freemasons' society first sprang up in 1717; that such a mass of curious ceremonies, bearing on their very front the most palpable marks of remote antiquity, was then for the first time concocted by doctors of divinity and other learned men, is to my mind preposterous.

Freemasonry is based on Sabeism, the worship of the stars; but, as before observed, its original intention has long since been lost sight of and abandoned. Modern masons not only continue the ceremonies of ancient masonry, consisting of seven degrees, which relate exclusively to pagan rites, but have added thereto about fifty others. These are founded partly upon pagan mysteries, and partly upon Jewish and Christian doctrines; forming altogether an incoherent medley of opposite principles. The partisans, however, of opposing sects seem to be reconciled to it, not stopping to inquire into the meaning of the symbols, or willing to be deceived by the false explication given of them, congregate together in great harmony. And, although the ceremonies relate wholly to religion, either Pagan, Jewish, or Christian, discussion on the subject is absolutely prohibited in the lodge.

CHATER VII.

ANALYSIS OF FREEMASONRY.*

Introduction.

I shall now proceed to analyse Freemasonry. And as I conceive it to be no other than the forms and ceremonies of the ancient Pagan religion; that is, Sabeism or the worship of the stars, the following remarks of Volney, on the natural causes which led to this species of worship, will not be amiss:

"The unanimous testimony of all ancient monuments, presents us a methodical and complicated system, that of the worship of all the stars, adored sometimes in their proper forms, sometimes under figurative emblems and symbols; and this worship was the effect of the knowledge men had acquired in physics, and was derived immediately from the first causes of the social state, that is, from the necessities and arts of the first degree which are among the elements of society.

"Indeed, as soon as men began to unite in society, it became necessary for them to multiply the means of subsistence, and consequently to attend to agriculture; agriculture, to be carried on with success, requires the observation and knowledge of the heavens. It was necessary to know the periodical return of the same operations of nature, and the same phenomena in the skies; indeed, to go so far as to ascertain the duration and succession of the seasons and the months of the year. It was indispensable to know in the first place, the course of the sun, who, in his zodiacal revolutions, shows himself the first and supreme agent of the whole creation; then, of the moon, who, by her phases and periods, regulates and distributes time; then of the stars, and even planets, which by their appearance and disappearance on the horizon and nocturnal hemisphere, marked the minutest divisions; finally, it was necessary to form a whole system of astronomy, or a calendar; and from these works there naturally followed a new manner of considering these predominant and governing powers. Having observed that the

---

* The author of "the Master Key to the door of Freemasonry," has judiciously remarked, "that the word *free* was added to masonry by the society, because none but the *freeborn* were admitted into it." And for a very obvious reason, for there could be no safety in confiding secrets to slaves, which might at any time be extorted from them by their masters. Besides, this was in conformity with the rule established in the Egyptian mysteries.

productions of the earth had a regular and constant relation with the heavenly bodies; that the rise, growth, and decline of each plant kept pace with the appearance, elevation, and declination of the same star, or group of stars; in short, that the languor or activity of vegetation seemed to depend on celestial influences, men drew from thence an idea of action, of power in those beings, superior to earthly bodies; and the stars dispensing plenty or scarcity, became powers, genii, gods, authors of good and evil.

"As the state of society had already introduced a regular hierarchy of ranks, employments and conditions, men, continuing to reason by comparison, carried their new notions into their theology, and formed a complicated system of gradual divinities, in which the sun, as first god, was a military chief, a political king; the moon was his wife, and queen; the planets were servants, bearers of commands, messengers; and the multitude of stars were a nation, an army of heroes, genii whose office was to govern the world under the orders of their chiefs; and all the individuals had names, functions, attributes drawn from their relations and influences;* and even sexes, from the gender of their appellations.†

"If it be asked to what people this system is to be attributed, we shall answer that the same monuments, supported by unanimous traditions, attribute it to the first tribes of Egypt; and when reason finds in that country all the circumstances which could lead to such a system; when it finds there a zone of sky, bordering on the tropic, equally free from the rains of the equator and the fogs of the north; when it finds there a central point of the sphere of the ancients, a salubrious climate, a great, but manageable river, a soil fertile without labor or art, and placed between two seas which communicate with the richest countries it conceives that the inhabitant of the Nile, addicted to agriculture from the nature of his soil, to geometry from the annual necessity of measuring his lands, to commerce from the facility of communications, to astronomy from the state of his sky always open to observation, must have been the first to pass from the savage to the social state, and con-

---

* A pretty fair description of a masonic lodge, with the *worshipful master* at the head, personifying the sun, and taking his place in the east; surrounded by the senior warden, who acts the part of the moon; the junior warden, who takes that of Orion, and the other subordinate officers and privates, all under the command of their chief, the worshipful master.—Edit.

† According as the gender of the object was in the language of the nation masculine or feminine, the divinity who bore its name was male or female. Thus the Capadocians called the moon god, and the sun goddess; a circumstance which gives to the same beings a perpetual variety in ancient mythology.

sequently to attain the physical and moral sciences necessary to civilized life.

"It was then on the borders of the upper Nile among a black race of men, that was organized the complicated system of the worship of the stars considered in relation to the productions of the earth and the labors of agriculture; and this first worship, characterized by their adoration under their own forms and natural attributes, was a simple proceeding of the human mind; but in a short time, the multiplicity of the objects of their relations, and their reciprocal influence, having complicated the ideas, and the signs that represented them, there followed a confusion as singular in its cause, as pernicious in its effects."

It has been sufficiently made to appear, it is believed, that the Society of *Freemasons*, has existed in England for upwards of six hundred years. How far its principles and objects were generally understood by its members in the early stage of its establishment, is unknown. But, judging from the enigmatical manner in which its ritual, as handed down to us, is explained, we may conclude that the brethren, particularly the craftsmen of the three first degrees, were kept as closely hoodwinked in respect to its true import, after, as they were before their initiation. The personal safety of its founders required this course. Hence the awful oaths exacted of them to keep secret the rites and ceremonies in which they were permitted to participate.

These ceremonies were manufactured for the occasion; and were so obscurely framed as to be rendered incomprehensible to all those not intrusted with the secret object of the institution. Besides artifice was made use of to mislead the brethren, answers to questions propounded being often given that have no relation to their true interpretation. In short, freemasonry is allegorical throughout, and is an imitation of the astronomical worship of the Egyptians, Hiram being substituted for Osiris. There are occasional departures from the original, to accommodate it to the craft or trade of masonry, which, as before observed, is a mere finesse to cover the real design. There, otherwise, would have been no necessity for dividing the subject matter of the three first degrees; which may be considered as substituted for the ceremonies and secrets of the *lesser* mysteries; and that of the royal arch and its appendages, for those of the *greater*. It may, however, have been the policy of the Druids, to deal out their mysteries in small parcels, to try the good faith of their pupils by degrees, and to stop short, or proceed with them accordingly.

No account of the secret practices of masonry, had been given to the public, till after its revival in 1717. The first writers who undertook to expose them, were Prichard, in 1730; Master Key to the door of Freemasonry, in 1768; and Jachin and Boaz, in 1776. As material alterations in the ritual have been made since the report of Prichard, whatever may be said of "old land marks," in making this Analysis, I shall rely chiefly upon him and the two following expositions for an explanation of the three first degrees, which was the extent of their labors, although the author of Master Key, signs himself "A member of Royal Arch."

On the revival of the institution, the surviving heirs of the mystery, no doubt, gave to the society as far as recollected, the very words and ceremonies as delivered to them; and which Prichard testifies under oath, to be truely reported by him.

This expose particularly indicates the order to be of ancient date. After perusing it, it would seem impossible to believe that men of learning, talents, and standing in society, would, in the eighteenth century of the Christian era, seriously form *de novo* such a medley, void of the least claim to wit or rationality, except in reference to the scientific worship of the heavenly bodies and other physical powers of nature. According to Prichard, many of the questions and answers, are in verse, which sufficiently indicate their Druidical formation; the sense of which, however, has been changed to prose, thereby rendering the dialogue more conformable to the present taste, and at the same time divesting it of its Druidical dress.

In adapting this parody of the mysteries to the uninformed state of the initiated to the three first degrees of masonry, although a trinity is acknowledged under the title of *wisdom, strength* and *beauty*, still the *true* first person is kept out of view.

"The maintainers of the Egyptian philosophy held, that the *Supreme Being*, the infinitely perfect and happy, was not the creator of the world, nor the alone independent Being. The Supreme Being, who resides in the *immensity of space*, which they call *peteroma* or fullness, produced from himself, say they, other immortal and spiritual natures, styled by them Æons, who filled the residence of the Deity with beings similar to themselves."—(Key to the New Testament.— Hutchinson, p. 36.)

This Divinity is spoken of by Jamblichus, under the name of *Emeph* or *Kneph*. He says, that "*This God is an intellect, itself intellectually perceiving itself, and converting intellections to itself;* and is to be worshipped through silence alone."—(Taylor's Trans. Jam. p. 302.)

Altho this god was secretly acknowledged by the philosophers and learned priests of Egypt, he was utterly unknown to the common people; and this is supposed to be the case with the mason of the three first degrees. But when he arrives at the *holy royal arch*, the discovery is made known to him. This is the awful Divinity, on coming into whose presence, the shocking exhibitions of thunder, lightning, etc. produce such excessive trepidation and fear. This is the *Wisdom*, the first person of the Egyptian trinity; Osiris the sun, the *Strength*, the Demiurgus or supposed maker of the world, is the second person; and Isis the moon, the *Beauty* of masonry, is the third. But as the first person is not revealed to the initiates of the minor degress, the trinity for these grades is made up wholly of visible, physical powers, adapted to the gross conceptions of the uninlightened; viz. Osiris, Isis, and Orus; that is the sun, moon, and Orion.

To prevent that satiety arising from the perusal of long rituals, particularly those in which the reader has no faith, I shall confine myself to as few items in that respect, as is consistent with the necessary developement of the subject. This analysis is not intended as a regular expose of the ceremonies of masonry.

After these preliminary remarks, I commence with the

Manner of Opening a Lodge;

and preparing a candidate for initiation, taken from Jachin and Boaz.

Masonry throughout is in the catechetical form, in the same manner as instruction is given to novices in all other religions. The master, before opening the lodge, demands of the officers their various stations and duties (which will appear in what are called lectures further on,) ending with those of the master; whose station is in the east, because the sun *rises* in the east to open the day, so the master *stands* in the east to open *his* lodge, and set the men to work.

After the conclusion of this ceremony, the master puts on his hat, and declares the lodge to be opened, in the name of holy St. John, forbidding all cursing, swearing, whispering, and all profane discourse whatever. He then gives three knocks upon the table, and puts on his hat, the brethren being uncovered. Provided a candidate has received the approval of the lodge for admittance, the master asks, if the gentleman proposed last lodge-night is ready to be made; and on being answered in the affimative, he orders the wardens to go out and prepare the person, who is generally waiting in a room at some distance from the lodge room by himself, being left there by his friend who proposed him. He is conducted into another room, which is *totally dark*; and then asked, whether he is conscious of having the vocation necessary to be received? On answering yes, he is asked his name, surname, and profession. When he has answered these questions, whatever he has about him made of metal is taken away, as buckles, buttons, rings, etc. and even the money in his pocket. Then they uncover his right knee and put his left foot with his shoe on into a slipper, (this is not practised in every lodge, some only slipping the heel of the shoe down;) hoodwink him with a handkerchief, and leave him to his reflection for about half an hour. The chamber is also guarded within and without by some of the brethren who have drawn swords in their hands. The person who proposed the candidate stays in the room with him; but they are not permitted to converse together.

During this silence, and while the candidate is preparing, the brethren in the lodge are putting every thing in order for his reception there; such as drawing the annexed figure [omitted] on the floor at the upper part of the room; which is generally done with chalk and charcoal intermixed. It is drawn east and west. The Master stands in the east, with the square hanging at his breast, the holy bible opened at the gospel of St. *John*, and three lighted tapers are placed in the form of a triangle in the midst of the drawing on the floor.

The proposer then goes and knocks three times at the door of the apartment, in which the ceremony is to be performed. The Master answers within by three strokes with the hammer, and the Junior warden asks, who comes there? The candidate answers (after another who prompts him) "One who begs to receive part of the benefit of this Right Worshipful Lodge, dedicated to St. *John*, as many brothers and fellows have done before me." The doors are then opened, and the senior and junior wardens, or their Assistants, receive him, one on the right, and the other on the left, and conduct him blind-folded three times round the drawing on the floor, and bring him up to the foot of it, with his face to the master, the brethren ranging themselves on each side, and making a confused noise, by striking on the attributes of the order, which they carry in their hands.*

In some lodges the candidates are led nine times round; but as this is very tiresome to the person who is to undergo the operation, his patience being pretty well tried by being blinded so long beforehand, it is very justly omitted.

---

* This custom is not observed in all Lodges.

Apprentice's Degree.

I commence this degree with Prichard's report, called "Masonry Dissected," as inserted in the Antimasonic Review; which Mr. Ward, the Editor, informs me, he printed from a manuscript copy. It is evidently an abridgment of the original: for it opens with the examination of an Apprentice previously initiated. It contains, however, enough for the present purpose.—An attestation to the truth of the statement is prefixed to the document, as follows :

" Samuel Prichard maketh oath, that the copy hereunto annexed is a true and genuine copy in every particular. Jur. 13 Die Oct. 1730, Coram me R. Hopkins."

I shall not confine myself to any one of the books on the subject in regular order, but take the questions and answers, or the purport of them, from either as may best suit my purpose.

Question. From whence came you ? Answer. From the *Holy Lodge of St. John*. [Why the Druids gave this name to the lodge will be explained in the sequel.] What recommendations brought you from thence ?—The recommendation which I brought from the right worshipful brothers and fellows of the right worshipful and holy lodge of St. John; from whence I came, and greet you *thrice* heartily well.

What do you come here to do ?—

> Not to do my own proper will,
> But to subdue my passions still;
> The rules of masonry in hand to take,
> And duly progress therein to make.

Are you a mason ?—I am so taken and accepted to be 'mong brothers and fellows. Where were you made a mason?—In a just and perfect lodge. What makes a lodge ?—*Five*.—Masons are deceived by the reason given for this number's making a lodge. " The ancient theology (as before observed) being nothing more than a system of physics, a picture of the operations of nature, wrapped up in mysterious allegories and enigmatical symbols," a solution of the enigma must be sought for from that source.

" The Egyptians represent the world by the number *five*, being that of the elements, which, says Diodorus, are earth, water, air, fire and ether or spiritus (they are the same amongst the Indians ;) and according to the mystics, in Macrobius, they are the supreme God or primum mobile, the intelligence or meus born of him, the soul of the world which proceeds from him, the celestial spheres and all things terrestrial. Hence, adds Plutarch, the analogy between the Greek pente, five, and Pan, all." (See Ruins, p. 236.)

What makes a *just* and *perfect* Lodge? *Seven.*—This is in consequence of its being formed by the union of *three* and *four*; which, as before observed, renders this number superlatively perfect.

Masonry teaches that the above numbers are required to make a lodge, because man has five senses, and there are seven liberal sciences; and much ridiculous parade is made in the definition of these sciences; which are thus arranged:—Grammar, rhetoric, logic, arithmetic, geometry, music, and astronomy. What doth geometry teach?—The art of measuring whereby the Egyptians found out their own land, or the same quantity which they had before the overflowing of the Nile.—How were you prepared to be made a mason?—I was neither naked nor clothed, barefoot nor shod; deprived of all metal; hoodwinked, with a *cable-tow* about my neck, when I was led to the door of the lodge, in a halting moving posture.—This preparation, as before noticed, is in conformity to the ancient usage in the mysteries: it is a scenical representation of the forlorn condition of man in a state of nature. The *rope* about the neck of the candidate, like the *chain* required by the Druids to be carried by their followers in the performance of their sacred rites, was, as before stated, in testimony of his submission to the will of God. [See Mayo's Myth. v. 2d. p. 220.

How got you admittance?—By *three* great knocks.—Who received you?—A junior warden.—How did he dispose of you?—He carried me up to the northeast part of the lodge, and brought me back again to the west, and delivered me to the senior warden. (Why the candidate begins his labors at the northeast part of the lodge has already been explained.)

Where did our ancient brethren meet, before lodges were erected?—Upon *holy ground*, or the highest hill or lowest vale, or in the vale of *Jehoshaphat*, or any other secret place; the better to guard against cowans* and enemies, either ascending or descending, that the brethren might have timely notice of their approach to prevent being surprised.

These ancient brethren were Druids; and the places mentioned are such as they used to assemble at, before the edict of Canute entirely

---

* Cowan seems to be a corruption of Covin, which the author of *The Secret Discipline*, &c. noticed above, substitutes for it. This word is thus defined by Webster:— "Covin (Qu. Arabic—to defraud.) More probably this word belongs to some verb in Gb.' signifying to conceal, or to agree. In Norm. Fr. covyne is a secret place or meeting."

prohibited their public meetings. In consequence of which Druidism was changed into freemasonry, and lodges were erected. It cannot be shown, that a lodge of masons ever held a meeting for the performance of their mystic rites, except in a close room, properly tiled. The groves and other places where the Druids assembled for worship, were consecrated to some divinity, and considered *holy ground*.—The vale of Jehoshaphat is here introduced as a mere juggle. It is a valley near Jerusalem, where, or in Jerusalem itself, a lodge of freemasons never held a meeting. The following extract from Holwell's Mythol. Dict. will show the reasons given by the ancients for worshiping the gods upon high hills or mountains.

High Places.

Many of old worshiped upon hills, and on the tops of high mountains; imagining that they thereby obtained a nearer communication with heaven. Strabo says (I. 15.) that the Persians always performed their worship upon hills. (Some nations instead of an image worshiped the hill as the deity. Max. Tyr. Dissert. 8. v. Appian. de bello Mithridatico.) In Japan most of their temples at this day are upon eminences; and often upon the ascent of high mountains: commanding fine views, with groves and rivulets of clear water; for they say, that the gods are extremely delighted with such high and pleasant spots. (Kæmpfer's Japan. v. 2. b. 5.) This practice in early times was almost universal; and every mountain was esteemed holy. The people, who prosecuted this method of worship, enjoyed a soothing infatuation, which flattered the gloom of superstition. The eminences to which they retired were lonely, and silent; and seemed to be happily circumstanced for contemplation and prayer. They, who frequented them, were raised above the lower world; and fancied that they were brought into the vicinity of the powers of the air, and of the deity who resided in the higher regions. But the chief excellence for which they were frequented, was the Omphi, interpreted *Theia cledon*, vox divina, being a particular revelation from heaven. In short, they were looked upon as the peculiar places where God delivered his oracles.

Many times when a reformation among the Jews was introduced by some of the wiser and better princes, it is still lamented by the sacred writer (1 Kings xxii.) that *the high places were not taken away; the people still offered, and burnt incense on the high places.*

The lodge is described as extending in length from east to west; in breadth from north to south; as high as the heavens; as deep as from the surface to the center; and supported by three large columns or pillars, named *Wisdom, Strength,* and *Beauty.*

"Our institution is said to be supported by wisdom, strength, and beauty; because it is necessary that there should be wisdom to contrive, strength to support, and beauty to adorn, all great and important undertakings. Its dimensions are unlimited, and its covering no less than the canopy of heaven. To this object the mason's mind is continually directed, and thither he hopes at last to arrive, by the aid of the *theological ladder,* which Jacob, *in his vision,* saw ascending from earth to heaven; the three principal rounds of which are denominated *faith, hope,* and *charity.*" (Webb.)

It is evident from the foregoing, that a masonic lodge is supposed to represent the world; upon which plan the ancient pagan temples were formed. The flooring of the lodge is intended to resemble the face of the earth, and the principal ceremonies performed in it, are an imitation of the movements of the heavenly bodies, particularly of that great luminary the Sun, the god of Egypt.

The Rev. R. Taylor, in his Lecture on masonry, very ingeniously solves the enigma of the three principal rounds of the aforesaid theological, or rather astronomical ladder, thus:

"Faith is the Genius of Spring; Hope of Summer; and Charity of Autumn.—Faith, in Spring, because faith and works must always come together.—Hope, of Summer, because from that point, the sun looks vertically down upon the seeds which have been committed *in faith* to the fertilizing womb of the earth.—Charity, of autumn, because then the sun empties his cornucopia into our desiring laps.—Faith is the eastern pillar; charity the western; and hope the key stone of this *royal arch.*"—This theological ladder has seven rounds, and is enigmatically described in the degree called Knight of Kadosh, which I shall hereafter notice. It marks the course of the sun through seven signs of the zodiac, commencing at the vernal equinox, and ending at the autumnal, both inclusive. The semicircle made by the sun in passing these signs, forms the celebrated *royal arch;* and a mason to attain the degree so called, must pass through the seven grades of the order. The three principal steps above noticed, allude to the equinoxes, and the northern solstice.

"Why should the master represent the pillar of *wisdom,* and be stationed in the east? As the sun rises in the east to open and adorn the day, so rises (at these words the master rises,) the worshipful master in the east to open and adorn his lodge, and set the craft to work. Why should the senior warden represent the pillar of *strength?* As the sun sets in the west, to close the day, so stands the senior warden in the west, to close the lodge, and dismiss the men from labor, paying them their wages. The junior warden represents the pillar of *beauty*, because he stands in the south, at high twelve at noon, which is the glory and beauty of the day, to call the men off from labor to refreshment, and to see that they come on again in due time.

The above arrangement is evidently deceptive. *Wisdom*, applicable to the true God, who, according to pagan theology, resides in the *immensity of space*, is kept out of view, and Osiris the sun is substituted in his place. *Strength* which is required for labor, at the opening of the day, and which is applicable to the sun, is transferred to its close, when the men are called from labor. The senior warden properly personates Isis, indicating the productions of the earth in the fall, which ornaments and beautifies the creation. The sun, moon, and Orus or Orion, (which lies directly over the equator,) form the wisdom, strength and beauty of the three first degrees; and they also composed the vulgar trinity of the Egyptians.

The two principal pillars are called Jachin and Boaz, and are supposed to be placed at the equinoctial points; Boaz in the east, and Jachin in the west; the former being on the left hand, and the latter on the right, to the inhabitants of the northern hemisphere, the seat of masonry. "The equinoctial points are called pillars, because the great semicircle, or upper hemisphere, doth seem to rest upon them." (R. Taylor.)

In the degree of *perfect master*, these two pillars are said to be *fixed crossways*. It is asked, are you a perfect master? *Ans.* I have seen the *circle* and the *square* enclosing the two columns. What do the columns represent? Jachin and Boaz, through which I must have passed to arrive at the degree of perfect master. What have you done in entering the lodge? I came to the altar, worked as an entered apprentice, fellow-craft, and master, to cross the two columns. "Now, (says Taylor,) what are cross-ways but two ways of which one crosses the other? These cross-ways, Boaz and Jachin, are the equinoctial points, at which the line of the ecliptic crosses the line of the equator—that is, the sun in his apparent path, the ecliptic, comes to shine directly over the line of the equator: this he does in spring and autumn, and only then."

The fellow-craft is said to receive his wages in the middle chamber, at which he arrives by seven winding stairs, passing the two pillars of

286　　　　　　　ANALYSIS OF FREEMASONRY:

Boaz and Jachin. This is embematical of the seven circular stages, made by the sun in his tour round those imaginary columns. The emerging of the sun from the lower hemisphere, on the 21st of March, and his return on the 27th of September, may, in figurative language, be denominated his rising and setting in regard to our hemisphere. Thus Osiris, the sun, sets the husbandmen to work on his rising at the former period, and Isis, the emblem of harvest, pays them in the fruits of the earth, on his return to the latter.

The following figure is that by which the symbol of harvest is represented in mythology; The torch, however, was peculiar to Ceres.

Isis, Ceres, Cybele, etc.

So the master of the lodge, who stands in the east, representing the sun, rises and sets his men to work; and the senior warden, who stands in the west, representing Isis, pays them their wages. To render this personification of Isis perfectly plain, a painting of a sheaf of wheat, is hung back of the senior warden's seat.*

It is also worthy of remark, that as the pagans constructed their temples in a manner to represent the world, they would naturally for that purpose, imagine the world to be divided into three departments or chambers; the upper, the middle, and the lower. The middle chamber would of course include the autumnal equinox: and on the arrival of the sun at that point of the heavens, the laborer, the husbandman, is paid his wages in the fruits of the earth.

Freemasons hall, in London, is a partial imitation of a pagan temple. "In the center of the roof of this magnificent hall, says Smith, a splendid sun is represented, surrounded with the twelve signs of the zodiac." And he adds, "The scientific freemason only knows the reason why the sun is thus placed in the center of this beautiful hall."

How is the lodge situated? Due east and west, because all churches and chapels are or ought to be so.

All pagan temples were so situated in consequence of the sun's being the universal object of worship. "The Egyptians, Chaldeans, Indians, Persians, and Chinese, all placed their temples fronting the east, to receive the first rays of the sun. Hence the worship of the sun has been the religion of the ancient people from which these, [the present race] are descended."—Tytler's Elem. of Hist.

It is true this custom continued long after the cause which produced it, ceased to be respected. Preston, in his illustrations of masonry, in giving a description of St. Paul's Cathedral, says, "A strict regard to the situation of this edifice, due east and west, has given it an oblique, appearance in respect to Ludgate street in front." This building was finished in 1696. Its architect, Sir Christopher Wren, in a letter dated 1707, addressed to a joint commissioner with himself for building churches to supply the places of those destroyed by the conflagration of

---

* Henry O'Brien A. B. in a late work entitled: "Phenecian Ireland," Dublin, 1833; after treating of some other of the pagan divinities, says:

"But our decision on the word sibbol, a name by which the Irish, as well as almost all other nations, designated and worshiped Cybele, must be guided altogether by another principle. For here I at once recognise the Syriac character as derived from *sibola,* an ear of corn, under which guise the Phenecians used to worship the earth as the mother of all harvests, and vegetables. All nations, therefore, by one common consent, represented Cybele holding in her right hand some ears of corn." [wheat] (p. 107.)—Now, Cybele has been shown to be but another name for Isis.

1666, observes, "As to the situation of the churches, I should propose they be brought forward as far as possible into the larger and more open streets. Nor are we, I think, *too nicely* to observe east or west in the position, unless it falls out properly." See Anderson's Const. of freemasonry.

Have you any ornaments in your lodge? Yes, the masonic pavement, the blazing star, and the indented or tesseled border. The Mosaic pavement is the flooring of the lodge. This points out the diversity of objects which decorate and adorn the creation, the animate as well as the inanimate parts thereof. "The same divine hand which hath blessed us with the sights of his glorious works in the heavens, hath also spread the earth with a beautiful carpet: he hath wrought it in various colors, fruits and flowers, pastures and meads; he hath wrought it as it were, in mosaic work, giving a pleasing variety to the eye of man."—Smith.

The blazing star in the center, indicates that prudence which ought to appear conspicuous in the conduct of every mason. The indented or tesseled border refers us to the planets which in their various revolutions, form a beautiful border of skirt-work round that grand luminary the sun. The furniture of the lodge is the volume of the *sacred law*, the compass, and the square.

The origin of what is called *mosaic work*, as well as the term by which it is designated, appears to be lost through the lapse of time.

"The ancients, especially the Greeks, says Bailey, adorned their floors, pavements of temples, palaces, etc., with mosaic, or rather *musaic* work. A work composed of many stones, or other matters of different colors, so disposed as to represent divers shapes of ornaments, birds, etc." Dr. Rees observes, "The critics are divided as to the origin and reason of the name mosaic." He then gives unsatisfactory hypotheses of several writers on the subject, and concludes by saying, " Mosaic appears to have taken its origin from paving:" leaving the question as to the propriety of thus denominating any kind of paving unsolved. This matter having eluded the researches of the learned for so many ages, that it is with diffidence I offer the following remarks

"The rural works, says Pluche, not being resumed in Egypt till after the Nile had quitted the plain, they for this reason, gave the public sign of husbandry the name of Moses or Museus, *saved from the waters ;* and on the same account, the nine moons during which Horus, Apollo, or husbandry continued his exercises, went by the same name." Hence, as we have seen, originated the fable of the nine muses. " Isis says the same writer, was so far the proclamation of the year, that she put on such clothes and dresses as were agreeable to the four seasons. To announce the beginning of spring that overspreads and enamels the earth with flowers and verdure, she wore carpets of different colors," etc.

Now, what could be more appropriate than to denominate the variegated and beautiful face of the earth in Egypt, during the nine months that bore the name of Moses or Museus, *mosaic* or *musaic* work, and to give the same appellation to its imitation?

The Egyptians and other ancient nations held high hills, groves, etc. in superstitious veneration; and although when more civilized, in order to shelter themselves from the weather, they quitted these favorite retreats, and worshipped their gods in temples; still it was natural that they should endeavor to imitate the scenes which they venerated, and had been accustomed to contemplate in their former devotions. With this view then, they decorated their temples so as, in some measure, to resemble the works of creation as exhibited in the places where they before assembled for religious worship. And the name Mosaic or Musaic would naturally occur to them as proper to be given to this ornamental work, intended to represent the face of the earth during the nine mosaic months.

How many principles are there in masonry? Four: point, line, superfices, and solid. Point the center, round which the master cannot err; line, length without breadth; solid comprehends the whole, (Prichard.) This as before observed, is the definition of the science of geometry.

A point within a Circle.

"In all regular, well constituted lodges, there is a point within a circle, which is bounded between north and south by two parallel lines one representing *Moses*, the other *king Solomon*. On the upper part of this circle rests the volume of the *sacred law*, which supports *Jacob's ladder*, the top of which reaches *to heaven*." In going round this circle

---

* "In the factitious caves, which priests every where constructed, they celebrated mysteries which consisted, says Origen against Celsus, in imitating the motion of the stars, the planets, and the heavens. The initiated took the name of constellations, and assumed the figure of animals. In the cave of *Mithra* was a ladder of *seven steps*, representing the seven spheres of the planets, by means of which *souls* ascended and descended; this is precisely the ladder in Jacob's vision; which shows that at that epoch, the whole system was formed. There is in the royal library a superb volume of pictures of the Indian gods, in which the ladder is represented with the souls of men ascending it. See Bailey's ancient astronomy." (Ruins, p. 239.)

I apprehend that the author is mistaken in regard to the steps of this allegorical lad-

we must necessarily touch on both these parallel lines, and on the sacred volume, and while a mason keeps himself thus circumscribed, he cannot err."—Carlile.

Although our ancient brethren dedicated their lodges to king Solomon, yet masons professing Christianity, dedicate theirs to St. John the Baptist, and St. John the Evangelist, who were eminent patrons of masonry; and since their time there is represented in every regular and well governed lodge, a *point within a circle;* the *point* representing an individual brother, the *circle* representing the boundary line of his duty to God and man, beyond which he is never to suffer his passions, prejudices, or interest, to betray him on any occasion. This circle is embroidered by two perpendicular parallel lines, representing *St. John the Baptist, and St. John the Evangelist,* who were perfect parallels in Christianity as well as masonry; and upon the vertex rests the book of Holy Scriptures, which point out the whole duty of man. In going round the circle, we necessarily touch upon these two lines, as well as upon the Holy Scriptures; and while a mason keeps himself thus circumscribed, it is impossible that he should materially err. (Webb.)

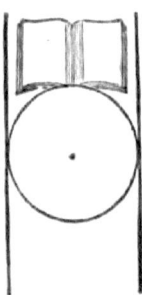

That expositors of masonry should differ in their interpretation of this figure, is not surprising. It is an astronomical enigma, the sense of which was probably lost sight of during the centuries in which the

---

der. The spheres of the planets being mere imaginary lines, and not so well adapted as the permanent constellations. And, in order to imitate the sun, the principal object of the pagan religious ceremonies, these would naturally be fixed upon for the purpose. The actors, in the scenical representations in the cave of Mithra, by taking the name of constellations, and assuming the figure of animals, corroborate this opinion.

affairs of the lodge, with very few exceptions, were in the hands of ignorant craftsmen.

The solution of the symbol I take to be as follows: The point in the center represents the Supreme Being; the circle indicates the annual circuit of the sun; and the parallel lines mark out the solstices within which that circuit is limited. The mason by subjecting himself to due bounds, in imitation of that glorious luminary, will not wander from the path of duty. The device is ingenious, and its meaning ought to be restored in the lodge to its original intention.

The assertion that lodges were formerly dedicated to Solomon, is gratuitous, and I believe will not admit of proof. I am not sensible of any historical document that substantiates the fact. We know very little of masonry prior to the revival of the order in 1717. And we learn by the earliest report of its practices, that the old masons hailed from the *holy lodge of St. John*. It is evident, as before observed, that the Druids adopted the names of their solstitial festivals, which had been assumed for them by the Christians, calling them St. Johns' days; and it is highly probable that they resorted to the same finess to delude their enemies, as well as those of the fraternity who were not fully initiated into their mysteries, in dedicating their lodges to these saints.

This artifice of introducing the St. Johns among the symbols of masonry, has put the craft to their wits to invent a plausible story to meet the case, and they have come, it is presumed, to an erroneous conclusion, that this was done by Christian masons.

What do you learn by being a *gentleman mason?* *Secrecy, morality,* and *good fellowship.* What do you learn by being an operative mason? To hew, square, and mould stone; lay a level and raise a perpendicular. Have you seen your master to-day? Yes. How was he clothed? *In a yellow jacket and blue pair of breeches.* (The master is the compasses, the yellow jacket is the brass body, and the blue breeches are the steel points.) How old are you? Under seven. ("Denoting he had not passed master.") Or rather that he had not passed to the fellow-craft's degree, seven years being formerly the term of an apprenticeship in freemasonry as in other trades.

The five last questions and answers are from Prichard; and from the simplicity of the dialogue, it may be concluded the original language and facts have not been perverted, and consequently that there were accepted, *gentlemen masons*, that is not of the craft, from the foundation of the institution.

Fellow-Craft's Degree.

Are you a fellow-craft? I am. Why were you made a fellow-craft? For the sake of the letter G. What does the letter G denote? Geometry, or the *fifth science*. In another part of the same degree, G is said to denote "the grand architect and contriver of the universe."[*] On being further questioned, the respondent replies, by letters four and science five this G aright doth stand, in a due art and proportion. You have your answer, friend. (N. B. Four letters are Boaz, fifth science, geometry.) (Prichard.) The importance bestowed upon geometry, the fifth science, according to masonic classification, may be another reason why five should compose a lodge.

How did you attain to this degree?—By the benefit of a grip and pass-word. The name of the grip is *Jachin*; that of the pass-word *Shibboleth*, which denotes plenty, and is represented by a sheaf of wheat suspended near a water-ford. (Allyn.) Did you ever work? Yes, in the building of the temple. Where did you receive your wages? In the middle chamber, which I entered through the porch, by *seven winding stairs*, where I discovered two great columns or pillars. The name of the one on the left hand is Boaz, and denotes *strength;* that on the right, Jachin, which denotes *to establish;* and when combined, *stability;* for God said, in strength will I establish this *mine house*, to stand firm forever. The *house* of God is the universe, which is doubtless established upon principles that will sustain it forever. The pillars Boaz and Jachin are imaginary props, standing at the two equinoxes east and west, to support the world. Here it may be remarked, that the pillar representing Boaz, or the sun, is properly said to denote strength, whereas in the apprentice's degree it is made to denote *wisdom*. Jachin signifying Isis the moon, was a necessary appendage to the creation, and perhaps may be applied metaphorically, to *establish*.

---

[*] It has been seen, that by the doctrine of the Pythagoreans, as well as that of masonry, the Supreme Being is often confounded with geometry as containing the principles of the material world. This is in conformity to the source from which both derive their origin.

"The secret doctrine of the Egyptian priests, like that of the Brahmins of India and the Magi of Persia, presents itself under the double form of a Theological and Cosmogonical system. It had for a basis, a species of *pantheism*, at one moment more physical, at another more intellectual in its character, and at times, again combining both of these attributes; a personification of the powers of nature more or less identified with the powers of mind, and conceived in a point of view having reference to a mysterious unity in which the Deity and the universe were blended together," (Professor Anthon's Class. Dict.)

"The sun is the creator and father, the moon the mother of all things. These two deities govern, produce, and nourish every thing connected with the visible universe. The sun is the third Demiurgus, the supreme creative intelligence under the third form: incarnate he becomes Osiris, the author of all good, and it is he that completes the Egyptian trinity." (Anthon's Class. Dict.)

Osiris, the sun, by his genial influence in the spring season, prepares the earth for cultivation, gives life to its various productions, and consequently enables the husbandman to commence his labors. Isis, the *teeming mother*, who personifies the earth as well as moon, nourishes during the summer, the seeds committed to her bosom, and in the fall season rewards the laborer.

The pillars of Boaz and Jachin, are described to be *eighteen cubits* high, *twelve* in circumference, and *four* in diameter.

The eighteen cubits refer to the inundation of the Nile, being the highest elevation it is known to have attained. The twelve cubits relate to the twelve signs of the zodiac, through which the sun passes; and the four cubits have reference to the *tetractys*, which comprehends the principles of geometry, point, line, superfices, and solid.

The pillars are adorned with two large chapiters, which are ornamented with net-work, denoting unity; lily-work, denoting peace; and pomegranates, which from the exuberance of their seeds, denote *plenty*. It is only the pillar of Jachin, which represents Isis, the emblem of harvest, that is decorated with pomegranates in the figures of these columns among the masonic symbols. They are further adorned with two globes, one celestial, the other terrestrial.

This display of *globes*, like most of the customs of masonry, may be traced to Egypt. Dr. Richardson, as recorded in a former part of this work, in describing the gateway or porch, leading to the temple of Isis, in Tentyra, says "Immediately over the centre of the *doorway*, is the beautiful *Egyptian ornament* usually called the *globe*, with serpents and wings, emblematical of the glorious sun poised in the airy firmament of heaven, supported and directed in his course by the eternal wisdom of the Deity."

Voltaire, however, is of opinion that this globe indicated the Supreme Being; he says, "It may be remarked, that the *globe* placed over the door of the temple of Memphis, represented the unity of the divine nature, under the name of Knef."—(Oeuvres—T. 16, p. 100.)

The candidate having learned the grip, token, and pass-word (Shibboleth, *plenty*,) of the fellow-craft, receives his wages, and passes the pillar of Jachin. He is then placed in the south-east part of the lodge, and thus addressed by the master:

Brother, masonry being a *progressive science*, when you were made an entered apprentice, you were placed in the north-east part of the lodge, to show that you were newly admitted. You are now placed in the south-east part, to mark the *progress* you have made in the *science*.

Thus the candidate commences his labors at that point where the sun is supposed first to have risen at the period of the creation, and by pursuing the course of that luminary till he has completed the circuit, becomes then worthy of the master's degree.

Master Mason's Degree.

The degree of master mason follows that of fellow-craft. And as it contains the story of the *murder* of Hiram upon which the entire fabric of masonry is erected; the very *gist* of the order, to which all other considerations are subordinate; which meets us at every turn through all the varied scenes of the institution, it becomes necessary to possess a due knowledge of the original upon which it is founded. This is the fable of Osiris and Isis; which I, therefore, place as an introductory preface to the master's degree. I take the fable from L'Origine de tous les Cultes, par Dupuis.

Explanation of the Travels of Isis, or the Moon.

The moon was associated, by the ancient Egyptians, with the sun in the general administration of the world, and it is she who represents the character of Isis in the sacred fable, known by the title of the history of Osiris and Isis. The first men who inhabited Egypt, says Diodorus of Sicily, struck with the grandeur of the heavens, and the admirable order of the universe, thought they perceived two primary and eternal causes, or two grand divinities, and they called one of them, or the sun, Osiris; and the other, or moon, Isis.

The denomination of Isis, given to the moon, is confirmed by Porphyry, and other authors; whence we draw a necessary conclusion, that the courses or journeying of Isis are no other than the courses of the moon; and as the regions of the heavens are those she traverses in her monthly revolutions, we will there fix the scene of her adventures.

This conclusion is justified by the passage from Cheremon, where this learned Egyptian tells us, that the Egyptians explained the fable of Osiris and Isis, as well as all other sacred fables, by the celestial bodies, by the phases of the moon, by the increase and diminution of her light, by the division of time and of the heavens into two parts, by the *paranatellons* or the stars which rise and set in aspect with the signs. It is upon this principle we have explained the poem of the Twelve Labors of Hercules; we shall follow the same principle in the explication of the Legend of Isis; of which we shall give also a comparative table, with those presented by the heavens, at the moment when the sun has departed from our hemisphere, and left to the moon, then at her full, the empire over long nights, up to the moment when he returns again to our regions.

Let us take then Isis at the epoch of the death of Osiris, her husband, and let us follow her steps, from the moment when she is deprived of him, up to that when he returns to her from hell; or, to drop the figure, from the moment when the sun has passed into the southern or inferior regions of the world, up to that when he repasses conqueror into the northern or superior hemisphere.

Plutarch supposes that Osiris, after his travels, being on his return through Egypt, was invited to a repast by Typhon, his brother and rival. The latter put him to death and threw his body into the Nile. The sun, says Plutarch, then occupied the sign Scorpio, and the moon was full; she was then in the sign opposite to Scorpio, that is to say, to Taurus, which lent its forms to the sun of the spring equinox or to Osiris; for at that distant period, Taurus was the sign which answered to the spring equinox. As soon as Isis was informed of the death of the unfortunate Osiris, whom all the ancients had denominated the same god as the sun, when she learned that the genius of darkness had shut him up in a *coffin*, she commenced a search after his body. Uncertain of the route she ought to pursue, uneasy, agitated, her heart lacerated with grief, in mourning garb, she *interrogates every one she meets.* She is informed by some young children that the coffin which contains the body of her husband, had been carried by the waters out to sea and thence to Biblos, where it was stopped; and was now reposing upon a *plant, which had immediately put forth a superb stalk.* The coffin was so enveloped, as to bear the appearance of being but a part of it. The king of the country, astonished at the beauty of the bush, had it cut, and made of it a column for his palace without perceiving the coffin which had become incorporated with the trunk. Isis actuated by a divine impulse, arrives at Biblos,; bathed in tears, *she seats herself near a fountain,* where she remained *overwhelmed with grief,* speaking to no one until the arrival of some of the queen's women. She salutes them politely, and commences dressing their hair in such a manner as to spread in it, as well as over their whole body, the odour of an exquisite purfume.

The queen learning from her women what had happened, and perceiving the exquisite odour of the ambrosia, desired to know this stranger. She invites Isis to her palace, attached her to her household; and placed her as nurse to her son. The goddess then made herself known and demanded that the precious column should be given to her.

She drew from it easily the body of her husband, by disengaging the coffin from the branches which covered it; these she found to be of light texture, which she perfumed with essences; she sent to the king and queen this envelope of strange boughs, which was deposited at Biblos, in the temple of Isis. She then embarked and returned to Egypt, to Orus her son; and deposited the body in a secluded place. Typhon having gone that night to the chase, finds the coffin, recognized the corpse, and cuts it into *fourteen pieces*,* which he scattered here and there.

The goddess seeing this, returned to collect these dispersed fragments; she interred each part in the place where it was found. Of all the parts of the body of Osiris, those of propagation were the only ones Isis could not find. She substituted for them the *phallus*, which was the image of them, and which was consecrated in the mysteries.

This is the precise Egyptian legend concerning Isis, which has not been handed down to us without much mutilation, and which make part of a sacred poem upon Osiris, Isis, and Typhon, their enemy.

Notwithstanding the immense deficiencies discoverable in this allegorical history, it will not be difficult for us to trace a perfect correspondence between the principal features of this sacred fable which remain to us, and the representations which the heavens offer, at the

---

* That is, into as many parts as there are days between the full moon and the new. This circumstance, says Plutarch, has reference to the gradual diminution of the lunary light, during the *fourteen days* that follow the full moon. The moon at the end of fourteen days, enters Taurus and becomes united to the sun, from whom she collects fire upon her disk, during the fourteen days which follow. She is then found every month in conjunction with him in the superior parts of the signs.

The equinoctial year finishes at the moment when the sun and moon are found united with Orion, or the star of Orus, a constellation placed under Taurus, which unites itself to the Neomenia of Spring.

The moon renews herself in Taurus, and a few days after, is seen in the form of a crescent, in the following sign, that is, Gemini, the home of Mercury. Then Orion, united to the sun, in the attitude of a formidable warrior, precipitates Scorpio, his rival, into the shades of night; for he sets every time Orion appears above the horizon. The day becomes lengthened, and the germs of evil are by degrees destroyed. It is thus that the poet Nonnus pictures to us Typhon conquered at the end of winter, when the sun arrives in Taurus, and when Orion mounts into the heavens with him.

different epochs of the movements of the two great *stars* which regulate the course of the seasons; the periodical march of vegetation, the division of time, and the succession of days and nights.—We will now proceed as in the poem on Hercules, to bring together these different representations, those which are presented by the fable, as well as those exhibited by the heavens. We will divide them into twelve parts.

[Here follows a critical comparison between the wanderings of Isis in search of the dead body of Osiris, and the courses of the moon in the heavens; but as the fable alone answers the purpose here intended, I omit the comparative representations. The foregoing note, however, is drawn from the part omitted. The author concludes as follows:]

A conformity so complete, and one which bears so many points of resemblance between the representations of the legend and those of the heavens, and which, mutilated as the legend or this sacred history may be, is so well sustained from one end to the other, as not to permit us to doubt that the astronomical priest who composed it, did nothing more than write down the courses of the moon in the heavens, under the title of the wanderings of Isis; especially when it is known that Isis is the name given to the moon in Egypt. We have, in our explanation, only made use of the method laid down for us by Cheremon to analyse these sacred fables, and especially that of Osiris and Isis, which he said was relative to the increases and diminutions of the light of the moon at the superior and inferior hemispheres, and to the stars in aspect with the signs, otherwise called *paranatellons*. The learned men of Egypt have themselves traced out the plan which we have adopted.

Here we have then an ancient queen of Egypt and an ancient king, whose imaginary adventures have been described in the form of history, but who, however, as the Hercules of the Greeks, are only physical beings, and the two principal agents of nature. We are led to judge, by these examples, of the allegoric character of antiquity, and to consider how much we should be on our guard against traditions which place physical beings as characters in history.

It is important not to lose sight of the fact, that formerly the history of the heavens and particularly of the sun, was written under the form of a history of men, and that the people, almost universally, received it as such, and looked upon the hero as a man. The tombs of the gods were shown, as if they had really existed; feasts were celebrated, the object of which seemed to be to renew every year the grief which had been occasioned by their loss.

Such was the tomb of Osiris, covered under those enormous masses, known by the name of Pyramids, which the Egyptians raised to the star which gives us light. One of these has its four fronts facing the four cardinal points of the world. Each of these fronts, is one hundred and ten fathoms wide at its base, and the four form as many equilateral triangles. The perpendicular height is seventy-seven fathoms, according to the measurement given by Chazelles, of the Academy of Sciences. It results from these dimensions, and the latitude under which this pyramid is erected, that *fourteen days* before the spring equinox, the precise period at which the Persians celebrated *the revival of nature*, the sun would cease to cast a shade at midday, and would not again cast it till *fourteen days* after the fall equinox. Then the day or the sun would be found in the parallel or circle of southern declension, which answers to five degrees fifteen minutes; this would happen twice a year, once before the spring equinox, and once after the fall equinox. The sun would then appear exactly at mid-day upon the summit of this pyramid. Then his majestic disk would appear for some moments, placed upon this immense pedestal and to rest upon it, while his worshippers, on their knees at its base, extending their view along the inclined plane of the northern side of the pyramid, would contemplate the great Osiris, as well when *he descended into the darkness of the tomb*, as when *he arose from it triumphant*.* The same might be said of the full moon of the equinoxes, when it takes place in this parallel.

It would seem that the Egyptians, always grand in their conceptions, had executed a project the boldest that was ever imagined, of giving a pedestal to the sun and moon, or to Osiris and Isis, at midday for the one, and at midnight for the other, when they arrived in that part of the heavens near to which passes the line which separates the northern from the southern hemisphere, the empire of *good* from that of *evil*, the region of *light* from that of *darkness*. They wished that the shade should disappear from all the fronts of the pyramid at mid-day, during the whole time that the sun sojourned in the *luminous* hemisphere, and that the northern front should be again covered with shade when night began to attain her supremacy in our hemisphere, that is, at the moment when Osiris descended into the tomb or into hell. The tomb

---

* Here we find an explanation of the time that it is said the body of grand master Hiram reposed in the tomb before it was discovered, and raised by king Solomon. Which, says Bernard, "it is said, had lain there *fourteen days*; some say fifteen." To have suffered the body of Hiram to have remained in this tomb *fifteen days*, would have marred the original design: it would have entirely destroyed the astronomical allusion intended by the incarceration.—Edit.

of Osiris was covered with shade nearly six months; after which light surrounded it entirely at mid-day, as soon as Osiris, returning from hell, regained his empire in passing into the luminous hemisphere. Then he had returned to Isis and to the god of spring, Orus, who had at length conquered the genius of darkness and of winter. What a sublime idea! In the centre of the pyramid is a vault, which is said to be the tomb of an ancient king. This king is the husband of Isis, the famous Osiris, this beneficent king whom the people believed to have reigned formerly over Egypt, while the priests and learned men saw in him the powerful planet which governs the world and enriches it with his benefits. And, in fact, would they have ever gone to so great an expense if this tomb had not been reputed to contain the precious remains of Osiris, which his wife had collected, and which she confided, say they, to the priests, to be interred at the same time that they decreed to him divine honors? Can we suppose that there was any other object among a people who spared nothing to give all pomp and magnificence to their worship, and whose greatest luxury was a religious luxury?* It is thus that the Babylonians, who worshipped the sun under the name of Belus, raised him a tomb which was hid by an immense pyramid; for as soon as the powerful planet which animates nature, became personified, and in the sacred fictions was made to be born, to die and to rise again, imitative worship, which sought to retrace his adventures, placed tombs beside their temples.

Thus is shown that of Jupiter, in Crete; of Mithra, in Persia; of Hercules, in Cadis; of the Coachman, the Celestial Bear, of Medusa, of the Pleaides, etc., in Greece. These various tombs prove nothing for the historical existence of the feigned personages to whom the mystic spirit of the ancients had consecrated them.

They show, also, the place where Hercules burned himself up, and we have shown that Hercules was no other than the sun personified in the sacred allegories; at the same time that we have proved that the

---

* This seems to me to be the most reasonable conjecture that has appeared, respecting the motives which caused the erection of those stupendous monuments, the pyramids.

On the subject of the Sphynx, which has also caused great speculation in regard to its origin and purport, the author of the "Identity of the Druidical and Hebrew religions," gives the following solution:

The Sphynx was a representation of the signs Leo and Virgo joined together, in commemoration of the inundation of the Nile, which occurs when the sun is in those signs. The Egyptians had always a sort of astronomical mystic reverence for the three signs, Cancer, Leo, and Virgo." M. Maillet is of the same opinion. (See Anthon's Class. Dict.) The great utility of the overflowing of the Nile to Egypt, which was considered a providential occurrence, was sufficient, among a superstitious people, to cause its commemoration in this manner.—Edit.

adventures of the queen Isis were those of the moon, sung by her worshippers.

I now proceed with the

Master Mason's Degree.

This degree, as before observed, is chiefly occupied in the pretended assassination of Hiram Abiff.*

The Temple of Solomon, like the temples of the Egyptians and other nations of the east, is said to have been constructed with a view to a representation of the world in miniature; thereby the better to adapt it to the popular prejudice in favor of performing religious rites in places where the operations of nature were exhibited before the worshippers. This temple, therefore, was well adapted for those astronomical allusions which composed the mystic rites of the ancients; and was for this reason probably selected, by the Druids, as an appropriate place in which to lay the scene of masonic mysteries.

The equinoxes and solstices are called the gates of heaven through which the sun passes. It was only at the latter, however, that any obstructions were believed to occur to his free egress and regress. The scene, therefore, of the death of Hiram, who takes the part of Osiris, as now acted in the lodges, is not a close imitation of the original, which has been lost sight of, but is sufficiently so to show from whence the copy is derived.

Are you a master mason?—I am; try me; prove me; disprove me, if you can. Where were you passed master?—In a *perfect lodge* of masters. What makes a perfect lodge of masters?—*Three.* Why do three make a lodge? Because there were *three grand Masons* in *building* the *world.* (Master Key, and Jachin and Boaz.)

Here the Kneph, Osiris, and Isis of the Egyptians; the Agathon, Logos, and Psyche of the Platonists; and the Wisdom, Strength, and Beauty of masonry, are too clearly indicated to admit of misinterpretation.

From whence came you?—From the east. Where are you going?—To the west. For what purpose?—To search for that which

---

* There is no propriety in the addition of Abiff or Abbif to the name of Hiram. In the original Hebrew from which it is taken, the affix is Abbi, the possessive case of Abba; which signifies father, and figuratively, a superior. His proper address, therefore is *my father*, or, in court style, *my lord.* In this sense, it is equivalent to Adonis, Baal, or Osiris, all names of the sun. And as Solomon's temple was built so as to imitate the world, the grand architect was very properly entitled.

was lost. What was that which was lost?—The master mason's word. How was it lost?—By three great knocks, or the death of our master Hiram. Where do you hope to find it?—With a center. What is a center?—A point within a circle, from which every part of the circumference is equally distant. Why with a center?—Because, from that point, no master mason can err.

The allusion here to Osiris the sun is very plain: and, when found, it is evident he must be on the imaginary circle made by his annual course, unless he should deviate from the order of nature. And the point in the center of that circle, according to the meaning evidently intended, it is equally certain, would be found in its proper place.

The story of Hiram is as follows:

At the building of Solomon's temple, fifteen fellow-crafts, perceiving that the work was nearly finished, and not having received the master's word, grew impatient, and agreed to extort it from their master Hiram the first opportunity they could find of meeting him alone, that they might pass for masters in other countries, and receive wages as such; but before they could accomplish their scheme, twelve of them recanted. The other three, being of a more determined character, persisted in their design: their names were Jubela, Jubelo, and Jubelum.

Hiram having entered the temple at twelve at noon, as was his custom, to pay his devotion to God, the three assassins placed themselves at the east, west, and south doors; Hiram having finished his prayer, came to the east door, which was guarded by Jubela, who demanded of him the master's grip and word in a *resolute manner;* he received for answer from Hiram, that it was not customary to ask it in *such a strain;* that he himself did not receive it so. He told him farther, that it was not in his power alone to reveal it, except in the presence of Solomon, and Hiram, king of Tyre. Jubela being dissatisfied with this answer, struck him across the throat with a twenty-four inch guage. Hiram then flew to the south door, where he received similar treatment from Jubelo; and thence to the west door, where he was struck on his head by Jubelum, with a gavel or setting maul, which occasioned his death. (Jachin and Boaz.)

Carlile places the conspirators at the east, north, and south entrances of the temple; and makes Hiram receive the finishing stroke at the east door. Whereas, to render the parallel in strict accordance as an allegory of the death of Osiris, Hiram should expire at the north or south gate or door.—The story is badly conceived, as there is no pretext for confining the word to Solomon and the two Hirams, nor for requiring that it should not be communicated except in the presence of the three. Besides, according to masonic tradition, there were at the same time 3,300 master masons employed on the temple, who must of course have been furnished with the master's word. To make out the parody, however, it was necessary that Hiram be put to death, and a cause must be invented to procure it; and altho the one fixed upon for the purpose, appears very mal á propos, it seems to be satisfactory to the craft.

It may be remarked, however, that Solomon and the two Hirams are here intended to represent the *trinity in unity*, and therefore, it may be supposed, could not act separately.

How did the ruffians dispose of the body?—They carried it out at the *west* door (according to the apparent course of the sun) and hid it till twelve o'clock the next night, when they met by agreement, and buried it on the side of a hill, in a grave six feet perpendicular, dug due east and west; and stuck down a sprig of cassia,* to mark the place.

Master Hiram not coming to view the workmen as usual, king Solomon caused search to be made for him in and about the temple; which proving ineffectual, he ordered the roll of workmen to be called; when it was found that *three were missing*, namely, Jubela, Jubelo, and Jubelum. The twelve fellow-crafts who had recanted, then went to Solomon with white aprons and gloves, emblems of their innocence, and informed him of every thing relating to the affair, as far as they knew, and offered their assistance to discover the three others who had absconded.

Solomon then ordered twelve trusty fellow-crafts to be selected, and sent three east, three west, three north, and three south, in search of Hiram. Elder Bernard gives fifteen as the number selected for this purpose, and adds, "In some lodges they send only twelve, when their own lectures say fifteen were sent." The Elder was not aware of the vast importance of confining the number to precisely twelve. Those who were deputed for this service represented the twelve signs of the zodiac; one of whom would be sure to find their grand master Hiram, the personification of Osiris the sun.

The party that took a westerly course, fell in with a way-faring

---

* "Cassia, my friends, did not grow about Jerusalem." (Dr. Dalcho.)

man, near the coast of Joppa, who, on being interrogated, informed them that he had seen three men pass that morning, whom from their appearance, he took to be workmen from the temple. They had been seeking for a passage to Ethiopia, and not being able to obtain it, had turned back into the country. This party then returned, and made their report to Solomon. Of the three who steered an easterly course, one, being weary, sat down at the *brow of a hill to rest and refresh himself;* and in rising, he caught hold of a twig, which coming easily up, excited his suspicions, and perceiving the ground to have been recently broken, he hailed his companions, and on searching, they found the body of their grand master Hiram, decently buried in a handsome grave, six feet east and west, and six feet perpendicular; and its covering was *green moss* and *turf,* which surprised them: whereupon they exclaimed, *muscus domus Dei gratia,** which, according to masonry, is, thanks be unto God, our master has got a *mossy house.* So they covered him closely, and went and acquainted king Solomon.

In regard to the conspirators, it shall suffice here to say, that according to the story, they were discovered, arrested, and executed. "Jubelum's body was severed in two, and scattered in south and north."—(Jachin and Boaz.)

After which Solomon ordered twelve crafts to take up the body of Hiram, in order that it might be interred in a solemn manner in the *sanctum sanctorum;* he also told them, if they could not find a *keyword* about him, it was lost; for there were only three in the world to whom it was known; and unless they were present it could not be delivered; and Hiram being dead, it consequently was lost. But the first sign and word that were made and spoken at his raising should be the master's word ever after. The twelve crafts went and cleared the rubbish, and found their master in a mangled condition, having lain *fourteen days;* upon which they lifted up their hands above their heads and exclaimed, O Lord my God! They failed in their attempts to raise the body, either by the grip of the apprentice, or that of the fellow-craft, the flesh cleaving from the bone: upon which they all raised their hands, and exclaimed, O Lord my God! I fear the master's word is forever lost; was there no help for the widow's son?

King Solomon then ordered a lodge of master masons to be summoned, and said, I will go myself in person, and try to raise the body by the master's grip or *lion's paw.* Some say, by the *strong grip or*

---

* The Latin tongue seems to have been familiar to the Hebrew masons of king Solomon's temple.

lion's paw. (Bernard.) By means of this grip the body of grand master Hiram was raised.*

The raising of Osiris, the prototype of Hiram. (*See page* 15.)

If this affair would admit of serious criticism, upon the supposition that this *word* was a mere name, term, or phrase, it might be asked what was the use in seeking for that which when found, could not be made use of, unless the fingers turned traitors, and exposed it unlawfully. The story, as before observed, wants plausibility.

This word, however, is not a name, it is the personified *Logos*, the *key stone* of the arch, the absence of which rendered the structure incomplete.

That Solomon and the two Hirams are made to personate the pagan trinity is evident from the following:

Master—What supports our lodge? Ans. Three pillars. Pray what are their names, brother?—*Wisdom, Strength,* and *Beauty.* What do they represent?—Three grand masters; Solomon, king of

---

* The author of the *Secret Discipline,* &c. before noticed, remarks on the password of this degree that, "By a singular *lapsus linguæ,* the moderns have substituted *Tubal Cain* in the third degree for *Tymboxein,* to be entombed. This in the ancient *Catechesis Arcani,* was the pass-word, from the symbolical representation of the state of death, to the restored and undying existence."

MASTER MASON'S DEGREE.

Israel; Hiram, king of Tyre; and Hiram Abiff; the three grand masters concerned in the building of Solomon's temple. And we were before told, there were three grand Masons in building the world;—of which Solomon's temple was an epitome.

The names Jubela, Jubelo, Jubelum, given to the pretended assassins of Hiram, I take to be a play upon the word Jubilum, the Latin term answering to Jubilee. They were of course formed at the time freemasonry was first established. The inflections of this word will give Jubili, Jubilo, Jubilum. That a slight variation should have taken place in their pronunciation, will not appear surprising, when it is considered that they have been handed down orally, by illiterate men, through many ages. Jubilum is derived from *jubeo*, to appoint; it also signifies to *bid, order, charge,* or *command*. Now, these reputed assassins are represented as demanding, in an imperious and authoritative tone, of grand master Hiram, the master's grip and word; and their names were probably given in allusion to this circumstance, being appropriate to the character assumed for them.

Besides the relation which the story of Hiram bears to that of Osiris, there is a singular fancy set forth in ancient astronomy in regard to the reputed murderers of Chrisna, which contains a strict analogy to the supposed assassination of Hiram.—Chrisna, among the Hindoos, is the same as Osiris with the Egyptians, and is worshipped by them in like manner. Nothing could be more explanatory of the fable of Hiram than this astronomical notion; which is given in Mackey's mythological astronomy, as follows:

"The stories which have been the result of the particular method made use of by ancient historians to express the various changes of the constellations and seasons of the year; and the causes of those changes, may be worth our while to examine.

"The Elohim, the Decans, or the Symbols which presided over the thirty-six subdivisions of the zodiac, or more properly speaking, of the year, each month having three, were those gods, whose care it was to regulate the weather in the different seasons, and who were supposed to vary it according to their will.

"These Decans or Elohim are the gods, of whom it is said, the Almighty created the universe. They arranged the order of the zodiac. The Elohim of the summer were gods of a benevolent disposition: they made the days long, and loaded the sun's head with topaz. While the *three wretches* that presided in the winter, at the extreme end of the year, hid in the realms below, were, with the constellation to which they belong, cut off from the rest of the zodiac; and, as they were *missing*, would consequently be accused of bringing Chrisna into those troubles which at last ended in his death.*"

Eleven is one of the numbers singled out to make a lodge, which like the rest, must have an astronomical allusion; and there is little doubt that it refers to the fanciful notion just detailed in regard to the defection of one of the great gods composing the zodiaz, with his attendant satellites, the Decans or Elohim. In consequence of this treachery, but eleven of these great chiefs remained faithful to their lord, the supreme ruler, the sun. This circumstance would be sufficient to cause the commemoration of that number, in the manner it is done in masonry.

It may be remarked, that the lamentations uttered for the death of grand master Hiram, is in exact accordance with the customs of the Egyptians in their celebrations of the fabled death of Osiris the sun; of the Phenicians for the loss of Adonis; and of the Greeks, in their mystic rites of the Eleusinian Ceres.

It is through the instrumentality of Leo, that Osiris, the sun, is relieved from his perilous condition. The strong *paw* of the *lion* wrests him from the clutches of Typhon, and places him in his wonted course. Anubis, the dog-star, is the herald of this event. Here we see the archetype of the raising of grand master Hiram, by the "*strong gripe or lion's paw.*"

In short, the attentive reader must have perceived, that the story of Hiram, is only another version, like those of Adonis and Astarte, and of Ceres and Proserpine, of the fable of Osiris and Isis. The likeness throughout is so exact as not to admit of doubt. The search for the body of Hiram;—the inquiries made of a wayfaring man, and the intelligence received;—the sitting down of one of the party to rest and refresh himself, and the hint conveyed by the *sprig* over the grave;—the body of Hiram remaining *fourteen days* in the grave prepared by the assasssins, before it was discovered, all have allusion to, and comport with the allegory of Osiris and Isis. The condition even in which the grave of Hiram is found, covered with green *moss* and turf, corresponds very much with that in which Isis found the coffin of Osiris.

Again, the cutting up and *scattering* the parts of the body of Jubelum, is a *fac simile* of the treatment which the body of Osiris is said to have received. By the way, the oath imposed upon the master

---

* This is a sketch of the life of the sun, who, finishing his career at the winter solstice, when Typhon and the rebel angels gain the dominion, seems to be put to death by them; but who soon after is born again, and rises into the vault of heaven where he reigns.—*Ruins*, p. 165.—Edit.

mason very likely grew out of the fable of Typhon's murder of Osiris, and afterwards cutting up the body into *fourteen* pieces, and *scattering* them hither and thither on the plains of Egypt.

Select Master's Degree.

Mr. Cole, Editor of "The Freemasons' Library," says, "There are, I am bold to assert, but four degrees in ancient freemasonry. This opinion accords, not only with the sentiments of the oldest and best informed masons, with whom I have conversed, but is also agreeable to written and printed documents; some of the latter of which are almost as old as the art of printing itself." The intermediate degrees between the master's and that of royal arch, which he considers the fourth, which have, he says, within a few years past, been manufactured into degrees, are merely elucidatory of the second, third, and fourth. Why, Mr. Cole need not have gone farther back into antiquity than to 1750, to learn that, at that time, but three degrees of masonry were known to the world. The party who styled themselves ancient masons, about this time, discovered the royal arch among the archives of the order, as has been shown above; but which those called moderns were strangers to, and did not then acknowledge.

The division of masonry into degrees is entirely arbitrary, and since operative masonry is no longer taught in the lodge, unnecessary. The reasons which governed in the administration of the pagan rites, which concealed from the initiates of the *lesser* mysteries the *aporreta* or *grand secret*, which was communicated to those of the *greater*, are inapplicable to masonry. For that secret, the existence of one Supreme God, and the error of polytheism, is now openly taught amongst all nations where freemasonry is established. The affectation, therefore, of confining this knowledge to the companions of the royal arch, is at this time extremely absurd.

What Mr. Cole advances, however, in regard to the connection in the matter of the several degrees which he notices, is evidently very correct; and the same might be said of the two first degrees, which are merely preparatory to the third. Still, I am inclined to believe that the founders of the order divided its secrets or ceremonies originally into seven grades. It was incumbent upon them to move slowly, and to manage the subjects, with whom they had to deal, with much caution, for fear of a disclosure. Besides seven steps seem necessary to complete the rounds of the holy royal arch, the grand desideratum of masonry.

Of the mark and pass-masters' degrees there is nothing worthy of notice, excepting one circumstance in that of the latter; which is, the electing of a newly initiated member, on the night of his admission, to preside, *pro tempore*, as master of the lodge. And then for the brethren to exercise their wit at his expence, by exposing his ignorance of the duties of the office imposed upon him; finally knocking off his hat, and dragging him from the master's chair.

This, as has been noticed above, is in perfect accord with the customs of the Pythagorean school, which treated novitiates in like manner.

In regard to the select master's degree, Mr. Cole observes, " We know of no degree in masonry, that has a more needful, or more important connection with another, than the select with the royal arch. It fills up a chasm, which every intelligent mason has observed, and without it, it seems difficult, if not impossible, to comprehend clearly some of the mysteries that belong to the august degree of royal arch. Indeed, such is the nature of the degree, that we cannot feel freedom to allude remotely to its secrets." And Mr. Cross remarks, " Without this degree, the history of the royal arch cannot be complete. It *rationally* accounts for the concealment and preservation of those *essentials* of the craft, which were brought to light at the erection of the second temple, and which lay concealed from the masonic eye, 470 years."

The fact is, the grand omnific (*all-creating*) *lost word*, it will be seen in the sequel, was eventually found in a vault under the ruins of Solomon's temple; and the difficulty was *rationally* to account for the manner in which it got there. This, therefore, is the grand object of the select master's degree; and at the same time so to locate the word as symbolically to represent its archetype, the sun *lost* in the inferior hemisphere. For this purpose, a history of the order was manufactured by its founders, of which the following is a sketch :

The three grand masters, at the building of the temple, entered into a solemn agreement not to confer the master's degree until the temple should be completed, that all three must be present when it should be conferred, and if either should be taken away by death prior to the finishing of the temple, the master's degree should be lost.

After this *wise* arrangement, lest the knowledge of the arts and sciences, together with the patterns and valuable models which were contained in the temple, should be lost, they agreed to build a *secret vault* under ground, leading from Solomon's most retired apartment, *a due west course*, and ending under the *sanctum sanctorum* of the temple, to be divided into *nine separate arches*. The ninth arch was to be the place for holding the grand council, and also for a deposit of a true copy of all those things which were *contained in the sanctum sanctorum above.*

After the ninth arch was completed, the three grand masters deposited therein those things which were important to the craft, such as the ark of the covenant, a pot of manna, the rod of Aaron, the book of the law, etc.

Prior to the completion of the temple, grand master Hiram Abiff was assassinated, and by his death, the master's word was lost. The two kings were willing to do all in their power to preserve the *sacred Word*, and as they could not communicate it to any, by reason of the death of Hiram, they agreed to place it in the *secret vault*, that if the other treasures were ever brought to light, the *Word* might be found also.

The *all-creating* or omnific Word was deposited in the *royal vault*, (the term used in this degree,) as is said, in three languages, Jah, Bel, On, which are all names of the sun. The direction of the arches, from east to west, is following the apparent course of that luminary; the *royal* vault therefore, is a symbol of the lower regions, in which the sun, the *king* and governor of the world, was supposed to be lost. Who "under the name of Osiris, persecuted by Typhon and the tyrants of the air, was put to death, shut up in a dark tomb, emblem of the hemisphere of winter; and aftewards, ascending from the inferior zone towards the zenith of heaven, arose again from the dead triumphant over the giants and the angels of destruction."—[Ruins, p. 139.]

The *nine* arches have an astronomical allusion in regard to the latitude of the place where the scene is intended to be laid.

Mackey accounts for the origin of the mysterious numbers among different nations in the following manner:—" In the Asiatic Researches (vol. 8, p. 289,) we are told, that '*seven* was formerly a favorite and fortunate number among the Hindus; *eight* among the Baudhists; and *nine* formerly in the west, and in the north of Asia. Nine was held a *sacred* and *mystical number* in the northern parts of the continent, from China to the extremity of the west.' And why? Because the people there lived under the same elevation of the pole. They all saw the great *Dial* of the *Deity* from the same point of view;—they all saw the pole from the *ninth stage* of the world, that is, the ninth climate, from which, it would be seen as a pyramid with *nine steps;* while from the lattitude of 32, the eighth stage of the world, it would be seen as a cone or pyramid with eight steps. At Delhi, in latitude 28, which is in the seventh stage, or climate, the pole was represented by a cone of seven steps. Hence, we find, the cause which induced the ancients, in the above latitudes, to venerate the numbers 7–8–9, was *astro-geographical;* and hence also we see the impossibility of making the astronomical numbers of a large empire agree with one capital.

"According to Herodotus, the Tower of Babel, which was in the latitude of 32 degrees, had a road-way up on the outside, which went eight times round in its ascent, so as to give the whole the appearance of eight towers, one above another. These were no doubt intended to commemorate the eight revolutions of the pole, which represented a serpent coiled eight times round a mountain. Besides the eight volved Tower of Babel, in the latitude of 32 degrees, we find at Pekin, a Tower of Porcelain *ten stories* high, thereby indicating its latitude to be 40 degrees; for in that situation, the north pole is so far elevated above the horizon as to admit *ten volves* of the serpent.

"Again, in Egypt, we find the statue of Pluto with a serpent coiled six times round him, which represents the six volves of the pole of the ecliptic round the south pole of the earth; which shows that the statue must have been erected at or near Thebes or Elephantine. Thus we see, that from Pekin to Elephantine, the men of learning agree in coupling the histories of their countries with that of the heavens."— [Mytho. Astro. part 1st, p. 68.]

I am induced to add the following curious remarks of the same writer, as, in some measure, explanatory of the preceding.

"The stories of the Pagans concerning the ascension of their gods into heaven, and their descent into hell, have produced in the minds of modern Europeans the most absurd notions,—such as never entered the minds of the first astronomers, who divided the heavens into three grand divisions, in the most simple manner imaginable. They observed towards the north, that a circuit in the heavens always appeared above the horizon: this they denominated one great empire; and as there is a point in the middle of it which is always stationary, this they made the seat of that empire, and subjected it to the government of a monarch, who could from his throne, that is the pole, behold all the nations of the earth, both by night and by day.*

"They could not but be sensible of that part of the vast concave that is forever hid from our sight, surrounding the south pole; this was distinguished as another grand division, and called the *pit,* in contra-dis-

---

* This notion doubtles gave rise to the custom of symbolizing the Deity by a circle with a dot in its center.—Edit.

tinction from the opposite, which was called the mountain.† Hence among the ancients, arose the epithets of *Helion* and *Acheron*, which meant nearly the same; as *Heli-on* is the sun in his highest, which the Greeks pronounce Heli-os, that is, *Elios*, the *most high*. Acheron is generally translated *hell*. It is compounded of *Achar, the last state or condition*, and *On*, the sun. Achar-on, therefore, signifies the last state or condition of the sun, alluding to his annual disappearance in those constellations which were in the neighborhood of the south pole.

" We see, by the precession of the equinoctial points, that while one sign is sinking into the *bottomless pit*, another sign is ascending into heaven, that is, rising up towards the pole. And as the inhabitants of the earth are insensible of its motion, they thought the pole of heaven revolved round that of the earth, describing a figure like a serpent coiled eight times; which would seem like a ladder with eight rounds, reaching from the earth up to the pole, that is, the *throne of Jove*. Up this ladder then the gods, that is, the signs of the zodiac, ascended and descended."—[Myth. Astr. part 1, p. 55.]

Most Excellent Master's Degree.

This degree is introduced in masonic books as follows:

" None but the meritorious and praiseworthy, none but those who through diligence and industry have advanced far towards perfection, none but those who have been seated in the *oriental chair* by the unanimous suffrages of their brethren, can be admitted to this degree of masonry.

" In its original establishment, when the temple of Jerusalem was finished, and the fraternity celebrated the cope-stone with great joy, it is demonstrable that none but those, who had proved themselves to be complete masters of their profession, were admitted to this honor; and indeed the duties incumbent on every mason, who is accepted and acknowledged as a most excellent master, are such as render it indispensable that he should have a correct knowledge of all the preceding degrees."

This degree contains a detail of the ceremony in the celebration of the passage of the sun through the first *celestial gate*, the winter solstice, that is the twenty-fifth day of December, which, as we have seen, was commemorated as the birth day of the *god Sol*.——The sun was

---

† An allusion to this idea seems to be made in the expression, " Who shall ascend to the *hill* of the Lord?" or as Cole, in his Freemasons' Library, has it, " *scale the mount of God*."

the key or cope-stone required to complete (or rather to form) the arch; and this raised by masons, is a symbol of that made by the sun in the heavens, and is commemorative of the commencement of his return to the upper hemisphere, in which that arch is formed. This degree, in some measure, anticipates the subject of the royal arch, in which the story of the finding of the *lost* sun, *logos* or *word*, is consummated.

For the purpose of opening the lodge, the brethren assemble round the altar, and form a circle, leaving a space for the master. All then kneel and join hands, and the master reads the following passages from scripture:

"Psalm xxiv. The earth is the Lord's and the fullness thereof; the world, and they that dwell therein. For he hath founded it upon the seas, and established it upon the floods. Who shall ascend into the hill of the Lord? or who shall stand in his holy place? He that hath clean hands, and a pure heart; who hath not lifted up his soul unto vanity, nor sworn deceitfully. He shall receive the blessing from the Lord, and righteousness from the God of his salvation. This is the generation of them that seek him, that seek thy face, O Jacob. Selah. Lift up your heads, O ye gates, and be ye lift up, ye everlasting doors, and the King of Glory shall come in. Who is this King of Glory? The Lord, strong and mighty; the Lord, mighty in battle. Lift up your heads, O ye gates, even lift them up ye everlasting doors, and the King of Glory shall come in. Who is this King of Glory? The Lord of Hosts, he is the King of Glory. Selah."

"2 Chron. vi. Then said Solomon, the Lord hath said that he would *dwell in the thick darkness.* But I have built a house of habitation for thee, and a place for thy dwelling forever. And the king turned his face, and blessed the whole congregation of Israel."

As the master reads the words, "lift up your heads, O ye gates," each brother raises his head; and as he continues, "and the king of glory shall come in," he steps along a few steps towards the space left for him in the circle.

The foregoing passage from the Psalms is very appropriate to the object of commemoration in this ceremony. For, although the Psalmist alluded to the true God, the language made use of, would equally apply to the Pagan god, the sun. The Abbe Pluche observes, as before noticed, that the *tongue* and *religion* of the Hebrews, were originally the same as the Egyptians: and, notwithstanding the variations which afterwards took place between them, "the forms of prayer remained the same." So in this case, the expressions, *the hill of the Lord; the king*

MOST EXCELLENT MASTER'S DEGREE. 313

of glory; the Lord mighty in battle, may be applied to the course of the sun; the veneration in which he was held, and his *wars* and *victories* over Typhon, the genius of evil. *King*, moreover, was one of the peculiar titles bestowed upon Osiris the sun. He was denominated, says Pluche, "the leader, the *king*, the moderator of the stars, the soul of the world, the governor of nature." Besides, the term made use of above, Hazis or Hesus, and translated Lord, is a pagan name of the Deity, and answers, says the same author, to the Warts or Mars of the Sabines and Latins.

So the idea in Chronicles, of the Lord's *dwelling in darkness*, might anciently, among the pagans, have alluded to the sun, in the lower hemisphere, or enveloped in clouds for a time, in the tropic of Cancer.

The reading being ended, the master kneels, and joins hands with the others, which closes the circle. They then rise, disengage their hands, and lift them up above their heads; cast up their eyes, and then suffer their hands to fall by their sides.

This sign, it may be presumed, is intended to express admiration and gratitude for the return of the sun.

After some further ceremonies, the senior warden demands of the most excellent, if this be not the day set apart for the celebration of the cope-stone? Which being ascertained to be the fact, the brethren form a procession double file, and march *six times* round the lodge, *against* the course of the sun, singing the following song:

> All hail to the morning, that bids us rejoice;
> The temple's completed, exalt high each voice;
> The *cope-stone* is finished—our *labor* is o'er,
> The sound of the gavel shall hail us no more.
>
> *   *   *   *   *   *   *
> Companions, assemble on this joyful day,
> The occasion is glorious, the key-stone to lay;
> Fulfilled is the promise, by the *ancient of days*,*
> To bring forth the cope-stone, with shouting and praise.
>
> *   *   *   *   *   *   *
> Thy *wisdom* inspired the great Institution;
> Thy *strength* shall support it till nature expire;
> And when the creation shall fall into ruin,
> Its *beauty* shall rise through the midst of the fire.

The *key-stone* is now brought forward, and two pillars or columns are set up, and an arch placed on them, made of plank, in imitation of block work; in the center of which is a mortice left for the reception of a *key-stone*, which the master takes, and, placing it in the arch, drives it down, by giving it *six raps* with his gavel.

---

* This is a title given to Isis.

The *ark*, which all this time had been carried round by four of the brethren, is now put upon the altar, and a *pot* of *incense* placed on it.

The members all kneel, and while in this attitude the master reads the following passage of scripture: 2 Chron. vii. 1, 4. Now when Solomon had made an end of praying, the fire came down from heaven, and consumed the burnt offering and the sacrifices; and the glory of the Lord filled the house, and the priests could not enter into the house of the Lord, because the glory of the Lord had filled the Lord's house. And when all the children of Israel saw how the fire came down, and the glory of the Lord upon the house, they bowed themselves with their faces to the ground upon the pavement, and worshipped and praised the Lord, saying, *for he is good, for his mercy endureth forever.*

As the master reads the last clause of the above extract, a brother touches a piece of gum camphor to a candle, and throws it into the *pot of incense*, of the same combustible matter, which stands on the altar before the kneeling brethren, which immediately ignites and makes a very brilliant light.

Here the emblem of the restoration of the lost sun, is too plain to be mistaken. The reader may recollect the account, given in a former part of this work, of a similar ceremony in the ancient mysteries; in which, after great lamentation for the loss of Adonis or Osiris, the sun, there was also great joy at his finding. "It is said, that this lamentation was performed over an image in the night season; and when they had sufficiently lamented, a candle was brought into the room, which ceremony might mystically denote the return of the sun, then the priest with a soft voice, muttered this form of words, ' *Trust ye in God, for out of pains salvation is come unto us.*' "

After the above, the brethren all repeat in concert the words, *For he is good, for his mercy endureth forever, six times, each time bowing their heads low towards the floor.**

The members then balance six times as in opening, rise and balance six times more, and the lodge is closed.

Ancient freemasonry could have no connection with the Hebrew Scriptures, any farther than they contained sentiments and expressions in common use among other nations. Or if the founders of the institution adopted passages of scripture, they perverted them to suit their own peculiar views. We have seen that the prospect of the return of the sun to the northern hemisphere, caused great rejoicings among the ancient pagan nations ; and the expression, " For he is good, for his mercy endureth forever," is peculiarly applicable to that circumstance.

The sentiment conveyed in the first verse of the foregoing song, calling upon the brotherhood to rejoice in consequence of having arrived at the end of their *labors*, is well illustrated in the following extract from Bryant's mythology, (vol. iii. p. 38.) which alludes to a fact noticed above.

" Part of the ceremony in the Eleusinian mysteries was a night scene, attended with tears and lamentations, on account of some person who was supposed to have been lost ; but at the close a priest used to present himself to the people who were mourning, and bid them to be of good courage, for the Deity whom they lamented as lost, was preserved; and that they would now have some *comfort*, some *respit* after all their *labor*. To which was added, I have escaped a calamity, and

---

* The companions of royal arch, previously to giving the *grand omnific word*, balance three times three, with their hands joined, bringing them down on their knees *nine times*, making a *pause* between each three.--Similar customs prevail in China at this day, which no doubt are derived from the same source as those of masonry. The following extract from the Chinese Courier, published at Canton, Nov. 1832, establishes this fact.

"Peking—— His Majesty, a few days ago, when worshipping and offering sacrifice on the altar of *Hwang Te*, the *Yellow Emperor*, and *divine originator of agriculture*, drank the '*cup of bliss*,' and performed the *grand ceremony of thrice kneeling*, and *nine times putting his forehead to the ground*.

It seems he did not much like it, for he has censured the master of the ceremonies for giving the words, *kneel—knock ;—kneel—knock ;—kneel—knock*, too slowly. He complains also, that the man who read the prayer, had but a poor voice, and commands that another be chosen who has a strong, clear voice, and is perfectly acquainted with the *detail of rites and ceremonies*.

On the 13th of May, the Emperor went in person to the altar of the *Black Dragon to pray for rain ;* and appointed select Budh priests, with several princes and kings, to form two parties, and alternately lodge at the temple, to *continue their supplications till rain should be granted*.

met with a better portion. This is the same rite as that which was called in Canaan, the death and revival of Adonis or Thamuz, who was the Osiris and Thamas of Egypt."

Again the same author observes, (vol. 3. p. 179.) " The principal rites in Egypt were confessedly, for a person lost, and consigned for a time to *darkness;* who was at last found. This person I have mentioned to have been described under the character of Osiris. Hence these exclamations at the feast of Isis: *Eurekamen, Sugcharomen.* [We have found him, and we rejoice together.]

"After Osiris had been reputed for some time lost, it was a custom among the Egyptians to go in quest of him; and the process, as described by Plutarch, was very remarkable; upon the nineteenth of the month, the Egyptians go down at night to the sea: at which time the priests and supporters (the Pateræ) carry the sacred vehicle. In this is a golden vessel in the form of a ship, or boat, into which they pour some of the river water. Upon this being performed a shout of joy is raised, and Osiris is supposed to be found."

The blaze of the gum-camphor of masonry seems more appropriate than the above, to typify the restoration of the lost sun.

The last verse of the song cited above, contains a beautiful allusion to the masonic trinity; and at the same time forcibly conveys the idea that the writer meant by the establishment of *the great institution*, the creation of the world, planned by infinite *wisdom*, supported by *strength*, and adorned by *beauty.*

Jubilee at Rome.

The church of Rome practices a rite very similar to that of the masonic order in laying the cope-stone. It is called the Jubilee, and the manner of performing it, says Bailey, is as follows:

"The Pope goes to St. Peter's church, to open what they call the *holy gate*, knocking at it three times with a *golden* hammer, repeating the 19th verse of the 118th psalm, "Open to me the gates of righteousness, and I will go unto them and praise the Lord." At this time the masons break down the wall, and the pope kneels before it, while the penatentiaries of St Peter wash him with *holy water*, then taking up the cross, he begins to sing the *Te Deum*, and enters the church, the clergy following him.

"In the mean time the cardinal legates are sent to open three other *holy gates*, with the same ceremonies, in the churches of St. John of **Lateran,** St. Paul, and St. Mary *the greater.* This is performed at the first vespers of Christmas eve, and the next morning the pope gives his *benediction* to the people, in the *Jubilee form*. When the *holy year* is ending, they shut the gates again in the following manner: the pope after he has blessed the *stones and mortar, lays the first stone*, and leaves there *twelve* boxes of gold and silver medals.

"Formerly *much* people resorted from all parts to Rome, to enjoy the *benefits* of the jubilee, but now-a-days but few, except those who dwell in Italy, the pope *allowing* them to observe the Jubilee in their own country, granting the *same benefits* as if they came to Rome."

There can be no possible meaning in this ceremony, unless an astronomical bearing be attributed to it, by considering the *four gates* as symbols of the equinoctial and solstitial points, which by the pagans were denominated gates of heaven; and through which souls were supposed to pass to arrive at the mansions of bliss. And as the popes hold the keys of these gates, it is kind in them occasionally to open them, in order to admit a few at least of their own flock.

The twelve boxes of medals deposited by his holiness, are emblematical of the twelve signs of the zodiac; which he, perhaps considers, as resting places on his celestial turnpike.

This farce is still continued at Rome, of which a late traveler in Italy, gives the following account:

Closing the holy door.

At four o'clock on the day of the Jubilee, the sound of trumpets was heard; in the midst of a procession which issued from the church passing through the holy door, was his holiness the pope, clothed in white robes, and wearing a golden mitre. He seated himself on his *white* throne, and remained quiet for a minute or two. He then descended from his throne and performed some ceremonies or mummeries. I sincerely pitied the poor old man, he looked the picture of death, and had been raised from his bed to personate St. Peter; he appeared to sink under the weight of his robes; his cumbrous mitre oppressed his aching head; he raised his heavy eyes and held up his skinny fingers, and seemed to say,—"How painful are hypocrisy, folly, and fraud, to a sick and dying man." The cardinals came about him in a fawning manner, and changed for him a part of his dress. At the closing of the holy door, we were somewhat disappointed. We beheld only the feeble pattering of an impotent old man: he blessed the golden trowel and its handle of mother-of-pearl; he blessed the mortar and the bricks. He contrived to lay three bricks in the holy door-way, using his holy mortar sparingly as though it were lip-salve. The door-way being then closed, a white satin curtain, decorated with a cross in golden embroidery, was drawn over it. The holy father, with as much theatrical jesticulation as he was capable of, gave his blessing, which concluded the farce of closing the *holy door*.

The opening and closing of the holy gates or doors, must be an annual ceremony, and therefore differs from what is generally called the Jubilee.

Jubilees were formerly celebrated, by the Jews, every fiftieth year. Pope Sextus IV. in 1475, appointed it to be held every twenty-fifth year, to give a greater chance for every person to receive the benefit of it once in his life. They afterwards became more frequent, and the popes granted them as often as the church, or themselves, had occasion for them. There is usually one at the inauguration of a new pope. At these Jubilees, the pope grants full pardon to all sinners who are present at their celebration.—See Rees' Cycl.

We have seen in the masonic ceremonies a constant reiteration of the number *three*, and sometimes thrice repeated, which is called giving the grand honors of masonry. There must have been some cause or reason for this custom, now unknown. And I will venture to say that, (as suggested by the author of the Defence of Freemasonry, before noticed,) its original intention was in honor and out of reverence to the ancient trinity. The practice seems to be kept up by the church of Rome, which goes to corroborate this opinion. One of the rules established by the reverend mother abbess of the Ursuline Convent at Charlestown, as reported by Miss Reed, one of the novices in that institution, is, "before entering the room to give *three knocks* on the door, accompanied with some religious ejaculation, and wait until they are answered by *three* from within." The mason will see that this is an exact copy of his rules and practice.

The reader has observed, that the number *six*, in the degree under consideration, is particularly respected. In the opening scene of initiations, not noticed above, the candidate is prepared with a rope wound six times round his body, and is then conducted to the door of the lodge, against which he gives six distinct knocks, which are answered by the same number from within; and when admitted, he is walked six times round the lodge, *moving with the sun*. On the contrary, the brethren more advanced, form a procession, as above stated, and march six times round the lodge, *against* the course of the sun. Masons from habit pass through these ceremonies, without stopping to examine into their meaning and original intention.

The Druids also paid great veneration to the number six. "As to what remains, says Mayo,—vol. ii. p. 239, respecting the superstitions of the Druids, I know not what was the foundation of the religious respect which they had for the number six; but it is certain they preferred it to all other numbers. It was the sixth day of the moon, that they performed their principal ceremonies of religion, and that they began the year. They went six in number to gather the Misseltoe; and in monuments now extant, we often find six of these priests together."

In every movement of the masonic order we discover traits of its derivation from a religion founded on astronomy. The Egyptians worshiped astronomy. They were the first people known to have acquired a knowledge of it. Their priests, shut up in the labyrinth, had nothing else to do but to study the movements of the heavenly bodies, and they communicated their discoveries in such a manner as to be incomprehensible to the common people.

So in masonry, the novice is marched round the lodge in conformity to the apparent movement of the sun; but afterwards the direction of the procession is reversed, showing that this appearance is produced by the actual movement of the earth, from west to east, round the sun. But this explanation is not given, and consequently the purport of the ceremony is not understood by the brethren.

Making the processions six times round the lodge, is in honor of the six benevolent divinities of the upper hemisphere. Volney, in treating of the notion the Persians had of the future world, and that paradise is placed under the equator, with this singular attribute, that in it the blessed cast no shade, observes, " There is on this subject a passage in Plutarch so interesting and explanatory of the whole of this system, that we shall cite it entire; having observed that the theory of good and evil had at all times occupied the attention of naturalists and theologians, he adds: 'Many suppose there are two gods of opposite inclinations, one delighting in good, the other in evil; the first of these is called particularly by the name of God, the second by that of Genius or Demon. Zoroaster has denominated them Oromaze and Ahrimanes, and has said that of whatever falls under the cognizance of our senses, light is the best representative of the one, and darkness and ignorance of the other. He adds that Mithra is an intermediate being, and it is for this reason that the Persians call Mithra the Mediator or intercessor.

'The Persians also say that Oromaze was born or formed out of the purest light; Ahrimanes on the contrary, out of the thickest darkness, that Oromaze made six gods as good as himself, and Ahrimanes opposed to them six wicked ones. That afterwards Oromaze trebled himself (Hermes tris-megistus,) and removed to a distance remote from the earth; that he there formed stars, and among others, Syrius, which he placed in the heavens as a guard and sentinel. He made also twenty-four other gods whom he inclosed in an egg; but Ahrimanes created an equal number who cracked the egg, and from that moment good and evil were mixed (in the universe.) But Ahrimanes is one day to be conquered, and the earth to be made equal and smooth, that all men may live happy."

Royal Arch Degree.

The royal arch degree seems not to have been known to what are called *modern* masons as late as about 1750. That portion of the old freemasons who met at the famous Apple Tree tavern, in 1717, and formed the society upon somewhat new principles; that is, so far as to admit into fellowship indiscriminately respectable individuals of all professions, were denominated by the non-adherents to this plan, *modern masons*. This affair caused the division of the masonic society into two parties, which continued till 1813, nearly one hundred years. To the rivalry occasioned by this schism, masonry, it is presumed, is mainly indebted for the great celebrity it has obtained in the world.

It appears, that the non-conformists to this new scheme, who considered themselves the orthodox party, by rummaging among the old records of the order, first discovered the royal arch degree, which had probably lain dormant for centuries. During which time, it would appear, the society had been confined almost exclusively to operative masons; who continued the ceremonies only of the apprentice, fellowcraft or journeyman, and master mason, these being deemed appropriate to their occupation.

This fact Dermott proves, by the production of an answer of a Mr. Spencer, one of the grand secretaries of a lodge of modern masons, to an application of W. C., a petitioner from Ireland; which is as follows:

" Your being an *ancient* mason, you are not entitled to any of our charity. The ancient masons have a lodge at the Five Bells in the Strand, and their secretary's name is Dermott.—Our society is neither *arch, royal arch,* nor *ancient,* so that you have no right to partake of our charity."

" Such (says Dermott) was the character given of them by their own

ROYAL ARCH DEGREE.

grand secretary, about fourteen years ago."—Dermott published his book in 1764.

If the knowledge communicated in this degree had not been recovered, the loss to the society would have been incalculable, provided its value be not overrated in the following estimation of it by masonic writers:

Webb says, "This degree is indescribably more *august*, *sublime*, and *important*, than all which precede it; and is the *summit* and *perfection* of ancient masonry. It impresses on our minds a *belief* of the *being* and *existence* of a *Supreme Deity*, without beginning of days or end of years; and reminds us of the reverence due to his holy name." Dermott calls it the *root, heart*, and *marrow* of masonry.

Cole adopts the following sentiment of a brother mason:—" In the R. A. [royal arch] mason's degree I beheld myself exalted to the top of *Pisgah*, an extensive scene opened to my view of the glory and goodness of the M. E. H. P. [most excellent high priest] of our salvation. I dug deep for *hidden treasures*, found them, and *regained* the *omnific word*."

"If we pass on to the royal arch, (says the Rev. G. Oliver, in his Lectures on Freemasonry,) we receive a wonderful accession of knowledge, and find every thing *made perfect*; for this is the *ne plus ultra* of masonry, and can never be exceeded by any human institution."

By the manner in which this subject is treated, it would seem that a mason is supposed to be ignorant of the existence of the one Supreme Being till admitted into the royal arch. This arises from copying after an institution established when this doctrine was not taught to the common people. Polytheism was the prevailing religion. The one Supreme was revealed only to a select number who were initiated into the greater mysteries, the royal arch of the ancients.

The members of this degree are denominated *companions*, and are "entitled to a full explanation of the *mysteries* of the order;" whereas, in the former degrees they are recognized by the common, familiar appellation of brothers, and kept in a state of profound ignorance of the *sublime secret* which is disclosed in this chapter. This accords with the custom of Pythagoras, who thus distinguished his pupils. After a probation of five years, as before stated, they were admitted into the presence of the preceptor, called his *companions*, and permitted freely to converse with him. Previously to the expiration of that term, he delivered his instructions to them from behind a screen.

The royal arch degree owes its title to the imaginary arch made in the heavens by the course of *king* Osiris, the sun, from the vernal to the autumnal equinox. The signs through which he passes in forming this semicircle, including those of the equinoxes, being seven, the number of grades or steps required to be taken by the mason, to entitle him to the honors of this degree.

This order is called a chapter, which requires *nine* officers; the principal of which are three, who compose what is called the *grand council*, and one denominated *captain of the host*.

There is, or should be, when convenient, an organ in the room in which the chapter is held. The companions enter the chapter in procession. At the entrance each gives the sign of *sorrow*, which is done by bowing the head and body, placing the right hand on the forehead. This sign is repeated as they approach the altar. They then place their scepters in their left hands, with the right on the left breast, and make the following declaration:—In the beginning was the *word*: and the *word* was with God: and the *word* was God. The sign of *sorrow* is now given the third time, and each advances to his proper place. They are so arranged as to form an arch or semicircle.—[Carlile.]

The sorrow here expressed, is an imitation of that of the ancients for the loss of the *word*, *logos*, or Osiris, personated by Hiram. The use of the organ agrees with the ancient manner of celebrating the orgies, and is in accordance with the custom of the Pythagorean school. The semicircle formed by the companions, confirms my opinion in regard to the name of this degree.

The grand council consists of the *most excellent high priest*, *king*, and *holy scribe*. The high priest is dressed in a *white robe*, with a *breast-plate* of cut glass, consisting of twelve pieces, [to represent the twelve signs of the zodiac,] an apron and a *miter*. The king wears a *scarlet robe*, apron and *crown*. The miter and crown are generally made of pasteboard; sometimes they are made of most splendid materials, gold and silver velvet; but these are kept for public occasions. The miter has the words *Holiness to the Lord*, in gold letters, across the forehead. The scribe wears a *purple robe*, apron and *turban*.

The color of the robes worn by the respective members of the grand council, the reader may be assured, has not been fixed upon through the mere fancy of the masonic order. There must be a mythological authority to sanction it.—'The ancient astrologers, says the most learned of the Jews, (Maimonides,) having consecrated to each planet a color, an animal, a tree, a metal, a fruit, a plant, formed from them all a figure or representation of the star, taking care to select for the purpose a proper moment, a fortunate day, such as the conjunction or some other favorable aspect; they conceived that by their (magic) ceremonies they could introduce into those figures or idols the influences of the superior beings after which they were modelled. These were the idols that the

Chaldean Sabeans adored; and in the performance of their worship they were obliged to *be dressed in the proper color*——. Thus, the astrologers, by their practices introduced idolatry, desirous of being regarded as the dispensers of the favors of heaven.

"The Egyptians, says Porphyry, call Kneph, the intelligence or efficient cause (of the universe.) They represent him under the form of a man in *deep blue*, (the color of the sky,) having in his hand a sceptre, a belt round his body, and a small bonnet royal of light feathers on his head, to denote how very subtile and fugacious the idea of that being is." Upon which I shall observe that Kneph in Hebrew signifies a wing, a feather, and that this color of sky blue is to be found in the majority of the Indian gods, and is, under the name of *narayan*, one of their most distinguished epithets.—See Ruins, p. 230—234.

Porphyry, I presume, is mistaken in supposing this god dressed in blue, to be Kneph; for as he was the Supreme God of the Egyptians, his proper dress would be white.

"The Roman Catholic cardinals, (says Mr. Buck, in his Theol. Dict.) dress in *scarlet*, to signify, that they ought to be ready to shed their blood for the *faith* and *church*, when the defence and honor of either require it." This, I imagine, is a mere conjecture, and not founded in fact. The custom, has, doubtless, an astronomical bearing. The pope, on gala days, is clothed in a *white* robe, wearing a golden miter, and is seated on his *white* throne ; and as the cardinals are second in rank, like the king in the royal arch, their appropriate color is, no doubt, scarlet.

The habit required for the person representing the sun; in the Dyonisian mysteries, says Taylor, is thus described in the Orphic verses preserved by Macrobeus in the first book of his Saturnalia, cap. 18.

> He who desires in pomp of sacred dress
> The sun's resplendent body to express,
> Should first a veil assume of purple bright,
> Like fair white beams combin'd with fiery light:
> On his right shoulder, next, a mule's broad hide,
> Widely diversifi'd with spotted pride
> Should hang, an image of the pole divine,
> And dædal stars, whose orbs eternal shine.
> A golden splendid zone, then, o'er the vest
> He next should throw, and bind it round his breast;
> In mighty token, how with golden light,
> The rising sun, from earth's last bounds and night
> Sudden emerges, and, with matchless force,
> Darts through old Ocean's billows in his course.
> A boundless splendor hence, enshrin'd in dew,
> Plays on his whirlpools, glorious to the view;
> While his circumfluent waters spread abroad,
> Full in the presence of the radiant god:
> But Ocean's circle, like a zone of light.
> The sun's wide bosom girds, and charms the wond'ring sight.
> Eleus. and Bac. Myst. p. 160.

The officers and companions of the chapter being stationed, the high priest says, companions, I am about to open a chapter of royal arch masons, and will thank you for your attention and assistance. If there is any person present who is not a royal arch mason, he is requested to retire. Companion captain of the host, the first care of congregated masons?—Captain. To see the tabernacle duly guarded. High priest. Attend to that part of your duty. The captain of the host stations the guard at the outside of the door, gives him his orders, closes the door, and makes an alarm of three times three, on the inside, to ascertain that the guard is on his post; the guard answers by nine corresponding raps; the captain then gives one, and the guard doe the same. He then reports that the chapter is duly guarded, by a companion of this degree at the outer avenue, with a drawn sword in his hand. The high priest then gives two raps with his gavel, and asks the following questions: Captain of the host, are you a royal arch mason?—I am, that I am. How shall I know you to be a royal arch mason?—By three times three. He thus proceeds, as is done in the other degrees, to demand the stations and duties of the officers of the chapter; which are as follows:

The captain of the host is stationed at the right hand of the grand council, *to receive their orders*, and see them duly executed.

The station of the *principal sojourner* is at the left hand of the grand council, to bring the *blind*, by a way they know not, to *lead* them in paths they have not known, to make *darkness light* before them, and *crooked things straight*.*

The duties of the two last mentioned officers, in the ancient mysteries, appertain to one character, Mercury, who was the *messenger* of the gods, and the *conductor* of *souls* to the other world, through the *dark* regions below.

The royal arch, like the greater mysteries, contains a scenical representation of a journey from this world to the next. In the way are four guarded passes, called *vails*, emblematical of the equinoxes and solstices, allegorically denominated *gates* of heaven, through which lies the sun's course.

Three of the officers stationed at these passes, are called *grand masters* of the first, second, and third vail; who require certain tokens and pass-words of the candidates on their admission through them. The fourth officer is styled *royal arch captain*. He is stationed at the inner vail, or *entrance* of the *sanctum sanctorum*, to guard the same, and see that none pass but such as are duly qualified, and have the proper pass-words and *signet* of *truth*. The colors of their several banners are, the first blue, the second purple, the third red, and the

---

* In the lower degrees, the duty of messenger, as well as that of regulating and conducting the ceremonies, is performed by two officers who are denominated deacons. These, like the rest of the masonic drama, I find to be astronomical characters. "The ancient Egyptians, says the astrologer Julius Firmicus, (Astron. Lib 2, c. 4,) divide each sign of the zodiac into three sections; and each section was under the direction of an imaginary being whom they called *Decan*, or chief of ten : so that there were three decans in a month, and thirty-six in a year. Now, these decans, who were also called gods (Theoi,) regulated the destinies of mankind,—and were placed particularly in certain stars." (Ruins p, 237.)

In the course of time, a trifling variation in the orthography of the name of these officers, admitting of little or none in the pronunciation, has taken place. The duties of the decans and those of the deacons are sufficiently allied to identify them. "Among the Greeks, those youths who served the tables were called *diaconoi*, deacons; that is ministers, attendants." (Calmet's Dict.)

fourth white; which have the same astronomical reference as the dresses of the grand council. The white banner, as masonry asserts, is emblematical of that *purity of heart*, and *rectitude of conduct*, which is essential to *obtain admission* into the divine *sanctum sanctorum* above.

In the duty assigned to the royal arch captain, there is evidently an allusion to that required of the "severe and incorruptible boatman, Charon;" who was prohibited from transporting souls across the lake or river *Acheron* to the *Elysian fields*, the heaven of the ancients, without the *signet* of the *judges*, who were appointed to examine into the characters of the deceased, and to allow or withhold their permission accordingly.—"To arrive at Tartarus, or Elysium, souls were obliged to cross the rivers Styx and Acheron, in the boat of the ferryman Charon, and to pass through the *gates* of horn or ivory, guarded by the dog Cerberus." (Ruins p. 148.)

Nine companions must be present at the opening of a royal arch chapter. Not more nor less than *three* are permitted to take this degree at the same time. The candidates are prepared by tying a bandage over their eyes, and coiling a rope *seven* times round the body of each, which unites them together, with *three* feet of slack rope between them.

Thus prepared, they are led into the royal arch chapter; which, they are told, is dedicated to enlighten those that are in darkness, and to show forth the *way*, the *truth*, and the *life*.

On entering the chapter they pass under what is called *a living arch*, which is formed by a number of companions arranging themselves on both sides of the door, each joining hands with the one opposite to himself. The conductor says, stoop low, brothers; remember that he that humbleth himself shall be exalted; stoop low, brothers, stoop low; we are about to enter the arch; which is raised up for him, but lowered when the candidates come under it. They seldom pass the first pair of hands without being obliged to support themselves on their hands and knees. Their progress may well be imagined to be very slow; for, notwithstanding their humble condition, they are under the necessity of sustaining on their backs, nearly the whole weight of the living arch above. The conductor, to encourage them, calls out occasionally, stoop low, brothers, stoop low! If they go too slow to suit the companions, it is not unusual for some one to apply a sharp point to their bodies, to urge them on; after they have endured this humiliating exercise as long as suits the convenience of the companions, they pass from under the living arch.

The reader will readily perceive, that this scene is an imitation of the trials of the greater mysteries: and although a faint one, the likeness is too apparent to be mistaken. It was anciently a religious rite, and the ceremony has outlived the principle that produced it.

Having got through the arch, the candidates are conducted once round the chapter, and directed to kneel at the altar to receive the obligation. The principal sojourner then thus addresses them: Brethren, as you advance in masonry, your obligation becomes more binding. You are now kneeling at the altar for the seventh time, and about to take a solemn oath or obligation: if you are willing to proceed, say after me:

I, A. B., of my own free will and accord, in presence of Almighty God, and this chapter of royal arch masons, erected to God, and dedicated to Zerubbabel, do hereby, etc. At the conclusion of the oath, the candidates kiss the book *seven* times.

Here the farce of dedication to St. John, which was originally intended as a sheer hoax upon the mystics of the minor degrees, is no longer continued. I shall hereafter endeavor to analyze the name of Zerubbabel.

The candidates are now conducted once round the chapter, and directed to kneel; while the sojourner reads a prayer. (See Webb's Monitor, p. 134.)

After prayer, the principal sojourner says, 'Companions, arise, and follow me.'

He conducts them once round the chapter, during which time he reads from Exodus, iii. 1—6.

'Now Moses kept the flock of Jethro, his father-in-law, the priest of Midian; and he led the flock to the back side of the desert, and came to the mountain of God, even Horeb. And the angel of the Lord appeared unto him in a flame of fire, out of the midst of the bush; and he looked, and behold the bush burned with fire, and the bush was not consumed.'

By the time this reading is ended, the candidates have arrived in front of a representation of the burning bush, placed in a corner of the chapter: when the principal sojourner directs them to halt, and slips up the bandage from their eyes.

A companion who performs this part of the scene, viz: personating Deity, steps behind the burning bush, and calls out vehemently, 'Moses! Moses!!' The principal sojourner answers for the candidates, 'Here am I.'

The companion behind the bush exclaims still more vehemently, 'Draw not nigh hither; put off thy shoes from off thy feet, for the place where thou standest is holy ground. [Their shoes are now taken off.] I am the God of thy fathers, the God of Abraham, the God of Isaac, and the God of Jacob.'

The principal sojourner then directs them to kneel down and cover their faces, and says, 'And Moses hid his face, for he was afraid to look upon God.'

The principal sojourner then says to the candidates, 'Arise and follow me,' and leads them three times round the chapter, during which time he reads from 2 Chorn. c. 36—v. 11—20.

The terror in which the initiated into the ancient mysteries were thrown, by the counterfeiting of thunder, lightning, etc., is here imitated. This occurs after the words, "and brake down the walls of Jerusalem;" the companions then make a tremendous noise, by firing pistols, clashing swords, overturning chairs, rolling cannon balls across the floor, etc. The candidates being blindfolded, must of course be surprised and terrified at such a scene.

In the meantime, the candidates are thrown down, bound, and dragged out into the preparation room, and the door closed. On being brought again into the chapter, they pass under the living arch. This is formed on one side of the hall or chapter; on the other side is what is called the *rugged road*, which is generally made of blocks of wood, old chairs, benches, etc. The conductor consoles the candidates, by observing, this is the way many great and good men have traveled before you; never deeming it derogatory to their dignity to *level themselves* with the fraternity. I have often traveled this road from Babylon to Jerusalem, and generally find it rough and rugged. However, I think I never saw it much smoother than it is at the present time.

By this time, the candidates have stumbled over the rugged road, and arrived again at the entrance of the living arch. The conductor says, companions there is a very difficult and dangerous pass ahead, which lies directly in our way. Before we attempt to pass it, we must kneel down and pray.

Sundry prayers and passages of scripture are recited before the rugged path is got rid of. There are clauses in one of them, which make it appear that it was originally addressed to the sun when in the lower hemisphere, imploring his return to the upper regions, as follows:

"Hear my prayer, O Lord! give ear to my supplications: for the enemy hath persecuted my soul: he hath made me *to dwell in darkness.* Therefore is my spirit overwhelmed within me; my heart within me is desolate. Hear me speedily, O Lord! my spirit faileth: *hide not thy face from me,* lest I be like unto them that *go down into the pit.* Cause me to hear thy loving kindness in the *morning;* for in thee do I trust. Bring my soul out of trouble. And of *thy mercy cut off my enemies; for I am thy servant.*"

The most appropriate prayer, as regards the mysteries of masonry, is, perhaps, that recorded by Dermott, which is used in the lodge of Jewish freemasons.

"O Lord, excellent art thou in thy truth, and there is nothing great in comparison to thee; for thine is the praise, from all the works of thy hands, forevermore.

"Enlighten us, we beseech thee, *in the true knowledge of masonry;* by the sorrows of Adam, thy first made man; by the blood of Abel, the holy one; by the righteousness of Seth, in whom thou art well pleased; and by thy covenant with Noah, in whose architecture thou was pleased to save *the seed of thy beloved;* number us not among those that know not thy statutes, nor *the divine mysteries of the secret Cabala.*

"But grant, we beseech thee, that the ruler of this lodge may be endued with knowledge and wisdom, to instruct us and explain his secret mysteries, as our holy *brother Moses*† did, *in his lodge,* to Aaron, to Eleazar, and Ithamar, the sons of Aaron, and the seventy elders of Israel.

"And grant that we may understand, learn, and keep all the stat-

---

* Cabal or Cabala is a secret science, professed by the Hebrew Rabbins, concerning the allegorical interpretation of the bible.—Edit.

† In the preface to the Mishna, we find this tradition of the Jews, explained as follows:

God not only delivered the law to Moses on Mount Sinai, but the explanation of it likewise: when Moses came down from the mount, and entered into his tent, Aaron went to visit him; and Moses acquainted Aaron with the laws he had received from God, together with the explanation of them; after this Aaron placed himself at the right hand of Moses, and Eleazar and Ithamar, the sons of Aaron, were admitted, to whom Moses repeated what he had just before told to Aaron: these being seated, the one on the right hand, the other on the left hand of Moses; the seventy elders of Israel, who composed the Sanhedrim, came in; and Moses again declared the same laws to them, with the interpretation of them, as he had done before to Aaron and his sons. Lastly, all who pleased of the common people were invited to enter, and Moses instructed them likewise in the same manner as the rest: so that Aaron heard four times what Moses had been taught by God upon Mount Sinai, Eleazar and Ithamar three times, the seventy elders twice, and the people once. Moses afterwards reduced the laws which he had received into writing, but not the explanations of them; these he thought it sufficient to trust to the memories of the above-mentioned persons, who, being perfectly instructed in them, delivered them to their children, and these again to theirs from age to age.

utes and commandments of the Lord, and this *holy mystery*, pure and undefiled unto our lives end. Amen, Lord."

The candidates after having passed the four vails, by giving the signs and pass-words appropriated to each, are admitted into the presence of the grand council, by means of a *signet*, being a *triangular* piece of metal with the word *Zer-ubba-bel* engraved upon it.

I have had the curiosity to look into the derivation and meaning of the word Zer-ubba-bel. As it is a compounded word, some of its compounds are of course abbreviated. Zer, it is likely, is a contraction of *zerah*, which means *east, brightness:* ubba is probably a corruption of *abba*, father, which the Deity is sometimes styled; and *bel* is well known to mean the sun, or lord. Zerubbabel is defined *dispersion* of *confusion*.

What could more clearly point out the glorious luminary of day, rising in the east, and dispersing the clouds and darkness? His seal ought, of course, to entitle the bearer to admittance into the *sanctum sanctorum*.

Finally, the grand council, being satisfied as to the pretensions of the candidates, directs them to repair to the *north-west corner* of the ruins of the old temple, and commence removing the rubbish, to lay the foundation of the new. (The reader will remember, that it was in the *north-west* that the Deity was supposed to have commenced his operations in the erection of the world.) While thus engaged, they discover a secret vault, in which is found the *key stone* of the *arch*; which, by the by, had already been put in its place, in the preceding degree.* On a second descent of one of the party, he discovers a small box or chest, standing on a pedestal, curiously wrought and overlaid with gold: he involuntarily found his hand raised to guard his eyes from the intense light and heat reflected from it. This proved to be the *ark*, containing the lost *word, logos,* or *sun;* which accounts for the *intense light and heat reflected from it.*† It contained also, *the book of the law—Aaron's rod—a pot of manna,* and *a key* to the ineffable characters of this degree.

---

* This circumstance, as well as that of the pass-word, Rabboni, being the same in the most excellent master's degree as in this, shows, as noticed by Mr. Cole, the intimate connection between the two degrees.

† "The god of day, personified in the sacred allegories, was subjected to all the destinies of man; he had his cradle and his *tomb*, under the names of Hercules, Bacchus, Osiris, etc. He was an infant at the winter solstice, at the moment when the day began to increase: it was under this form that his image was exposed in the ancient temples, there to receive the homage of his adorers. 'Because then, says Macrobeus, the day being the shortest, this god seemed to be but a feeble child. This is the child of the mysteries, he *whose image the Egyptians drew from the bottom of their sanctuaries every year on a fixed day.*'" (Origine de tous les Cultes, p. 313.)

Here is the original of the drawing up, from beneath the foundation of Solomon's temple, of the *omnific* (all-creating) word, logos, or sun.

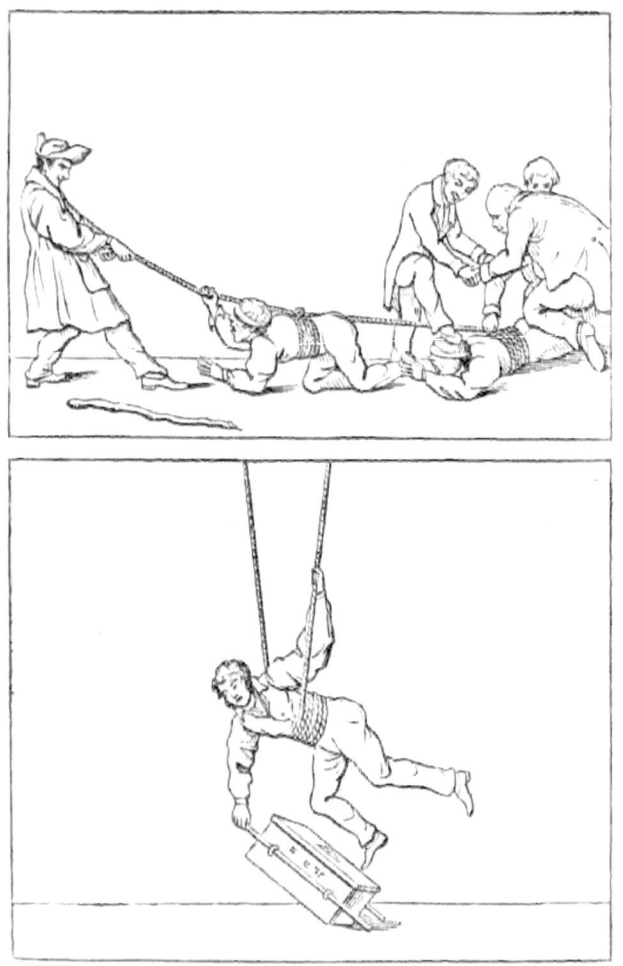

The candidates passing under the living arch; also, the descent of a companion into the vault of nine arches.

This ark of masonry is but a copy of the old *mysterious chest* of the ancient Egyptians; which, among other monuments of the ancient state of mankind, contained "acorns, heads of poppies, bay-berries, branches of fig-tree," etc.; which, like the manna of the Jews, are said to have served as their main sustenance, in the early ages of the world.

Although the masons pretend to inherit Aaron's rod; in their hands it has lost its miraculous powers. And as to the book of the law, by which modern masons at least, mean the law of Moses, it was not in the Jewish ark; for, according to 1 Kings c. 8, v. 9, "There was nothing in the ark save the two tables of stone."

The following questions and answers occur, in what is called lectures, after the ceremonies of initiation are passed; which are, in fact, statements of what had been before detailed. I have endeavored to avoid repetitions, by previously omitting part of what takes place at initiations.

After receiving the obligation, what was said to you? We were told that we were now obligated and received as royal arch masons, but as this degree was infinitely more important than any of the preceding, it was necessary for us to pass through many *trials*, and to *travel* in *rough* and *rugged ways*, to prove our fidelity, before we could be entrusted with the more important secrets of this degree. We were further told, that, though we could not *discover the path we were to travel*, we were under the direction of a *faithful guide, who would bring the blind by a way they know not, and lead them in paths they had not known; who would make darkness light before them, and crooked things straight; who would do these things, and not forsake them.* (See Isa. 42, v. 16.) *Follow your leader and fear no danger.* Let your advance be by *seven* solemn steps, and at each step, you must halt and make obeisance, with the awe and reverence suited to this *grand and solemn occasion;* for every step brings you nearer to the *sacred name of God.*

The following remarks of Plato, in his "Phædon, or Dialogue on the immortality of the soul," will tend to explain the inference intended to be drawn from the above passage, by showing the idea entertained by the ancients in regard to the difficulties to be encountered in the journey to the other world; to which the extract from Isaiah is here made to apply.

" If the soul is immortal, it stands in need of cultivation and improvement, not only in the time that we call the time of life; but for the future, or what we call the time of eternity. For if you think justly upon this point, you will find it very dangerous to neglect the soul. Were death the dissolution of the whole man, it would be a great advantage to the wicked after death, to be rid at once of their body, their soul, and their vices. But forasmuch as the soul is immortal, the only way to avoid those evils and obtain salvation, is to become good and wise. For it carries nothing along with it, but its good or bad actions, and its virtues or vices, which are the cause of its eternal happiness or misery, commencing from the first minute of its arrival in the other world. And it is said, that after the death of every individual person, the demon or genius that was partner with it, and conducted it during life, *leads* it to a certain place, where all the dead are obliged to appear in order to be judged, and from thence are *conducted by a guide* to the world below. And after they have there received their good or bad deserts, and continued there their appointed time, *another conductor* brings them back to this life, after several revolutions of ages. Now this road is not *a plain road*, else there would be no occasion for guides, and nobody miss their way. But there are several *by-ways, and crossways*, as I conjecture from the method of their sacrifices and *religious ceremonies.* So that a temperate wise soul *follows its guide*, and is not ignorant of what happens to it; but the soul that is nailed to its body, that is inflamed with the love of it, and has been long its slave, after much struggling and suffering in this visible world, is at last dragged along against its will by the demon allotted for its guide. And when it arrives at that fatal rendezvous of all souls, if it has been guilty of any impurity, or polluted with murder, or has committed any of those atrocious crimes that desperate and lost souls are commonly guilty of, the other souls abhor it and avoid its company. It finds neither companion nor guide, but wanders in a fearful solitude and horrible desert; till after a certain time, necessity drags it into the mansions it deserves. Whereas the temperate and pure soul has the gods themselves for its guides and conductors, and goes to cohabit with them in the mansions of pleasure prepared for it."

What further was said to you? The high priest first read the following passage, (Exodus vi. 2, 3.) "And God spake unto Moses, and said unto him, I am the Lord, and I appeared unto Abraham, unto Isaac, and unto Jacob, by the name of God Almighty, but by my name Jehovah, was I not known to them."

He then informed us that the name of Deity, *the divine Logos, or word*, to which reference is had in John, (1, v. 1, 5.) "In the beginning was the *word*, [Logos] and the word was with God, and the *word was God*; the same was in the beginning with God: all things *were made* by him, and without him was not any thing made that was made; in him *was life*, and the *life* was the *light of men:* and the *light shineth in darkness*, and the *darkness comprehended it not.*" That this Logos, or *word*, was anciently written only in these sacred characters, (showing them,) and thus preserved from one generation to another. That this was the true *masonic word*, which *was lost* in the *death of Hiram Abiff*, and was restored at the building of the temple, in the manner we had at that time assisted to represent.

Here the whole mystery of masonry is unveiled; here is a candid confession of what the masons had been so long in search of, which proves to be the *lost Logos*, the second person in the pagan trinity. Logos is the same as Osiris, the sun, considered as the Demiurgus, the maker of the world, under the direction of the Supreme Being.

It has been asserted by Dr. Priestly and others, that the above passage in John, is an interpolation; and the use here made of it, by an institution derived from paganism, corroborates the fact.

"Those who believe that the Logos was the personification of the divine intellect, or of the divine attributes of wisdom, power, etc., trace this doctrine to the ancient Platonists; from whom, as they conceive, it was adopted by the Christian fathers." * * * "In the writings of Plato, Logos has two acceptations, viz. those of speech, and of reason, such as is found in man. But when this philosopher speaks of *nous* or *Logus*, as something distinct from the Divine Being himself, as a power or property belonging to him, and all divine powers and properties being *substance*, it would be very natural and easy to transform this divine power into a substantial person; and this we shall find to have been the case with respect to the latter Platonists, agreeably to one of the Platonic maxims, viz. that *being* and *energy* are the same thing."—(Rees' Cycl.)

"Never any *philosophy* was so *fashionable*, as that of *Plato* during the first ages of the church : the *Pagans* interested themselves amongst all the different sects of *philosophers*, but the conformity which *Plato's* was found to have with religion, made almost all the knowing Christians of that sect. Thence came the mighty esteem they had of *Plato*: they looked upon him as a sort of prophet who had foretold many important points of Christianity, especially that of the holy Trinty: nay, they went so far as to take his works for comments on the scripture; and to conceive the nature of the *Word*, as he conceived it. He represented *God* so elevated above his *creatures*, that he did not believe that they were immediately made by his hands; and therefore he put between them and him this *Word*, as a degree by which the actions of God might pass down to *them;* the Christians had the like idea of *Jesus Christ:* and this may perhaps be the reason why no heresy has been more generally received and maintained with greater heat than *Arrianism*.

This *Platonism* then (which seems to honor the Christian religion by countenancing it) was very full of notions about *Demons:* and thence they easily passed into that opinion which the old Christians had of *oracles.*

Plato said, that Demons were of a middle nature, between God and man; that they were the aerial *genii* appointed to hold a commerce between God and us; that although they were near us, yet we could not see them; that they penetrated into all our thoughts; that they had a love for the good, and a hatred for the bad; and that it was for their honor that such variety of sacrifices, and so many different ceremonies were appointed: but it does not at all appear, that Plato acknowledged any evil demons, to which might be attributed the management of the illusions of oracles. Plutarch, notwithstanding, assures us, that Plato was not ignorant of them; and amongst the Platonic philosophers, the thing is out of doubt. Eusebius, in his Evangelical Preparations, recites a great number of passages out of Porphyrius, where that Pagan philosopher assures us, that evil demons are the authors of *enchantments, philtres* and *witch-crafts;* that they cheat our eyes with *spectres, phantoms,* and *apparitions;* that lying is essential to their nature; that they raise in us the greatest part of our passions; and that they have an ambition to pass with us for gods; that their aerial and spiritual bodies are nourished with suffumigations, and with the blood and fat of sacrifices; and that it is only these that employ themselves in giving oracles, and to whom this task so full of fraud is assigned: in short, at the head of the troop of evil demons he places *Hecate* and *Serapis.*

Jamblichus, another Platonist, has said as much. And the greatest part of these things being true, the Christians received them all with joy, and have added to them besides a little of their own: as for example, that the demons stole from the writings of the prophets some knowledge of things to come; and so got honor by it in their oracles.

This system of the ancient Christians had this advantage, that it discovered to the Pagans, by their own principles, the original of their false worship, and the source of those errors which they always embraced. They were persuaded that there was something supernatural in their oracles; and the Christians, who were always disputing against them, did not desire to confute this opinion. Thus by demons (which both parties believed to be concerned in the oracles,) they explicated all that was supernatural in them. They acknowledged indeed that this sort of ordinary miracles were wrought in the Pagan religion: but then they ruined this advantage again, by imputing them to such authors as evil spirits. And this way of convincing, was more short and easy, than to contradict the miracle itself, by a long train of inquiries and arguments. Thus I have given you the manner how that opinion which the first ages of the church had of the Pagan oracles, was grounded, I might, to the three reasons which I have already brought, add a fourth of no less authority perhaps than those: that is, that in the supposition of oracles being given by demons, there is something miraculous: and if we consider the humor of mankind a little, we shall find how much we are taken with any thing that is miraculous. But I do not intend to enlarge myself on this reflection; for those that think upon it, will easily believe me, and those that do not, will perhaps give it no credit, notwithstanding all my arguments."

The physical properties of the sun are plainly set forth in the extract from John.—The language is in the mystic style of the Platonic school, and not in the plain, simple manner of the gospel writers; but notwithstanding, if put in the shape of interrogatory, "What is that which contains the principles that produce *life*, and is at the same time, the *light* of men?" It would not form a *conundrum* difficult of solution.—"The light shineth in darkness, and the darkness *comprehended* it not," alludes to a time past, when the sun was enveloped with clouds in either of the tropics ; and his extrication, and triumph over Typhon, the *prince* of *darkness*, was the very cause of the celebration here imitated by the masons.

Besides, it is said, "*That* was the true light, which lighteth every man that cometh into the world." Now, this could not properly be said of Christ, as it would not apply to those who never heard of his name; but is very applicable to the sun, which lighteth every one in all parts of the earth.

Mr. Dupuis, taking for granted that the above passages are genuine, that is, actually written by St. John, makes great account of them, as well he might, to prove that *Christ* and the *sun* are the same, and consequently that Christianity is sun-worship. He says,

"The theology of Orpheus taught that *light*, the most ancient and the most sublime of all beings, is God, that inaccessible God, who envelopes all things in his substance, and who is called *reason*, (conseil) light and life. These theological ideas have been copied by the evangelist John, when he said 'That the life was the light, and that the light was the *life*, and that the light was the Word, or the reason, and the wisdom of God.' "

Again, "The Guebres still at this day reverence the light as the most beautiful attribute of the divinity. 'Fire, say they, produced the light, and the *light is god*." This is the ethereal fire, in which ancient theology placed the substance of the divinity, or universal soul of the world, from whence emanates light and life, or, to use the expressions of the Christians, the *Logos*, or the *word*, which *lighteth every man that cometh into the world, and giveth life to all beings*."

But, admitting the passages above quoted from St. John's gospel, to be interpolations, as I believe has been made evident, the argument of Dupuis on this head, falls to the ground.

There is much confusion, after all, in regard to the *omnific word*. Whether this was created by the original founders of the order, for the purpose of deception, or has been introduced by modern masons, is unknown. After declaring the *Logos* to be the recovered *long lost word*, another compound name, intended to bear the same import, is substituted in its place.

This the English masons call Jao-Bul-On, and the American masons, Jah-Buh-Lun. They both say the word is compounded of the names of Deity in three languages, Hebrew, Chaldean, and Syriac; leaving Egypt, the mother of the mysteries, from which masonry is derived, out of the question, although On, which composes part of the compound word, used by English masons, was one of the names of the Deity, peculiar to that country.

Neither *Buh* nor *Lun*, it is believed, was ever the name of a Deity in any language; and although the sun was worshipped under the symbolical figure of the bull, either on account of his great use in agriculture, or because the celestial sign of the bull was formerly in the vernal equinox at the opening of the year; yet it is evident that the bull was looked upon merely as a symbol, and not as actually constituting the name of the Supreme Being. Whereas Jah-Bel-On, were permanent names, universally, and at all times bestowed upon the Deity, by one or other of the nations above mentioned.

"The chief varieties of this sacred name [of God] amongst the inhabitants of different nations (says Oliver,) were Jah-Bel or Baal, and On or Om."

"Bel or Baal, (says Mayo,) was the same god with Moloch. Their names, both of which signify the *king*, the *lord*, are titles applicable to the sun."

It is not permitted to utter this *omnific word* above the breath, and three companions are required to perform it, each pronouncing a syllable alternately. And admitting Jah-bel-on to be the word, one would say Jah, another Bel, and the third On; and then interchangeably until each had pronounced the whole compound. A similar superstition prevails among the Jews, in regard to what is called the Tetragammaton, or word of four letters, which, in Hebrew, compose the name Jehovah. The Jews, however, are not permitted to pronounce this name, even by dividing the syllables in the manner of the companions of royal arch masonry.

The very attribute given to the lost word, *omnific*, (all-creating,) indicates the Demiurgus, the Creator of the world, which as before observed, was believed by the ancients to be the sun.

It was of no importance to investigate the composition of the *omnific word* of masonry, any further than to show, that in all the movements of the order, the sun is kept constantly in view; and that the lost master mason's word meant nothing but the lost influence of that luminary, when in his greatest northern, or southern declination.

But to return to the lecture: it is stated by the candidates, that the high priest placed *crowns* upon their heads, and told them they were now invested with all the important secrets of this degree, *crowned and received as worthy companions, royal arch masons.*

This custom, it has been shown, is not without authority, or precedent, in the ancient mysteries.

I will repeat, from Dupuis, the purport and end of the mysteries:—
" The mystagogues make *darkness* and *light* successively to appear before the eyes of the initiates. Night the most obscure, accompanied with frightful spectres, is replaced by a brilliant day, whose light environs the statue of the divinity. This sanctuary is approached with trembling, where all was prepared to exhibit the spectacle of Tartarus and Elysium. It is in this *last stage* that the initiated, being ultimately inducted, perceives the picture of beautiful prairies enlightened by a clear sky; there he hears harmonious voices, and the charming songs of the sacred choirs. It is then that, become absolutely free and disfranchised from all evil, he mixes with the crowd of the initiates, and when, *his head being crowned with flowers*, he celebrates the holy orgies with them.

" Thus the ancients represented here below, in their initiations, that which would, they said, one day happen to souls when they should be disengaged from bodies, and drawn from the obscure prison in which destiny had enchained them in uniting them to terrestrial matter."—(Orig. de tous les Cultes, p. 501.)

As this crowning is the closing ceremony of initiations into the mysteries, so is its imitation in the royal arch included in the last act of the drama of ancient freemasonry.

The following address, copied from Webb's Freemason's Monitor, is delivered to the newly initiated companion:

"Worthy companion, by the consent and assistance of the members of this chapter, you are now exalted to the sublime and honorable degree of a royal arch mason. Having attained this degree, you have arrived at the *summit* and *perfection* of ancient masonry, and are consequently entitled to a full explanation of the mysteries of the order.

"The *rites* and *mysteries* developed in this degree have been handed down through a chosen few, unchanged by time, and uncontrolled by prejudice; and we expect and trust they will be regarded by you with the same *veneration*, and transmitted with the same scrupulous purity to your successors.

"No one can reflect on the ceremonies of gaining admission into this place, without being forcibly struck with the important lessons which they teach.

"Here we are necessarily led to contemplate with gratitude and admiration the sacred source from whence all earthly comforts flow; here we find additional inducements to continue steadfast and immoveable in the discharge of our respective duties; and here we are bound, by the most solemn ties, to promote each other's welfare, and correct each other's failings, by advice, admonition, and reproof."

I shall conclude the notice of this chapter, with a few remarks on the Jewel and Badge of the order. The following is an abridgment of a description given by Carlile:

The jewel is composed of two intersecting triangles, surrounding another triangle, with the sun in the center, an emblem of the Deity.*

Under these is the compound character, |⊥|, the *Triple Tau*, (triple T,) which is the royal arch mason's badge; by which the wearer acknowledges himself the servant of the *true* god.

The T, it has been seen, is the figure of the old Egyptian Nilometer, used to ascertain the height of the inundation, on which depended the subsistence, the *life* of the inhabitants. The Nilometer, in consequence, became the symbol of *life, health*, and *prosperity;* and was

---

* Or rather a deity itself.

supposed to possess the power of *averting evil*. It was, therefore, in an abbreviated form, suspended to the necks of the sick as an *amulet or charm*.*

Thus has originated the badge of royal arch masonry: its triple form, as usual, relates to the Egyptian trinity.

It is generally conceded by masonic writers, that ancient masonry closes with the royal arch. In an edition of "The Illustrations of Masonry," by the late Mr. Preston, published in London, 1829, the editor, Mr. Oliver, author of the lectures from which quotations have been made above, observes:

"All degrees beyond the royal arch ought to be carefully separated from *genuine* masonry, as they are mostly founded on vague and uncertain traditions, which possess not the *shadow* of *authority* to recommend them to our notice."

The additional degrees, including those considered legitimate, amount to upwards of fifty. These are founded, partly upon astronomical principles, agreeing with the ancient worship of the Egyptians; and partly upon the Hebrew and Christian doctrines; of two or three of which a slight notice will be taken.

It may be remarked in general, that many of the degrees of knights are founded on the Christian knighthoods, got up in the time of the crusades, in the twelfth century; and that the ceremonies thereof are an imitation of those superstitious establishments. A former grand high priest of the chapters in the state of New-York, informs me, that he initiated a French gentleman into the degree of knight of Malta, who told him he was a member of the ancient order of that name, and that the ceremonies were very similar.

At the time those old knighthoods were founded, "Superstition mingled in every public and private action of life; in the holy wars, it sanctified the profession of arms; and the order of chivalry was assimilated in its rights and privileges to the sacred orders of priesthood. The *bath* and the *white* garment of the novice were an indecent copy of the regeneration of baptism; his sword, which he offered on the altar, was blessed by the ministers of religion; his solemn reception was preceded by *fasts* and *vigils*; and he was created a knight in the name of God, of St. George, and of St. Michael the archangel."—(Rees's Cycl.)

---

* The letter T (*Tau*) was used by captains and heralds, and signed on their names, who remained alive after a battle; as the letter *Theta* (Θ) was used as a mark of death, so was T of life.—(Bailey.

Order of High Priesthood.

The ancient priests of Egypt, and the Druids of Gaul and Britain, of course, officiated in the administration of the mysteries. Soon after Druidism was extinct, it is probable, the royal arch was neglected, and lay dormant for several centuries. On its revival, about the middle of the eighteenth century, it was found that priests, or persons to officiate as such, were necessary to preside in this chapter. Accordingly they were chosen from the laity among the brethren, or from such clergymen as had joined themselves to the order ; and there were doctors of divinity among the first promoters of the revival, or revolution of the society.

Here the English clergy had an opportunity, which they did not neglect, to mould the ceremonies connected with the order of priesthood, to suit their purpose. The odious tithes-system is openly advocated, and the awful fate of Korah, Dathan, and Abiram, held out as the due punishment of all those who should dare to resist it.

The following remarks upon his subject are abstracted from Cross and Webb:

This order appertains to the office of high priest of a royal arch chapter : it should not be conferred when a less number than *three* high priests are present. Whenever the ceremony is performed in *due and ample form*, the assistance of at least *nine* high priests, are requisite. A convention notified to meet at the time of any communication of the grand chapter, will afford he best opportunity of conferring this important and *exalted* degree of masonry, with *appropriate solemnity*.

The reading of the following passages of scripture composes a part of the ceremonies appertaining to this order.

The first passage read is the 14th chapter of Genesis, relating to the successful expedition of Abram against certain kings, and on his return, giving to Melchisedec thithes of all he had obtained.—A reference is then made to Hebrew 7, v. 1–6 ; wherein it is said, " This Melchisedec, king of Salem, which is king of peace, was *without father, without mother, without descent ; having neither beginning of days, nor end of life;* but abideth a priest continually. Now consider how great this man was, unto whom even the patriarch Abraham gave the tenth of *the spoils.* And verily they that are of the sons of Levi, who receive the office of the priesthood, *have a commandment to take tithes of the people, according to the law, that is, of their brethren.*"

Now, this alludes particularly to the Levitical law, and had a special reference to that portion of the tribe of Levi who were admitted into the sacerdotal order, and is totally inapplicable to the Christian dispensation. It was a peace-offering of St. Paul, the author of the book of Hebrews, to the Jewish priests, to prevent their persecution: for surely the apostle did not pretend to the right of demanding tithes of the Christian laity of his day; for he boasts of having been of no charge to them, laboring for his own support. The English clergy, however, claim the benefit of *this law*, and have duped the masons into an acknowledgement of their pretensions.

The next passage cited is Numbers 16, v. 1—33; which gives the horrid catastrophe of Korah and company, for resisting Moses and Aaron. This example is evidently adduced to deter the laity of England from opposing the tithes-claimers, the would-be legitimate heirs of the sons of Levi, *who receive the office of the priesthood.*

Moses here accuses the body of the Levites of *seeking the priesthood*, and asks, "What is Aaron, that ye murmur against him?" Which shows that tithes were the bone of contention, even in the time of Moses, the priesthood obtaining a greater share, in proportion to their numbers, than the rest of the tribe. The passage concludes as follows:—"And it came to pass, as he (Moses) had made an end of speaking all these words, that the ground clave asunder that was under them: and the earth opened *her mouth*, and swallowed them up, and the houses, and all the men that appertained unto Korah, and all their goods. They, and all that appertained to them, went down alive into the *pit*, and the earth closed upon them: and they perished from among the congregation."

The American masons ought, at least, to have so modified the ordination of priests into the order, as to render it consistent with our republican institutions, and not given the least countenance to the iniquitous exaction of clerical tithes.

It may be said, that there is no immediate cause of alarm on this head; yet the reiterated admission of such a claim, by a numerous, respectable society, may in time be the means of rendering it popular. It may be remarked, that Christian clergymen who are inducted into this order, assume the duties of pagan priests, and of course perform ceremonies appropriate to the worship of the heavenly bodies, *all the host of heaven.* This, to be sure, may be done very innocently, as they are not necessarily diverted from the integrity of their faith; and moreover, are probably not aware of the real import of the rites and ceremonies in which they participate.

After the election of a candidate to the office of high priest, he is thus addressed by the grand high priest:—"You are appointed chaplain to this chapter, and I now invest you with this *circular jewel*, the badge of your office. It is emblematical of eternity, and reminds us that here is not our abiding place," etc. Now, we have seen, that a circle, owing to its figure, was esteemed by the ancients, a symbol of their god, the sun.

" Let the *mitre*, with which you are invested, remind you of the dignity of the office you sustain, and its *inscription* impress upon your mind a sense of your dependence upon God," etc.—The inscription upon it is *holiness to the Lord;* the same as that which surrounds the mitre of the hierophant of the mysteries, and also that of the Roman pontiff.

" The *breast-plate*, with which you are decorated, is in imitation of that upon which were engraved the names of the twelve tribes, and worn by the high priest of Israel," etc.—The breast plate is the same as that worn by the hierophants of Egypt, which had described upon it the twelve signs of the zodiac.*

" The *various colors* of the *robes* you wear, are emblematical of every grace and virtue, which can adorn and beautify the human mind."—The various colors of the robes of the high priest are symbolical of the seasons, when the sun is in the different constellations of the zodiac.—" Ye priests! (says Volney, alluding to Catholic priests,) you wear his [the sun's] emblems all over your bodies ; your tonsure is the disk of the sun, your stole is his zodiac, your rosaries are symbols of the stars and planets. Ye pontiffs and prelates! your mitre, your crosier, your mantle, are those of Osiris."—(Ruins, p. 139.)

Although, after the extinction of Druidism, it was necessary for masonry to create an order of priests to officiate in the royal arch chapter as representatives of the deity, still it is evident that the English clergy, who undoubtedly took a principal part in arranging the ceremonies appropriated to initiations into the order, have managed the affair to suit their own sinister purposes. They made up a medley, compounded of Paganism, Jewism, and Christianity. Little of ancient masonry is to be seen in it, excepting the dress of the high priest, which is purely of pagan origin. And here it may be proper to remark, that although it has been shown, that the prayers of the ancient pagans and those of the Jews were couched in the same terms, the

---

* Volney, in taking notice of some customs of the Hebrews, which are also strictly masonic, observes:—" In vain did Moses proscribe the worship of the symbols which prevailed in lower Egypt and Phenicia; in vain did he wish to blot from his religion every thing which had relation to the stars; many traits call them to mind in spite of all he has done." He cites as instances, " The seven *luminaries* or *planets* of the great candlestick; the *twelve stones* or *signs* in the urim of the high priest, and the feast of the two *equinoxes, entrances* and *gates* of the two *hemispheres*."

objects to whom they were addressed only being changed, nevertheless it may be doubted that the frequent introduction of texts of scripture in the ceremonies, is in strict conformity to original masonry. Two doctors of divinity, Dissanguliers and Anderson, were engaged in the collection, or forming anew, of the ceremonies, and had it in their power to mould them at will.

Whether innovations, in this respect, were made or not upon this occasion, is of no consequence any farther than thereby to give an impression that masonry might have some connection with the Jewish religion. These observations are, therefore, made to guard against such a conclusion.

Knight of the Eagle and Sovereign Prince of Rose-Croix de Heroden.

This degree is a parody on the royal arch; and, as such, tends to confirm our interpretation of the purport of that chapter.— Here the *lost word* is *Jesus of Nazareth*, instead of *Hiram*.

The time and circumstances attending the *losing* of the word, are thus stated:

The moment when the vail of the temple was rent; when darkness and consternation covered the earth; when the stars disappeared, and the *lamp* of day was darkened; when the implements of masonry were lost, and the cubic stone sweated *blood* and *water*; *that was the moment when the great Masonic Word was lost.*

Nevertheless, says the master, we will endeavor to recover it, and, addressing the candidate for initiation, says, are you disposed to follow us? Answer.—Yes, I am. Master,—Brother wardens, make the candidate travel for *thirty-three years*, to learn the beauties of the *new law*. The junior warden then conducts the candidate thirty-three times round the lodge without stopping. (Bernard reduces the number to seven.) The candidate is now conducted to the darkest of places, from which *the word* must come forth *triumphant*, to the *glory* and *advantage* of *masonry*. He is then ordered to parade the room three times, in memory of the *mysterious descent*, which lasted *three days*.

After some further ceremony, the master questions the candidate as follows:

From whence came you?—From *Judea*. Which way did you come?—By *Nazareth*. Who conducted you?—*Raphael*. Of what tribe are you descended?—The tribe of Judah.

What do these four initial letters, I. N. R. I., signify?—Jesus Nazarenus, Rex Judæorum. (*Jesus of Nazareth, King of the Jews.*)

Master. My brethren, *what happiness!* the word is recovered; *give him the light.* The vail is taken off, and all the brethren clap their hands *three* times, and give *three* huzzas.—(Carlile.)

The master says to the candidate, approach, *my brother*, I will communicate to you our *perfect mysteries.* I congratulate you on the recovery of the word, which entitles you to this degree of *perfect masonry.* I shall make no comment or eulogium on it. Its *sublimity* will be duly appreciated by you. The impression which, no doubt, it has made on your mind, will convince you that you were not deceived when you were informed that the *ultimatum* of *masonic perfection* was to be acquired by this degree. It certainly will be a source of very considerable satisfaction to you, that *your merit alone* has entitled you to it.

The above is a mere sketch of this degree: its scenery, some parts of which has already been noticed, is very imposing. In the representation of the infernal regions, the awful sights of the *greater mysteries* are more closely copied than is done in the royal arch. Whether the inventors of the order expected any serious effects to be produced by it; or whether it was got up for amusement, and to show the ingenuity of its projectors, is uncertain. But it is pretty evident that such exhibitions, introduced amidst scenes of merriment and recreation, would not tend to make a very strong impression.

Knight of Kadosh.

Chapter of the grand Inspectors of Lodges, grand elected Knights of Kadosh, or the White and Black Eagle. The chief is entitled Grand Commander.

Altho this degree is not recognized in ancient masonry, it has nevertheless, such a decided astronomical bearing as to render it probable that it is derived from the Egyptian rites. I will, therefore, attempt to give an explication of its enigmatical allusions.

When a reception into this degree is made, the grand commander remains alone in the chamber, and must be so situated that the candidate cannot see him, as he is not to know who initiated him. A part of this obligation is, that he never will declare to any one who received him or assisted at his reception to this *sublime* degree. This is sheer affectation, and intended for no other purpose than to impress upon the candidate the *awfulness* of the mysteries in which he is about to be instructed. It is, however, an imitation of an ancient custom. Warburton says, "A passage in Eunapius seems to say, that it was unlawful to reveal the *name* of the hierophant." And Pythagoras, it has been seen, gave his lessons from behind a screen to his newly entered pupils.

The saluting sign of Knights of Kadosh is, to hold the sword in the left hand, and place the right hand on the red cross which covers the heart. The question, *Are you Kadosh?* is answered by placing the right hand on the *forehead*,* and saying, *Yes, I am.*

The mounting of what is called the *mysterious ladder*, is the most distinguished ceremony in this degree. It is thus represented:

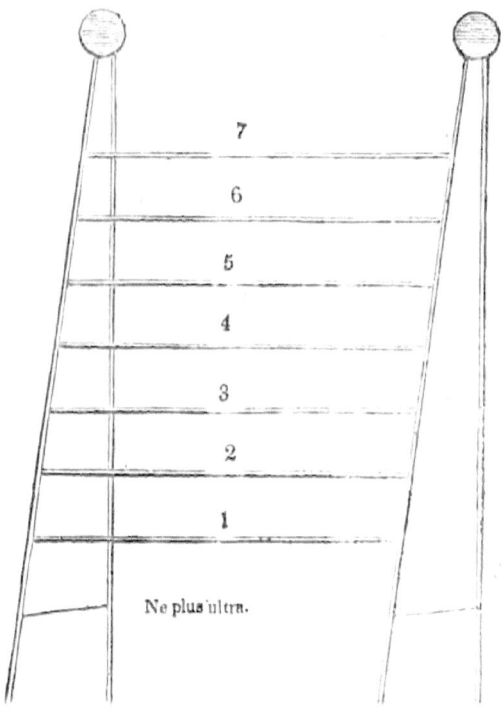

This ladder is an astronomical riddle, founded on the progress of the sun through seven signs of the zodiac, namely from Aries to Libra inclusive.

In expounding this riddle, I shall avail myself of the solution, by

---

* In the East, any person preferred to honors, bore a scepter or staff of honor, and sometimes a plate of gold on the *forehead*, called *Cadosh*, or *Caduceus*, signifying a *sacred* person. (See supra.)

Dupuis, of the fable of Hercules, one of the names of the sun, whose pretended labors are shown to be a mere allegory of the course of that luminary.

* Whether the names given to the steps of the ladder, have a meaning in any language, or are here used arbitrarily, I know not. I give them as published by Bernard, with the significations annexed.

Previously to the candidates mounting the ladder, he is taught to pronounce the names of the seven steps, and is sworn to observe the injunctions pretended to be indicated thereby. After he has pronounced the last word, in the seventh step, the Grand Commander says, by the seven conditions, and by the power that is transmitted to me, which I have acquired by my *discretion*, my *untired travels*, *zeal, fervor* and *constancy*, I receive you *Grand Inspector* of all lodges, *Grand Elect Knight Templar*, and to take rank among the *Knights of Kadosh*, or *White and Black Eagle*, which we bear the name of: I desire you not to forget it. It is indispensable for you, my brother, to mount the *mysterious ladder*, which you see there; it will serve to instruct you in the *mysteries* of our order, and it is absolutely necessary that you should have a true knowledge of it. The candidate then ascends the ladder. When he is on the seventh or highest step, and has pronounced the three last words, the ladder is lowered and the candidate passes over it, because he cannot retire the same way, as he would in such case be obliged to go back, against which he has taken an obligation. He then reads the words at the bottom of the ladder, *ne plus ultra*.

It has been the custom of the manufacturers of masonic degrees to entitle the last, for the time being, the ne plus ultra; which being succeeded by others, the latter, like *more of the last words of Mr. Baxter,* throw the former into the back ground. So, the Grand Commander, in addressing the candidate, calls "This order the last degree of masonry." The attention, therefore, of the candidate, when arrived at the top of the ladder, is directed to the ne plus ultra below.

The candidate's retiring by a different way from that by which he ascended, is in imitation of the course of the sun. The following fanciful description of the laws which govern the stellary system, is given by Mackey, (p. 139.)

"In the oblong zodiac of Tentyra, each of the twelve signs is divided into three parts of ten degrees, and each part is represented by a human figure, (with attributes expressive of his functions,) called a Decan; and as each sign of the zodiac has three of these, the first of each was called a powerful leader of three. To this company of thirty-six Decans they attributed the management of the seasons. These were the *powers* whose functions were more durable than those of the twelve zodiacal constellations, which are still found to alter their position every 2,000 years, relative to the season: and to move, in that time, through a space of thirty degrees from the equinoctial points. Not so the more powerful and constant gods, called the Decans, or Eloim; those of that rank which are fixed at the equator, are still supposed to compel the sun to shine twelve hours a day all the world over; and those at the opposite parts of the equator, constantly *propel the sun the same way* through their dominions, that is, those at the *spring node* will not suffer the *sun* to pass out of their palace the same way by which he entered; but order him to move on to the sign more northward. This is known to be the constant order of the sun, moon, and planets."

First Step of the Mysterious Ladder.

The name designating the first step, is *Isedakah*, which is defined *righteousness.*

This, I apprehend, has an allusion to the sun in the vernal equinox, in the month of March, when the days and nights are equal all over the world, and when the sun, after having been long in the southern hemisphere, passes the line, in order to dispense his favors equally to the north; which is doing justice to all, agreeably to the above definition.

Second Step.

The second step is *Shor-laban*, (*white ox, figuratively.*) This is the only step, the definition of which is literally true; which, as it might lead to an interpretation of the meaning of the mysterious ladder, is thus falsely denominated figurative.

Taurus, the bull, is the second sign of the zodiac, into which the sun enters on the 21st of April. His entry into this sign is marked by the setting of Orion, who, in mythological language, is said to be in love with the Pleiades; and by the rising of the latter.

Third Step.

The third step is called *Mathok*, (*sweetness.*)

The third sign of the zodiac is Jemini, into which the sun enters in the mild, pleasant month of May. "'Canst thou hinder the sweet influences of Pleiades or loose the bands of Orion.'—(Job.) Now, the Pleiades were denominated, by the Romans, Vergilia, from their formerly rising when the spring commenced; and their sweet influences blessed the year by the beginning of spring."—(Identity of the Hebrew and Druidical religions.)

Fourth Step.

The fourth step is *Emunah*, (*truth in disguise*.)

The fourth sign is Cancer, into which the sun enters in the month of June. Egypt, at this period, is enveloped in clouds and dust, by which means the sun is obscured or disguised; and which figuratively may be denominated truth.

Fifth Step.

The fifth step is "*Hamal saggi*, (*great labor,*) *advancement to the practice of Heaven.*"

The fifth sign is Leo, or that of the celestial lion, called the lion of *Nemea*, under which the sun passes in July.—The *great labor* and difficulties to which the sun was supposed to be subjected in passing this sign, have before come under notice: which, also, is in perfect accord with the fable of the eminent exploit of Hercules, in killing the lion of Nemea.

The sun, when in the sign Leo, is on his *advance* towards the equator, where the ancients supposed heaven to be situated.

Sixth Step.

The sixth step is *Sabhal*, (*a burden, or patience*.)

The sixth sign through which the sun passes is Virgo, marked by the total disappearance of the celestial Hydra, called the hydra of Lerna, from whose head springs up the great dog and the crab.

Hercules destroys the hydra of Lerna, but is annoyed in his operation by a sea-crab which bit him in the foot.—Appolodorus says, that whenever Hercules lopped off one of the monster's heads, two others sprang up in the place of it, so that this labor would have been endless, had he not ordered his companion Iolas to sear the blood with fire, and thereby put a stop to their reproduction; and thus was that event actually represented in a fine picture in the temple of Delphi.— (Mayo.)

Seventh Step.

The seventh step is named *Gemulah, Binah, Tebunah,* (*retribution, intelligence, prudence.*)

The seventh sign is *Libra*, into which the sun enters at the commencement of autumn, indicated by the rising of the celestial Centaur, the same that treated Hercules with *hospitality*. This constellation is represented in the heavens with a *flask full of wine*, and a thyrsus, ornamented with *branches of leaves and grapes*, the symbol of the productions of the season.

The sun has now arrived at the autumnal equinox, bringing in his train the fruits of the earth; and *retribution* is made to the husbandman, in proportion to his *intelligence* and *prudence*.

The allegory is certainly beautiful, and the *mysterious ladder* is well worthy to be called the *ne plus ultra* of masonry.

Since preparing the above, my attention has been drawn to a learned article on the same subject, in a work, before noticed, by the Rev. G. Oliver; which confirms my conjecture that the ladder composed a part of the machinery of the *mysteries*, and consequently has a legitimate standing in masonry. It probably constituted a component part of the royal arch degree, illustrating the seven steps required to consummate that exalted grade.—The following is a sketch of this article:

The *ladder* with *seven steps*, was used in the Indian mysteries to designate the approach of the *soul* to perfection. The steps were usually denominated *gates*. The meaning is undoubtedly the same; for it is observable that Jacob, in referring to the lower *stave* of his *ladder,* exclaimed, "this is the house of God, and the *gate* of heaven." Here we find the notion of ascending to heaven by means of the practice of moral virtue, depicted by the Hebrew patriarchs, and by a remote idolatrous nation, under the idea of a *ladder*. These gates were said to be composed of different metals of gradually increasing purity: the uppermost stave, which constituted the summit of perfection, and opened a way to the residence of the celestial deities, was composed of the pure and imperishable substance of gold, and was under the protection of *their most high god, the sun.*

The ascent to the summit of the paridisaical mount of God, by means of a pyramid consisting of seven steps, was an old notion, certainly entertained before the vision of Jacob; for it prevailed amongst the Mexican savages[*]; and the original settlers on the vast continent

---

[*] See Humboldt's Researches in America, vol. 1, p. 86.

of America could have no knowledge of this vision, either by tradition or personal experience.

In these mysteries, during the ceremony of initiation, the candidate was passed successively through seven dark and winding cavern; which progress was mystically denominated, *the ascent of the ladder.* Each cavern terminated in a narrow stone orifice, which formed an entrance into its successor. Through these gates of purification, the mortified aspirant was compelled to squeeze his body with considerable labor; and when he had attained the summit, he was said to have passed through the transmigration of the spheres, to have accomplished the ascent of the soul, and to merit the favor of the celestial deities.

In the Persian mysteries, the candidate, by a similar process, was passed through seven spacious caverns, connected by winding passages, each opening with a narrow portal, and each the scene of some perilous adventure, to try his courage and fortitude before he was admitted into the splendid *Sacellum*, which being illuminated with a thousand torches, reflected every shade of color, from rich gems and amulets, with which the walls were copiously bedecked. The dangerous progress was denominated, *ascending the ladder* of perfection.

From this doctrine has arisen the tale of Rustam, who was the *Persian Hercules*, and Dive Sepid, or the White Giant.—(Fab. Pag. Idol. v. iii, p. 328.)

" Cai-Caus, the successor of Cai-Cobab, the first monarch of the Caianian dynasty, is instigated by the song of a minstrel to attempt the conquest of Mazenderaun, which is celebrated as a perfect earthly Paradise."

This celestial abode refers to the splendid sacellum of the Persian *Epoptæ*, which was an emblematical representation of heaven.

" Cai-Caus fails in his enterprize; for the sacred country is guarded by the White Giant, *who smites him and all his troops with blindness*, and makes them his prisoners."

This is a literal account of the first stage of initiation, which in the mysteries always commences with *darkness.* In those of Britain, the candidate is designated as a *blind man.* And the captivity of Cai-Caus and his Persians in the cavern, under the rigid guardianship of the Dive, is but a figurative representation of the candidate's inclosure under the Pastos; and this place of penance in the Celtic mysteries, which had many ceremonies in common with those of Persia, (Borl· Ant. of Corn., b. ii. c. 22,) was said to be guarded by the gigantic deity Buanawr, armed with a drawn sword, who is represented as a most powerful and vindictive being, capable in his fury of making heaven, earth, and hell to tremble.—(Dav. Notes on Taliein's Cad Goddeu.) In the Gothic mysteries, the same place of captivity and penance is fabled to be guarded by Heimdall, whose trumpet emits so loud a blast, that the sound is heard through all the worlds.—(Edda Fab.)

"In this emergency the king sends a messenger to Zaul, the father of the hero Rustam, begging his immediate assistance. For the greater despatch, Rustam takes the shorter, though more dangerous road, and departs alone, mounted on his charger Rakesh."

Here Rustam enters upon the dreadful and dangerous business of initiation, mounted, says the legend, upon the charger Rakesh, or more properly Rakshi. This was a horrible winged animal, whose common food is said to have been serpents and dragons. Now these reptiles, together with monsters compounded of two or more animals, were the ordinary machinery used in the mysteries to prove the courage and fortitude of the aspirant, during his progress through the seven stages of regeneration.

"The course which he chooses is styled, *the road of the seven stages;* and at each of the first six he meets with a different adventure, by which his persevering courage is severely tried."

At each of the seven stages the candidate really encountered many dangers; and vanquished a multitude of Dives, dragons, and enchanters, who in succession opposed his progress to perfection.—(Shah name, in Richardson's Dissert. East. Nat.) Being *pantomimically enacted during the process of initiation*, and the reiterated attacks prosecuted with unrelenting severity, instances have occurred where the poor affrighted wretch has absolutely expired through excess of fear.

"Having at length however fought his way to *the seventh*, he discovers his prince and the captive Persians; when he learns from Cai-Caus, that nothing will restore his sight but the application of *three drops of blood* from the heart of the *White Giant*."

The symbolical *three* drops of blood, had its counterpart in all the mysteries of the ancient world; for the number *three was ineffable*, and the *conservator of many virtues*. In Britain, the emblem was three drops of water; in Mexico, as in this legend, three drops of blood; in India, it was a belt composed of three triple threads; in China, the three strokes of the letter Y, etc. etc.

"Upon this, he attacks his formidable enemy *in the Cavern* where he was accustomed to dwell; and *having torn out his heart*, after an obstinate combat, he infuses the prescribed three drops into the eyes of Cai-Caus, *who immediately regains his powers of vision.*"

In this tale we have the theological ladder connected with the system of Persian initiation transferred from mythology to romance; and the coincidence is sufficiently striking to impress the most ordinary observer with the strict propriety of the application. The candidate comes off conqueror, and is regularly restored to light, after having given full proof of his courage and fortitude, by surmounting all opposing dangers. Father Angelo, who went out as a missionary into the East about 1663, says, that in the midst of a vast plain between Shiraz and Shuster, he saw a *quadrangular* monument of stupendous size, which was said to have been erected in memory of this great enterprize of the hero Rustam. The fact is, that this quadrangular inclosure was an ancient place of initiation; and from a confused remembrance of the scenes of mimic adventure which were reprepresented within its *seven secret caverns*, the fabulous labors of Rustam had doubtless their origin.

Here the author has evidently mistaken the copy for the archetype. *The scenes of mimic adventure*, alluded to, undoubtedly originated from *the fabulous labors of Rustam, the Persian Hercules*. It has been shown that Hercules was one of the names by which the sun was designated,[*] and that the perilous adventures attributed to a fabulous character to whom the name was given, was a mere allegory on the progress of that luminary through the signs of the zodiac; of which the tale of Rustam is another version.

The order of Noachites, or Chevaliers Prussian.

This order, there is reason to believe, was instituted by the ancient Prussians. It claims priority over that of the freemasons of England. The author of an expose of the ritual of that institution, which will be noticed below, gives just fifty-three years between the periods of the two establishments; and says, " This tradition is firmly believed." In corroboration of this fact, Dr. Anderson observes, " The first name of Masons, according to some old traditions, was Noachidæ."

The ceremonies of the Noachites seem to have served in some measure, as a model upon which those of freemasonry are founded. Although the scene of the establishment of this order is laid at the Tower of Babel, instead of the Temple of Solomon, the craft of masonry, as in the freemasons' society, is made use of to cover the real design of

---

[*] Osiris, Bacchus, Cronus, Pluto, and Hercules, are all equally the sun.—(Faber Dis. on the Myst. of the Cabiri, v. 1, p. 17.)

the institution, the maintaining of religious dogmas, if not the recovery of independence.

The following remarks, in Guthrie's sketch of the history of ancient Prussia and Poland, will tend to show at what time this institution was probably formed.

Speaking of Poland, he says, "From this period [830] for some centuries we have no very certain records of the history of Poland. The title of duke was retained till the year 999, when Boleslaus (the I.) assumed the title of king, and conquered Moravia, Prussia, and Bohemia, making them tributary to Poland."

Of Prussia.—"The ancient history of Prussia, like that of other kingdoms, is lost in the clouds of fiction and romance. The inhabitants appear to have been a brave and warlike people. They were descended from the Sclavonians, and refused to submit to the neighboring princes, who, on pretence of converting them to Christianity, wanted to reduce them to slavery. They made a noble stand against the kings of Poland; one of whom, Boleslaus IV. they defeated and killed in 1163. They continued Pagans, till the time of the latter crusades, about the year 1227."

From the foregoing statements, it appears that the sway of Poland over Prussia, obtained in 999, was not of long duration; and it is reasonable to conjecture, that soon after the conquest, the people of Prussia established the order of Noachites. It was evidently a military institution, and undoubtedly intended as a rallying point, to operate as occasions might occur, for the recovery of the civil and religious liberties of the nation.

Admitting that the society of Noachites was founded in the year 1000, which is highly probable, and provided the foregoing tradition be correct, the establishment of freemasonry in England, would have occurred about the middle of the eleventh century, which is as late as it is likely to have been neglected, after the edict of Canute prohibiting the open worship of the Druids.

Bernard, in his account of this order, says, "The grand master, general of the order, whose title is chevalier grand commander, is Frederic William, king of Prussia. His ancestors, for three hundred years, have been protectors of this order. The knights were formerly known by the name of Noachites.

"The Noachites, now called Prussian Chevaliers, are descended from *Peleg*, the grand architect of the tower of Babel, their origin being more ancient than that of the masons descended from Hiram.—

The knights assemble on the night of the full moon in the month of March, [the vernal equinox] in a *secret place*, to hold their lodges; and they cannot initiate a candidate into the mysteries of this order unless by the light of the moon."

Great innovations have been introduced into the ceremonies of this order. I have a copy of its ritual, which, from its antiquity and Druidical style, may be presumed genuine. It was reprinted from a London copy, by John Holt, New-York, 1768. As a curiosity, and as bearing a relationship to the ancient mysteries, I will give an abstract of it.

The order consists of two degrees, called *Minor* and *Major;* and the officers form what masonically may be termed a *Chapter*, to which the other members are not admitted. This chapter comports with the royal arch of freemasonry; for here the *secret word, Belus*, is revealed, which, the reader is aware, is the same as Osiris, personated by Hiram. The expounder of the order appears to have committed an error, in giving this word at the opening of the minor's degree; because it is expressly said afterwards, that *it was unknown to all but officers*.

Minor's Degree.

Examiner. When did Masonry begin? Respondent. About one hundred and fifty four years after Noah's flood, at the building of Babel's tower. Who was grand master there? Nimrod,* called by masons *Belus*. [Not *Peleg*, as modern masons have it.] Where was the first lodge held?—In a pleasant plain of Babylon, called *Shinar*, on the banks of the river Tygris.

In what manner were you made?—I was led to a door, where a man stood with a drawn sword in his hand, who asked my friend what he wanted. What did your friend reply?—To have me made a mason. Did he admit you?—Yes, he struck the door with his sword, upon which it instantly flew open; my friend then led me by the hand into a *very dark room*, and then the door was shut. What succeeded this?—My friend then said with a loud voice,

> Here stands a candidate for masonry,
> Who fain would know our art and mystery:
> Shew him the light by which we work, and then
> Perhaps he'll learn the art, like other men.

---

* Nimrod, which signifies a rebel in the Jewish and Chaldean language, was the name given him by Moses; but in Chaldea he was called Belus, which signified *lord;* and afterwards was worshiped as a god by many nations, under the name of Bel, or Baal, and became the Bacchus of the ancients, or Bar-Chus, the son of Chus.

ORDER OF NOACHITES.

Upon this a door flew open, and discovered a *room extremely light*, out of which came three men, with drawn swords, one of whom said, *deliver your friend to us.* Upon this my friend delivered me into their care, and I was ushered into the lodge, one walking before, and one on each side, and my friend in the rear. Thus was I brought out of *darkness into light.*

What was done after this?—I was *stripped naked*, in order that all the lodge might be well assured they were not imposed upon by a woman.* What was then done?—The master clothed me with the badge of *innocence.* (This is a loose white garment, generally made of fine linen, and sometimes of silk.) He then took me by the right hand, and placed me in the centre of the brethren; he then ordered me to kneel down on both my knees, and held to my throat the point of a sword which he had in his hand, and then addressed me as follows:

"Sir,—You are now going to be admitted a member of this ancient and honorable fraternity, and it is expected that you will lay yourself under the subsequent obligation.

"You shall not reveal to any person or persons, either by word of mouth, or your own hand-writing, or cause to be revealed in any manner whatever, any part or parts, point or points, or any traditions, which have been, are now, or shall hereafter be held as a secret among masons, unless to an honest man, who you know is a mason, or to the master or wardens of any regular Lodge.

"And as it was always esteemed by the masons of old, that to swear by the sword was the most binding of all obligations, so we do insist and require you solemnly to kiss the edge of this sword presented to your throat, as a signification of your full consent to, and approbation of, the above particulars.

"Your well performing this injunction, will make you ever esteemed by this venerable body, as the contrary will render you guilty of a breach of the most sacred band of human society, and consequently degrade you from the character of a man of honor, which every mason ought to preserve more carefully than his life."*

Are you desirous of knowing the Major's secrets?—Yes. Ex. Your good behaviour alone will not obtain them.

---

* This is a sheer hoax upon the order. The real intention, as in the mysteries and freemasonry, is to represent man in a state of nature, before the arts, and particularly that of making clothing, were invented. The candidate before initiation is looked upon as an uncultivated savage; his initiation civilizes and regenerates him.—Edit.

* The freemasons, at the revival of the order in 1717, would have done well to have adopted this oath, instead of those of Hiram-masonry.—Edit.

> R. By that alone they could not be obtain'd,
> But I by that a Golden Signet gain'd;
> Which will admit me into that degree,
> That I may work among the Majors Free.

What is that signet?—A ring. Ex. Produce it?—R. Behold it here. (Showing the ring.)

> Ex. Attend, my brethren, all that round me stand,
> While I obey great Belus' dread command.
> Our brother here, upon examination,
> Desires I'll place him in a higher station;
> A Minor's character has well maintain'd,
> And answer'd all things well; by which he's gain'd
> The Signet rare, which Belus did ordain
> For such as could the Minor's art attain,
> That they may to the tow'r repair, and be
> Receiv'd to work among the Majors Free.
> 'Tis then my will and pleasure that he may
> Begin to work, and enter into pay.

Ceremony of Installment of Officers.

Where were you installed?—In the observatory. How high was it?—On the top of the tower. How got you there?—By a winding ascent. In what manner were you installed?—I first passed the Minor's examination, and then the Major's; after which Belus informed me, the brethren had unanimously agreed to elect me into the office of which he invested me with the badge. Have the officers a *secret word?*—Yes. How did you receive it?—

> On my two knees he ordered me to kneel,
> Before he could the *secret word* reveal;
> *A word to all but officers unknown,*
> Because we give it when we *are alone;*
> The word is *Belus,* be it known to thee,
> *'Twas* that great man *gave birth to Masonry.*

CHAPTER VIII.

MISCELLANEOUS ARTICLES.

Ceremonies observed in laying the foundation stone of Freemason's Hall, London, 1775; and its dedication, in 1776.

The similarity of practices in masonry and the ancient rites of Bacchus, is fully exemplified in these ceremonies. The *Caduceus* or *magical wand* of Mercury, the *mysterious chest*, and the *three pitchers*, containing corn, wine, and oil, are appropriately used. This will appear by the following short abstract of the transactions on those occasions, as published by Smith:

"The first stone of mason's hall was laid by the Rt. Hon. Robert Edward Lord Peter, baron of Writtle, grand master of the masons of England, accompanied by the *worshipful* Rowland Holt, etc.

About twelve o'clock the procession arrived, and continued *three times* round the ground, where the hall was to be erected. The grand master then deposited the *foundation stone* with the usual formalities. After which the deputy grand master presented the *square* to the grand master, when his *lordship* tried the corners of the stone, and then returned it to the deputy, who gave it to the architect. The senior grand warden next presented the *level* to the grand master, who therewith tried the stone *horizontally*, and returned it as before. The junior grand warden then presented the *plumb-rule* to the grand master, who applied it *properly*, and returned it as before. His *lordship* then *struck* the stone *three times* with a *mallet*, on which the grand treasurer *waved his wand*, and the brethren joined in the *grand honors* of masonry. (This is done by clapping hands three times three.)[*] The following anthem was then sung:

> To Heaven's high Architect all praise,
> All praise, all gratitude be given,
> Who deigned the human soul to raise,
> By *mystic secrets* sprung from heaven.
>   Chorus. *Thrice* repeated.
> Sound aloud the great Jehovah's praise,
> To him the dome, the temple raise.

---

[*] On laying the foundation of the Royal Infirmary of Edinburgh, in 1738, each of the brethren in their turns gave *three* strokes upon the corner stone with an iron mallet, which was succeeded by *three* clarions of the trumpet, *three* huzzas, and *three* claps of hands.—(See Lawrie, p. 155.)—Edit.

An oration was then pronounced. At the conclusion of which, the grand treasurer again *waved his wand*, and the grand honors were given as before. A grand piece of music was then performed by the instruments, and an ode on masonry rehearsed; after which the procession was resumed, and continued *three times round* as before.

The whole ceremony was conducted with the greatest order and decorum. The grand master and the rest of the brethren then proceeded through the city in procession in their carriages, without *exposing* any of the *ensignia* of the order, to Leathersellers hall, where an elegant entertainment was provided, and the evening concluded with great joy and festivity."

Dedication of the Hall, in 1776.

At half past twelve the procession entered the hall in the following order:

Grand Tiler, with a drawn sword—four tilers, carrying the *lodge* [the mysterious chest,] covered with white satin—master of the seventh lodge, carrying two silver *pitchers*, containing *wine* and *oil*—the master of the sixth lodge, carrying a gold *pitcher*, containing *corn*—the first *light* carried by the master of the fifth lodge—architect, carrying *square, level*, and *plumb-rule*—master of the fourth lodge, carrying the *bible, compasses*, and *square*, on a velvet cushion—grand chaplain,—grand secretary, with the *bag*, [purporting to contain private papers appertaining to the affairs of the lodge—a mere formality]—grand treasurer, with the staff [wand,]—second *light*, carried by the master of the third lodge—the third *light*, carried by the master of the second lodge—master of the senior lodge, carrying the book of constitutions—grand sword-bearer, carrying the sword of state—grand master.

On the procession reaching the grand master's chair, the brethren who formed it were proclaimed, and from that station walked round the hall *three times*. The *lodge* was then placed in the center of the hall, and the three lights, with one gold and two silver pitchers, containing corn, wine, and oil, were placed thereon; the bible, compasses, square, and book of constitutions, on a velvet cushion, being placed on a pedestal, the foundation stone anthem was sung.

His lordship then expressed his approbation of the architect's conduct, and commanded the proper officers to receive back the implements which had been delivered him at laying the foundation stone. A solemn piece of music was next performed, during which the ladies, and those who were not masons, retired. The grand master then ordered the hall to be tiled, on which the *lodge* [the little chest,] was uncovered, and the grand secretary informed the grand master, that it was the desire of the society to have the hall dedicated to *masonry;* on which the grand master *commanded* the grand officers to assist in that ceremony, during which the organ kept playing solemn music. The grand officers then walked round the *lodge* in procession *three times,* stopping each time for the *ceremony* of *dedication;* when the grand master in solemn form declared the hall dedicated to *masonry,* to *virtue,* and to *universal charity and benevolence;* which being proclaimed, the grand honors were given as before: the *lodge* was then *covered,* and the ladies introduced amidst the *acclamation* of the *brethren:* next a grand anthem was sung. An oration on masonry was then delivered by William Dodd, L. L. D. grand chaplain."

As the method of disposing of the *corn, wine,* and *oil,* is not stated in the foregoing account, I will subjoin the custom in this respect, which is observed at laying the foundation stone of public structures, and at the dedication of mason's halls, as given by Webb and others.

"The gold and silver vessels are presented to the grand master; and he, *according to ancient ceremony,* pours the corn, the wine, and the oil, which they contain, on the stone, saying,

"May the all bounteous Author of Nature *bless* the inhabitants of this place with all the necessaries, conveniencies, and comforts of life; *assist* in the erection and completion of this building; *protect* the workmen against every accident, and *long preserve* this structure from decay; and *grant* to us all, in needed supply, the corn of *nourishment,* the wine of *refreshment,* and the oil of *joy.*

'*Amen! So mote it be! Amen!*'

"He then strikes the stone *thrice* with the mallet, and the *public honors* of masonry are given."

In the dedication of mason's halls, the *corn, wine,* and *oil,* are poured upon the *lodge,* that is, as before observed, the little mysterious chest, Aaron, or ark.

The processions three times round the foundation, and the hall when finished; the three lights; the clapping hands three times; striking the stone thrice, etc. are in conformity to the customs of the ancients; which was done by them in reverence of the deity, and in acknowledgment of their belief in the triplicity of his nature or attributes.

"The Druid priests, in their worship, looked towards the sun—they retained many of the Ammonian rites,—they are said to have made *mystical processions* round their *consecrated fires sunwise* before they proceeded to sacrifice."—[Hutchinson, p. 69.]

In short, the agreement of the foregoing customs of masons with the observances of the ancients on similar occasions, will appear evident from the following historical facts:

"We learn from Festus, that the Etrurians had books concerning the ceremonies observed at the founding of *cities, altars, temples, walls,* and *gates.* Plutarch tells us, that Romulus, before he laid the foundation of Rome, sent for men from Etruria, who informed him in all the punctilios of ceremony which he was to observe. According to Dionysius, they began with offering a sacrifice. They then dug a ditch, into which they threw the *first fruits* of all things that served for *human nourishment;* at the same time they consulted the gods, to know if the enterprise would be acceptable to them, and if they approved of the day chosen to begin the work. They then chalked out the boundaries by a score of white earth, which they called *Terra pura.* While they were forming the boundary, *they stopped at certain intervals to renew the sacrifices.* In these sacrifices they invoked, besides the gods of the country, the gods to whose protection the new city was recommended, which was done secretly, because it was necessary that the tutelar gods should be unknown to the vulgar. In fine, so much regarded was the day on which a city was founded, that they kept up the memory of it by an anniversary festival.

Among the Romans, when they were to build a temple, the Auruspices were employed to choose the place where, and time when, they should begin the work. This place was purified with great care; they even encircled it with fillets and garlands. The Vestals accompanied with young boys and girls, washed this spot of ground with water, pure and clean, and the priest expiated it by a solemn sacrifice. Then he *touched the stone that was to be first laid in the foundation,* which was bound with a fillet; when the people, animated with enthusiastic zeal, threw it in with some *pieces of money or metal* which had never passed through the furnace. When the edifice was finished, there was also a *consecration of it, with grand ceremonies,* wherein the priest, or, in his absence, some of his college presided.—(Mayo's Myth. vol. 1, p. 141 and 297.)

"The same author, in treating of the festivals and processions of the Egyptians, observes;—"The Hebrews, who derived from the Egyptians that fatal propensity which they had towards idolatry, imitated them but too often, not only in the solemnity of the *golden calf,* but also in the ceremony of their *processions.* The prophet Amos upbraids them for having *led about* in the wilderness, the *tabernacle of the god*

Moloch, the image of their idol, and the star of the god Remphan. St. Stephen, in the acts of the apostles, taxes them with the same piece of idolatry.—Several other people practised the same ceremonies, whether they had learned them from the Egyptians, as is very probable, or had invented them themselves."—(Vol. 1, p. 303.)

In regard to sacrifices, Harwood, in his Grecian Antiquities, says,— "When the fruits of the earth were the only food of men, care was taken to reserve a certain portion for the gods. The same custom was observed when they began to feed upon the flesh of animals. Sometimes water was poured on the altar or the head of the victims, sometimes honey or *oil*; but in general they were sprinkled with *wine*, and then the wood of the fig tree, the myrtle, or the vine, were burnt upon the altar.—There was scarce any sacrifice without *corn* or bread, and more particularly *barley*, as it was the first sort of corn used by the Greeks, after the diet of acorns was given up."—(p. 146.)

Although masonry copies the customs of the ancient nations, it must not be supposed that there is any idolatry connected with it. It is merely an idle imitation of their rites and ceremonies, without any reference to the original import of them.

Antimasonic Writers.

The Abbé Barruel and Professor Robison, by their malignant and false allegations against the masonic society, have so far prejudiced the minds of a portion of the reading public, as to cause a belief that freemasonry was hostile to christianity, to good order, and to civil government. This calumny was founded solely upon the aid given by the freemasons of France to the revolution of government in that country. A revolution which certainly in its commencement, met with the approbation of every friend of liberty throughout the civilized world.

Both these writers were ultra royalists. Barruel was a French Jesuit priest, who, on the breaking out of the revolution in France fled to England, where he published his phillipic against republicanism and freemasonry, under the title of "Memoirs, illustrating the history of Jacobinism." Robinson was Professor of natural philosophy, and secretary to the Royal Society of Edinburgh. His attack on masonry and free governments, is entitled " Proofs of Conspiracy against all the religions and governments of Europe, carried on in the secret meetings of Freemasons, Illuminati and Reading Societies."

These writers pursue the common, hackneyed course of aristocracy against liberty, by calumniating and vilifying its supporters. No crime is too infamous to be laid to the charge of the most talented and virtuous of men. This disengenuous course shows the turpitude of the cause they espouse. It is most base to divert the reader from principles to men, and by false allegations against them, to prejudice him against their principles. Many an unsuspecting reader has suffered his mind to be perverted, by this flagitious mode of argument.

Barruel makes the following charge against the order of masons:

"I saw masons, till then the most reserved, who *freely* and *openly* declared, 'Yes, at length the grand object of freemasonry is accomplished, *equality and liberty;* all men are *equal* and *brothers;* all men are *free.* [Monstrous.] That was the whole substance of our doctrine, the object of our wishes, *the whole of our grand secret.* Such was the language I heard fall from the most zealous masons, from those whom I have seen decorated with all the insignia of the deepest masonry, and who enjoyed the rights of *venerable,* to preside over lodges. I have heard them express themselves in this manner before those whom, masons could call the *profane* (uninitiated,) without *requiring* the *smallest secrecy,* either from the men or women present. They said it in a tone as if they wished all France should be acquainted with this glorious achievement of masonry.—(Vol. ii. p. 149.—Hartford ed. 1799.)

Barruel also extracts the following sentiment, from Condorcet's "Progress of the human mind," as worthy of reprobation. Condorcet, speaking of the secret associations which existed in France, previously to the revolution, says, "They were the associations of those generous men who dare examine the foundations of all power or authority, and who revealed to the people the great truths, that their *liberty* is *inalienable;* that no prescription can exist in behalf of tyranny; that no convention can irrevocably subject a nation to any particular family: that magistrates, whatever may be their titles, functions or powers, are only the officers, and not the masters of the people: that the people always preserve the right of revoking those powers emanating from them alone, whether they judge it has been abused, or consider it to be useless to continue them. In short, that the people have the right of punishing the abuse as well as well as of revoking the power."

"Thus we see (says Barruel,) Condorcet tracing back the germ at least of all the principles of the French revolution, to these secret associations, which he represents as the benefactors of nations."

Had not masons a right equally with other citizens, to take part in the glorious cause of freeing their country from despotism? Was it not their duty, and would they not been infamous not to have done so?

The American masons were as zealous, I believe, in the cause of their country in our revolution as other men, and have never, to my knowledge, as a distinct class, been reproached for it.

The French revolution, however objectionable its course in some stages of its progress, and however unfortunate its termination, was holy and just. Its projectors and the French people as a nation, are no more responsible for the atrocities of Robespierre, than are the society of masons for the murder of Morgan.

But how were the enormities complained of, produced? By the combination of the despots of Europe for the purpose of reducing the French nation to its former state of bondage. Among the means employed, a civil war was fomented in La Vendee, comprehending three departments of the republic, and money was furnished to the rebels against their country, by England, to prosecute this nefarious warfare.

Besides, almost all the nobility and clergy of France, were in opposition to the cause of liberty, and carrying on every possible intrigue to reinstate the monarchy. They were sensible of the benefits resulting to them from the services of an enslaved people, and they wished to bring them back to their former debased state.

Thus was the French nation situated: surrounded by external foes, and harrassed by those within; to kill or be killed became the only alternative, and acts were committed, under the sway of Robespierre, that tarnished the glorious cause in which they were engaged.

But, after all, it is a pretty well ascertained fact, that Robespierre was in the interest of the powers combined against France, which caused him to disgrace the revolution in the manner he did.

If any country ever had cause to revolutionize its government, it was France, under the ancient regime. Where America had one just complaint against the abuses of government, France had a hundred: it would require a volume to enumerate them. I have not a list before me, but one was so degrading to the character of man, that it made a strong impression upon my mind when examining the catalogue. It was this: in some places, in certain seasons of the year, the peasants, by the law called the *Gabelle*, were obliged in turn, to beat the ponds and brooks all night, to prevent the seigneur or lord of the manor and family's being disturbed by the *croaking of the frogs*.

By this single example the debased state of the people of France may easily be imagined.

The horrors of the Bastile, the famous prison at Paris, is pretty well understood. A Mr. Caritat, well known in the city of New

York, as a bookseller, informed me, that he had been employed as a clerk in one of the offices of government in Paris, and that he had filled up hundreds of *letters de cachet*, signed in blank by the king. These letters were orders to the keeper of the Bastile, to receive under his charge the persons named in them; and which might be obtained for a few guineas, by any influential character. Thus were persons thrown into this dismal place, without trial and without any charge of crime. One man released from it, on its demolition, had suffered confinement for forty years, and was entirely ignorant of the cause of his imprisonment.

In the mean time the king, good easy soul, was enjoying the pleasures of the table and the chase, unmindful of the sufferings of his fellow men, inflicted through his instrumentality. In fact, whatever may be said of Louis XVI, it is very evident, that he was a complete *gourmand*, and very little endowed with the active virtues.

Thomas Paine, in his "Rights of Man," in answer to Edmond Burke's attack on the French revolution, observes, "Through the whole of Mr. Burke's book, I do not observe that the Bastile is mentioned more than once, and that with a kind of implication as if he was sorry it is pulled down, and wished it was built up again. 'We have rebuilt Newgate, says he, and tenanted the mansion; and we have prisons almost as strong as the Bastile for those *who dare to belie the Queen of France.*'

"Not one glance of compassion, not one commiserating reflection, that I can find throughout his book, has he bestowed on those that lingered out the most wretched of lives, a life without hope, in the most miserable of prisons. It is painful to behold a man employing his talents to corrupt himself. Nature has been kinder to Mr. Burke than he has been to her. He is not affected by the reality of distress touching his heart, but by the showy resemblance of it striking his imagination. *He pities the plumage, but forgets the dying bird.* Accustomed to kiss the aristocratical hand that hath purloined him from himself, he degenerates into a composition of art, and the *genuine soul of nature forsakes him.* His hero or his heroine must be a tragidy-victem, expiring in show, and not the real prisoner of misery, sliding into death in the silence of a dungeon."

Mr. Burke for his apostacy from the whig cause, and writing his philippic against the French revolution, received from the British king of the people's money, a pension of fifteen hundred pounds sterling: Six thousand, six hundred and sixty dollars.

By this work, says Joel Barlow, in a note to his "Conspiracy of

Kings," " He (Burke) conjured up a war, in which at least two millions of his fellow creatures must be sacrificed to his unaccountable passion. Such is the condition of human nature, that the greatest crimes have usually gone unpunished. It appears to me that history does not furnish a greater one than this of Mr. Burke ; and yet all the consolation that we can draw from the detection, is to leave the man to his own reflections, and expose his conduct to the execration of posterity."

Many misstatements have been published, charging the legislatures of France in the time of the revolution, with an open avowal of infidelity to the Christian religion, and with persecuting the clergy, with a view of prejudicing mankind against their cause. All this has been grounded upon a single expression of Anacharsis Cloots, one of the assembly, which received, however, no countenance from the other members. Robespierre, who, above all others, deserves the severest censure, professed the greatest regard for religion, and introduced to the assembly a long report, expressly upon that subject, which was received with approbation.

The following extract from the History of the Revolution, by M. Rabaut de St. Etienne, will correct the errors that have been circulated respecting the treatment of the priests.—Rabaut was a protestant clergyman, a member of the National Assembly, and a man of first rate character and talents.—He says,

" The oath required of the clergy was one of the pretexts used for endeavoring to create one of those quarrels which are termed schisms, and in which men separate into parties, and then fight, for the sake of abstract questions which they do not understand. The National Assembly had given the title of *Civil Constitution of the Clergy*, to what was nothing but its organization. It should seem that the Assembly would have done better, in not engaging in this affair, since each profession and each professor can arrange themselves agreeably to their own mode of proceeding, saving the superintending power of the government. It ran the hazard of reviving, under one form, a body which it had destroyed under another. But priests maintain such a fast hold of all temporal affairs, and attach themselves so closely to the interests of the government, that it is difficult to separate them from these affairs and these interests ; and, take the matter up in what shape you will, the the priesthood still meets you at every corner : this creates a degree of embarrassment in every country, where the sovereign, be it what it may, hath a serious inclination to be master.

"The National Assembly, then, having organized the clergy, according to the principles of the French constitution, required of the priests the oath, which had been taken by every citizen, to support the constitution; but it required, at the same time, that they should swear to maintain the civil constitution of the clergy. Of all the military men who have taken, and broken, the civic oath, not one ever thought of saying, that Heaven was injured by the military organization, their pretext hath been, that they had already taken an oath to the king, which rendered the latter null and of no effect. But priests are in the habit of identifying themselves with God, and whoever offends them, offends heaven. Accordingly, certain subtle minds soon discovered the means of creating a schism, in asserting, that this constitution was a spiritual affair, nay more, that it was another religion; that to require such an oath was a restraint of the freedom of conscience, that it was putting priests to the torture, and exposing them to suffer *martyrdom*. They even desired death, and that they might be led to execution, well assured that the national convention would never do any such thing.

"There was found in the Kingdom a considerable number of well-meaning persons, who imagined, that their consciences had received a material injury by this new organization of the clergy: for what men most believe, is very often, what they least understand. Meanwhile the nonjuring priests were obliged to quit their parishes, and *pensions* were allotted to them: but they endeavored to preserve their influence over their parishioners, and to interest them in their favor, by all those means which continually lie within reach of those, to whom men have committed the government of their reason. This division inspired the enemies of the constitution with the hope, that the French might be seduced into a civil war for the sake of the priesthood, since they would not go to war for the sake of the nobility, which, in truth, had no abstract ideas to present to the subtle minds of the discontented. The courtiers and the friends of privileges, on a sudden became *devout;* they were devout even at court; nay, they were devout even at Worms and at Coblentz. But the citizens of Paris, even such as were least enlightened, did not become the dupes of this mummery; now without Paris, there can be no civil war."—(Lond. ed. p. 200.)

Mr. Robison maintains the same tyrannical doctrines as Barruel; in support of which he quotes the arguments of one of the kings of France in vindication of his claims to power.

"Hear, says he, what opinion was entertained of the sages of France by their Prince, the father of Louis XVI. the unfortunate martyr of monarchy. 'By the principles of our *new* philosophers the throne no longer wears the *splendor of divinity*. They maintain that it arose from violence, and that by the same justice that force erected it, force may again shake it, and overturn it. The people can never give up their power. They only let it out for their own advantage, and always retain the right to rescind the contract, and resume it whenever their personal advantage, their only rule of conduct, requires it. Our philosophers teach in public what our passions suggest only in secret.'"—Then follows the reasoning of Louis, intended to show this doctrine to be heretical and absurd; and Robison adds, " This opinion of a prince is unpolished indeed, and homely, *but it is just.*" (p. 343.)

The author attempts, without a shadow of proof, to connect freemasonry with the Order of Illuminati; and then, by calumniating the latter, to disparage the former. But in this he has miserably failed: for, after all that has been said against the society of Illuminati, it appears to have been instituted for the sole purpose of lessening the evils which result from the want of information, by enlightening the public mind, and diffusing useful knowledge among all classes of the community.

To suppose, as the author pretends, that this society, composed of men of the first respectability and standing, wished to destroy all order and government, is too preposterous for a moments consideration.

The order is said to have been founded in Germany about the year 1777; and Dr. Adam Weishaupt, professor of Canon Law in the university of Ingolstadt, was the projector.

The author gives Dr. Weishaupt's prospectus of his views, by which the reader may form his own opinion of the merits of his scheme.

" The order of ILLUMINATI appears as an accessory to freemasonry. It is in the lodges of freemasons that the Minervals are found, and there they are prepared for Illumination. They must have previously obtained the three English degrees. The founder says more. That his doctrines are the only true freemasonry. He was the chief promoter of the *Eclectic System*. This he urged as the best method for getting information of all the explanations which have been given of the masonic mysteries. He was also a *Strict Observanz*, and an adept Rosycrucian. The result of all his knowledge is worthy of particular remark, and shall therefore be given at large.

'I declare, says he, and I challenge all mankind to contradict my declaration, that no man can give any account of the order of freemasonry, of its origin, of its history, of its object, nor any explanation of its mysteries and symbols, which does not leave the mind in total uncertainty on all these points. Every man is entitled, therefore, to give an explanation of the symbols, and any system of the doctrines, that he can render palatable. Hence have sprung up that variety of systems, which, for twenty years have divided the order. The simple tale of the English, and the fifty degrees of the French, and the knights of Baron Hunde, are equally authentic, and have equally had the support of intelligent and zealous brethren. These systems are in fact but one. They have all sprung from the blue lodge of three degrees; take these for their standard, and found on these all the improvements by which each system is afterwards suited to the particular object which it keeps in view. There is no man, nor system, in the world, which can show by undoubted succession that it should stand at the head of the order. Our ignorance in this particular frets me. Do but consider our short history of one hundred and twenty years.—Who will show me the mother lodge? Those of London we have discovered to be self-erected in 1716. [1717.] Ask for their archives. They tell you they were burnt. They have nothing but the wretched sophistications of the Englishman Anderson, and the Frenchman Desaguiliers. Where is the lodge of York, which pretends to the priority, with their king Bouden, and the archives that he brought from the East? These too are all burnt. What is the chapter of Old Aberdeen, and its holy clericate? Did we not find it unknown, and the mason lodges there the most ignorant of all the ignorant, gaping for instruction from our deputies? Did we not find the same thing at London? And have not their missionaries been among us, prying into our mysteries, and eager to learn from us what is true freemasonry? It is in vain, therefore, to appeal to judges; they are no where to be found; all claim for themselves the sceptre of the order; all indeed are on an equal footing. They obtained followers, not from their authenticity, but from their conduciveness to the end which they proposed, and from the importance of that end. It is by this scale that we must measure the mad and wicked explanations of the Rosycrucians, the Exorcists, and Cabalists. These are rejected by all good masons, because incompatible with social happiness. Only such systems as promote this are retained. But alas, they are all sadly deficient, because they leave us under the dominion of political and religious prejudices; and they are as inefficient as the sleepy dose of an ordinary sermon.*

'But I have contrived an explanation which has every advantage; is inviting to Christians of every communion; gradually frees them from all religious prejudices; cultivates the social virtues; and animates them by a great, a feasible, and *speedy* prospect of universal happiness, in a state of liberty and moral equality, freed from the obstacles which subordination, rank, and riches, continually throw in our way. My explanation is accurate, and complete, my means are effectual, and irresistible. Our secret association works in a way that nothing can withstand, *and man shall soon be free and happy.*

'This is the great object held out by this association; and the means of attaining it is Illumination, enlightening the understanding by the sun of reason, which will dispel the clouds of superstition and of prejudice. The proficients in this order are therefore justly named the Illuminated. And of all Illumination which human reason can give, none is comparable to the discovery of what we are, our nature, our obligations, what happiness we are capable of, and what are the means of attaining it. In comparison with this, the most brilliant sciences are but amusements for the idle and luxurious. To fit man by Illumination for active virtue, to engage him to it by the strongest motives, to render the attainment of it easy and certain, by finding employment for every talent, and by placing every talent in its proper sphere of action, so that all, without feeling any extraordinary effort, and in conjunction with and completion of ordinary business, shall urge forward, with united powers, the general task. This indeed will be an employment suited to noble natures, grand in its views, and delightful in its exercise.

'And what is this general object? THE HAPPINESS OF THE HUMAN RACE. Is it not distressing to a generous mind, after contemplating what human nature is capable of, to see how little we enjoy? When we look at this goodly world, and see that every man *may* be happy, but that the happiness of one depends on the conduct of another;

---

* Dr. Weishaupt has made a declaration rather too bold in the opening of his views, in respect to freemasonry. He might possibly be justifiable in saying that the origin of the order had not been discovered; but that it *can not be*, remains to be proved. He, however, had not, perhaps, perused the German work, noticed in the introduction of this volume; the author of which, I will venture to say, had found the right clue to lead to a development of the secret. Whether it conducted him to a result satisfactory to his readers, or whether his book fell into the hands of those "*who can understand,*" I know not.

when we see the wicked so powerful, and the good so weak; and that it is vain to strive, singly and alone, against the general current of vice and oppression; the wish naturally arises in the mind, that it were possible to form a durable combination of the most worthy persons, who should work together in removing the obstacles to human happiness, become terrible to the wicked, and give their aid to all the good without distinction, and should by the most powerful means, first fetter, and by fettering, lessen vice; means which at the same time should promote virtue, by rendering the inclination to rectitude, hitherto too feeble, more powerful and engaging. Would not such an association be a blessing to the world?

'But where are the proper persons, the good, the generous, and the accomplished, to be found? and how, and by what strong motives, are they to be induced to engage in a task so vast, so incessant, so difficult, and so laborious? This association must be gradual. There *are* some such persons to be found in every society. Such noble minds will be engaged by the heart-warming object. The first task of the association must therefore be to form the young members. As these multiply and advance, they become the apostles of beneficence, and the work is now on foot, and advances with a speed increasing every day. The slightest observation shows that nothing will so much contribute to increase the zeal of the members as secret union. *We see with what keenness and zeal the frivolous business of freemasonry is conducted, by persons knit together by the secrecy of their union.* It is needless to inquire into the causes of this zeal which *secrecy* produces. It is an universal fact, confirmed by the history of every age. Let this circumstance of our constitution therefore be directed to this noble purpose, and then all the objections urged against it by jealous tyranny and affrighted superstition will vanish. The order will thus work silently, and securely; and though the generous benefactors of the human race are thus deprived of the applause of the world, they have the noble pleasure of seeing their work prosper in their hands.'

"The candidate, before his admission, is required to peruse and sign the following oath:"

'I, N. N., hereby bind myself, by my honor and good name, forswearing all mental reservation, never to reveal, by hint, word, writing, or in any manner whatever, even to my most trusted friend, any thing that shall now be said or done to me respecting my wished-for reception, and this whether my reception shall follow or not; I being previously assured that it shall contain nothing *contrary to religion, the state, nor good manners.* I promise, that I shall make no intelligible extract from any papers which shall be shewn me now or during my noviciate. All this I swear, as I am, and as I hope to continue, a man of honor.'

"The urbanity of this protestation must agreeably impress the mind of a person who recollects the dreadful imprecations which he made at his reception into the different ranks of freemasonry."

The difference in the style of the oath, administered in the two orders, must be attributed to the customs of the times in which they were formed.

Mr. Robison, after bestowing the most vulgar abuse upon the learned and amiable Dr. Priestly, adds, "But I do not suppose that he has yet attained his acmé of illuminatism. His genius has been cramped by British prejudices. These need not sway his mind any longer. He is now in that *'rara temporis (et loci) felicitate, ubi sentire quæ velis, et quæ sentias dicere licit.'*"—That is, he now enjoys the rare felicity of time and place (America) where it is lawful to think what one pleases, and to speak what one thinks.

The liberty of speech which we claim in this country, must be very grating to the feelings of a man possessing the principles of Robison. He would have no person, except the mean eulogists of power, like himself, permitted to utter his sentiments.

"Does Dr. Priestly think (says he) that the British will part more easily than their neighbors in France with their *property and honors, secured by ages of peaceable possession, protected by law,* and *acquiesced in* by all who wish and hope that their own descendants may reap the fruits of their *honest industry.*"—(p. 367.)

The following deed of the ferocious robber, William of Normandy, will serve as a general example of the manner in which the British nobility obtained their property. It is taken from the National Portrait Gallery, London, 1829:

Francis Rawdon Hastings, Marquis of Hastings, K. B. The family of Rawdon is of great antiquity, and of Norman extraction. But the English pedigree is deduced from Paulin, or Paulinus Roydon, who commanded a body of archers, in the army of William, at the battle of Hastings. For this service he received from the Conqueror a grant of lands in the West Ridings of Yorkshire, near Leeds. The tenure was by grand sergeantry; and the condition, that of presenting to the king and his successors a cross-bow and arrow, whenever any of them should come to hunt there. Of the title deed conveying these manorial rights, Weever, in his "Funeral Momuments," gives the following as a faithful transcript:

> I, William Kyng, the thurd yere of my reign,
> Give to thee Paulyn Roydon, Hope and Hopetowne,
> With all the bounds both up and downe;
> From heaven to yerthe, from yerthe to hel,
> For thee and thyne there to dwel,
> As truly as this *king-right* is *myn*:
> For a crosse-bow and an arrow,
> When I sal come to hunt on yarrow.
> And in token that this thing is sooth,
> I bit the whyt wax with my tooth,
> Before Meg, Maud, and Margery,
> And my third sonne Henry.

The armorial bearing is that of fess between three pheons, or arrow-heads, with this motto,—*Et nos quoque tela sparsimus*: We too have scattered our arrows.

The following statement exhibits the amount drawn annually from the hard earnings of the people, to support the profligate luxury of the nobility and clergy of Great Britain.

Nice British Pickings,—Expressed in British Pounds.

399 Peers sitting in Parliament, and their families, receive from the taxes	£2,754,336
309 Peers not sitting in Parliament, and their families, receive	978,000
	£3,732,336
The Marquis of Bute and family receive	65,811
Lord Eldon	50,400
The Duke of Beaufort,	48,600
The Earl of Lauderdale	33,600
Lord Baresford	29,000
The Duke of Newcastle	19,900
Archbishop of Canterbury	41,100 and 176 livings
Bishop of Durham	61,700 livings unknown
Bishop of London	10,200 with 95 livings
Bishop of Litchfield	12,590 with 48 livings
Bishop of St. Asaph	7,000 with 90 livings
Bishop of Bath and Wells	7,330 with 27 livings
Bishop of Chester	4,700 with 30 livings
Bishop of Chichester	6,770 with 36 livings
Bishop of Ely	21,340 with 108 livings

Bishop of Lincoln	8,280 with 36 livings
Bishop of Norwich	8,370 with 40 livings
Bishop of Oxford	3,500 with 11 livings
Bishop of Rochester	5,400 with 21 livings
Bishop of Salisbury	14,420 with 40 livings
Bishop of Cloyne	7,500 and great patronage.
	467,511
Which added to the aforesaid sum of	3,732,336
Amounts to the sum of	£4,199,847

Which will maintain 83,997 families, at £50 a year and upwards each family.

Here we see the *honest industry* by which the privileged orders acquire their property. By livings are to be understood parishes, in which curates are located by the bishops, and from which the latter receive every tenth animal, sheaf of wheat, etc., which are raised therein; whilst the famished curates, who actually do all the service, in reading prayers, sermons, etc., receive but sixty or seventy pounds a year. This is English Christianity, but it is not the religion of Christ.

I will add to these notable instances of acquiring wealth, in England, by *honest industry*, a late communication from a writer in Liverpool to an editor of a paper in New-York. After giving a list of the present Cabinet and other officers of state, he says:—" American notions of economy will be shocked, when I add that for the privilege of being *mis*-governed by these gentlemen, the tax-ridden, church-rate, and tythe-stricken people of England, Scotland, and Ireland *must* pay the enormous yearly sum of *six hundred thousand dollars*! Yes, the mere salaries to the members of the government—I say nothing of the fees, perquisites, peculation and patronage—amount to this sum. Nor is this all: supposing the members of the government remain in office only a week—a day—an hour—nearly every one of them is entitled to a retiring pension varying from one-half to one-third of his salary. Thus Lord Brougham, after a Chancellorship of four years, receives a pension of twenty-five thousand dollars a year *for life!*—The Duke of Wellington, who has obtained grants, amounting to upwards of five millions of dollars, allows his mother to draw a small pension from the country.

" These things are worth knowing, in case any attempt should be made—as made it one day will be—to trammel the free institutions of America with the trappings of royalty. If you are wise, remain as you are—blessed with a cheap government, and a corrective control over it."

For opposing these outrageous impositions, is Dr. Priestly abused, by this defender of the oppressions and degradation to which the people of European monarchies are subjected.

"The Assembly, says Robison, had given the *illumination warwhoop*—'*Peace with cottages, but war with palaces.*' A *pouvoir revolutionaire* is mentioned, which supercedes all narrow thoughts, *all ties of morality*. Lequinio publishes the *most detestable book* that ever issued from a printing press, *Les Pejugés vaincus*, containing all the principles, and expressed in the very words of *Illuminatism*"—(p. 317.)

Any pretence of regard for the *ties of morality*, by Mr. Robison, after having vindicated the most tyrannical and pernicious doctrines, is adding insult to injury.

There was never a more moral and humane sentiment proclaimed by any government in the world, than that quoted above. What animosity existed between the people of France and those of other countries? None at all. The crowned heads supported by the privileged orders of Europe, had combined against France, with a view of destroying her free institutions, and thereby secure their own ill-gotten power and emoluments. They alone were her enemies.

Lequinio and Robison were antipodes to each other in principle. While the one wished to destroy prejudices, the other endeavored to cultivate and support them.

Lequinio was a member of the National Convention of France, and published the book in question, *Prejudices Vanquished or Destroyed*, in 1794. It has not, to my knowledge, been translated into English, nor have I a copy of the original before me. It was, however, favorably noticed by a British Review, at the time of its publication; from which the following sentiments are extracted. These will show the tenor of the work, and enable the reader to determine which book, that of Robison or Lequinio, is entitled to the epithet *detestable*.

Of Prejudices. "Prejudices arise out of ignorance and the want of reflection ; these are the basis on which the system of despotism is erected, and it is the master piece of art in a tyrant, to perpetuate the stupidity of a nation, in order to perpetuate its slavery and his own dominion. If the multitude knew how to think, would they be dupes to phantoms, ghosts, hobgoblins, spirits, etc., as they have been at all times, and in all nations? What is *nobility*, for example, to a man who thinks? What are all those abstract beings, children of an exalted imagination, which have no existence but in vulgar credulity, and who cease to have being as soon as we cease to believe in them.

"The greatest, the most absurd, and the most foolish of all prejudices, is that *very prejudice* which induces men to believe that *they are necessary* for their happiness, and for the very existence of society.

Of Kings. "Kings have ever been tyrants, more or less despotic, more or less cruel, more or less unjust, but equally smitten with a love of power, intoxicated by the spirit of domination, forgetful that they were men, anxious to place themselves on a level with gods, and averse to recollect that all their power and authority was derived from the very nations whom they oppressed.

"It may easily be perceived, that by the word *tyrant*, I do not mean solely those monsters of the human race, such as Nero, Caligula, Charles IX., etc., my definition extends to almost all kings, past and present; I do not even except that king of France so often vaunted as the 'good Henry;' (Henry IV.) although less cruel than most of his predecessors, he was assuredly no less despotic, and thought no less than they, that all France was destined for his pleasure and his glory; if an innovator during his reign had dared to have recalled the memory of their unalienable rights to the minds of the people, he would have been crushed under the weight of the royal authority. Let any one recollect the game laws enacted by this monarch, and then ask himself if he were really a good king. By an article of his *ordonance* on this subject, it was decreed, that every peasant, found with a gun in his hand, near a thicket, should be stripped naked, and beaten with rods around it. It was thus that the life of man was sacrificed to the repose and the existence of hares and patridges, destined for the pleasures of a prince, more culpable, perhaps, in respect to this barbarous *law*, than any of his predecessors, because, educated among the indigent and unfortunate, he ought never to have permitted any other sentiments than those of gentleness and humanity to penetrate into his mind.

"What should a king be, if he were as he ought? A man covered with a paper jacket, on which is written, (*De par la nation & la loi.*) 'By order of the people and the law;' the herald of the nation, the proclaimer of its orders, and nothing more. It is ridiculous enough to see royalty propagated from father to son, like the king's evil; it is still more ridiculous to see nations so deceived by being accustomed to slavery, as to become the servile idolators of that power by which they are oppressed, without once recollecting that it is their own.

Of War. "Who is that perverse, and ever execrable man, who first invented the murderous art of war, and that famous science of tactics, which consists in the best means of massacreing whole nations? One creature may assassinate another in a moment of passion, and, however barbarous this act really is, and however much it may be repugnant to the sensibility of a good man, yet he can conceive it: but for two men, in cool blood, to think of assassinating one another, or thousands of men of assassinating other thousands, with whom they are utterly unconnected, and can have no quarrel or even difference with; of this he can form no idea.

"O shame to the human species! Nations, blind, and asleep, will you never awake? What? shall not an individual whom you have placed upon the throne, and whom you have overwhelmed with your bounties, be satisfied with consuming the fruit of your sweat and of your toils, in the bosom of indolence and voluptuousness, and with laying your industry and your fortune under contribution! And shall he wish to dispose of your very existence? must you be the instruments of his anger and his vengeance, of his ambition and his mad desires?

"He wishes to conquer a province, that is to say, to usurp the dominion over a country, and pillage the inhabitants; and it is to assist this audacious robbery, of which you will enjoy no lucrative portion, that you are about to desolate the territories of a people who never offended you, to burn their villages, and to spread death and desolation over their fields; while in this attempt you expose yourselves to excessive fatigues, to continual privations, and even to death itself; or, what is still worse, to wounds, which but prolong a miserable existence!"

A philanthropist, a man who wishes to promote the general happiness of his fellow men, can see nothing *detestable* in the foregoing sentiments of Lequinio. But professor Robison, as well as the Abbè Barruel, had his own private interests to subserve. He possessed a lucrative office in the university of Edinburgh; which he could neither have obtained nor held, had he advocated the cause of oppressed humanity. Thus, unhappily for mankind, it becomes the interest of the learned in monarchies, to support the power of tyrants.

Barruel held a place, perhaps, equally lucrative in the church; and although the republic, as has been seen, exercised much forbearance and generosity towards the nonjuring priests, he did not possess sufficient liberality of soul to make the least sacrifice for the benefit of the nation under its embarrassed situation. He would neither take the oath of allegiance to the republic, nor retire upon a moderate pension.

I shall now make some remarks on the calumnies that have been industriously spread throughout the world against the French revolution. And although none can reflect without detestation on the tyranny and cruelties of Robespierre, and some others who obtained power in the course of that revolution, I shall be able to show that these are inferior in atrocity to the barbarities which took place in the American revolutionary war.

It should be remembered, also, that a great part of the enormities which occurred in France, were perpetrated by mobs. The people, driven to madness by the intrigues of their internal foes, gave a loose to their fury, which the government could not control.

It was the policy of kings and their adherents, to stigmatize the actors in the French revolution, as well as the just principles upon which it was founded. Hence the cry of *awful, horrible, detestable*, revolution, was echoed from court to court throughout Europe; and, without correct information, relying upon the reports of the corrupt presses of the enemies of France, the same cry, I am sorry to say, was reverberated by a portion of the press, from the republican shores of America.

The same course was pursued to scandalize the American revolution; and Europe was filled with the lies which were daily issued from " Rivington's *lying* Gazette," printed in New-York when in possession of the British.

Which is most criminal, it may be asked, to rebel against one's country, against a nation, or to rebel against one man, a king, who arrogantly claims the right to govern a country, because one of his ancestors, in a former age, like William, the Norman, or Canute, the Dane, compelled the people of that country by force of arms, to submit to his authority?

The grand and ultimate object of these writers was to bring the French revolution into disrepute among the people of Europe, in order to check its progress in other countries. And to effect this, no means were thought too vile to be resorted to. The principle of liberty itself, as though mankind were unworthy of enjoying it, was to be calumniated and denounced. " The French officers and soldiers, says Robison, who returned from America, imported the American principles, and in every company found fond hearers who listened with delight and regret to their fascinating tale of American independence. During the war, the minister was obliged to allow the Parisians to amuse themselves with theatrical entertainments, where every extravagance of the

Americans was applauded as a noble struggle for native freedom. All wished for a taste of that liberty and equality which they were allowed to applaud on the stage; but as soon as they came from the theatre into the street, they found themselves under all their former restraints. The sweet charm had found its way into their hearts, and all the luxuries of France became as dull as common life does to a fond girl when she lays down her novel.

"In this irritable state of mind a spark was sufficient for kindling a flame. To import this dangerous delicacy of American growth, France had expended many millions, and was drowned in debts."

The author then states sundry circumstances, either true or false, to prove that the Illuminati and Freemasons took a part in the revolution of France; and says, "After all these particulars, can any person have a doubt that the order of Illuminati formerly interfered in the French revolution, and contributed greatly to its progress?" He at the same time acknowledges that, "There is no denying the insolence and oppression of the crown, and the nobles, nor the misery and slavery of the people, nor that there were sufficient provocation and cause for a total change of measures and of principles."

But he finds fault with "The rapidity with which one opinion was declared in every corner, and that opinion as quickly changed;" as though it were to be expected that a whole people, who had just burst the bonds which had held them enchained for centuries, should simultaneously adopt the same opinions in regard to the manner of securing their future liberties.

"In 1789, or the beginning of 1790, a manifest was sent from the grand National Lodge of Freemasons (so it is entitled) at Paris, signed by the duke of Orleans as grand Master, addressed and sent to the Lodges in all the respectable cities of Europe, exorting them to unite for the support of the French Revolution, to gain it friends, defenders, and dependents; and according to their opportunities, and the practicability of the thing, to kindle and propagate the spirit of revolution through all lands. This is a most important article, and deserves a very serious attention. I got it first of all in a work written by L. A. Hoffmann, Vienna, 1795.

"The author says, 'That every thing he advances in these memorandums is consistent with his own personal knowledge, and that he is ready to give convincing proofs of them to any respectable person who will apply to him personally. He has already given such convincing documents to the Emperor, and to several Princes, that many of the machinations occasioned by this manifesto have been detected and stopped; and he would have no scruple at laying the whole before the public, did it not unavoidably involve several worthy persons who had suffered themselves to be misled, and heartily repented of their errors.' He is naturally (being a Catholic) very severe on the Protestants (and indeed he has much reason) and by this has drawn on himself many bitter retorts. He has however defended himself against all that are of any consequence to his good name and veracity, in a manner that fully convinces any impartial reader, and turns to the confusion of the slanderers.

"Hoffmann says, that 'he saw some of those manifests; that they were not all of one tenor, some being addressed to friends, of whose support they were already assured.' One very important article of their contents is earnest exhortations to establish in every quarter secret schools of political education, and schools for the public education of the children of the people, under the direction of well-principled masters; and offers of pecuniary assistance for this purpose, and for the encouragement of writers in favor of the Revolution, and for indemnifying the patriotic booksellers who suffer by their endeavors to suppress publications which have an opposite tendency."

There is nothing in all this but what common prudence would dictate. Shall monarchs and their satellites be applauded for exerting every means to secure their power, and to prevent the spread of liberal political opinions; and shall the friends of liberty be reproached for using the same means for the support and security of free governments?

From what is said of Hoffmann, here spoken of, it is probable he was a worthless character, on whose word no reliance could be placed. His complaints against the Protestants were, doubtless, that they favored the revolution, which, in the eyes of Professor Robison, would be sufficient to justify every abuse. He was, no doubt, rewarded for his base officiousness.

"I conclude, says Mr. Robison, this article (on the French revolution) with an extract or two from the proceedings of the National Assembly and Convention, which make it evident that their principles and their practice are precisely those of the Illuminati, on a great scale.

"On the 19th of November, 1792, it was decreed, 'That the Convention, in the name of the French nation, tenders help and fraternity to all people who would recover their liberty.'

"On the 21st of November, the President of the Convention said to the pretended deputies of the Duchy of Savoy, 'Representatives of an independent people, important to mankind was the day when the National Convention of France pronounced its sentence, *Royal dignity is abolished.* From that day many nations will in future reckon the era of their political existence. From the beginning of civil establishments Kings have been in opposition to their nations—but now they rise up to annihilate Kings. Reason, when she darts her rays into every corner, lays open eternal truths—she alone enables us to pass sentence on despots, hitherto the scare-crow of other nations.'

"But the most distinct exhibition of principle is to be seen in a report from the diplomatic committee, who were commissioned to deliberate on the conduct which France was to hold with other nations. On this report was founded the decree of the 15th of December 1793. The reporter addresses the Convention as follows:

"'The Committees of Finance and War ask in the beginning, What is the object of the war which we have taken in hand? Without all doubt the object is *the annihilation of all privileges, war with the palaces, and peace with the cottages.* These are the principles on which *your declaration of war* is founded. All tyranny, all privilege must be treated as an enemy in the countries where we set our foot. This is the genuine result of our principles. But it is not with Kings alone that we wage war—were these our sole enemies, we should only have to bring down ten or twelve heads. We have to fight with all their accomplices, with the privileged orders, who devour and have oppressed the people during many centuries.

"'We must therefore declare ourselves for a revolutionary power in all the countries into which we enter, (loud applauses from the Assembly)—nor need we put on the cloak of humanity, we disdain such little arts. We must clothe ourselves with all the brilliancy of reason, and all the force of the nation. We need not mask our principles—the despots know them already. The first thing we must do is to ring the alarm bell, for insurrection. We must, in a solemn manner, let the people see the banishment of their tyrants and privileged casts—otherwise, the people, accustomed to their fetters, will not be able to break their bonds. It will effect nothing, merely to excite a rising of the people—this would only be giving them words instead of standing by them.

"'And since, in this manner, we ourselves are the Revolutionary Administration, all that is against the rights of the people must be overthrown, at our entry—we must display our principles by actually destroying all tyranny; and our generals, after having chased away the tyrants and their satellites, must proclaim to the people that they have brought them happiness; and then, on the spot, they must suppress tithes, feudal rights, and every species of servitude.

" 'But we shall have done nothing if we stop here. Aristocracy still domineers—we must therefore suppress all authorities existing in the hands of the upper classes. When the revolutionary authority appears, there must nothing of the old establishment remain. A popular system must be introduced—every office must be occupied by new functionaries—and the Sansculottes* must every where have a share in the administration.

" 'Still nothing is done, till we declare aloud the precision of our principles to such as want only a half freedom. We must say to them—if you think of compromising with the priviledged casts, we cannot suffer such dealing with tyrants—they are our enemies, and we must treat them as enemies, because they are neither for liberty nor equality. Show yourselves disposed to receive a free constitution—and the Convention will not only stand by you, but will give you permanent support; we will defend you against the vengeance of your tyrants, against their attacks, and against their return. Therefore abolish from among you the Nobles—and every ecclesiastical and military incorporation. They are incompatible with equality. Henceforward you are citizens, all equal in rights—equally called upon to rule, to defend, and to serve your country. The agents of the French Republic will instruct and assist you in forming a free constitution, and assure you of happiness and fraternity.'

" This report was loudly applauded, and a decree formed in precise conformity to its principles. Both were ordered to be translated into all languages, and copies to be furnished to their generals, with orders to have them carefully dispersed in the countries which they invaded."

---

* Sansculotte literally means without small clothes. It was bestowed in derision by the well dressed royalists upon the republicans of France; who acknowledged its applicability, and assumed the term; saying our condition is the result of the iniquitous system of government, which hitherto has been conducted for the benefit of a few, to the degradation and bebasement of the great mass of the people. The French republicans were also styled Jacobins, which arose merely from the circumstance of their meetings being held in a monastery formerly belonging to an order of monks thus denominated. And this name, in foreign countries, has been made to mean something awfully atrocious. The apostate, Cheetham, attempted to play this pitiful game, by styling the republicans of New-York, Martlingmen, in consequence of their meeting at a house kept by Abraham Martling. Such contemptible resorts show the baseness of the cause intended to be benefited by them.

The reader is aware, that the principal powers of Europe had combined for the purpose of putting down the French Republic, and restoring the ancient regime; and still they complained of these retaliatory measures.

What course did the American revolutionists take, under similar circumstances? In the confederation of the American States, in 1781, the 11th article says, "Canada acceding to the confederation, and joining the measures of the United States, shall be admitted into the Union." An army was sent into Canada, for the purpose of inducing and aiding the people of that province to assert and maintain their independence.

Let us see how the government of the United States treated this revolutionary principle in latter times. The following is an extract of a speech delivered by Henry Clay, in the House of Representatives, in 1818, in favor of acknowledging the independence of the provinces of La Plata, in South America:

"I maintain, said he, that an oppressed people are authorized, whenever they can, to rise and break their fetters. This was the great principle of the English revolution. It was the great principle of our own. We must, therefore, pass sentence of condemnation upon the founders of our liberty;—say that they were rebels, traitors,—and that we are, at this moment, legislating without competent powers, before we can condemn the cause of Spanish America. Our revolution was mainly directed against the theory of tyranny. We had suffered comparatively but little,—we had in some respects been kindly treated,—but our intrepid intelligent fathers saw, in the usurpations of the power to levy an inconsiderable tax, the long train of oppressive acts that was to follow. They rose—they breasted the storm—they conquered, and left us the glorious legacy of freedom. Spanish America, for centuries, has been doomed to the practical effects of an odious tyranny. If *we* were justified, *she* is more than justified."

The sentiments of Mr. Clay were responded to by Congress, and La Plata was declared by our government free and independent.

The French revolution was hailed with joy by the friends of liberty, in England, as appears by the following document. Mr. Robison states, that while his book was printing, he obtained a work then just published in Paris. It confirms, says he, all that I have said respecting the use made of the freemason lodges. It gives a particular account of the formation of the Jacobin Club, by the Club Breton. The author writes: We may judge of what the duke of Orleans could do in other places, by what he did during his stay in England. He gained over to his interest Lord Stanhope and Dr. Price, two of the most respectable members of the *Revolution Society*. This society even sent to the Assembly an ostensible letter, in which are the following passages:

"The Society congratulates the National Assembly of France on the Revolution which has taken place in that country. It cannot but earnestly wish for the happy conclusion of so important a Revolution, and, at the same time, express the extreme satisfaction which it feels in reflecting on the glorious example which France has given to the world.

"The Society resolves unanimously to invite all the people of England to establish Societies through the kingdom, to support the principles of the Revolution, to form correspondences between themselves, and by these means to establish a great concerted Union of all the true Friends of Liberty."

Accordingly (says the French author) this was executed, and Jacobin Clubs were established in several cities of England, Scotland, and Ireland.

The following passages are quoted by Mr. Robison from a vindication published by Professor Weishaupt, against the charges brought against him, by those who wished to retain the mass of the people in a state of vassalage:

'All men, says he, are subject to errors, and the best man is he who best conceals them. I have never been guilty of such vices or follies: (as he had been accused of) for proof, I appeal to the whole tenor of my life, which my reputation, and my struggles with hostile cabals, had brought completely into public view long before the institution of this Order, without abating any thing of that flattering regard which was paid to me by the first persons of my country and its neighborhood; a regard well evinced by their confidence in me as the best instructor of their children.

'It is well known that I have made the chair which I occupied in the University of Ingolstadt, the resort of the first class of the German youth.

'The tenor of my life has been the opposite of every thing that is vile; and no man can lay any such thing to my charge. I have reason to rejoice that these writings have appeared; they are a vindication of the order and of my conduct. I can, and must declare to God, and I do it now in the most solemn manner, that in my whole life I never saw or heard of the so much condemned secret writings; and in particular, respecting these abominable means, such as poisoning, abortion, etc., was it ever known to me in any case, that any of my friends or acquaintances ever even thought of them, advised them, or made any use of them.

'It was the full conviction of what could be done, if every man were placed in the office for which he was fitted by nature and a proper education, which first suggested to me the plan of illumination.

'I am proud to be known to the world as the founder of the Order of Illuminati: and I repeat my wish to have for my epitaph,

> '*Hic situs est Phaethon, currûs auriga paterni,*
> '*Quem si non tenuit, magnis tamen excidit ausis.*"

This is the resting place of Phaëton, son of Apollo; he failed to guide the chariot of the sun, and fell—yet nobly fell, so lofty the attempt.

It is reproachful to human nature, that men respectable for their acquirements, and of good standing in society, should be induced through self-interest, to use every possible means by calumny and falsehood to destroy the character and usefulness of persons like professor Weishaupt, who exert their talents with a view of bettering the condition of their fellow men. And it is to be lamented that many of those for whose benefit such philanthropists labor, join in the hue and cry against them.

The following appropriate language is applied to the writings of Messrs. Barruel and Robison, in an address of De Witt Clinton, past grand master of the State of New York, at the installation of Stephen Van Rensselaer, as grand master of the lodges of this State, September, 1825.

"Our fraternity has suffered under the treatment of well-meaning friends, who have undesignedly inflicted more injuries upon it than its most virulent enemies. The absurd accounts of its origin and history, in most of the books that treat of it, have proceeded from enthusiasm operating on credulity and the love of the marvellous. An imbecile friend often does more injury than an avowed foe. The calumnies of Barruel and Robison, who labored to connect our society with the Illuminati and to represent it as inimical to social order and good government, have been consigned to *everlasting contempt*, while exaggerated and extravagant friendly accounts and representations continually stare us in the face, and mortify our intellectual discrimination, by ridiculous claims to unlimited antiquity. Nor ought it to be forgotten, that genuine masonry is adulterated by sophistications and interpolations foreign from the *simplicity* and *sublimity of its nature*. To this *magnificent Temple of the Corinthian order*, there have been added Gothic erections, which disfigure its beauty and derange its symmetry. The adoption in some cases of frivolous pageantry and fantastic mummery, equally revolting to good taste and genuine masonry, has exposed us to much animadversion: but our institution, clothed with celestial virtue, and armed with the *panoply of truth*, has defied all the storms of open violence, and resisted all the attacks of insidious imposture; and it will equally triumph over the errors of misguided friendship, which, like the transit of a planet over the disk of the sun, may produce a momentary obscuration, but will instantly leave it in *the full radiance of its glory.*"—(Freemason's Library, p. 338.)

Horrors of the American Revolution, etc.

The revolution of France was agreeable to the will, doubtless, of ninety-nine out of a hundred of its inhabitants. The republic was the rule of the people; the French citizens, therefore, who resisted it, were rebels, were traitors to their country. And although the severities exercised towards them in many cases, can by no means be justified, yet reproaches against the republic, on the score of cruelty, come with a very ill grace from its enemies.

In proof of which, I will call to remembrance some of the appalling scenes of the American revolutionary war, showing how rebels to a king were treated by his myrmidons; which ought to be often recurred to, and held up to the eternal execration of posterity. This would be more becoming Americans than to dwell upon the horrors of the French revolution, relying on the garbled accounts of its domestic and foreign foes. For this purpose I shall give the following indubitable facts.

The policy of the British government evidently was to waste away the small number of troops which America had raised, and to deter others from entering into the war, by the inhuman means here detailed.

Extracts from Mrs. Warner's History of the American Revolution, (v. iii, p. 34.)

" Many of the captured Americans were sent to Great Britain, where they were for a time treated with almost every severity short of death. Some of them were transported to the East Indies; others put to menial services on board their ships: but after some time had elapsed, those in general who were conveyed to England, might be deemed happy, when their sufferings were compared with those of their countrymen who perished on board the prison ships in America, under the eye of British commanders of renown, and who in many respects, were civilized and polite.

"No time will wipe off the stigma that is left on the names of Clinton and Howe, when posterity look over the calculations, and find that during six years of their command in New-York, *eleven thousand* Americans died on board the Jersey, a single prison ship, stationed before that city for the reception of those victims of despair. Nor was the proportion smaller of those who perished in their jails, dungeons, and prison hulks.

"It is true that in England, the language of government held up all the American prisoners as *rebels, traitors, insurgents,* and *pirates;* yet this did not prevent the compassionate heart from the exercise of the benign virtues of charity and brotherly kindness. The lenient hand of many individuals was stretched out for their relief. While their sorrows were thus softened, their brethren in America, in the neighborhood of parents, children, and the most affectionate partners, *not being permitted to receive from them the necessary relief, were dying by thousands, amidst famine, filth and disease.*"

In speaking of the ravages of the British on the borders of the state of Connecticut, under the command of the traitor Arnold, Mrs. Warren observes:

"New London was more seriously attacked; and after a short and brave resistance, plundered and burnt. As soon as the town had surrendered, a number of soldiers entered the garrison: the officer who headed the party inquired who commanded it? The valiant Colonel Ledyard stepped forward, and replied with ease and gallantry, 'I did, but you do now;' and at the same time delivered his sword to a British officer. The barbarous ruffian, instead of receiving his submission like the generous victor, immediately stabbed the brave American. Nor was his death the only sacrifice made in that place, to the wanton vengeance of the foes of America: several other officers of merit were assassinated, after the surrender of the town; while their more helpless connexions experienced the usual cruel fate of cities captured by inhuman conquerers."—(Vol. iii, p. 90.)

Fort Griswold, above alluded to, was probably defended with as much bravery as was exhibited on any occasion during our revolutionary war. The whole garrison, with the exception of one who secreted himself, were inhumanly butchered. Those who had been wounded during the action, were crammed into carts, and precipitated down the steep hill on which the fort stands among the rocks below; where those who were not instantly killed, were left to perish. This is the manner in which British officers reward bravery in an enemy. The statement here made I have from an eye witness, Thomas Herttell, Esq., who will substantiate the facts, if denied. Mr. Herttell was in sight of the fort at the time of the action, and learnt all the particulars soon after.

The following account of the treatment and sufferings of the American prisoners on board of the Jersey prison ship, is taken from the recently published Narrative of the Rev. Mr. Andros, of Berkley Massachusetts:

"We were captured, on the 27th of August, by the Solebay Frigate, and safely stowed away in the old Jersey prison ship at New-York. This was an old 64 gun ship, which through age had become unfit for further actual service. Her dark and filthy external appearance perfectly corresponded with the death and despair that reigned within; and nothing could be more foreign from the truth than to paint her with colors flying, or any circumstance or appendage to please the eye. She was moored about three quarters of a mile to the eastward of Brooklyn Ferry, near a tide mill on the Long Island shore. The nearest distance to land was about twenty rods. And doubtless no other ship in the British navy ever proved the means of the destruction of so many human beings. It is computed that no less than *eleven thousand* American seamen perished in her! But after it was known that it was next to certain death to confine a prisoner there, the inhumanity and wickedness of doing it was about the same as if he had been taken into the city and deliberately shot on some public square. But as if mercy had fled from the earth, here we were doomed to dwell. And never, while I was on board, did any Howard, or angel of pity, appear to inquire into, or alleviate our woes. Once or twice, by the order of a stranger on the quarter deck, a bag of apples were hurled promiscuously into the midst of hundreds of prisoners crowed together thick as they could stand; life and limbs were endangered by the scramble. This, instead of compassion, was a cruel sport. When I saw it about to commence, I fled to the most distant part of the ship. On the commencement of the first evening, we were driven down to darkness between decks secured by iron gratings, and armed soldiery. And now a scene of horror, which baffles all description, presented itself. On every side wretched, desponding shapes of men could be seen.

Around the well room an armed guard were forcing up the prisoners to the winches, to clear the ship of water and prevent her sinking, and little else could be heard but mutual execrations, reproaches and insults. During this operation there was a small dim light admitted below, but it served to make darkness more visible, and horror more terrific.

"When I became an inmate of this span abode of suffering, despair, and death, there were about four hundred prisoners on board, but in a short time they amounted to twelve hundred. And in proportion to our numbers, the mortality increased. All the most deadly diseases were pressed into the service of the king of terrors, but his prime ministers were dysentery, small pox, and yellow fever. There were two hospital ships near the Old Jersey, but these were soon so crowded with the sick, that they could receive no more. The consequence was, that the diseased and the healthy were mingled together in the main ship. In a short time we had two hundred or more sick and dying, lodged in the fore part of the lower gun deck, where all the prisoners were confined at night. Utter derangement was a common symptom of yellow fever, and to increase the horror of the darkness that shrouded us, (for we were allowed no lights betwixt decks,) the voice of warning would be heard, 'Take heed to yourselves. There is a mad-man stalking through the ship with a knife in his hand.' I sometimes found the man a corpse in the morning, by whose side I lay down at night. At another time he would become deranged, and attempt in darkness to rise, and stumble over the bodies that every where covered the deck. In this case I had to hold him in his place by main strength. In spite of my efforts he would sometimes rise, and then I had to close in with him, trip up his heels and lay him again upon the deck. While so many were sick with raging fever, there was a loud cry for water, but none could be had except on the upper deck, and but one allowed to ascend at a time. The suffering then from the rage of thirst, during the night, was very great. Nor was it at all times safe to go up. Provoked by the continual cry for leave to ascend, when there was already one on deck, the sentry would push them back with his bayonet. By one of these thrusts, which was more spiteful and violent than common, I had a narrow escape of my life.—In the morning the hatchways were thrown open and we were allowed to ascend, all at once, and remain on the upper deck during the day. But the first object that met our view in the morning was a most appalling spectacle. A boat loaded with dead bodies, conveyed them to the Long Island shore, where they were slightly covered with sand. I sometimes used to stand to count the number of times the shovel was filled with sand to cover a dead body. And certain I am that a few high tides or torrents of rain must have disinterred them. And had they not been removed, I should suppose the shore, even now, would be covered with huge piles of bones of American seamen. There were probably four hundred on board, who had never had the small pox,—some, perhaps, might have been saved by inoculation. But humanity was wanting to try even this experiment. Let our disease be what it would, we were abandoned to our fate.

"Now and then an American physician was brought in as a captive, but if he could obtain his parole he left the ship, nor could we much blame him for this. For his own death was next to certain, and his success in saving others by medicine in our situation, was small. I remember only two American physicians who tarried on board a few days. No English physicians, or any one from the city, ever, to my knowledge, came near us. There were thirteen of the crew, to which I belonged, but in a short time all but three or four were dead. The most healthy and vigorous were seized first with the fever, and died in a few hours. For them there seemed to be no mercy. My constitution was less muscular and plethoric, and I escaped the fever longer than any of the thirteen, except one, and the first onset was less violent. There is one palliating circumstance as to the inhumanity of the British, which ought to be mentioned. The prisoners were furnished with buckets and brushes to cleanse the ship, and with vinegar to sprinkle her inside. But their indolence and their despair was such that they would not use them, or but rarely. And, indeed, at this time, the encouragement to do it was small. For the whole ship, from her keel to the tafferel, was equally affected, and contained pestilence sufficient to desolate a world; disease and death were wrought into her timbers. At the time I left her, it is to be presumed a more filthy, contagious, and deadly abode for human beings, never existed among Christianized people."

The following is extracted from an account of the war, by an English historian, William Gordon, D. D.

"Great complaints are made of the horrid usage the Americans met with after they were captured. The garrison of Fort Washington surrendered by capitulation to general Howe, the 16th of November. The terms were, that the fort should be surrendered, the troops be considered prisoners of war, and that the American officers should keep their baggage and side arms. These articles were signed and afterwards published in the New-York papers. Major Williams, of Rawling's rifle regiment, in doing his duty that day, fell into the hands of the enemy. The haughty, imperious deportment of the officers, and the insolent scurrility of the soldiers of the British army, soon dispelled his hopes of being treated with lenity. Many of the American officers were plundered of their baggage, and robbed of their side arms, hats, cockades, etc., and otherwise grossly ill-treated. The fourth day of their captivity, Rawlings, McIntire and himself, all wounded officers, were put into one common dirt cart, and dragged through the city of New-York, as objects of derision, reviled as rebels, and treated with the utmost contempt. From the cart they were set down at the door of an old *waste* house, the remains of Hamden Hall, near Bridewell. The privates in the coldest season of the year were closely confined in churches, sugar houses, and other open buildings, which admitted all kind of weather, and were subjected to the severest kind of persecution that ever unfortunate captives suffered. Officers were insulted and often struck for attempting to afford the miserable privates some relief.

" Major Williams verily believed, that not less than fifteen hundred prisoners perished in the course of a few weeks in the city of New-York, and that this dreadful mortality was principally owing to the want of provisions and extreme cold.—(Vol. ii. p. 427.)

An extract from Gen. Ethan Allen's narrative of his capture and treatment by the British, in the American revolutionary war:

" I next invite the reader to a retrospective sight and consideration of the doleful scene of inhumanity, exercised by Gen. Sir William Howe, and the army under his command, towards the prisoners taken on Long Island, on the 27th of August, 1776; sundry of whom were, in an inhuman and barbarous manner, murdered after they had surrendered their arms; particularly a Gen. Woodhull, of the militia, who was hacked to pieces with cutlasses, by the light horsemen, and a Capt. Fellows of the Continental army, who was thrust through with a bayonet, of which wound he died instantly.

" Sundry others were hanged up by the neck till they were dead, five on the limb of a white oak tree, and without any reason assigned except that they were fighting in defence of the only blessing worth preserving: and, indeed, those who had the misfortune to fall into their hands at Fort Washington, in the month of November following, met with but very little better usage, except that they were reserved from immediate death to famish and die with hunger; in fine, the word rebel, was thought, by the enemy, sufficient to sanctify whatever cruelties they were pleased to inflict, death itself not excepted; but to pass over particulars, which would swell my narrative far beyond my design.

"The private soldiers who were brought to New-York, were crowded into churches, and environed with slavish Hessian guards, a people of a strange language, who were sent to America, for no other design but cruelty and desolation. I have gone into the churches, and seen sundry of the prisoners in the agonies of death, in consequence of very hunger, and others speechless, and near death, biting pieces of chips; others pleading for God's sake, for something to eat, and at the same time, shivering with cold. Hollow groans saluted my ears, and despair seemed to be imprinted on every of their countenances. The filth of these churches, in consequence of the fluxes, was almost beyond description. I have seen in one of them, seven dead, at the same time, lying among the excrements of their bodies.

"It was a common practice of the enemy, to convey the dead from these filthy places, in carts, to be slightly buried; and I have seen whole gangs of tories making derision, and exulting over the dead, saying, 'there goes another load of d—d rebels.' I have observed the British soldiers to be full of their insulting jokes, and vaunting on those occasions; but they appeared to me less malignant than tories.

"The provisions dealt out to the prisoners, were by no means sufficient for the support of life: It was deficient in quantity, and much more so in quality. The prisoners often presented me with a sample of their bread, which was damaged to that degree, that it was loathsome, and unfit to be eaten. Their allowance of meat (as they told me) was quite trifling, and of the basest sort. I never saw any of it, but was informed, bad as it was, it was swallowed almost as quick as they got hold of it. I saw some of them sucking bones after they were speechless; others who could yet speak, and had the use of their reason, urged me in the strongest and most pathetic manner, to use my interest in their behalf; 'for you plainly see,' said they, 'that we are devoted to death and destruction;' and, after I had examined more particularly into their truly deplorable condition, and had become more fully apprized of the essential facts, I was persuaded that it was a premeditated and systematical plan of the British council, to destroy the youths of our land, with a view thereby to deter the country, and make it submit to their despotism; but that I could not do them any material service, and that, by any public attempt for that purpose, I might endanger myself by frequenting places the most nauseous and contagious that could be conceived of. I refrained going into the churches, but frequently conversed with such of the prisoners as were admitted to come out into the yard, and found that the systematical usage still continued. The guard would often drive me away, with their fixed bayonets.

"The integrity of these suffering prisoners, is hardly credible. Many hundreds, I am confident, submitted to death, rather than enlist in the British service, which, I am informed, they most generally were pressed to do."

"The success of the American arms at Princeton, had a mighty effect on Gen. Howe and his council. Their obduracy and death-designing malevolence, in some measure, abated or was suspended. The prisoners who were condemned to the most wretched and cruelest of deaths, and who survived to this period, were immediately ordered to be sent within the American lines for exchange. Several of them, however, fell dead in the streets of New York, as they attempted to walk to the vessels in the harbor for their intended embarkation. Most of the residue, who reached their homes, having received their death wound, could not be restored by the assistance of physicians and friends; but, like their brother prisoners, fell a sacrifice to the relentless and scientific barbarity of Britain. I took as much pains as my circumstances would admit of, to inform myself not only of matters of fact, but likewise of the very design and aims of Gen. Howe and his council: The latter of which I predicated on the former, and submit it to the candid public."—(See Moore's Memoir, p. 157.)

Journals of Congress.

The following is an abstract of a report made to Congress, by the Board of War, January, 1778:

"It appears that the general allowance of provisions for each prisoner per day, does not exceed four ounces of meat and the same quantity of bread, and ofttimes much less, and frequently so damaged as not to be eatable; although the professed allowance is from eight to ten ounces; and that the prisoners have been treated in general, officers not excepted, with a cruelty scarce to be paralleled, and with the most studied and illiberal insult.

"That it has been a common practice with the enemy, on a prisoner's being first captured, to keep him three, four, and even five days without a morsel of provisions of any kind, and then to tempt him to enlist with the new levies, in order to save his life:—that there are numerous instances of prisoners of war perishing in all the agonies o hunger:—that, being generally stript of what clothes they have when taken, they have suffered greatly for want thereof during their confinement."

The British prisoners, on the contrary, were treated with the greatest humanity, as appears by the following resolution of Congress, passed January 27, 1776:

"Resolved, That the committee of inspection of Esopus, or Kingston, be directed to supply the prisoners there with necessary clothing, and also provide them with lodgings and provisions, not exceeding the rations allowed to privates in the continental army, on the most reasonable terms they can."

But the worst is not yet told. The most horrible, the most appalling to civilized humanity, is the employment of savages as auxiliaries in war, and then paying them a stipulated price for the scalps of men, women and children. This was done in the American revolutionary war. A graduated price was fixed upon by British commanders for the scalps of soldiers, farmers, women and children.

The late Col. Willet, who was second in command, at a period of the war, of a body of American troops stationed at Fort Stanwicks, at the head of the Mohawk river, and hearing one day the firing of muskets in the woods adjacent to the fort, he issued out with a party of the garrison and soon met a little girl running with a basket of blackberries in her hand,—on advancing further he found her companion tomahawked and scalped. He afterwards overtook a party of Indians, some of whom he killed, and made prisoners of others; on one of whom he found an official paper, signed by a British officer, stating the amount that was paid for the various scalps as above enumerated.

He sent this document to Gov. Livingston of Jersey, who then contemplated to write a history of the war; but which he did not accomplish, and the paper, perhaps, has never been published.

This statement was made by Col. Willet, a short time before his death, in the office of the Recorder of this city, in the presence of Mr. Riker the Recorder, Gen. Lamb, and several others, among whom was myself.

Even in the last war of America with England, at the taking of Little York, in Upper Canada, a woman's scalp, with long hair, was found in the council chamber, hanging behind the Speaker's chair along side the mace. This must have been a signal to the Indians to prepare for profitable employment.

This fact is officially stated by Gen. Dearborn and Commodore Chauncey.

The scalp agent in this war resided at Malden, and was well known to a friend of mine, the late Dr. LeBaron, United States' apothecary general; who told me that the office and duty of its incumbent, were notorious, and admitted of no doubt. After, however, the American government had taken into pay some Indian tribes, and a retaliation was apprehended, a council of war of British officers was convened at Kingston, when it was determined to pay the Indians in future for prisoners brought to the camp alive, instead of scalps.

The legislature of New-York passed an act granting a bounty on wolves' heads, on account of the depredations made by them on the sheep of the farmers. This was a justifiable mode of warfare against wolves; but the British government, it is believed, stands pre-eminent, without a parallel among nations, in paying a bounty on *human scalps*.

And, however barbarous were the native executioners of its vengeance, they never violated the chastity of females that fell into their power, as the British soldiers were permitted to do, at sundry places during the last war; and they were led also to expect an opportunity to commit the same outrage at New-Orleans, as appears by the watchword, *beauty* and *booty*, given out on the night of the attack.

I will make a short extract from the Memoirs of William Sampson, Esq., as an example of the manner in which kings treat rebels to their assumed authority, in case they do not succeed in ridding themselves of it.

"I remained in Dublin until the 16th of April, when the terror became so atrocious that humanity could no longer endure it. In every quarter of the metropolis, the shrieks and groans of the tortured were to be heard, and that, through all hours of the day and night. Men were taken at random without process or accusation, and tortured at the pleasure of the lowest dregs of the community. Bloody theatres were opened by these self-constituted inquisitors, and new and unheard of machines were invented for their diabolical purposes. Unhappily, in every country, history is but the record of black crimes; but if ever this history comes to be fairly written, whatever has yet been held up to the execration of mankind, will fade before it. For it had not happened before, in any country or in any age, to inflict torture and to offer bribes at the same moment. In this bloody reign, the coward and the traitor were sure of wealth and power; the brave and the loyal to suffer death or torture. The very mansion of the viceroy was peopled with salaried denouncers, kept in secret, and led out only for purposes of death. Some of them, struck with remorse, have since published their own crimes, and some have been hanged by their employers. Men were hung up until their tongues started from their mouths, and let down to receive fresh offers of bribe to betray their neighbor or discover themselves. If they neither knew nor would discover any thing, these intervals of relaxation were followed by new and more poignant inflictions. And when that courage, which is the noble attribute of my unhappy countrymen, spurned in the midst of agony at the tempter and the bribe ; the nearest and the tenderest relatives were often brought to witness these horrors; that out of their feelings might be extorted some denunciation, true or false, which the virtue of the sufferer had withheld."

Among other means of torture made use of for the above purpose, I am told by an Irish gentleman, who now holds a respectable office in our republic, that caps made of pitch mixed with powder were not unfrequently placed upon the heads of these unfortunate victims, and then set on fire.

Unfortunate Poland, like Ireland, made a brave but ineffectual effort to shake off the despotism with which it is oppressed ; and the following statement shows the humanity of its conquerors :

"Poland fell, neither from the valour nor from the number of her enemies; she fell from their all-pervading intrigues and the power of their gold. There was treachery in the midst of her camp, and in the bosom of her councils ; and to this foe, no citadel was ever impregnable. Her fall was followed by greater outrages upon civilization and humanity than have ever been perpetrated in modern ages. Warsaw immediately became a pandemonium of massacre, rapine, and cruelty, of which not half the horrors have been breathed or written. The Russian prisoners were liberated, and revenge added its fury to the tide of their passions. Fathers and husbands, pinioned for the dungeon and the gallows, witnessed the dishonor of their daughters and wives. The sleeping infant attracted no compassion, and kneeling children were not spared. Similar scenes occurred in all the principal cities of the kingdom. Of the military and civil officers, great numbers were shot or hanged: hundreds of others were chained together and marched off to the mines of Siberia. Some, however, escaped, and are fugitives in England, France, and the United States. An English traveller who has very recently passed through Poland, met on its northern frontier, some hundreds of Poles, many of them apparently of the higher class of the population, chained five abreast, to an iron bar, and marching to hard labor for life, in mines where the light of day never enters. But one of the latest means employed for the destruction of the Polish people, is the exportation of children. The imperial ukases for this measure spread terror and desolation throughout the kingdom. Entire schools of children have been seized, and hurried off in caravans to the interior of Russia, without being allowed a sight of their parents; and parents, whose natural yearnings over their little ones impelled them to attempt their rescue, were immediately delivered over to the military tribunal, to be tried for insubordination. But a peculiarly diabolical feature of this ukase remains to be developed. It only mentions orphan children; yet it defines these to be either children without fathers, though having fortunes, or those having fathers but in indigent circumstances. Thus the two branches of this definition are made to embrace nearly the whole youthful population. The commissaries of police, in the cities, and the *commissaires d'arrondissmens* in the provinces, were ordered to invite all parents, having families in distress, to send in declarations to that effect, that they might obtain relief from the government. Many, suffering from the prevailing misery of the country, were seduced by this apparently benevolent offer, to do so. The children of all these came within the regulation of the ukase, and were speedily torn from their arms. An eye witness has assured us that out of 450 children of the first division transported, scarcely 115 reached Bobruysk alive. They were compelled to walk the moment they crossed the frontiers; and when any were unable, from sickness or fatigue, to proceed further, they were abandoned, with a portion of bread and water. Several persons recently arrived from Siberia, have fallen in with the corpses of many of these unfortunate innocents, stretched beside the bread of which they could not avail themselves. The next step was to seize all the male children of the parochial schools; and by this means, and that of the recent military conscription, the population of brave but unhappy Poland has already been reduced to half its former number."

Extracts from Foreign Papers.

The whole province of Lithuania was traversed in different directions by the Russian troops, who burnt the towns and villages, massacred the prisoners, and killed even the women and children.

"Three of the confederates of Dziewicki, who has poisoned himself, have been shot at Warsaw, in the public place of execution, without the walls. They all died with a display of courage and firmness, hoping that their deaths might be useful to their unhappy country. Olkowski, in particular, showed great self-command. While on his way to execution, he gathered up a handful of the soil, and exclaimed, 'For this we have fought, and for this we are willing to die!' The tombs of these young heroes have become objects of veneration to the people, who strew flowers and garlands upon them. Many women have compromised themselves. A young lady, named Helen Nowakowska, has received 200 stripes, for having sent provisions to some unfortunate insurgents who were dying of hunger in the woods. The horrible punishment was inflicted in one of the barracks of Lublin, to the sound of military music; and to render it more severe, they afterwards shaved her head, and confined her in a convent, and no one can tell when she will be released. The wife of Orlowska had been condemned to receive 500 stripes for having sheltered one of her relations. She entreated that her punishment might be inflicted publicly at Warsaw, in order that it might inflame the courage of the patriots. This favor, however, being denied her, on the day her sentence was to have been executed, she was found dead in her prison, having forced pins into her bosom." (The Polonaise.)

"Gallicia, of all the provinces of Poland, seems to be suffering under the most cruel persecutions, and that at the hands of the coldblooded diplomate, Metternich. Count George Tyskiewiez, though an old man, has been confined in a subterranean cell for more than a year; his wife, who went to Vienna to supplicate the late emperor, was received by him just before his death, but repulsed by Metternich. Colonel Lariski is attached to a wall by an iron bar in another dungeon; etc."

We see nothing in revolutionary France, like the cruelties I have detailed. Many rebels and traitors to the republic were executed, but there was no torture, no protracted sufferings.

And shall the autocrat of Russia, and his miserable slaves, the instruments of his vengeance:—shall the government of England, and those who approve and support it, exclaim against the *horrors* of the French revolution? And will the present generation in America, forgetful of the consideration due to themselves, and the toils and sufferings of their virtuous fathers in purchasing their liberties at so dear a rate, bestow all their sympathies upon the sufferings of a few crowned heads, and others impudently styling themselves *noble*,—who are the enemies of freedom, and whose sole aim is to support rank and privileges, at the expense of the degradation and misery of the rest of mankind, with whom they have no feelings in common.

Above all, while irreligion is urged against France as the cause of cruelties in her revolutionary struggle, let not the profession of piety in other nations sanctify the commission of deeds infinitely more atrocious; for well might the French exclaim, in the language of a Scotch marshal, " If we are sinners, our enemies are *na saints*."

It is, moreover, worthy of remark, that the atrocities imputable to France, were committed during the sway of Robespierre, who professed as great regard to religion, as did the monarchs that combined against the republic, under a pretence of preserving it. He denounced the Moderates, commonly called the Geronde party, for want of faith in Christianity: the most prominent characters of which were Condorcet, Brissot, Lafayette, Thomas Paine, etc. Religion, in fact, has been the hobby-horse of tyrants in all ages and in all countries; and mankind have too easily been gulled by their hollow pretensions. In the practice of monarchs professing Christianity, we do not perceive the humble, charitable, forgiving spirit recommended by its benevolent founder. These virtues, they seem to think, do not properly belong to them. They must be arrogant, proud, and vindictive; and the most appropriate ensigns of their escutcheon would be a bloody cross, supported by deaths-heads and cross-bones.

An Abstract of " A Defence of Masonry ;"

Occasioned by a Pamphlet called Masonry Dissected." London, 1730.

This pamphlet is that written by Samuel Prichard, and made use of in this volume.—The Defence was published by Dr. Anderson, and appended to his History of the Constitutions of freemasons. The author, though probably a member of the masonic society, would wish to make it appear, that he drew all his information of it from the work he pretends to answer.

" I was exceedingly pleased (says he) to find the Dissector lay the original scene of masonry in the East, a country always famous for symbolical learning supported by *secrecy*. I could not avoid immediately thinking of the Egyptians, who concealed the chief mysteries of their religion under signs and symbols, called hieroglyphics.

" Pythagoras, by travelling into Egypt, became instructed in the mysteries of that nation; and here he laid the foundation of all his symbolical learning. The several writers that have mentioned this philosopher, and given an account of his sect and institutions, have convinced me fully, that freemasonry, as published by the Dissector, is very nearly allied to the old Pythagorean discipline; from whence, I am persuaded, it may in some circumstances, very justly claim its descent." Here the author details some of the leading doctrines and customs of the Pythagoreans, in proof of his opinion; which have been before noticed. After mentioning some other sects whose practices corresponded, he says, in many particulars with those of the fraternity, he adds, " The last instance I shall mention, is that of the Druids of our own nation, who were the only priests of the ancient Britons. In their solemnities they were clothed in *white*; and their ceremonies always ended with a good feast."

" The number *three* is frequently mentioned in the Dissection; and I find that the ancients, both Greeks and Latins, professed a great veneration for that number. Theocritus thus introduces a person who dealt in secret arts:

> "' Thrice, thrice I pour, and thrice repeat my charms!
> Verbaque ter dixit : Thrice he repeats the words. (Ovid.)
> Three colors in three knots unite.' (Virg.)

" Whether this fancy owes its original to the esteem the Pythagoreans and other philosophers had for the number *three*, on account of their *triad* or *trinity*; or to its aptness to signify the power of all the gods, who were divided into three classes, celestial, terrestrial and infernal; I shall leave to be determined by others.

" The gods had a particular esteem for this number, as Virgil asserts:

"' Numero Deus impare gaudet.' Unequal numbers please the gods. The sons of Saturn, among whom the world was divided, were *three:* and for the same reason we read of Jupiter's *Fulmen trifidum*, or three-forked thunderbolt; and Neptune's *trident*, with several other tokens of the veneration they bore to this particular number.

" A particular ceremony belonging to the oath, as declared by the Dissector, bears a near relation to a form of swearing among the ancients, mentioned by a learned author. The person who took the oath was to be upon his bare knees, with a *naked sword pointed to his throat*, invoking the *sun, moon*, and *stars* to be witnesses to the truth of what he swore." (Alex. ab Alexandro, Lib. V. cap, 10.)

" The accident, by which the body of Master Hiram was found after his death, seems to allude in some circumstances, to a beautiful passage in the sixth book of Virgil's Eneid." The author here recites the story of the *golden bough*, as being a necessary passport for Eneas's descent into the infernal regions, and adds:

"Anchises, the great preserver of the Trojan name, could not have been discovered but by the help of a *bough*, which was plucked with *great ease* from the tree; nor, it seems, could Hiram, the grand Master of masonry, have been found but by the direction of a *shrub*, which, says the Dissector, *came easily up*. The principal cause of Eneas's descent into the *shades*, was to inquire of his father the *secrets* of the *fates*, which should sometime be fulfilled among his posterity: the occasion of the *brethren's* searching so diligently for their *master* was, it seems, to receive from him *the secret word of masonry*, which should be delivered down to their fraternity in after ages. This remarkable verse follows:

"The body of your friend lies near you dead, Alas, you know not how!—This was Misenus, that was murdered and buried, *Monte sub aerio*, under a high hill; as, says the Dissector, *master Hiram* was.

"But there is another story in Virgil, that stands in a nearer relation to the case of Hiram, and the accident by which he is said to have been discovered; which is this: Priamus, king of Troy, in the beginning of the Trojan war, committed his son Polydorus to the care of Polymnestor, king of Thrace, and sent with him a great sum of money; but after Troy was taken, the Thracian, for the sake of the money, killed the young prince, and privately buried him. Eneas coming into that country, and accidentally plucking up a *shrub* that was near him on the side of a hill, discovered the murdered body of Polydorus. Eneid, III.

"By Dryden:

> "'Not far a rising hillock stood in view,
> Sharp myrtles on the sides and cornels grew;
> There while I went to crop the Sylvan scenes,
> And shade our altars with the leafy greens,
> I pull'd a plant: with horror I relate
> A prodigy so strange and full of fate!
> Scarce dare I tell the sequel! from the womb
> Of wounded earth, and caverns of the tomb,
> A groan, as of a troubled ghost, renew'd
> My fright; and then these dreadful words ensued:
> Why dost thou thus my buried body rend?
> O spare the corpse of thy unhappy friend!'

"The agreement between these two relations is so exact, that there wants no further illustration."

Rosycrucian Degree.

I have lately noticed that some writers, (and particularly William L. Stone, Esq., who is the author of a very interesting work on freemasonry,) have conjectured that this institution sprung from the famous society of Rosycrucians, I will, therefore, here add a short account of that association, as well as of the masonic degree founded upon it.

"The Rosycrucians, that is to say, brothers of the Rosy-Cross, were, says Bailey, a sect or cabal of hermetical philosophers; who bound themselves together by a solemn secret, which they swore inviolably to observe, and obliged themselves, at their admission into the order, to a strict observance of certain established rules. Their chief was a *German* gentleman educated in a monastery, where, having learned the languages, he travelled to the holy land, *Anno* 1378, and being at Damascus, and falling sick, he had the conversation of some Arabs and other oriental philosophers, by whom he is supposed to be initiated into this mysterious art. At his return into Germany, he formed a society, and communicated to them the secrets he had brought with him out of the East.

"They pretended to know all sciences, and especially medicine, of which they published themselves the restorers; they also pretended to be masters of abundance of important secrets; and among others that of the philosopher's stone; all which they affirmed they had received by tradition from the ancient Egyptians, Chaldeans, the Magi, and Gymnosophists. They pretended to protract the period of human life by means of certain *nostrums*, and even to restore youth. They pretended to know all things; they are also called the *invisible Brothers*, because they have made no appearance, but have kept themselves *incognito* for many years.

"This society is frequently signified by the letters *F. R. C., Fratres Roris Cocti*, it being pretended that the matter of the philosopher's stone is dew, concocted and exhaled."

The mystical importance which this society had obtained, rendered it a fit subject for the manufacturers of masonic degrees to found an order upon, which, therefore, was not neglected.

The Rosycrucian degree seems, in Carlile's report, to be confounded with that of the Knights of the Eagle, and Sovereign Prince of Rose-Cross, before noticed. The subject of both is the death and resurrection of the Saviour. The master bears the same title in each In the latter he is said allegorically to represent the person of *Wisdom* and *Perfection*, which gives him the title of *most wise and perfect master*. The wardens are styled *most excellent and perfect*. The other officers *most puissant and perfect brothers*. The brethren are called *most respectable and perfect masons.* The allegory of the pelican forms a part of both degrees. The Jewel of that of the Rosycrucian is a triangle formed by a compass and a quarter of a circle. In the center is a cross, upon which is a rose, and upon the quarter of the circle is a pelican, bleeding to feed her young. The Jewel is tied to a black rose, and pendant to a black collar, in the first point, and to a crimson in the second.

The decorations of the lodge, in the principal apartment, are first, a triangular altar on seven steps. Behind it is a large transparency, with a cross and a rose painted on its middle, and this inscription over it, " Jesus of Nazareth, the King of the Jews." Broken columns are visible on one side of the transparency, and a tomb on the other in the east, with three large lights in the west.—*Jam satis.*

The Rosycrucian society is of a very different cast from that of ancient freemasonry, which bears the most palpable marks of a descent from an institution established anterior to the Christian era.

In concluding my work, I repeat that the freemasons' society was founded for the purpose of concealing the rites of the ancient pagan religion, under the cover of operative masonry; and that, although the religion is extinct, its ceremonials remain, and clearly develope the origin of the institution. Sabeism, or the worship of the stars, is conspicuous in every grade of the order: the frequent quotations from the bible betray its religious cast, and, moreover, confirm, what has before been advanced, that the forms of prayer, and consequently other acts of devotion among the Pagans and Hebrews, were delivered in the same terms, tho applied to different objects.

The ceremonies of masonry, however, by no means impeach the morality it inculcates, which is unexceptionable, whatever may have been the conduct of some of its deluded members, impelled by a fanatical zeal for the preservation of its supposed secrets, or whatever innovations may have been introduced by aspiring, political demagogues, adverse to the established principles of the order. But at the same time, it must be confessed, that its moral precepts are conveyed in a style mal à propos at the present day. Moral action can now be taught without the aid of the Mosaic or Musaic pavement, the tesseled border, the square, the compass, the bee-hive, the plumb-line, etc. And as to any useful art or science, about which great parade is still made in masonic books, nothing of the kind is now practised in lodges. Among the ancient ignorant, operative masons, a little instruction in the rudiments of learning, including rough architecture, were, no doubt, given; but operative freemasonry has been abandoned for upwards of one hundred years, and no more of it remains to the order than the record of its former practice.

I will close the volume with the following apposite remarks of Dupius, applied to the original school, from which masonry received its lessons.

The author, after giving a specimen of the extravagant and absurd cosmogonies of different nations, observes:

"We will not pursue farther the parallel of all the philosophical opinions which each of the mystagogues has delivered in his own manner. We confine ourselves to this example, which is sufficient to give an idea of the allegorical genius of the ancient sages of the east, and to justify the use which we have made of the philosophical dogmas that are known to us, to discover the sense of these monstrous fictions of oriental mysticism. This manner of instructing men, or rather of imposing upon them under the pretext of instruction, is as far removed from our customs as hieroglyphics are from our writing, and as the style of the *sacred science* is from the philosophy of our days. But such was the language that was held to the initiates, says the author of the Phenician cosmogony, in order to excite in mortals astonishment and admiration."

THE END.

www.ingramcontent.com/pod-product-compliance
Lightning Source LLC
Chambersburg PA
CBHW020940230426
43666CB00005B/92